Just Sustainability

Catholic Theological Ethics in the World Church

James F. Keenan, Series Editor

Since theological ethics is so diffuse today, since practitioners and scholars are caught up in their own specific cultures, and since their interlocutors tend to be in other disciplines, there is the need for an international exchange of ideas in Catholic theological ethics.

Catholic Theological Ethics in the World Church (CTEWC) recognizes the need to appreciate the challenge of pluralism, to dialogue from and beyond local culture, and to interconnect within a world church not dominated solely by a northern paradigm. In this light, CTEWC is undertaking four areas of activity: fostering new scholars in theological ethics, sponsoring regional conferencing, supporting the exchange of ideas via our website (catholicethics.com), and publishing a book series.

The book series will pursue critical and emerging issues in theological ethics. It will proceed in a manner that reflects local cultures and engages in cross-cultural, interdisciplinary conversations motivated by mercy and care and shaped by shared visions of hope.

Just Sustainability
Technology, Ecology, and Resource Extraction

Edited by

Christiana Z. Peppard

and

Andrea Vicini, SJ

Founded in 1970, Orbis Books endeavors to publish works that enlighten the mind, nourish the spirit, and challenge the conscience. The publishing arm of the Maryknoll Fathers and Brothers, Orbis seeks to explore the global dimensions of the Christian faith and mission, to invite dialogue with diverse cultures and religious traditions, and to serve the cause of reconciliation and peace. The books published reflect the views of their authors and do not represent the official position of the Maryknoll Society. To learn more about Maryknoll and Orbis Books, please visit our website at www.maryknollsociety.org.

Published by Orbis Books, Maryknoll, New York 10545-0302.
Manufactured in the United States of America.

Library of Congress Cataloging-in-Publication Data

Just sustainability : technology, ecology, and resource extraction / edited by Christiana Z. Peppard and Andrea Vicini, S.J.
pages cm. — (Catholic theological ethics in the world church; 3)
Includes bibliographical references and index.
ISBN 978-1-62698-132-4 (pbk. : alk. paper)
1. Human ecology—Religious aspects—Catholic Church. 2. Sustainable development—Religious aspects—Catholic Church. I. Peppard, Christiana Z.
BX1795.H82J87 2015
241'.691—dc23

2014035465

To James F. Keenan, SJ,

for initiating, leading, and accompanying

Catholic Theological Ethics in the World Church

and to future generations of CTEWC scholars

who will promote just sustainability

Contents

Acknowledgments

This volume on sustainability in the world church is the outcome of a global collaboration in Catholic theological ethics. Our first and fervent thanks go to all the contributors for their creative essays, prompt submissions, and diligent revisions. It has been an honor and a privilege to work with scholars from around the world on topics of shared concern. Of the life events that transpired during this time, we note especially the passing of João Batista Libanio, SJ (1932–2014), whose vocation as pastor and professor—including his work on globality, poverty, and neo-colonialism in South America—represents a vital direction for Catholic theological ethics in the twenty-first century.

The members of the Planning Committee of Catholic Theological Ethics in the World Church (CTEWC) conceived the original idea of a book series after two successful cross-cultural conferences in Padua (2006) and Trent (2010). This volume is the third in the series, and we owe a debt of gratitude to members of the Planning Committee for their insight and suggestions. Special thanks are due to Linda Hogan, Agbonkhianmeghe Orobator, SJ, and James F. Keenan, SJ, for editorial and strategic advice. We are grateful to our publisher, Orbis Books, and especially to editor James Keane for his commitment to the timely publication of this volume and his helpful comments along the way.

Finally, we want to acknowledge the contributions of James F. Keenan, SJ, who has been a leader in global theological ethics in ways both intellectual and practical. It is as the result of his ongoing labors and vision that CTEWC exists and is committed to a truly global set of conversations—through networking, conferences, books, monthly newsletter, a website, scholarships, and visiting professorships. There is profound value in these opportunities to explore, amplify, and engage the lived realities and theological/ethical commitments of people worldwide. We hope this volume helps to facilitate the task of global awareness and theological reflection in a changing world.

Introduction
On Just Sustainability and Its Challenges

Christiana Z. Peppard and Andrea Vicini, SJ

Few terms are as frequently and widely used in global discourse about economics, development, and the environment as "sustainability." Indeed, the many contemporary deployments of the term led one theorist to suggest in 2010 that "the term has become so widely used that it is in danger of meaning nothing"—which is to say it

> has been used variously to mean "politically feasible," "economically feasible," "not part of a pyramid or bubble," "socially enlightened," "consistent with neoconservative small-government dogma," "consistent with liberal principles of justice and fairness," "morally desirable," and, at its most diffuse, "sensibly far-sighted."[1]

In the contemporary world, then, a concern arises: If "sustainability" can mean so many different things, does it mean anything at all?

The notion of sustainability first crested into global policy discourse with the 1987 publication of the report of the Bruntdland Commission (composed on request of the United Nations General Assembly), which was titled *Our Common Future: Report of the World Commission on Environment and Development*.[2] The operative definition of sustainability in that report—to which many analyses in the general literature since then have referred, including this edited collection—is linked to the observation that economic development bears environmental and social impacts. Thus sustainable development is spelled out by *Our Common Future* as the ability to meet individuals' needs in the current world while protecting sufficient resources to allow future generations to meet their own needs. Among the report's noteworthy features, it seeks to link temporal connections between present and future generations, as well as spatial connections among geographically disparate populations.[3] The issues are not merely economic, or social, or ecological: they are also ethical, at least implicitly. To speak of relationships among current and future generations, to articulate concerns about unchecked forms of economic growth, to advocate for the interdependence of human societies and ecosystems: these are questions that fall within the ambit of ethical, philosophical, and theological discourse. These are not just social scientific reflections; they are descriptive and prescriptive questions and recommendations about the proper aims, limits, and contexts of human prowess in a changing world.

To read the chairperson's introduction and the first chapters of *Our Common Future* in the present day is to experience an uncanny sense of familiarity, for although that report was published nearly thirty years ago, it articulates social, economic, and environmental issues that resonate with—and in some cases exactly describe—the context of the present day. Indeed, the vast majority of issues identified by the consensus authors of *Our Common Future* have amplified in the intervening decades while diplomatic and global efforts to ameliorate those problems have, for the most part, yielded limited results.[4] Consider, for example, that since 1987, five Intergovernmental Panels on Climate Change have confirmed the anthropogenic causes, severity, and expected impacts of global warming; yet even while individual nations and the European Union have made progress on meeting climate targets, international accords have faltered due to vested political interests (especially in the United States) and the challenges of collective action toward matters of the common good. Industrialized nations have experienced accelerated growth in their domestic economies, while developing nations have registered different levels of economic and social development and grappled with the "resource curse."[5] Economics remains neoliberal in both theory and practice, with governmental assessments of Gross Domestic Product and growth failing to account for ecological realities in the creation of value (such as drawdown of natural resources).[6] The 2008 Stern Report, for example, advocated strong controls on carbon emissions, but the backlash to that report among economists and policymakers indicated that massive theoretical and practical disagreements persist among economic and political elites about how best to value the costs of climate action or inaction.[7]

Meanwhile, extreme weather events as well as ongoing drought and desertification have led to an increase in the numbers of internally displaced people as well as international environmental refugees. Fossil fuel corporations remain bastions of profit, political clout, and energy production in the present-day global economy; progress on renewables such as solar and wind remains relatively limited to a few centers of global innovation; and the 1986 nuclear meltdown at Chernobyl that formed one backdrop of the Bruntdland Report has been eerily echoed by the 2011 Fukushima nuclear reactor crisis. Social and economic inequality persists, and we are also at present in the midst of what experts have termed the "sixth great extinction" in the history of the planet—this broad eradication of species is, like climate change, unprecedented in that humans are its cause.[8] No wonder that some scientists and environmental theorists suggest renaming the current geological era as the "Anthropocene"—that is, the era of human-induced changes to earth's systems, the time of humans as a planetary force.[9]

Amid this litany of inaction and loss, and accounting for the diverse understandings of "sustainability," it may seem foolish to title a volume *Just Sustainability* and then to centrally invoke the contested term throughout the volume. Our view is that the challenge is to engage various understandings of both justice and sustainability, and to give a sober assessment of what notions ought to be carried with us into a future that is not only commonly shared but also quite uncertain.

Just Sustainability is thus an exercise in honing twenty-first-century sensibilities about sustainability from a particular, thick set of descriptions. It represents a collective inquiry into the contours of sustainability from Catholic thought, theology, and practices worldwide. As the play on words in the volume's title suggests, sustainability in this book strives to entail the norm of justice, which has become a central part of Catholic thought and magisterial teaching in the late twentieth-century contexts of economic development, technological innovation, and environmental degradation. Although there are many ways of parsing the content of justice in political philosophy and theology, for the purposes of this volume we employ an understanding of justice that is both temporally and geographically broad, entailing fairness to future generations as well as respect for ecosystems and the earth processes on which all forms of life (including but not limited to humans) depend. These notions are necessarily general and are parsed in a variety of ways throughout the chapters; but the thematic thread is evident and provides an important modifier to the complex idea of sustainability. In our view, any viable path to sustainability must also be just. Readers will find that ideas and norms of justice permeate parts 2 ("Structures") and 3 ("Theological Stances and Sustainable Relations") in ways that are more thoroughly developed than the place-based reflections in part 1 ("Locations"). Whether as norms guiding policy decisions or in the development of ecological virtue theory, concepts of justice and sustainability must mutually inform one another in the twenty-first century.

This volume does not attempt to offer a final word on ecology, technology, and resource extraction. Instead, it illuminates some of the conceptual terrain from within a particularly well-developed form of ethical discourse. As such, we have sought to create a volume in which each essay is clear about its bias, in at least one of two ways. First, some essays—especially those in part 1—are explicitly place-based reflections on sustainability challenges. Thus they are "biased" in the sense that they are contextual; that is, they emerge from certain geographic, political, economic, cultural, and social realities. Second, all the essays in this volume emerge from a rising theological and ethical discourse that has taken decisive shape within global Catholicism since the mid-twentieth century. This discourse on the intersections of environmental, social, and economic issues can be found in magisterial documents, especially since Vatican II and the encyclical *Populorum Progressio* (1967), where a notion of "integral development" was decisively articulated.[10] Those complex interactions can be found, too, beyond the hierarchical magisterium: they are also rising in the embedded practices and adaptations of particular communities, as well as in scholarly theological and ethical discourse.

Just Sustainability builds on the existing rich history of theological and ethical reflection by scholars from around the world in pursuit of articulating distinctly Catholic, and representatively global, perspectives.[11] This book is a project in search of a transformative ethics, oriented toward the common good and global flourishing, that seeks to challenge oppressive structures and relational dynamics. The chapters that offer these forms of reflection do so in relation to various contemporary discourses in natural and social science, ethics, economics, and global diplomacy.

As an attempt to be representatively global and to capture some of the complexities of current economic, social, and environmental systems, the book proceeds in three parts. Part 1, *Locations*, consists of essays from eleven different countries. Each short essay depicts and analyzes the challenges facing a particular region, reflects critically on contributing paradigms, and indicates how existing forms of thought and action (including economic, political, theological, and ethical dimensions) might need to be reframed. These reflections from six continents ground the global scope of *Just Sustainability*.

Part 1 begins with two chapters from Eastern Europe and the European Union: **Dzintra Ilisko** explores the significance of ecofeminism for sustainability education in the Baltic States. **Markus Vogt** summarizes the well-honed theological and ethical perspectives on responsible energy supply from the perspective of German churches after World War II. Next, from Oceania, **Francis X. Hezel, SJ,** reports on problems of economic development and environmental degradation in Micronesia. In Asia, **Osamu Takeuchi, SJ,** reflects philosophically and theologically on the impact of the earthquake and nuclear leakage at the Fukushima reactor in 2011, linking that crisis to the legacy of nuclear war and ongoing debates about nuclear power as an energy source. **John Karuvelil, SJ,** critiques several specific instances in which economic development programs have led to involuntary displacement of large populations in India, and explains how economic and political incentives must be accountable to standards of integral development.

From Africa, in a theological and spiritual reflection, **Viviane Minikongo Mundele** writes about the reciprocal but uneven relations of ecology, society, and moral theology in the Democratic Republic of the Congo, offering insights about the significance of biblical interpretation and theological anthropology in ecological action. Also writing on the Democratic Republic of the Congo, **Muhigirwa Rusembuka Ferdinand, SJ,** investigates mining as a major sector of the Congolese economy while shedding critical light on its human, social, and environmental impacts. **Benedict Chidi Nwachukwu-Udaku** also examines the multidimensional issues concerning resource exploitation and economic benefit in the context of Nigeria, where he calls for a new paradigm of value and worth to take root.

In the Americas, the late **João Batista Libanio, SJ,** observes how in Brazil, nature is among the poor and overlooked constituencies that deserve recognition and a preferential option among colonial legacies and neocolonial economic and extractive systems. **Miguel Ángel Sánchez Carlos** adds a perspective on social sustainability and political structures from Mexico, while farther north, **Kenneth M. Weare** reports on the perils of industrial agriculture in the United States.

Part 2, "Structures," discusses powerful and determinative systems, forces, and realities that shape the complex relations of environment, economy, and society. Any transformative ethic must first understand the context of concern and action; globalization's many interrelated, complex dynamics and systems present real structural challenges for remedying the worst of environmental degradation and human suffering. Some of these structures were introduced in part 1 and receive fuller treatment in part 2; others are introduced and explicated for the first time. Thus the eight essays in part 2, written by scholars from five countries, emphasize structural realities while evaluating them in light of Catholic theological and ethical resources.

John Sniegocki opens part 2 with a focused, trenchant analysis of the political economy of sustainability in the contemporary, globalizing world, employing Catholic social thought as a rigorous interlocutor. This chapter's conceptual groundwork amplifies the importance of many essays that follow. **Dennis T. Gonzalez** depicts new measures for justice, ecological wisdom, and integral development in light of ongoing environmental changes and challenges from economic development. **Constansia Mumma-Martinon** draws on the connections between urban growth and development to offer a constructive set of critiques and proposals regarding sustainability in urban planning in Kenya. Moving to the question of human food security, **Teresia Hinga** tackles the vexing problem of food scarcity in her powerful reflection on empty granaries, stolen harvests, and the "weapon of grain." **Mark Graham** depicts the environmental and social problems that flow from the "unsavory gamble" of contemporary industrial agriculture, especially in the United States.

The "resource curse" rises again as a focal topic and site of critique in the essay by **Peter Knox, SJ,** who challenges the very presumption that such a thing as extractive mining can be sustainable for the health of the land and human populations. Drawing on the theme of human health impacts, **Jacquineau Azétsop, SJ,** articulates why sustainability is a key concept correlating environmental and social well-being through a case study of health systems and HIV/AIDS public health policy in Chad. **Celia Deane-Drummond** turns the conversation to the enduring theme of technology and offers a critical appraisal of three different forms of emerging technologies through the lens of a theology of gratuitousness.

The nine authors of part 3, "Theological Stances and Sustainable Relations," hail from six different countries. While drawing on important global realities and trends described and analyzed in parts 1 and 2, part 3 is the most explicitly theological and constructive part of the volume. Each essay engages theological and ethical resources for transforming both local and global realities into a more just and sustainable world community. This part emphasizes the "ought" questions for which ethics is known—asking, for example: How do we properly understand the role of the human being in light of scientific reality as well as religious tradition? How ought we to construct a sustainable energy economy? What ought future generations be able to hope for, and what are our obligations in facilitating those conditions?

Denis Edwards augments his significant work in ecological theology by reflecting on the relationships between humans and other creatures in distinctly theological registers. **Randy J. C. Odchigue** explores connections between ecology and ecclesiology, asking what it would mean for the church to embody and perpetuate just, sustainable communities. **Ann Marie Mealey** depicts well-established relations between feminist thought and ecology, and constructively augments the discussion, both practically and theologically. The question of how human beings ought to behave, and what ecological virtues might promote just and sustainable communities, is at the heart of **Nancy M. Rourke**'s essay on Catholic virtues ecology: What are ecological virtues? And what does it mean to think ecologically about virtue theory?

Christine Firer Hinze employs Catholic social teaching's "stranded assets" of economic critique and advocacy for integral development as a central part of the project of just sustainability, namely, improving the character and categories on which human economic exchange is based. In a related way, **Edward Osang Obi, MSP,** foregrounds a "community-of-interests" perspective on natural resource exploitation to critique and reconfigure problematic economic relations. Among the most entrenched patterns of resource exploitation are those pertaining to fossil fuels; **Erin Lothes Biviano** presents the problem of fossil fuel extraction and combustion in light of climate change and then offers a theological analysis of renewable energy, suffused with contemporary energy scholarship as well as religious rhetoric. **Daniel R. DiLeo** participates in a time-honored Jesuit tradition by exploring what Ignatian spirituality can offer in the process of reconceptualizing sustainability on both personal and societal levels. And **Peter J. Henriot, SJ,** concludes the volume with a pragmatic reflection on the vital linkages among education, empowerment, and sustainability—a task befitting this and future generations that must learn to share the challenge of living together sustainably in a complex world.

Thus, through the iterative flow of sections—from the local, particular, and descriptive (part 1), to the structural and systemic (part 2), to the normative and even speculative (part 3)—*Just Sustainability* demonstrates several forms of ethical reflection that are necessary for global ethics in the twenty-first century. So too, in its composition—with authors from many countries and a range of areas of expertise, including many lay people and scholars, as well as Jesuits, other religious, and priests—*Just Sustainability* represents our best efforts to think collectively about environmental problems facing global humanity.

As editors, we come from two countries (the United States and Italy), with backgrounds in bioethics, environmental ethics, moral theology, and religion and science. The book's timely content intersects in some ways with other recent contributions to the burgeoning fields of religion and ecology as well as ecological theology and environmental justice. As a diverse compendium of reflections on value systems and worldviews in relation to ecological thought, this volume is a contribution to the emerging scholarship on religion and ecology and a source for environmental sociology. But insofar as it is specifically situated within scholarly discourse on Catholic theological ethics, it also appeals to a particular niche of academic work.

Finally, the insights contained here will also resonate with emerging voices in Catholic environmentalism and human development organizations, such as the Catholic Climate Coalition or Catholic Relief Services; perhaps they may be taken up by the Catholic magisterium under Pope Francis, whose namesake was identified as the patron saint of ecologists in 1979. Indeed, we hope that *Just Sustainability* serves as a catalyst for ongoing debate and articulation among scholars as well as faith communities about the multiple interactions of particular values—in this case, theological and ethical considerations—along with the pursuit of environmental and social flourishing in a complex, globalizing world.[12]

No account of what constitutes "sustainability" is truly value free, but there are better and worse ways of conceiving of the term. Our hope is that the particular and explicit values that surface throughout the volume can help shed both critical and constructive light on local and global issues in sustainability, especially at the intersections of ecology, technology, and resource extraction. Perhaps by making explicit the question of what is at stake in our normative uses of such terms, and by proceeding with epistemological humility, some incremental progress can be made in thinking and acting well as human beings on an increasingly human-dominated planet.

Notes

1. Eric Zencey, "Theses on Sustainability: A Primer," *Orion Magazine,* May/June 2010, http://www.orionmagazine.org.

2. World Commission on Environment and Development, *Our Common Future: Report of the World Commission on Environment and Development* (New York: United Nations, 1987). See http://www.un-documents.net.

3. See ibid.

4. The most compelling case for this claim in the context of climate change and international diplomacy is Dale Jamieson, *Reason in a Dark Time: Why the Struggle against Climate Change Failed—and What It Means for Our Future* (New York: Oxford University Press, 2014).

5. See, for example, Joseph E. Stiglitz, *Globalization and Its Discontents* (New York: W. W. Norton, 2003) and *Making Globalization Work* (New York: W. W. Norton, 2007).

6. See James Gustave Speth, *The Bridge at the End of the World: Capitalism, Crisis, and Crossing from Crisis to Sustainability* (New Haven, CT: Yale University Press, 2009). Alternative measures of economic growth and national well-being have been proposed by various experts. See the Gund Institute for Ecological Economics for further information, http://www.uvm.edu/giee/.

7. *Stern Review: The Economics of Climate Change* (London: Department of the Treasury, 2006), http://webarchive.nationalarchives.gov.uk.

8. Elizabeth Kolbert, *The Sixth Extinction: An Unnatural History* (New York: Henry Holt, 2014).

9. See Jan Zalasiewicz, Mark Williams, Will Steffen, and Paul Crutzen, "The New World of the Anthropocene," *Environmental Science and Technology* 44 (2010): 2228–31. The atmospheric chemist Paul Crutzen is credited with the term "Anthropocene." He is a Nobel Laureate, and since 1996 he has been a member of the Pontifical Academy of Sciences.

10. For a summary of these developments, see Christiana Z. Peppard, *Just Water: Theology, Ethics, and the Global Water Crisis* (Maryknoll, NY: Orbis Books, 2014), chaps. 1 and 4.

11. The existing literature is large and growing. Selected texts that address only Catholic theological ethics in light of contemporary environmental issues (such as climate change) include Jame Schaefer, *Theological Foundations for Environmental Ethics: Reconstructing the Patristic and Medieval Concepts* (Washington, DC: Georgetown University Press, 2009); Jame Schaefer, ed., *Confronting the Climate Crisis: Catholic Theological Perspectives* (Milwaukee, WI: Marquette University Press, 2011); Richard W. Miller, ed., *God, Creation, and Climate Change: A Catholic Response to the Environmental Crisis* (Maryknoll, NY: Orbis Books, 2010); Tobias Winright, ed., *Green Discipleship: Catholic Theological Ethics and the Environment* (Winona, MN: Anselm Academic, 2011); Jame Schaefer and Tobias Winright, eds., *Environmental Justice and Climate Change: Assessing Pope Benedict XVI's Ecological Vision for the Catholic Church in the United States* (Lanham, MD: Lexington, 2013). Beyond these texts, the literature on ecological theology, technology and ethics, and theological anthropology is robust.

12. Willis Jenkins, *The Future of Ethics: Sustainability, Social Justice, and Religious Creativity* (Washington, DC: Georgetown University Press, 2013); Mary Evelyn Tucker and John Grim, *Ecology and Religion* (Washington, DC: Island Press, 2014); Whitney Bauman, *Theology, Creation, and Environmental Ethics* (New York: Routledge, 2009) and *Religion and Ecology: Developing a Planetary Ethic* (New York: Columbia University Press, 2014).

Part I

Locations

Sustainability in the Baltic States

Insights from Ecofeminism

Dzintra Ilisko

In the twenty years since the fall of the Soviet Union, the Baltic States have undergone tremendous changes in their political and socioeconomic spheres of life. Katarzyna Kosmala has described this transition process as "a chaotic polysemy, full of paradoxes of progression and retrogression" in response to new challenges.[1] Women entered this time of transition believing that socialism had solved the issue of gender inequality and that democracy would automatically grant some additional rights for women. However, the consequences of Soviet policy are still visible with respect to negative attitudes about women and the environment.

The context of the Baltic States differs from that encountered by Western feminists. We need to open new spaces of discourse, to rewrite cultural narratives, and to define ecofeminist insights for the question of sustainability in the Baltic context.[2] This essay suggests that university education about sustainability and justice is an important component in addressing inequalities in the Baltic States. In particular, strategies suggested by ecofeminist thinkers indicate how universities can tackle both women's oppression and environmental degradation.

Although in one of the Baltic States, Latvia, legislation protects every individual from gender discrimination, much remains to be done to promote true equality. For example, female representation in politics is low; women's leadership is not possible in Catholic and Protestant churches; and most managerial positions are held by men. Moreover, the unequal sharing of household duties curtails women's participation in public life. Finally, with economic reforms and the introduction of a competitive market, women have become particularly vulnerable to harassment and exploitation in the workplace.

Latvia is also facing a number of severe ecological issues neglected under Soviet governance, such as air and water pollution, the emission of carbon dioxide, massive destruction of the Latvian forests, unsustainable agriculture, and handling the by-products of industrial production.

An ecological perspective for Latvia needs to be reimagined. It should encompass both a gender analysis of political, social, and religious dynamics within educational settings to counteract the exclusion and oppression of women, as well as a strong ecological commitment. Ecofeminism combines these two commitments. It encourages building a sustainable community that respects and honors all human beings—women and men—and fosters the well-being of the whole ecosystem.

Sustainability in an Ecofeminist Frame

With their roots in the Western feminist and environmental movements of the 1960s and 1970s, the contemporary ecofeminist theologians Rosemary Radford Reuther, Sallie McFague, and Ivone Gebara identify environmental sustainability and social justice as urgent goals.[3] They criticize the patriarchal aspects of Christianity that contribute to subduing both the earth and women. Because of the linkages among diverse forms of oppression, they stipulate that women's liberation and environmental justice are intertwined.[4]

Ecofeminist thinkers demonstrate the interplay among poverty, gender discrimination, and access to political and economic privilege.[5] Their assessment found an echo in *Agenda 21*, the document resulting from the 1992 United Nations Conference on Environment and Development in Rio de Janeiro, which focuses on the worldwide conditions that pose severe threats to the sustainable development of people. In this document, the traditional forms of economic development were recognized as sexist and saturated with patriarchal perspectives, and gender equality was urgently suggested as a requirement in all developmental activities.[6] Moreover, the commitment to ensure women's empowerment and agency was also expressed in the 2002 *Johannesburg Declaration on Sustainable Development*.[7] Environmental justice demands a voice for those who have been excluded from participating in the social decision-making process.

Sustainability in Higher Education

Ecofeminist theologians offer many different methodologies for building just communities. First, interlocking structures of oppression must be identified along with their causes and consequences. Next, sustainable alternatives must be articulated as priorities for action. The educational context is important because a community of care can be built by developing students' responsibility that extends further than their human neighbors and into the ecological contexts in which they live. Ideally, students should learn to perceive how moral vocation and responsibility reach out to all people and the whole creation. This approach expresses a transformative education that could lead to new behavioral patterns toward the other and the earth. Nel Noddings, for example, discusses how care begins both with oneself and people with whom we live privileged relationships, but then gradually grows outward to include caring for all the oppressed and excluded. This expanding awareness helps identify the connections between multiple forms of oppression.[8] Therefore, a primary educational task is to help students uncover hidden forms of oppression.

Second, there is an urgent need to reexamine critically the nature and structure of schooling in order to promote sustainability. Are current educational systems part of the problem or part of the solution in working toward a sustainable future? Both a deeper critique of current educational systems and a broader vision of the role of education in shaping the future are needed. Existing educational frameworks should be challenged and renewed, with the goal of promoting a sustainable future.

Universities can serve as key agents of change in transforming education and society. They can adjust their educational projects and shape the knowledge and skills of future generations. In particular, schools of education could stress concern for sustainability when they train new teachers, provide professional continuing education to already practicing teachers, and support regional and national ministries of education with their expert opinion. Moreover, in universities, sustainability education informed by ecofeminist principles can emphasize a multidimensional connectedness of human beings with nature on the affective, cognitive, spiritual, and behavioral levels through appropriate lifestyles; restore one's connectedness with one's locality; help individuals overcome alienation, fragmentation, and dislocation by replacing it with caring and nurturing attitudes toward the earth; and explore diverse ways of restoring human-nature relations.

Universities, in particular, must prepare students to build a more sustainable society based on principles of social justice and equality. They should also equip students with the needed competence to become agents of change; model sustainable thinking by forming values, attitudes, and behaviors; and transform institutions of higher education into creative learning communities whose learning culture is adaptive, creative, and flexible rather than solely product-oriented.

Strategic Approaches in the Baltic Context

Environmental degradation was a clear consequence of Soviet politics in the Baltic States. In particular, Latvia has encountered a number of severe environmental issues; air and water pollution are among its most significant environmental concerns, and are largely related to a lack of waste treatment facilities during the years of Soviet governance. Acid rain has contributed to the destruction of Latvia's forests. The country's water supply is perilously polluted with agricultural chemicals and industrial waste. The Gulf of Riga and the Daugava River are both heavily polluted. A majority of the nation's sewage does not receive adequate treatment. Almost half the nation's water contains bacteria levels that are beyond the accepted safety limits. The Baltic Sea, the youngest sea on the planet and one of the world's busiest maritime areas over the past one hundred years, has degraded quite dramatically. Vehicles also account for 70 percent of the country's air pollution.

In Latvia, sustainable development can also be characterized by the ecological footprint. According to a study by the World Wildlife Fund, the average ecological footprint of every inhabitant on this planet should not exceed 1.7 hectares. According to this study, Latvia was in thirty-fourth place among the 115 countries analyzed, with an average ecological footprint of 3.43 hectares per inhabitant. The inhabitants of Latvia overspend their globally available resources. Concrete action is required to foster sustainable development.

Consumption patterns and the pursuit of the ideal "good life" depicted by the media plague Latvian society. Instead of condemning the dynamics of consumption, it is necessary to supplement this dominant message with sustainable practices inspired by ecofeminist thinkers. Soundly communicated sustainable practices and beliefs may provide a platform where enlightened attitudes toward nature and the oppressed can be formed.

One of the strategies proposed by ecofeminist thinkers is to adopt a simpler lifestyle and reevaluate the notion of a "good life." This strategy is consistent with Sallie McFague's and Ivone Gebara's theological insights. Their proposals, however, do not recommend traditional forms of ascetism, such as leaving the world or denying our bodily needs and feelings, but rather focus on small but important actions that might include living in a modest household, abstaining from unnecessary shopping, and promoting respect for the environment.

Moreover, ecofeminist theologians suggest the transformation of relationships by avoiding a dualistic approach that opposes humanity to the earth. They suggest a contemplative attitude as an alternative. In this context, contemplation means appreciating the intrinsic beauty of nature and building the kinds of relations between human beings and the earth that are not based on patterns of domination. Stewardship is one possible model in which human beings are partners with God in the care of Creation, and with a responsibility to stand in solidarity with one another—particularly with the oppressed.

Ecofeminist methodology illuminates patterns of oppression and privilege that exclude women and other marginalized groups from all spheres of life, including the earth. As an intellectual as well as a political movement, ecofeminism seeks to reevaluate and eventually transform the social, political, and religious dynamics that oppress both human beings and the earth.

Notes

1. Katarzyna Kosmala, "Expanded Cities in Expanded Europe: Resisting Identities, Feminist Politics and Their Utopias," *Third Text* 24, no. 5 (2010): 541–55.

2. Dzintra Ilisko, "Ecofeminism—A Healing Perspective for Reshaping Religious Education," in *International Handbook of the Religious, Moral and Spiritual Dimensions in Education: Part One,* ed. Marian de Souza et al. (Dordrecht: Springer, 2006), 127–40.

3. Rosemary Radford Ruether, *New Women, New Earth: Sexist Ideologies and Human Liberation* (San Francisco: Harper and Row, 1975), and "Religious Ecofeminism: Healing the Ecological Crises," in *The Oxford Handbook of Religion and Ecology*, ed. Roger S. Gottlieb (New York: Oxford University Press, 2006), 362–75; Sallie McFague, *The Body of God: An Ecological Theology* (Minneapolis: Fortress, 1993).

4. Rosemary Radford Ruether, *Integrating Ecofeminism, Globalization and World Religions* (Lanham, MD: Rowman and Littlefield, 2005); Ivone Gebara, *Longing for Running Water: Ecofeminism and Liberation* (Minneapolis: Fortress Press, 1999).

5. Janet Biehl, *Rethinking Ecofeminist Politics* (Boston: South End Press, 1991); Carolyn Merchant, *The Death of Nature: Women, Ecology and the Scientific Revolution* (San Francisco: Harper and Row, 1980).

6. United Nations, *United Nations Conference on Environment and Development: Agenda 21* (1992), http://www.unep.org.

7. World Summit on Sustainable Development, *Johannesburg Declaration on Sustainable Development,* 17th Plenary Meeting (September 4, 2002), http://www.unescap.org/, no. 20.

8. Nel Noddings, *Caring: A Feminist Approach to Ethics and Moral Reasoning* (Berkeley: University of California Press, 1984).

Sustainability and Responsible Energy Supply from the Perspective of the Churches in Germany

Markus Vogt

Environmental concerns and the protection of creation are prominent topics in German society. German churches play an active and very specific role in this debate. In this brief essay, I focus on two relevant aspects: sustainability and nuclear energy.

Sustainability: A Principle of Catholic Social Teaching?

Sustainability has not yet become a systematic part of Catholic theology or even social doctrine on a global level.[1] On a national level in Germany, however, such change is occurring in social ethics and in applying Catholic social doctrine. Since the early 1990s, German theologians and the German Bishops Conference have postulated an extension of social principles: along with human dignity, solidarity, and subsidiarity, they suggested *sustainability*, which should address the challenges of human ecology within society.[2] For them, sustainability is the missing link between a theology of creation and environmental activism in today's society. Just as the Christian idea of charity was for many centuries understood merely as a personal virtue and only became politically effective and relevant in connection with the solidarity principle, the theology of creation needs to be translated into socially accepted categories so that it can become politically viable and justifiable, and can influence both organizational structures and economic decisions in contemporary society.[3] In other words, a theology of creation is not operative on the political level unless it is accompanied by a strong commitment to promote sustainability in structural and political ways. Conversely, sustainability without the belief in the goodness and dignity of creation (whether in a Christian theological account or not) runs the risk of lacking ethical depth.

The claim of sustainability is deeply challenging for society but also for the churches because it demands a comprehensive shift in people's way of life, as well as the understanding of the economy and of the relationship between humans and nature. In public discourse on sustainability, theologians and citizens are confronted with an ambivalent "green washing" because the term "sustainability" is very broad and therefore can be misunderstood and misused.[4] The churches have a significant duty to clarify the ethical and religious dimensions of the concept of sustainability. This includes global and intergenerational justice, respecting creation as a gift, and promoting the intrinsic value of nature. This ethical debate has been at the core of the initiatives of the churches in Germany over the last two decades.

The term "sustainability" is a translation of the German term Nachhaltigkeit, which was coined in 1713 by the German forester Hans Carl von Carlowitz, who was deeply inspired by his Christian faith.[5] Christians played an important role in developing the idea of sustainability as an integration of ecological, socioeconomic, and cultural aims.[6] There is a growing conviction that religions will play a key role in establishing a broad-based consensus and a deeper understanding of the basic ethical principles of a sustainable society. There are roots for this development, notably in the "Conciliar Process" for Justice, Peace, and the Integrity of Creation, which was initiated in 1983 in Vancouver, Canada.[7] The social doctrine of the Catholic Church also contains many promising directions but has yet to become fully operative.

Nuclear Energy as a Particularly Sensitive Issue in Germany

"Questions linked to the care and preservation of the environment today need to give due consideration to *the energy problem*," wrote Benedict XVI in *Caritas in Veritate*. This sentence is often quoted in sustainability conversations within the Catholic Church in Germany, where the controversial assessment of nuclear power as a means of energy production has been highly debated.[8]

Early contributions to this sustainability debate include the rational-economic approach of weighing costs against benefits, as suggested by Wilhelm Korff in 1979;[9] a more radical criticism voiced by Cardinal Höffner as early as 1980; and the coining of the term "bridge technology" by the commissariat of German bishops, which rejected the idea of nuclear energy as a beacon of hope for future progress and instead characterized it as a transition technology on the way to renewable energies.[10] A statement of the German Bishops' Conference in 2006 pointed out the "grave risks" of placing nuclear waste in temporary and permanent storage places, and called nuclear technology a "clear violation of the principle of precaution."[11] The bishops of Bavaria even found stronger words as a reaction to the nuclear disaster in Fukushima in March 2011:

> The catastrophe in the Japanese nuclear power plant Fukushima has again illustrated the limits of the power of humans. The residual risk of nuclear power is unforeseeable; the question of permanent storage has yet to be answered and cannot be imposed on future generations. The Bavarian Bishops do not consider nuclear power as a sustainable means of energy production. The phase-out of this technology is to be implemented as soon as possible, and the period of the utilization of nuclear technology as a bridge technology is to remain as short and limited as possible.[12]

The Evangelical church in Germany had already issued a categorical renunciation of nuclear power after the disaster in Chernobyl in 1986: "the utilization of nuclear energy is incompatible with our responsibility for creation."[13] This view is based on statements from the Protestant churches regarding the ethical responsibility of nuclear power, as well as more specific questions concerning permanent storage, risk assessment, and the relationship between climate change and nuclear energy.

Only months after the Fukushima Daiichi nuclear disaster, the German government decided to phase out nuclear power plants in a gradual process ending in the year 2022. This was a very difficult decision for a country whose economy is highly dependent on a secure and cheap energy supply. The German government declared it to be an ethical decision (the commission that advised the government was called the "Ethics Commission"), and the churches were strongly involved.[14] In the context of this broad public debate the German Bishops Conference published a book on the substantial impact that an energy turnaround would have on the realization of the goal of "responsibility for creation" at the beginning of the twenty-first century.[15]

There has to be high awareness of the ethical dilemma between the diverging goals of avoiding nuclear risks and fighting climate change; this should at least be addressed in statements of scientific, philosophical, and theological ethics.[16] Many members of churches in Germany believe that the solution of this dilemma is a new model of reduced resource consumption. This model needs to comprise not only an integrated view on risks, technology, and resource extraction but also a new social contract for global and intergenerational justice.[17]

Notes

1. The term is not mentioned in any encyclical, nor in the very impressive chapter on ecology in "Caritas in Veritate." Benedict XVI, *Caritas in Veritate* (Vatican City: Libreria editrice Vaticana, 2009), nos. 48–52. Hereafter *CV.*

2. See Die deutschen Bischöfe, *Handeln für die Zukunft der Schöpfung* (Bonn: Sekretariat der Deutschen Bischofskonferenz, 1998), nos. 106–50; Hans Münk, "Nachhaltige Entwicklung und Soziallehre," *Stimmen der Zeit* 216, no. 4 (1998): 231–45; Markus Vogt, *Prinzip Nachhaltigkeit: Ein Entwurf aus theologisch-ethischer Perspektive* (Munich: oekom, 2013), 471–81.

3. See Vogt, *Prinzip Nachhaltigkeit*, 456–70; Andreas Lienkamp, *Klimawandel und Gerechtigkeit: Eine Ethik der Nachhaltigkeit in christlicher Perspektive* (Paderborn: Schöningh, 2009); Thorsten Philipp, *Grünzonen einer Lerngemeinschaft: Umweltschutz als Handlungs-, Wirkungs- und Erfahrungsort der Kirche* (Munich: oekom, 2009).

4. Oliver Reis, *Nachhaltigkeit—Ethik—Theologie: Eine theologische Beobachtung der Nachhaltigkeitsdebatte* (Münster: Lit, 2003); Vogt, *Prinzip Nachhaltigkeit*, 29–39.

5. Hans Carl von Carlowitz, *Sylvicultura Oeconomica oder haußwirthliche Nachricht und Naturgemäße Anweisung zur Wilden Baum-Zucht* (Reprint of the first edition: 1713,

Freiberg: T. U. Bergakademie, 2000); Ulrich Grober, *Sustainability: A Cultural History* (Cambridge, UK: Green Books, 2012).

6. For biblical roots of the sustainability concept, see Alois Hüttermann, "Biology and the Law of Judaism," in *The Encyclopedia of Judaism*, ed. Jacob Neusner, Alan J. Avery-Peck, and William S. Green (Boston: Bloomsbury Academic, 2002), 4:1620–29. For a broad collection of early scientific theological reflections about environmental ethics and the role of the churches, see Hans Halter and Wilfried Lochbühler, *Ökologische Theologie und Ethik*, 2 vols. (Graz: Styria, 1999). See also Philipp, *Grünzonen einer Lerngemeinschaf*; Vogt, *Prinzip Nachhaltigkeit*, 180–214.

7. Vogt, *Prinzip Nachhaltigkeit*, 190–96.

8. *CV*, no. 49.

9. Wilhelm Korff, *Kernenergie und Moraltheologie: Der Beitrag der theologischen Ethik zur Frage allgemeiner Kriterien ethischer Entscheidungsprozesse* (Frankfurt: Suhrkamp, 1979); see also Wilhelm Korff, *Die Energiefrage: Entdeckung ihrer ethischen Dimension* (Trier: Paulinus-Verlag, 1992).

10. See Arbeitskreis Umwelt im Kommissariat der Deutschen Bischöfe, *Zur Bewertung der Kernenergienutzung* (Bonn: Sekretariat der Deutschen Bischofskonferenz, 1996).

11. The German Bishops—Commission for Society and Social Affairs and Commission for International Church Affairs, *Climate Change: A Focal Point of Global, Intergenerational and Ecological Justice*, Commission texts 29, 2nd ed. (Bonn: Sekretariat der Deutschen Bischofskonferenz, 2007), no. 54.

12. See http://www.erzbistum-muenchen.de. There are several statements of Catholic bishops that argue along the same line. Nonetheless, the Pontifical Academy of Sciences supports the peaceful utilization of nuclear energy. For the scientific debate and its ethical impact, see also Mylce Schneider, Antony Froggatt, and Steve Thomas, *Nuclear Power in a Post-Fukushima World: 25 Years after the Chernobyl Accident: The World Nuclear Status Report 2010–2011* (Washington, DC: Worldwatch Institute, 2011), 11–19; World Nuclear Association, *Facts and Figures*, http://www.world-nuclear.org; Markus Vogt, *Energy for Tomorrow: Perspectives of the Transition to a Post-Fossil Economy* (2010), http://www.ordosocialis.de.

13. The Evangelical church in Germany emphasized their categorical rejection of nuclear power in 1998 and 2006. For the many statements by representatives of Protestant churches in Germany, see http://www.ekd.de/.

14. Die Bundesregierung, *Deutschlands Energiewende—Ein Gemeinschaftswerk für die Zukunft: Abschlussbericht der Ethik-Kommission Sichere Energieversorgung* (Berlin: Bundesregierung, 2011).

15. Die deutschen Bischöfe, *Der Schöpfung verpflichtet—Anregungen für einen nachhaltigen Umgang mit Energie* (Bonn: Sekretariat der Deutschen Bischofskonferenz, 2011).

16. Jochen Ostheimer and Markus Vogt, *Die Moral der Energiewende: Risikowahrnehmung im Wandel—am Beispiel der Atomenergie* (Stuttgart: Kohlhammer, 2014); Dieter Gerten and Sigurd Bergmann, eds., *Religion in Environmental and Climate Change: Suffering, Values, Lifestyles* (London: Continuum, 2012).

17. Vogt, *Energy for Tomorrow*; Markus Vogt, *Climate Justice* (Munich: Rachel Carson Center, 2010); Potsdam Institute for Climate Impact Research, Institute for Social and Development Studies at the Jesuit University in Munich, Misereor, Munich Re Foundation, *Global Yet Equitable: Combating Climate Change, Enabling Development. A Report* (Munich: C. H. Beck, 2010).

The Case of Micronesia

Francis X. Hezel, SJ

Micronesia (Republic of Palau, Republic of the Marshall Islands, and Federated States of Micronesia [FSM]) has a cumulative landmass of 518 square miles spread over 2 million square miles of the western Pacific Ocean. The cumulative population of these three nations is about 175,000. The name "Micronesia" translates as "small islands." Their tiny size is indeed a defining characteristic, for these three nations as it is for their neighbors in the South Pacific, all of which are struggling to find a place for themselves in the modern world despite their serious limitations: their small size, a relatively uneducated population, scant resources, and remote location. These limitations suggest dubious prospects for strong economic development. There are substantial hurdles to the establishment of an economy and governance structures that can generate sufficient services, including education, health services, and public safety.

Because the three nations of Micronesia have a small Gross Domestic Product (GDP) relative to the cost of government services, they are heavily dependent on US financial assistance or other foreign aid.

With the insistent call to develop their economies to sufficient size to support the expensive modern governments that are now expected of today's nation-states, island nations in the Pacific Ocean are tempted to borrow against their future by commoditizing their natural resources (including minerals and fisheries). Papua New Guinea, for instance, is trading on its mineral resources (which are finite) but still maintains the lowest per capita income in the region. Nauru, an island once mined for its rich deposits of phosphate, is an object lesson in resource depletion: with its phosphate exhausted, the trust funds set up to provide for the future are today all but empty. The tiny nation has gone from riches to rags. The Solomon Islands depends heavily on a logging industry that provides about two-thirds of its export earnings, but overexploitation has resulted in a sharp decline in its economy in recent years.[1]

FSM and the Marshall Islands are among several nations in the Pacific that are attempting to cash in on the rich fishing grounds within their Exclusive Economic Zones (EEZ) by leasing rights to foreign tuna fishing companies. In 2011, the sale of fishing licenses to foreign fleets brought in a record USD 24 million for FSM, but this represented less than 8 percent of the total GDP for the nation.[2] The economic contribution of license fees is even less in other Micronesian nations. If the catch value does not generate sufficient income, then Micronesian nations are tempted to ratchet up the number of trawlers and purse-seiners they allow to fish in their waters, which increases the likelihood of overfishing and the drastic reduction of tuna stocks in the Pacific.

What other means of economic development are available? Tourism and service industries provide some options; but no Pacific island nation has been able to support itself on tourism alone. Moreover, the sale of services, especially offshore banking, has been restricted by the United States, Australia, and other large nations for fear that they will cater to terrorists and criminal interests. At core, a major challenge for sustainability in Micronesia is a structural problem that is not easily solved: the economic and political incentives lead small island nations to exploit what limited natural resources they have—whether by licensing overfishing in their waters, overcutting their forests, or depleting their mineral resources. The incentive for all this is not necessarily greed as much as the need for political survival.

To expect small nations with few resources to develop a self-sustaining economy without resorting to environmental depredation of some sort might be expecting too much of them. Small island nations like Kiribati, Tuvalu, and the three nations of Micronesia may face overwhelming odds in trying to grow the economy they need to support themselves in the future. Perhaps the solution is to apply to the global community of nations the same ethical principles liberal nations have adopted regarding their own people. Unemployment benefits and welfare have become standard features in modern nation-states throughout the West. Is it too much to hope that the same vision might be expanded to include less well-endowed nation-states?

Foreign aid is now perceived as a diplomatic tool used by wealthy nations to extract bargains from the aid recipients. In many other cases, it is regarded as a temporary measure that is expected to boost the economy to the point where the recipient nation is no longer dependent on aid. Perhaps in the future, we will regard foreign aid to the poorer nations not as enlightened self-interest on the part of rich nations, but as a right that extends as long as a nation is unable to support itself.

Meanwhile, island nations face the perils brought on by climate change and sea-level rise. In recent years FSM and the Marshall Islands have been experiencing king tides and saltwater surges in low-lying coral atolls. Salt-water seepage into taro patches has resulted in the loss of 80 percent of the taro crop on some islands.[3] Taro, known as the "potato of the Pacific," is the fallback staple of the region. Kiribati, an island nation of atolls, is already witnessing rising sea level and seepage of saltwater into its "freshwater lens" (a limited amount of freshwater that sits atop of seawater). Its president foresees the day when his people will be forced to move from their atoll homes to higher land elsewhere. Even as his people prepare for this event, island nations like FSM and the Marshalls are already experiencing the loss of traditional food stocks.

For Micronesia, then, the threat to environmental integrity is two sided. Sea-level rise is already reclaiming the food sources that enabled island populations to survive there, even as the high cost of a modern government for an island nation-state puts pressure on it to recklessly exploit other resources.

Notes

1. Francis X. Hezel, *Pacific Island Nations: How Viable Are Their Economies?*, Pacific Islands Policy 7 (Honolulu: East-West Center, 2012).

2. World Bank, Open Data, http://data.worldbank.org.

3. Francis X. Hezel, "High Water in the Low Atolls," *Micronesian Counselor* 76 (Pohnpei: Micronesian Seminar, 2009).

Nature, Human Beings, and Nuclear Power in Japan

Osamu Takeuchi, SJ

Within Japanese culture, there is a tradition of sensitivity to and sympathy for nature. The natural environment is a grace through which we live, though it can also bring natural disasters. This essay discusses the following three points: first, the influence of the Great East Japan Earthquake of 2011 on Japan; second, the inability of nuclear power as we know it to provide human beings with peace or prosperity; and third, the lessons we should learn for the future from the meltdown of the Fukushima nuclear power plant, including the reevaluation of the thinking that led to the construction of such power plants. Nuclear power as we know it has characteristics that are so destructive of nature as to render it incompatible with human and environmental well-being.

The Great East Japan Earthquake: A Natural Disaster

Nature blesses and supports our lives in many ways, but it can also bring destruction. The massive earthquake (magnitude 9.0 on the Richter Scale) off the coast of Japan in March 2011 triggered a destructive tsunami that left much loss and many problems. Many survivors lost homes, employment, and relatives. In addition to the 15,883 people confirmed dead, 2,667 were still missing by July 10, 2013. Many of the 344,000 evacuees still live in temporary housing. This severe natural disaster also exposed problems that affect a much larger proportion of the Japanese population.

The victims of the tsunami were engaged in primary production in a much higher proportion than that of the rest of the Japanese population: as agriculturists and fishermen, their livelihoods are linked to the environment. This connection is not experienced by consumers who purchase their food across the gulf of the distribution system at the supermarket.

Nuclear Meltdown: A Human-Made Disaster

The tsunami caused critical damage to the Fukushima No. 1 nuclear power plant, causing uncontrolled fission, meltdown, and explosions resulting in severe leaks both of radiation and of radioactive materials. This is not a natural disaster, but rather a completely human-made disaster resulting from human arrogance.

A nuclear power plant operates on the same principle as a nuclear bomb, except that the energy is released slowly and the dangerous by-products are contained as safely as possible. Although the radiation itself may be limited as long as the structures around it are undamaged, the radioactive waste is a disaster that can only be delayed, not eliminated. When the containment structures and systems are damaged, as in Fukushima, even radiation from the fission becomes a threat to human and biological life. The Fukushima accident showered 8 percent of Japan with radioactive materials and is still releasing radiation and radioactive materials into the air, ocean, and groundwater. Through the action of wind, currents, and food distribution, these problems may not be confined to Japan alone.

The Fukushima plant was constructed as a means of providing energy for the growing human population, in accordance with global trends that promoted nuclear power in the aftermath of World War II. Thus the very same technology that had been deployed for mass destruction with the atomic bombings of Hiroshima and Nagasaki was promoted as a productive means to generate energy. In terms of the relationship between the experience with atomic bombs and the use of the same nuclear technology for the manufacture of about a third of Japan's energy, Robert Jay Lifton says:

> There *was* resistance, much of it from Hiroshima and Nagasaki survivors. But there was also a pattern of denial, cover-up and cozy bureaucratic collusion between industry and government, the last especially notorious in Japan but by no means limited to that country. Even then, pro-nuclear power forces could prevail only by managing to instill in the minds of Japanese people a dichotomy between the physics of nuclear power and that of nuclear weapons, an illusory distinction made not only in Japan but throughout the world.[1]

The promotion of nuclear power plants comes from need and greed for energy. The value of the planet's environment and of the long-term good of human beings was not a substantial consideration when nuclear power was established in Japan. As a result, Japanese people have borne the brunt of nuclear devastation not just in World War II, but also in the twenty-first century.

In the wake of the Fukushima event, all fifty-four nuclear reactors in Japan were either shut down or left inoperative. The reactors in Tomari, Hokkaido, were the last to shut down on May 5, 2011, for routine maintenance, though two reactors at Ohi in Fukui were restarted on July 1, 2012. As nuclear power previously supplied a third of Japan's electricity, there is pressure to restart the plants. The government and power companies insist that the reduced capacity in electricity generation could lead to mandatory power cuts, especially at peak periods in hot weather. They have devised so-called "stress tests" that claim to show that a plant is safe to restart. The criteria used for these tests are not clear. Stress tests are not sufficient conditions to restart the reactors. Many people do not believe the reliability of these tests.

Opinion polls on March 11, 2012, the first anniversary of the earthquake and tsunami, found that 60 percent of the people opposed restarting the reactors, with 80 percent expressing distrust of the new safety measure.[2] According to a *Kyodo News* survey in July 2013, 58.3 percent of the people still opposed restarting the reactors.[3] However, people living near the plants have mixed feelings, as their livelihood depends on the nuclear power industry. One said, "Our jobs and daily life are more urgent than a disaster that may occur only once in a million years."[4]

Challenges for the Future

We need a new model: development and promotion of alternative, renewable energy sources. Wind and geothermal power can add to conventional thermal generation, which can also include the use of natural gas from wells or from shale. Wind in Japan could provide power equivalent to from seven to forty nuclear plants;[5] geothermal sources could provide the power of more than twenty.[6] Co-generation, which maximizes the reusability of the heat of engine exhaust, could increase the efficiency of mechanical engines. Taking waste disposal and safety into account, these options cost less than nuclear power, can provide equivalent energy, and are safer. The consequences will be felt in this generation as well as future ones.

Since 1963, nuclear reactors in Japan have produced 1.2 million times as much radioactive material as the Hiroshima atomic bomb and 4,000 times as much plutonium as was contained in the Nagasaki bomb. As Japan was the only country in the world to be attacked by these nuclear weapons and has now experienced the disaster of Fukushima, we should be ready to show the world how to avoid the temptations and excruciating burdens of nuclear power and nuclear disaster.

What should we do for the future? We should learn again who we are as human beings and live more humbly. We human beings have greater limitations than we think. We are responsible to God, who made everything, to care for the environment of the earth. Genuine attention must be given to the environmental and human costs of nuclear disasters. Our lives depend on other lives, as well as on the health of the environment. If we forget this, we become arrogant. Our lives also give life to others, and our decisions can protect the greater good. If we forget this, we lose hope. Our vision for sustainable energy should not resemble a nuclear disaster. Rather, energy sources should be safe for present and future generations.

Notes

1. Robert Jay Lifton, "Fukushima and Hiroshima," *New York Times*, April 15, 2011, http://www.nytimes.com.

2. David McNeill, "In Japan, the Lights Are Already Starting to Go Out," *Independent*, May 16, 2012, http://www.independent.co.uk.

3. *Tokyo Shimbun*, July 24, 2013, http://www.tokyo-np.co.jp.

4. "Fukui's 'Nuclear Alley' conflicted over restarting reactors," *Japan Times*, January 28, 2012, http://info.japantimes.co.jp.

5. *Asahi Shimbun*, April 22, 2011, http://www.asahi.com.

6. John Daly, "Will Japan Embrace Geothermal Power to Move Away from Nuclear?," *Oil Price*, December 31, 2012, http://oilprice.com.

Participation Is the Path to Sustainable Development

Developmental Projects and Involuntary Displacement in India

John Karuvelil, SJ

Development is a favorite mantra of Indian politicians. In the past decades, India has developed rapidly, at least in terms of its Gross Domestic Product. Although this development has helped some, especially the rich and the powerful, it has also caused immense misery for many of the poor and marginalized groups. Since gaining independence, India has uprooted and displaced more than sixty million people through its numerous dams, special economic zones (SEZs), mines, thermal and nuclear power plants, industrial complexes, sanctuaries, national parks, and more.[1] The displaced are mostly the poor: farmers, tribals, low castes, and other marginal groups. In the name of development they are herded out of their rich natural habitats and made to fend for themselves. In this essay, I first analyze the well-known Sardar Sarovar Project (SSP). In light of that analysis, I explain how without the participation of the people, the country's development is not possible. Last, I indicate the benefits of such participation. Overall, this reflection suggests that developmental projects in India can be authentic only when the affected people are taken care of and are made a part of such projects.

The Sardar Sarovar Project

The SSP is a part of the larger Narmada Valley Project, the most ambitious river valley development project conceived in the twentieth century. The plan is to build 3,200 dams (30 major, 135 medium, and the rest small) on the river Narmada and its tributaries, which span the three states of Gujarat, Madhya Pradesh, and Maharashtra.[2] Two of these, the Sardar Sarovar in Gujarat and Narmada Sagar in Madhya Pradesh, are multipurpose dams, intended for irrigation, domestic water supply, and hydropower.

The Sardar Sarovar dam is projected to irrigate 18,000 square kilometers of land, provide drinking water to over 8,200 villages (about 40 million people), and produce 1,450 megawatts of power annually.[3] However, all these figures are contested. Independent studies showed a huge disparity between these projections and the actual possible benefits. Lately, the government itself has admitted that these projections were exaggerated.[4] However, the project cost has constantly increased since construction began and is now estimated to be 400 billion rupees (USD 7.5 billion).[5]

Part of what has made the SSP controversial are the cost-benefit equations. Officially, the SSP was to displace about 41,000 families. However, independent sources estimate the project will displace about 85,000 families (about half a million people), of whom about 60 percent are tribals and Dalits, the poorest among the Indian population. Moreover, land, houses, crops, animals, and other resources have been forcefully snatched away: displacement is involuntary.[6] The project will also affect adversely another 25 million people who live in the valley. When the dam is full, it will submerge a stretch of about 13,000 kilometers of beautiful, rich forests, and some of the most fertile agricultural lands in India.[7]

Further, compensation has not been provided to the majority of displaced people, and even those who received some compensation obtained too little to restart their lives. It has also become clear that the actual beneficiaries of the project will be industrial houses, big businesses, and the main cities of the state of Gujarat. The recognition that millions of the poor and the marginalized have to pay dearly for the benefit of the rich has brought together various people's organizations under one umbrella body, the Narmada Bachao Andolan.

In the absence of real resettlement and proper compensation, most of the displaced people have become destitute, have migrated to cities for labor and survival, and have taken refuge in slums in and around major cities where civic amenities like drinking water, sanitation, and other basic needs are unmet. The poor and the uneducated are cheated and exploited not only in their removal from their lands, and in their share of compensation from the government, but also in cities and towns where they are forced to work like slaves.[8]

The Need for Participation

The SSP is one example of numerous developmental projects that add to the struggles of underprivileged groups while the rich and the influential classes, politicians, and bureaucrats thrive on the sufferings and helplessness of the poor. Therefore, while the rest of the world sees the monumental constructions and sprawling cities and appreciates the scale of India's development, the real India—the 80 percent of the population that lives in its villages—is, in fact, dying. They play no active part in the development of the country, except that they pay for it with their labor, livelihood, and even their lives. Therefore, if India is to really develop, the benefits of this development should first reach these 80 percent, the most affected by the kinds of negative impacts described above.

Participation and Integral Development

Participation is closely associated with social justice and the common good, and is a safeguard against the marginalization of people and communities; it protects them from the tendency of the state and other large institutions to unilaterally exercise power over common people, destroying their liberty and initiative. According to the *Catechism of the Catholic Church*, participation is an "obligation inherent in the dignity of the human person," and it is "necessary that all participate, each according to his position and role, in promoting the common good."[9] Leaving developmental projects completely in the hands of bureaucrats, especially in Third World countries like India where corruption is rampant, can only lead, as John Paul II says, "to a loss of human energies and an inordinate increase of public agencies which are dominated more by bureaucratic ways of thinking than by concern for serving their clients and which are accompanied by an enormous increase in spending."[10] If development is to be "integral," and not just economic, then it is crucial to attend to the people who bear the biggest burdens of major development projects.

In a country like India, which is fraught with class-caste-religious tensions, participatory projects can also help to strengthen state-citizen interactions as well as interpersonal relationships. Since state-citizen interactions are multisectoral and require multilevel (national, regional, and local) deliberations, they bring together all stakeholders, agents, and beneficiaries. This can break many sociopolitical, class-caste boundaries and promote holistic community development.

Thus, as the case of the SSP demonstrates, an integrated developmental program requires among other things a continuous increase in the economic and political participation of all people. It also requires a countereducation against greed and selfishness by the powerful who manipulate socioeconomic and religious elements in society for their own advantage at the cost of weaker segments in society.

Notes

1. See Asit Das, "Displacement: The Indian State's War on Its Own People," *Sanhati* (October 3, 2011), http://sanhati.com.
2. Rekha Oleschak Pillai, "Sardar Sarovar Injustices," *Forced Migration Review* 26 (August 2006): 68; Arundhati Roy, "The Greater Common Good," *Friends of River Narmada*, http://www.narmada.org/.
3. See S. Parasuraman, "Performance and Effectiveness of SSP Dam," *Association for India's Development* (August 2008), http://aidindia.org; Roy, "Greater Common Good."
4. See Roy, "Greater Common Good."
5. Ibid.
6. See ibid.; Medha Patkar, "An Open Letter" (1994), http://www.proxsa.org.
7. Patkar, "Open Letter."

8. See Roy, "Greater Common Good."

9. *Catechism of the Catholic Church* (Vatican City: Libreria Editrice Vaticana, 1993), no. 1913.

10. John Paul II, *Centesimus Annus* (1991), http://www.vatican.va, no. 48.

Ecology, Moral Theology, and Spirituality

A Perspective from the Democratic Republic of Congo

Viviane Minikongo Mundele

In the Democratic Republic of Congo, as elsewhere in Africa and around the world, we hear how the ecological crisis is affecting people and the planet—and yet the consequences of this crisis take on different dimensions in various places. This situation requires thinkers to reflect on the future of the planet. Everyone—doctors, lawyers, economists, ethicists, theologians, agriculturists, shopkeepers—must work for the consistent and sound management of nature. Here, I reflect on ecology and spirituality in light of Catholic moral theology. This perspective seems increasingly relevant to the plight of the earth today; it may be applicable in the context of the Democratic Republic of Congo as well as other places. First, I will try to dispel misconceptions about the biblical approach to ecology. Then I will address how Christianity condemns the ongoing ecological crisis. Finally, I will articulate four principles concerning human relationships with nature.

Pitfalls to Avoid

The Bible has long been considered a reference book and a source of action for Christians. But how useful is it in the present day? Biblical times did not feature highly refined industrial economies, with such a great capacity of polluting as is occurring during our age—including the ongoing transformation of raw materials and consumption of minerals, as well as the overload of pollutants and toxic waste disrupting our biosphere. Thus, it is important not to translate or equate the two eras. The Bible does not directly answer questions posed uniquely by our contemporary situation of environmental degradation.

Moreover, aren't biblical perspectives resolutely anthropocentric, viewing humans as superior to the earth? The anthropocentrism of Christianity is a criticism that was leveled by Lynn White in 1966 and renewed by, among others, Carl Amery in 1972.[1] To be sure, the emergence of the Judeo-Christian faith had implications for the relations between human beings and nature, and it is true that there are strong correlations between the ecological crisis and biblical ideas of human dominion.

What, then, can the Christian tradition speak to in this situation? Recently, scholars have begun to point out that the Bible is full of texts that could support a renewed ecological consciousness, in part because the writers of the Bible were deeply immersed in seasonal patterns and ecological realities. Thus both the Hebrew Bible and the New Testament contain passages that explicitly place humanity in solidarity with the universe, that is, with plants, animals, soil, and so on. These passages invite human beings to refrain from excess in their transforming activities. This invitation is well expressed especially in laws such as the Sabbath (Exod. 23:12), the sabbatical year (Exod. 23:10–11; Lev. 25:1–7), and the Jubilee year (Lev. 25:8–13).

Environmental Protection and Christian Responsibility

Human beings are able to exploit nature, the framework for the development of all forms of life. Human beings are also intimately part of the cycle, the process, and the order of nature—we can modify it, but not escape it, as many recent natural disasters demonstrate.[2] Consider, for example, how "more than 40 percent of drugs used have as an active ingredient a natural substance, which is extracted from a plant in two-thirds of cases. To this we need to add the substances obtained from animals, from mammals to insects."[3] Biodiversity is a monumental and invaluable resource for humanity. The reduction or disappearance of certain species has negative consequences on human survival.

Conversely, environmental degradation not only imperils ecosystems—it also negatively affects human communities. Consider, for example, that exposure to chemicals in the environment—in air, water, food, and soil—is linked to the emergence and aggravation of a range of diseases such as asthma and cancer, as well as genetic defects. The vector-borne diseases that affect more than 700 million people in the world each year are considered the most sensitive to changes in climate and the state of the environment caused by the misuse of nature.[4]

These facts remind us that the life possibilities of the human species are fundamentally conditioned by the state of nature. We should recognize the vitality of ecosystem health, if only as a matter of self-interest. But of course nature is more than a resource for human use. In theological perspective, it inspires wonder. Through admiration of flora and fauna, encounters with nature are long-attested sources of inspiration for art, literature, and poetry.

Ultimately, it seems that the preservation or protection of nature ought to be viewed, first, as a profession of one's faith, as well as the recognition of the greatness and majesty of God (Job 36:26). Second, since a stance of gratitude and stewardship is a favorable response to God's love, given the sacred origin of nature as well as the value it has for humanity, the expected logical attitude should be respect, protection, and conservation. As a result, the present generation needs to take into account the needs of its descendants and its impacts on ecosystems. Lack of respect for nature can be likened to the theft of the natural heritage of future generations; thus, distributive justice and solidarity between generations require giving to each generation their due.

If the present generation cannot accurately determine the interests and needs of future generations, it can at least recognize their right to have a world with its potentialities intact where they will exercise their choice. In fact, I agree with Pierre Gibert: "Even if God does not explicitly prohibit human beings to damage God's work, it is clear that God could not bear its destruction."[5] Humans should not bear it, either.

Ecological education is vital, and so too is spiritual awareness. The first principle of a Catholic spirituality, informed by moral theology, emphasizes the need *to protect and conserve nature and fulfill our responsibility of being loyal guardians toward God's creation, which has integrity and value apart from human beings*. The second principle affirms the need *to protect and conserve nature in light of human welfare.* The theory of intergenerational solidarity inspires the third principle of the spirituality of ecology: *to protect and conserve nature is to refrain from stealing the happiness and well-being of future generations.* A fourth and final principle is *to protect and conserve nature is equivalent to turning toward the One who is the origin and the ultimate end of humankind.* I am far from claiming that I have explored all the contours of this spirituality; it is a starting point and will find diverse expressions in a range of contexts, from my part of West Africa to many other countries and regions around the world. But any enrichment in this perspective will help Christians better understand the reasons for their commitment to the cause of nature.

Translated from the French by Andrea Vicini, SJ

Bibliography

Catéchisme de l'Église Catholique. Kinshasa: Médiaspaul, 1992.

Bastaire, Hélène et Jean. *Pour une écologie chrétienne.* Paris: Cerf, 2004.

César das Neves, João. *Dieu dans l'économie.* Nouan-Le-Fuzelier: Éditions des Béatitudes, 2005.

Coste, René. *Paix, justice, gérance de la création.* Paris: Nouvelle Cité, 1989.

Kahn, Axel. *Et l'homme dans tout ça? Plaidoyer pour un humanisme moderne*. Paris: Nil, 2000.

Poucouta, Paulin. "La théologie africaine au défi de l'écologie." *Revue Africaine de Théologie* 26, no. 56 (2004): 171–86.

Santedi Kinkupu, Léonard. "Pour une nouvelle sagesse d'habiter le monde." *Revue Africaine de Théologie* 26, no. 56 (2004): 167–70.

Saoût, Yves. *Dialogue avec la terre: L'être humain et la terre dans la Bible.* Paris: Éditions Ouvrières, 1994.

Schaefer-Guignier, Otto. *Et demain la terre: Christianisme et écologie.* Geneva: Labor et Fides, 1990.

Thévenot, Xavier. *Éthique pour un monde nouveau*. Références éthiques. Paris: Salvator, 2005.

Wénin, André. *L'homme biblique: Lectures dans le premier Testament*. 2nd ed. Paris: Cerf, 2004.

Notes

1. René Coste, *Dieu et l'écologie: Environnement, théologie, spiritualité* (Paris: Éditions de l'Atelier, Éditions Ouvrières, 1991), 43.

2. See Peter Eicher, ed., *Nouveau dictionnaire de théologie*, 2nd ed. (Paris: Cerf, 1999), 230–31.

3. Jacques Arnould, "Et Dieu créa la biodiversité . . . : Connaissance et beauté de la nature," *Revue d'éthique et de théologie morale, le Supplément* 235 (2005): 65.

4. See Félicien Lukoki Luyeye, "Le développement et les risques écologiques," *Revue Africaine de Théologie* 25, no. 56 (2004): 303–5.

5. Pierre Gibert, "Principe d'écologie et l'idée de création," *Lumière et vie* 214 (1993): 83.

Theological Perspectives on Governance in the Mining Sector in the Democratic Republic of Congo

Muhigirwa Rusembuka Ferdinand, SJ

The African continent has been blessed by God with immense natural resources.[1] In the context of economic globalization and climate change, the rational and equitable management of these natural resources has become a major theme in addressing integral human development.[2] One such country, considered one of the most potentially rich countries in the world, is the Democratic Republic of Congo (DRC), which has been called a "geological scandal," with 2.3 million square kilometers of the country and more than 1,100 different minerals extracted by about 300 mining companies.[3]

The DRC has multiple resources: forests (145 million hectares, that is, 56 percent of African forests); energy (the Inga Dam's capacity for hydroelectric power generation is 100,000 megawatts, representing 15 percent of global capacity); oil (with a reserve of 180 million barrels); natural gas (with a reserve of 55 billion cubic meters in Lake Kivu); and mining. According to Mupepele Monti, globally the DRC holds three-quarters of the world's cobalt reserves.[4] It also ranks first in industrial diamonds, second in iron, third in pyrochlore, fourth in copper, fifth in coltan, and eighth in cassiterite. In Africa, the DRC holds second place in coal, fifth for methane, and sixth in oil.

Yet despite this geological potential, the DRC is shockingly poor: according to Human Development Indicators of the United Nations Development Programme (UNDP), in 2012 the DRC was the very lowest in standards of development—placing 187th of 187 countries. This is alarming. The consequences can be seen in several realms.

At the political level, the mining code of 2002 was being revised at the time of this writing, and the hope was that in 2014 the DRC parliament would pass a new mining code that would take into account the UN Charter on Natural Resources, the African Mining vision, and the Southern African Development Community Mining Code.

On the economic front, the mining sector of the DRC is considered the leading sector of the Congolese economy. In 2012, its contribution to the state budget (USD 7 billion) was around 30 percent of Gross Domestic Product and 10 percent of budget revenues (USD 700 million). This seems low, considering the increase in mining production, the tax potential, and the upturn in world metal prices. The poor mobilization of revenues can be explained by corruption and the poor wages paid to workers.

On the environmental front, the mining companies that are present in the DRC do not completely fulfill their environmental responsibilities. Negative impacts on the environment are multiple. This situation can be largely attributed to the fact that companies take advantage of the weakness of the state's regulatory powers. The companies gain a financial advantage from avoiding the costs of environmental cleanup, and the legal and political enforcement mechanisms allow those companies to externalize the costs of mining. Downstream ecosystems and communities bear the costs instead.

Socioculturally, in the DRC the industrial mining sector produces multiple sociocultural impacts, the most prominent of which is, in the words of Msgr. Gaston Ruveli Kashala, "the exploitation of human beings by human beings, family imbalance, immorality, environmental pollution, the relocation of many villages and cemeteries."[5] In general, companies do not fulfill their social, economic, and environmental obligations to local communities.

In recognition of this dire situation, in July 2007 the Catholic bishops of the National Episcopal Conference of Congo created an ad hoc Episcopal Commission for Natural Resources. They affirmed that "instead of contributing to the development of our country and the benefit of our people, the minerals, oil, and forests have become the cause of our misery."[6] The proper management of national resources will be a determining factor in the revival of the DRC. Moreover, in January 2008, the bishops reaffirmed that "the exploitation of natural resources continues to raise serious issues of sovereignty, equity, legality, and respect for the local communities and the environment."[7] To promote good governance in the mining sector will require that all stakeholders work on specific causes locally (transparency, accountability, fight against corruption) and globally (fair trade agreements, implementation of corporate social and environmental responsibility).

Theological Insights

In theological perspective, *creation is a gift from God* entrusted to the stewardship of humankind. One of the principles of Catholic social teaching is respect for the universal destination of earthly goods, to indicate that "natural resources and the environment are a common patrimony for all humanity. They are a special gift from God to all humanity that all human beings present and future generations are required to guard jealously."[8] As a gift of God, all creation and the environment must be safeguarded and protected against harm and adverse environmental impacts that affect the nature, air, water, forests, wildlife, and the ecosystem.[9] At the heart of creation is the *centrality and dignity of the human person*, created in the image of God and charged with responsible stewardship of creation.[10]

In light of these principles, especially the universal destination of the goods of creation, the governance of mineral resources must involve promoting *economic justice* for all. This principled statement is a foundation of Catholic social teaching and was affirmed by the Second African Synod.[11] Moreover, this wealth should contribute to integral human development, justice for workers, social and economic well-being of the populations affected by the mining exploitation, and protection of the natural environment upon which all life depends.

In the DRC, the realization of God's plan for creation depends on the *good governance of natural resources* and on environmental protection. Therefore, the postsynodal apostolic exhortation *Africae Munus* invites all members of the church to work and advocate for an economy that cares for the poor and that respects the whole creation and the environment. This suggests that church leaders are called to understand the major challenges of climate change and the exploitation of natural resources and their implications for food security. Even further, church leaders must be a prophetic voice in advocating for just forms of distribution of resources, for fair governance, and for the protection of natural resources for the benefit of future generations as well as the present one. In communion with John Paul II, we can conclude:

> A new approach and a new culture are needed, based on the centrality of the human person within creation and inspired by environmentally ethical behavior stemming from our triple relationship to God, to self, and to Creation. Such an ethic fosters interdependence and stresses the principles of universal solidarity, social justice, and responsibility, in order to promote a true culture of life.[12]

Translated from the French by Andrea Vicini, SJ

Notes

1. Benedict XVI, *Post-Synodal Apostolic Exhortation Africae Munus* (Kinshasa: Medias Paul, 2011), no. 79.

2. Africa Progress Panel, *Equity in Extractives: Stewarding Africa's Natural Resources for All* (Geneva: Africa Progress Panel 2013); Revenue Watch Institute, *Resource Governance Index* (New York: Revenue Watch Institute, 2013); Synodus Episcoporum, *II Coetus Specialis Pro Africa: The Church in Africa in Service to Reconciliation, Justice and Peace* (2009): "Elenchus Finalis Propositionum," Propositions nos. 22, 29, 30, http://www.vatican.va.

3. Banque Mondiale, *République Démocratique du Congo: La bonne gouvernance dans le secteur minier comme facteur de croissance* (October 2007), http://documents.banquemondiale.org, 20.

4. Léonide Mupepele Monti, *L'industrie minière congolaise: Chiffres et défis* (Kinshasa: Harmattan, 2012), 1:290–92.

5. Mgr. Gaston Ruvezi Kashala, "Notre richesse est dans notre dignité et non dans le mining" (2008, unpublished).

6. Comité Permanent des Evêques de la République Démocratique du Congo, *Changeons nos coeurs (Jl 2,13): Appel à un engagement réel pour la reconstruction de la République Démocratique du Congo* (2008), http://www.consolata.org, no. 6.

7. Ibid., no. 9.

8. Polycarp Pengo, "The Church in Africa: Mission and Challenges" (December 5, 2011), http://www.zenit.org, no. 6 [edited by the translator]. See also Pontifical Council for Justice and Peace, *Compendium of the Social Doctrine of the Church* (2004), http://www.vatican.va, nos. 466–71.

9. See Benedict XVI, *Africae Munus*, no. 80.

10. See Pontifical Council for Justice and Peace, *Compendium*, no. 108.

11. See Synodus Episcoporum, *II Coetus Specialis Pro Africa*, Proposition no. 14.

12. John Paul II and Bartholomew I, *Common Declaration on Environmental Ethics* (2002), http://www.vatican.va.

The Problem of Economic Sustainability in Nigeria

A Call for a New Paradigm

Benedict Chidi Nwachukwu-Udaku

Like most of Africa, Nigeria is plagued by sociopolitical problems that hamper economic sustainability. Why is Nigeria poor? Who is impoverishing it? Why has its history remained a constant rehearsal of woes and inconsistencies in the areas of economic development, social integration, political stability, and religious bigotry?

This study highlights two major factors. First, I wish to argue that tribalism and political disintegration are evils that undermine authentic economic sustainability. A concrete example is the obvious effects of environmental degradation in the Niger Delta area of Nigeria, where crude oil exploration and extraction have left the populace impoverished through the pollution of bodies of water, land, and air in conjunction with an unhealthy tribal divide in the country. Second, I argue that the paradigm of domination, which characterized colonial dictatorship and carries over to present-day tribal politics and multinational corporations, hinders authentic economic development.

Which Nigeria? Decoding the Infamous Tribal Identity with Respect to Niger Delta

Nigeria has three major tribes—Yoruba, Hausa, and Igbo—that are referred to as the country's three-legged structure.[1] But each leg of the tripod structure is falling apart because of political rivalry, unjust distribution of goods, strife, and infighting, all of which foster a focus on short-term, small-group benefits and thereby undermine the common good for the entire nation.

In the political arena, the Yoruba people consider themselves Yoruba first, Nigerian second; this myopic view is true also of the Hausa and Igbo people, as well as other tribes in Nigeria, who place tribal agendas ahead of their country's national interest.[2] In fact, the spirits of domination, tribalism, and corruption are more prevalent in the national sphere than the pursuit of shared national prosperity. This tribal political agenda prevents policies that can address the issue of poverty caused by environmental degradation in Niger Delta.

The situation in Niger Delta presents compelling, significant moral quandaries. The Delta is home to twenty million people who directly or indirectly trace their ancestry to Igboland. It is the largest wetland in Africa, and maintains the third-largest drainage basin in Africa. In addition to supporting abundant flora and fauna, the Niger Delta possesses arable terrain that can sustain a wide variety of crops, lumber, or agricultural trees, and more species of freshwater fish than any ecosystem in West Africa. Yet the region could experience a loss of 40 percent of its inhabitable terrain in the next thirty years as a result of extensive dam construction in the region. The carelessness of the oil industry has also precipitated environmental decline, which can perhaps be best encapsulated by a 1983 report issued by the Nigerian National Petroleum Corporation in these words:

> We witnessed the slow poisoning of the waters of this country and the destruction of vegetation and agricultural land by oil spills which occur during petroleum operations. But since the inception of the oil industry in Nigeria, more than twenty-five years ago, there has been no concerned and effective effort on the part of the government, let alone the oil operators, to control environmental problems associated with the industry.[3]

This socioeconomic lament describes the cry of the people for over three decades. While people are lamenting, the government and the multinational oil operators are blinded by the huge amount of gains they unjustly make at the expense of the lives that are lost through water and air pollution. The police agencies that govern the activities of the oil companies reflect the tribal prejudices that make it possible for the "winning party" to develop, maintain, and expand dynasties through conquest. This situation reveals how those in political leadership or economic power continue to marginalize the weak and the disadvantaged, which leads to perpetual domination of the lower class, deters genuine human and economic development, and results in negative environmental and health outcomes.

A Call for a New Paradigm for Economic Sustainability

Considering the situation in Niger Delta, we observe that domination punctuates tribal political life and economic policies. The paradigm of domination, which triumphed during the era of the colonial masters and their policy of divide-and-rule in Nigeria, remains an enduring practice by the present leaders, especially in their economic policies. With the spirit of domination, some parts of the country are denied infrastructures and social conditions that can alleviate poverty and environmental degradation.

With the situation in Niger Delta, people are denied the opportunity to grow and be self-reliant. Everyone depends on what falls from the master's table, without seeking to eat with the "master" from the same table. Economic inequality becomes a norm in the so-called "master" and "slave" relationship of *nnukwu mmanwu* and *obere mmanwu*. The "master," invested with the arrogant mind-set of "we are here" and "you are there," remains a colossus who can manipulate the economic gains of the nation. Paternalism, which functions with great intensity in this setting, is grossly elevated to a pseudopolitical virtue that militates against authentic economic development.

In lieu of the paradigm of domination, I propose a paradigm of recognition that will enable Nigerians to realize their common identity without undermining local rationalities, cultural values, religious sensibilities, social epistemologies, and holistic worldviews that could foster economic growth in Niger Delta. For example, the cultural virtue of *dimkpa* among the Igbo, with the complementary tools of social epistemology and cultural hermeneutics, could be integrated into a model for environmental sustainability in Niger Delta.[4]

Dimkpa, literally meaning "the husband of necessity," shows that the Igbo expect their sons to be manly, efficient, enterprising, full of vigor, and capable of coping independently, no matter how cruel and unbearable the situation is. It is a recognition that one can persevere and achieve a result, a declaration that the problem in Niger Delta is not beyond repair. *Dimkpa* signifies that people ought to be masters of emergences, not by dominating people but by dealing with the situations that militate against the well-being of community. Hence, *dimkpa* could enable the Nigerian nation to address the situation in Niger Delta beyond tribalism by recognizing that Niger Delta is a home for many people in Nigeria. People ought to be the agents, means, and end of economic development. Adherence to *dimkpa* can help reduce forms of manipulation and social disabilities that paralyze economic progress and cause environmental degradation.

To heal the problems of environmental degradation and poverty in Niger Delta, there should be a reappreciation of the individual as agent, means, and end of economic development. This change will further constitute a balm to heal the wounds of bribery, corruption, tribalism, and nepotism that are inflicted on people by pseudotribal economic policies and trends.

The paradigm of recognition, with its openness to economic development, responsible leadership skills, and the use of social epistemic tools such as stories, narratives, cultural hermeneutics, and local wisdom as enshrined in the cultural virtue of *dimkpa,* will inaugurate a new moment for economic sustainability in Nigeria. It is morally imperative to reestablish a Nigerian nation that looks beyond racial, tribal, and village loyalties, and that is united by a constant search for the common good.

Notes

1. T. Nwalor, Foreword to *Igbos to Be or Not to Be? A Treatise on Igbo Political Personality and Survival in Nigeria,* by Jude N. Uwalaka (Enugu: SNAAP Press, 2003), vi.

2. This lack of unity and a common goal is fast undermining the ideals of political life in Nigeria. Today we have more ethnic politics than national politics. See Toyin Falola, *Culture and Customs of Nigeria* (Westport, CT: Greenwood Press, 2001), 165; R. E.

Mgbeahuruike, *The Ethical Challenges of Constant Military Intervention in Nigeria Politics: Studies in the Political Ethics of Nigeria from 1960 to 1989* (Rome: Lateran University Press, 1989), 50.

3. Quoted in *Shell Shocked: The Environmental and Social Costs of Living with Shell in Nigeria,* ed. Andrew Rowell and Andrea Goodall (Amsterdam: Greenpeace International, 1994), 11.

4. In my previous work, I have used the cultural virtue of *dimkpa* as an antidote against the spread of HIV/AIDS in Africa. See B. C. Nwachukwu-Udaku, *From What We Should Do to Who We Should Be: Negotiating Theological Reflections and Praxis in the Context of HIV/AIDS among the Igbos of Nigeria* (Bloomington, IN: AuthorHouse, 2011), 183–84.

The Cry of Nature in the World of the Poor

The Case of Brazil

João Batista Libanio, SJ

The ecological problem has two faces. One concerns humankind; the other concerns specific world regions. For all people are involved in and affected by ecological issues, and ultimately in an ecological frame we face "a crisis of civilization that challenges humankind to live within the principles and limits which nature provides."[1] The anguished "cry" is one that expresses the risks associated with the current type of development that leads the earth to exhaustion. This cry can be heard all over the world. With respect to the South American continent, negative effects include deforestation with progressive desertification, air pollution, contamination and destruction of water sources, soil poisoning by pesticides, destruction of ecosystems, feverish and predatory extraction of fossil fuels, food insecurity, global warming followed by extreme weather changes, and acidification of the seas.

In both its older and more recent forms, development is based on the triad of market, capital (profit), and technology. Its soul is the ideology of consumerism. What dominates is the simple and immediate sale for profit that aims at increasing capital and investing in technology—with dangerous implications for the environment. Even pursuing a green economy does not affect the ongoing problem of environmental degradation and of its social burden.[2] As Leonardo Boff pointed out, we distinctly hear two further "cries": of the earth and of the poor. Both cries result from colonial legacies and ongoing patterns of exploitation.

The current situation of globalized neoliberal capitalism extends the conquest mentality of previous centuries. Recall, for example, how the Amerindian territories became lands for mining gold and silver and, hence, *commodities*. Today, mining is still associated with negative impacts on land, water, and human communities. Yet it is highly profitable for national and transnational companies that sell natural resources to global markets.[3]

Of course, the deforestation of the Amazonian rainforest is the most famous example of the negative consequences of economic development in South America. The Brazilian National Institute for Space Research (INPE) notes that deforestation of the Amazon rose 26 percent from August 2012 to February 2013 compared with the same period the previous year. An area of 1,695 square kilometers was devastated; previously, 4,656 square kilometers of the Amazonian forest were lost between August 2011 and July 2012, which is more than three times the size of the city of São Paulo.[4]

Agricultural development, exploitation of the soil, and agribusiness also pose major problems. The Cerrado region is in the Mato Grosso territory, which originally stretched for more than two million square kilometers of contiguous areas and is a major site of biodiversity—indeed, it is the "most biologically rich savanna in the world."[5] The plight of this area is not visible to international viewers, who are more drawn to the famous example of rainforests. In recent decades, the Cerrado has been subject to large-scale agricultural development. The decline of native species accelerates every year. In 2008, studies by the Brazilian Ministry of Environment indicated that agricultural development had already devastated about 47 percent of the Cerrado.[6] In other regions, ongoing industrialization and development mean pollution: for example, in manufacturing cement (as in the area surrounding the enormous dam construction at Belo Monte).[7] It is not clear that new technologies alone will solve the ecological problems caused by consumption and pollution.

In response to the double cry for liberation of the poor and for the earth, an ethics of sustainability, care, and social justice is urgently needed.[8] Sustainability should be aimed at the survival of the earth and not of the current economic system. Moreover, a radical change of the current model of production and consumption is urgently needed. Caring for humanity and for the planet requires an inclusive and sustainable economy that will meet the needs and promote the rights of all human beings and living creatures. It supposes the equitable distribution of wealth. It also requires the fostering of opportunities, aimed at ensuring dignified living conditions for all humanity by eradicating poverty and by reducing social inequalities. It protects the ecosystem necessary for subsistence as well as the economic, social, physical, and cultural well-being of the poor.

In Brazil, economic centralization led to decisions whose ecological repercussions are only beginning to be manifested. Two cases have become paradigmatic: the change of the course of the São Francisco River and the construction of the Belo Monte hydroelectric plant. Brazil needs energy to maintain its pace of development. To produce this energy it has opted for hydroelectric power, with damaging effects on the local flora and fauna, because of reductions of water flow in the river. Expert studies judged the Belo Monte plant to be infeasible because of its social and environmental impact. The same is true with respect to changing the course of the São Francisco River, because it will seriously alter the whole ecosystem around the river.[9] Serious studies on the subject concluded that changing the river's course will not solve the area's water shortages. On the contrary, the water shortage could be addressed by implementing alternative solutions with lower environmental impact as well as lower financial and social costs. But in both cases, these major development projects have been approved.

Sustainability and social justice goals cannot be achieved without an educational process that aims at promoting true eco-literacy. Education does not change the world on its own, but educated people do change the world.[10] What the Christian vision may further add is an appreciation of the theology of creation and the significance of social liberation from structures of oppression.

Translated from the Portuguese by Andrea Vicini, SJ

Notes

1. Luiz Fernando Krieger Merico and Bernard Lestienne, "Conferência plenária: O que fazemos com a Terra que Deus nos confiou?," in *VIII Simpósio Nacional Filosófico-teológico* (Belo Horizonte: FAJE, 2012), http://www.faculdadejesuita.edu.br.

2. Leonardo Boff and several economists denounced the lure of the green economy that still remains hostage of, and even radicalized, the old paradigm of domination of nature in order to extract the greatest possible benefits for its business and the market. Leonardo Boff, "Economia verde versus Economia solidária," *Jornal do Brasil*, June 11, 2012, http://www.jb.com.br/. Pablo Solón Romero, former Bolivian Ambassador to the United Nations, criticized the green economy and remarked: "The current relation with nature is through the market. You have to buy it. The problem with the green economy is that they are saying capitalism has failed because we have not put a price on nature. The logic is that you do not take care of what does not have a price. We must change the paradigm of how we relate with Mother Earth. It is not a problem of compensation, but of restoration. . . . The *green economy* will include insurance so that if your environmental property is damaged you will be compensated. We need a citizens' tribunal for the environment." Pablo Solon, "At the Heart of Our Society Is Mother Earth," http://therightsofnature.org/.

3. In Brazil, mining mainly produces four categories of environmental problems: pollution in water and air, noise pollution, and land erosion. Carlos Eugênio Gomes Farias, "Mineração E Meio Ambiente no Brasil," http://www.cgee.org.br/.

4. "Desmatamento da Amazônia sobe 26% nos últimos 7 meses, diz Inpe" (2013), http://g1.globo.com/.

5. Fred Pearce, "The Cerrado: Brazil's Other Biodiverse Region Loses Ground," *Yale Environment 360* (2011), http://e360.yale.edu/.

6. See "Agronegócio e a devastação do cerrado," http://essetalmeioambiente.com/.

7. Several of these highly polluting plants are located around the urban megalopolis of Belo Horizonte. See Auxiliadora Maria Moura Santi and Arsênio Oswaldo Sevá Filho, "Combustíveis e riscos ambientais na fabricação de cimento; casos na Região do Calcário ao Norte de Belo Horizonte e possíveis generalizações," http://www.ifch.unicamp.br.

8. Luiz Fernando Krieger Merico, *Economia e sustentabilidade: o que é, como se faz* (São Paulo: Loyola, 2008), 11ff.

9. See "Brazil's Belo Monte Dam," http://amazonwatch.org/work/belo-monte-dam.

10. Paulo Freire, *Educação como prática da liberdade*, 13th ed. (Rio de Janeiro: Paz e Terra, 1982); Paulo Freire, *Pedagogia do oprimido*, 3rd ed. (Rio de Janeiro: Paz e Terra, 1975).

Social Sustainability in Mexico

Miguel Ángel Sánchez Carlos

The "rule of law" (*estado de derecho*) is a modern political notion. Under the rule of law, both political life and public administration are shaped by unavoidable ethical requirements. Moreover, the rule of law is the expression of the general will of the people. The separation of powers (i.e., executive, legislative, and judicial) mediates the people's will and prevents the concentration of power or any interference between one power and the other two powers. In this system, the recognition and exercise of the fundamental rights and freedoms of citizens are further examples of how the people's will is mediated.[1]

The notion of rule of law, which unfortunately in many societies is still a distant ideal, plays an important role in addressing the ecological deterioration of large regions of the planet, particularly when we consider that the presence of industrial development that exploits the environment necessarily involves political decisions that permitted or tolerated the exploitation.

In short, the existence of a strong rule of law is fundamental because it places the conservation and sustainability of life—particularly when the life of all creatures is wounded, threatened, or vulnerable—above any commercial interest (public or private) that threatens the sustainability of life on the planet.

Sustainability in a Systemic Perspective

To appreciate better the importance of the rule of law for sustainability, however, it is necessary to understand the rule of law systemically. Following the 1987 Brundtland Report released by the United Nations World Commission on Environment and Development, "sustainability" is defined as "The satisfaction of the basic needs of the present without threatening corresponding needs to future generations."[2] It is very important to emphasize the systemic nature of sustainability, that is, to realize that both the relations of production as well as the goods produced and consumed take place within the market economy, which is a system created by human beings. Moreover, the economic system is part of the whole political system. Hence, it is essential to think systemically in order to understand the relationship between these types of systems. Consequently, to analyze sustainability, an interdisciplinary methodology must take into account economics, politics, and sociology in both theory and in contemporary contexts.[3]

In other words, the promotion of sustainability is inseparable from an attentive critical analysis of the overall sociopolitical system. This analysis allows the identification of the interrelated forces (political, economic, cultural, social) that influence, or hinder, or prevent, or hamper, or even promote sustainability.

A crucial conflict to consider is that between a cyclic system, on the one hand, and a linear system, on the other. An example of a cyclic system is the ecosystem—where some factor that depends on the presence of one natural element (or on its degradation) promotes the persistence (or the appearance) of another natural element; whereas an example of a linear system is the market production system—which poses real threats and challenges to sustainable social development and life on the planet.[4] Despite many contemporary efforts to render high-yield economic growth compatible with sustainability, the main tenet of this system—"to produce efficiently and to consume with opulence"[5]—is unworkable. The current dynamics of the market production system would threaten both the efficiency of the system of production and the consumers' ability to buy goods.[6] As a consequence, individuals and groups could be impoverished to the point of being excluded from the marketplace, because they are neither able to produce more in the shortest time possible and at the lowest cost, nor have they the resources to consume compulsively what is produced.

Sustainability in Mexico

Sustainability in Mexico is still a work in progress, not only in the case of public policy aiming at industrial development, but in education.[7] In particular, two aspects need emphasis.

With respect to the rule of law in the industrial context, existing legal regulations might be inapplicable because of their generality and because they do not take into account a systemic structural dimension. A few examples: the difficulties of the small and medium manufacturing industry in the context of market competition;[8] the lack of regulatory frameworks concerning specific environmental issues and the presence of loopholes, as in the case of water pollution; and low compliance rates concerning existing environmental regulations, due to the high levels of government corruption or to weak incentives for compliance.[9] Hence, the importance of a "systemic approach" should be stressed, because while nations cannot live without industrial development, this should not result in economic development without appropriate ethical standards.[10]

However, the civic culture in Mexico is still weak, and the average Mexican citizen has a limited influence on public policy. Moreover, the notion of responsible consumption faces a theological and pastoral impasse in Mexico, because the potential of Christianity to form the citizen's conscience is underdeveloped with regard to ecological behavior: that is, encouraging people to consume in ways that would prioritize manufactured goods produced in sustainable ways and to challenge any type of production that would abuse the environment. Hence, what is missing is a more far-reaching education aiming at promoting responsible consumption within multiple relevant social contexts and institutional settings.

As an example, within the Christian communities this educational effort could occur both through catechesis and adults' formation centered on Catholic social teaching. It is also necessary to promote the people's participation in implementing the political dimension of Christianity, so that the citizens might influence public policy by promoting the observance of the rule of law, particularly in what concerns the regulations that protect sustainability within civil society.

It should be noted that, beginning in recent decades, various Christian groups have been engaged in implementing sustainable practices as well as in helping to articulate and to promote theological and ethical reflections focused on sustainability. Despite these positive examples, however, Christianity has not yet realized its potential to become actively engaged in promoting sustainability and in putting into effect concrete sustainable practices.

Sustainable Social Alternatives

The ethico-theological and pastoral process of promoting sustainability in Mexico has already begun, at least in some contexts. In recent decades, base communities and groups involved in pastoral social work have organized, both in the countryside and in cities. They have implemented a dual strategy.

The first strategy is characterized by practical formation and education that links theology and ecological action—including workshops on how to produce and to collect the goods needed for family and community life; ethical and theological conscientization about sustainability, justice, and peace; the concept of "respect for creation"; the dissemination of an ecological theology, which is rooted in sharing one's experience of Christ and of God as the provident Father-Mother, against the idolatry of the market and of consumption. Other concrete examples concern the creation of family gardens and green roofs, as well as a commitment to recycling all types of waste—by including projects that create ornamental works.

The second part of this strategy is sociopolitical activism by these groups and Christian movements aimed at influencing public policy. In this case, the commitment to address ecological concerns and promote sustainability is among the criteria for assessing the electoral proposals of the various political candidates and parties. Similarly, in the public arena it is common to notice social mobilization against industrial practices or the establishment of companies that pollute, both with their emissions and even by virtue of their location in neighborhoods. Among multiple possible examples, there are many instances of popular resistance against locating malls in green areas, as in the case of the plan to establish a Costco mall in the green area in the city of Cuernavaca (Morelos), or locating malls in archaeological areas; multiplying the number of gas stations; or changing the zoning codes from green to residential in order to build huge residential complexes.

This strategy can be considered a civic strategy as well as a Christian approach. A key aspect of this double Christian strategy is the positive interaction with a large number of local and global groups and movements (ecumenical, social, and political) that are committed to promote systemic sustainability within the market economy. As I indicated earlier, within the strategy of action of the ecclesial base communities, which is aimed at promoting a just society, respect for creation plays a relevant role.[11]

We can conclude by emphasizing that in Mexico sustainability—as a topic and as a social issue—is still an enormous challenge, both at the practical level and in theological ethics. An increasing commitment and concrete experiences and practices implemented individually and institutionally can further promote greater engagement in sustainability in Mexico. Renewed organizational support and more efficient dissemination of successful sustainable solutions are needed. The Catholic Church could play an important role in joining in this process of renewed and strengthened organization and dissemination.

Translated from the Spanish by Andrea Vicini, SJ

Notes

1. See Marciano Vidal, "Estado de derecho," *Diccionario de ética teológica* (Estella: Verbo Divino, 2000), 221–22.

2. Alfonso Mercado García and Ismael Aguilar Barajas, "Sustentabilidad ambiental en la industria," in *Sustentabilidad ambiental en la industria: Conceptos, tendencias internacionales y experiencias mexicanas*, ed. Alfonso Mercado García and Ismael Aguilar Barajas (México, D.F.: El Colegio de México/Tecnológico de Monterrey, 2005), 21.

3. See Annie Leonard, *La historia de las cosas: De cómo nuestra obsesión por las cosas está destruyendo el planeta, nuestras comunidades y nuestra salud. Y una visión del cambio* (Buenos Aires: Fondo de cultura económica de Argentina, 2010), 19–22.

4. Ibid., 23–25. For example, the eruptions of the volcano Popocatepetl in the State of Mexico fertilized the surrounding land with benefits for the regional agricultural production. They exemplify a cyclical phenomenon. In the same region, however, the waste of a denim maquiladora does not produce the same favorable effects. It releases contaminated water in the nearby streams. Moreover, it employs women from the surrounding villages, who are considered cheap labor; they are exploited and paid low wages. Finally, when the company finds another location where even lower wages can be paid, the maquiladora will relocate. This exemplifies a linear process.

5. Helio Gallardo, "América Latina en la década de los noventa," *Pasos* 59 (May–June 1995): 19–22.

6. For example, if cell phone factories would keep producing with great efficiency and would make available to the Mexican market a number of cell phones proportionately comparable to the number in the American market, the Mexican market would be saturated. Moreover, if the consumers aim at keeping up with the new types of cell phones that are advertised, the majority of the population would not be able to buy other basic commodities like food or clothing, while the extravagance of the buyer could lead to compulsive buying and debt.

7. "In Mexico, although there have been improvements in environmental policy since the implementation of NAFTA, the industrial development has generated intense pressures on the environment, including high levels of pollution and, occasionally, the not sustainable use of natural resources. In such circumstances, to achieve environmental sustainability is a major challenge for the future welfare of the country. In Mexico, despite the importance of the relationship between industrial development and environmental sustainability, the scarcity of information and of studies about this interaction is surprising." Mercado García and Aguilar Barajas, "Sustenabilidad ambiental en la industria," 19–20.

8. In Mexico, "there is a big difference between the large amount of regulations concerning atmospheric emissions and the limited number of regulations regarding water protection. This situation causes both an incomplete normativity and inequality between the big and middle size companies. These industries need to follow the same regulations despite their diversity. Morover, the large number of regulations on air pollution increases the costs of inspection and of mornitoring." Mercado García and Aguilar Barajas, "Sustentabilidad ambiental en la industria," 23.

9. Alfonso Mercado García and María de Lourdes Blanco Orozco, "¿Exigencia gubernamental y responsabilidad corporativa? Un estudio sobre las normas ecológicas aplicables a la industria mexicana," in *Sustentabilidad ambiental en la industria*, 244–46.

10. An example is the Mexican municipality of Tepetitla in the state of Tlaxcala. "The imbalance in developing and protecting the town's resources is visible. The town suffers from erosion, deforestation, contamination of surface and underground water, production of hazardous solid waste, and loss of biodiversity." Tepetitla has almost 19,000 inhabitants, and 90 percent of its production depends on the local manufacturing industry. This industry brought economic advantages to the population, who are employed in pottery production, sewing, food packaging, and, mostly, washing denim in the local company (Tarrant-Mexico). However, these economic activities generate large amounts of solid, liquid, and gas waste that, with the complacency of the local authorities, are not disposed of in sustainable ways. This explains the high levels of contamination in the whole community and the associated health problems, because of the contamination of the nearby river Atoyac. For more details, see Lilia Rodríguez Tapia and Jorge A. Morales Novelo, "Gestión ambiental a nivel local, una tarea pendiente: Tepetitla de Lardizábal, Tlaxcala," in *Reflexiones del desarrollo local sostenible*, ed. Gretchen A. González Parodi (México, D.F.: Ediciones Eón/Universidad Autónoma Metropolitana, 2012), 291–322.

11. See http://cebmx.org.

Can Agriculture Be Sustainable in the United States?

Kenneth M. Weare

For the human family, food is indispensable for life. The right to food is affirmed in the United Nations Universal Declaration of Human Rights and by the Catholic Church in Pope John XXIII's encyclical *Pacem in Terris* (1963). However, recent scientific investigative studies, analyses, and evaluations of the present and projected global ecological reality confront humanity with a devastating challenge in the realm of food security and systems of food production. Accordingly, while climate change itself is the most formidable obstacle to sustainability and global justice, agriculture remains in the forefront, not only for impoverished peoples, but locally for present and future farmers. And the future of agriculture is deeply intertwined with the effects of climate change.

Agriculture in the United States is characterized by high-yield, intensive, industrial-scale farming of monocultures, which has led to the depletion of soil quality and water supply, among other negative effects. In an era of climate change and water security, crop production is faltering in the United States, as it is elsewhere in the world. The US Catholic bishops have warned of the multiple dangers of industrial farming, from the devastating impact of chemical fertilizers to the near disappearance of the small family farmer. At the same time, even within the borders of the United States, a dramatically high proportion of young people go to bed hungry every night, and an even higher number suffer obesity due largely to the consumption of unhealthy foods. Food systems must be a top priority for civic and political representatives, religious leaders, farmers, and citizens. How will North America nourish itself in the future? And how will its farms be sustained?

In the United States, local food movements are taking root as people clamor for farmers' markets, fresh produce, and organic agriculture. Many people also support human rights for farm workers, many of whom are seasonal migrants working in low-paid, arduous conditions. Simultaneously, multitudes of small groups attempt (too often, in vain) to influence federal legislation on such related issues as fair prices for farmers, financial assistance for small farmers, funding for nutrition and conservation projects, and commodity subsidy reform. But the related issues of healthy food, sustainably produced food, and living wages for farmers appear removed from an agricultural arena increasingly manipulated and controlled almost exclusively by agribusiness, commodity interests, and a closely knit band of Midwestern legislators that virtually dictates the government's food and farming policies.

Is there, then, a just and sustainable solution for agriculture and for the small-scale farmer? Structural impediments at the level of the political economy are a real problem. Even so, in North America, one successful and adaptable project as a model solution is Community Supported Agriculture (CSA). The CSA model originated in Europe in the early 1960s with a focus on local, social, and sustainable relationships. CSA organizations have been developing in North America since the mid-1980s. Today there are upward of 6,500 CSAs throughout the United States. As a sustainable alternative to chemical-laden industrial farming, CSA is a locally based socioeconomic model of agricultural production and distribution. Ultimately, CSA arrangements aim at contributing to viable livelihoods of organized small family farmers by raising incomes from sustainable agriculture and by empowering them within the agricultural system.

Most CSA organizations provide top-quality foods for the local and wider community utilizing organic or biodynamic methods of farming. The CSA is an association of people who have committed themselves to supporting local farms, with both farmers and consumers jointly sharing the benefits as well as the risks of food production. Farmers and consumers work together on behalf of the earth and each other. The farmers function with an ecological consciousness, and the consumers share the financial costs of the growing season and the risks of variable harvests. The average price of a share in a CSA varies according to region, crops, and other variables, but it is ordinarily reasonable and competitive with the cost of an equal amount of fruit and vegetables from large agribusiness operations (due at least in part to the local nature of CSA organizations, there are fewer distribution costs). The consumers may receive weekly allotments of vegetables and fruit, as well as herbs, flowers, honey, eggs, and dairy products. Fruits and vegetables constitute the main crops produced.

Usually the CSA farms are family farms, relatively limited in size, functioning independently, and are labor intensive. They are thus an alternative to the large-scale, industrial agribusiness that constitutes the majority of US farm production. CSA consumers contribute to the economic side by supplying farmers with capital annually through prepaid purchasing agreements. The method frees farmers to devote themselves to quality production issues. It likewise gives farmers an edge in the competitive food market that is dominated by agribusiness and not receptive to local food production.

Although many advantages and other gains have resulted from the overall success of CSAs nationwide, most critical here are those benefits directly related to ecology. CSA philosophy affirms that the activities of every human affect the earth. The land is foundational to sustaining all of human life. The manner in which the earth is preserved affects not only people who presently survive on its food production, but future generations who will likewise depend on that soil for their future. Thus the responsibility for protecting and nourishing the land lies not only with the small-scale farmers who number under one percent of the population but also with the entire population. It is in humanity's self-interest, with a corresponding Christian-based ethical focus on the poor and marginalized, that farmers be encouraged and championed in their work to produce high quality, adequate quantity, and very nutritious food products while maintaining an exceptionally high environmental quality and land preservation.

There are other noteworthy CSA results. One ever-increasingly relevant CSA outcome directly relates to climate change: compared to industrial agriculture, the reduced and limited local transportation of crops results in a decline of carbon dioxide emissions. An expanding number of CSA farmers have ceased utilizing pesticides or nonorganic fertilizers, thus minimizing the destructive impact so harmful to the environment. They avoid the use of human-fixed nitrogen in widely applied fertilizers; these create massive quantities of chemical runoff, which lead to eutrophication, severely impairing sensitive aquatic ecosystems. CSA's program of organic farming also excludes biocides (a microorganism or chemical substance such as DDT used to destroy many different organisms), which have proven counterproductive since they eliminate only 1 percent of the intended targets.

Finally, with a view toward the future, many CSA groups provide educational opportunities that offer apprenticeships for young people from local rural communities as well as industrial urban centers who have expressed an interest in learning the art of organic farming within the context of a CSA methodology. Thus, in North America, the CSA model testifies to the realized feasibility of a just sustainable agriculture. The question for the future is: Can the political, economic, and ethical will be mobilized to scale up CSA agriculture as a real alternative to agribusiness?

Bibliography

Groh, Trauger, and Steven McFadden. *Farms of Tomorrow Revisited: Community Supported Farms, Farm Supported Communities*. Great Barrington, MA: Steiner Books, 2000.

Henderson, Elizabeth, with Robyn Van En. *Sharing the Harvest: A Citizen's Guide to Community Supported Agriculture.* Rev. and exp. ed. Great Barrington, MA: Steiner Books, 2007.

Karp, Robert "Toward an Associate Economy in the Sustainable Food and Farming Movement." *Biodynamics* (Spring 2008): 24–30.

McFadden, Steven, *The Call of the Land: An Agrarian Primer for the 21st Century.* 2nd ed. Bedford, IN: NorLights Press, 2011.

National Research Council, Committee on Twenty-First Century Systems Agriculture. *Towards Sustainable Agricultural Systems in the 21st Century.* Washington, DC: National Academies Press, 2010.

Poppen, Jeff. "Community Supported Agriculture and Associative Economics." *Biodynamics* (Spring 2008): 19–20.

Speth, James Gustave. *The Bridge at the Edge of the World.* New Haven, CT: Yale University Press, 2008.

Part II

Structures

The Political Economy of Sustainability

John Sniegocki

Our world is facing many deep and interrelated crises. Growing numbers of thoughtful analysts question the long-term economic, social, and ecological viability of the world's dominant structures. This essay will briefly highlight some of the major crises that our world confronts, examine competing understandings of root causes, and suggest possible constructive responses. The contributions made by Catholic social teaching to analysis of these problems and the quest for positive alternatives will also be explored.[1]

A World in Crisis

"No generation," argues Lester Brown, "has faced a challenge with the complexity, scale, and urgency of the one that we face."[2] While some may be inclined to skepticism concerning such a bold claim, there is much evidence to support Brown's assertion. Of particular concern is the reality of human-caused climate change. Current and predicted consequences of climate change include increased drought, severe storms and flooding, rising sea levels, shortages of drinking water, declining agricultural productivity in many regions, the spread of disease, and massive species extinction. These impacts are expected to lead to large numbers of environmental refugees and to the exacerbation of social conflicts around the world.[3]

Even more worrisome is that many climate scientists fear that we may be nearing critical "tipping points" with regard to the earth's climate. If these tipping points are reached, self-reinforcing feedback mechanisms may come into play that will make even more catastrophic forms of global warming virtually inevitable. For example, if large quantities of permafrost in the Arctic regions melt (a process that is already in its early stages), vast quantities of methane trapped underneath will be released. Methane is a very potent greenhouse gas, twenty-three times as powerful as carbon dioxide. Scientists fear that this methane will contribute to additional warming, more melting, and further release of methane, in an accelerating spiral. "If this happens," says Jeremy Rifkin, "there is nothing our species could do to prevent a wholesale destruction of our ecosystems and catastrophic extinction of life on the planet."[4]

Highlighting the dire urgency of climate change realities, the United Nations Development Programme has issued a sobering warning: "There is now overwhelming scientific evidence that the world is moving towards the point at which irreversible ecological catastrophe becomes unavoidable. . . . There is a window of opportunity for avoiding the most damaging climate change impacts, but that window is closing: the world has less than a decade to change course."[5] This warning was issued in 2008, and global greenhouse gas emissions since that time have continued to rise.

Along with climate change, our world also faces an array of additional serious ecological problems. These include extensive deforestation, desertification, soil erosion, declining soil fertility, air and water pollution, ocean acidification, and the death of coral reefs. It is estimated, for example, that the world is losing an area of arable farmland the size of the state of Nebraska each year. With regard to deforestation, over half of the world's temperate and tropical forests have already been lost. In recent decades tropical forests have been cut down at the rate of one acre per second.[6]

Overall, environmental analysts argue that humans are in a state of "overshoot" with regard to available ecological resources. Ecological footprint analysis, which seeks to quantify human use of natural resources, is one way that such realities can be measured. According to these studies, overall human use of the world's resources and waste sinks is already approximately 50 percent above sustainable levels.[7] The ecological footprint of an average person in the United States is even higher, more than 500 percent above sustainable per capita usage.[8] As population continues to rise (estimated to likely peak at around nine billion or more later this century), the amount of ecological resources available per person for sustainable use will be even lower. A recently conducted assessment of millennial global ecosystems provides additional evidence for the reality of ecological overshoot, finding that approximately two-thirds of global ecosystem services provided to humanity are currently in decline.[9]

Of course, there are very wide disparities among and within countries in the use of resources and production of wastes. On the one hand, a significant portion of humanity is unable to meet basic needs. Over 1.2 billion people, nearly a fifth of the world's population, live in extreme poverty, on the equivalent of under $1.25 per day. Around 2.5 billion live on under $2 per day. Nearly 900 million people, more than one in eight, are chronically hungry.[10] On the other hand, many people have significant excess, especially in the world's wealthier countries. Overall levels of inequality, both within and among countries, have generally been rising.[11]

Further compounding these problems are looming resource shortages of various kinds, ongoing economic instability due to recurring global financial crises, the realities of violent conflict, extremely high levels of world military spending, the spread of nuclear and biological weapons, and the ethical challenges of new technologies such as genetic engineering. Surveying the situation of our world as a whole, Sir Martin Rees disturbingly argues that "the odds are no better than fifty-fifty that our present civilization on Earth will survive to the end of the present century."[12] Rees is a former president of the Royal Society, Great Britain's most prestigious scientific body. Despite such deep concern on the part of scientists, however, politicians often seem oblivious to these realities. "It all seems a little unreal," says Graeme Taylor. "Although all the evidence indicates that our world is speeding toward disaster, most people, including most global leaders, are unaware of the urgency of the situation. . . . At a time when all of humanity needs to be mobilized to avert catastrophe, our leaders are asleep at the controls."[13] How have we come to the point where such a dire understanding of our predicament is increasingly common among knowledgeable analysts? What changes are needed to avoid these worst-case scenarios?

Exploring Root Causes and Needed Structural Changes

A central question concerning the political economy of sustainability is whether current structures are capable of overcoming the crises that we face. Would moderate reforms within existing systems be sufficient? Or are more fundamental transformations needed? What would be the nature of these reforms? The four subsections that follow highlight varying interpretations and convictions about the global political economy that give rise to differing answers to these questions.

Market Liberals

Market liberals assert that the current structures of global capitalism are overwhelmingly positive. "Liberal," it should be noted, is being used here in its classical economic sense, referring to a stance supportive of minimally regulated markets and so-called "free trade." These persons, such as the economists Julian Simon and Jagdish Bhagwati, assert that economic growth is essential for overcoming both poverty and ecological challenges. They stress also that capitalism is the system most capable of producing growth. Market liberals frequently appeal to the hypothesis known as the "environmental Kuznets curve." This theory asserts that although economic growth at first correlates with more pollution and ecological degradation, at higher levels of per capita income the resources ultimately become available to adequately address environmental problems through enhanced efficiency, new technologies, and mitigation efforts. Thus the solution to environmental problems caused by economic growth is understood by market liberals to be yet more economic growth.[14]

Although they acknowledge the importance of addressing negative ecological externalities, market liberals express confidence that market mechanisms and market-based incentives, rather than direct governmental regulations, are the best means by which to respond to environmental challenges. These persons also generally express deep faith in human ingenuity, science, and technology to save humanity from any possible human-caused ecological disasters.

Institutionalists

A second set of persons, sometimes termed "institutionalists," share much in common with the market liberals. These commonalities include emphasis on the importance of economic growth and a favorable overall attitude toward capitalist economic forms. At the same time, in contrast to the market liberals, institutionalists accept the need for strong government regulation on behalf of the common good, including strong environmental agreements at the international level. Some prominent persons and groups associated with this institutionalist perspective include the United Nations Environment Programme; Gro Harlem Brundtland, a former Norwegian prime minister; and Maurice Strong, a former UN official.[15]

Radical Political Economists

Other analysts, such as those influenced by the tradition of "radical political economy," are much more critical of the dominant system of global capitalism.[16] These radical critics view central features of capitalism, such as its need for perpetual economic growth, as being inherently incompatible with ecological sustainability. "Resolving the ecological crisis," John Bellamy Foster, Brett Clark, and Richard York assert, "requires in the end a complete break with the logic of capital and the social metabolic order it creates."[17] In order to maximize profits for shareholders and to triumph over competitors, these critics assert, capitalist firms have an irresistible need to grow and expand. This involves fostering consumerism, seeking to minimize the expense of labor and other inputs, and minimizing responsibility for broader social or ecological costs. Such pursuit of endless growth in a world of finite resources and waste sinks is a prescription for ecological disaster as well as heightened economic and social inequality. Ultimately, these critics contend, capitalism prioritizes the interests of the wealthy, not the broader common good. "The destruction of the environment and the degradation of human life," says Patrick Hossay, "are not accidental side effects of recent policy choices; they are entwined and unavoidable outcomes of the priorities, principles, and practices that define the global rules of the game."[18] For the radical political economists, sustainability is possible only through a transition to democratic socialist forms of social-economic organization that break with the growth imperative and that prioritize the meeting of human and ecological needs over the quest for profit maximization.

Grassroots Critics of Development and Neoliberal Globalization

Another strand of thought highly critical of global capitalism is represented by persons who are variously termed "social greens" or "grassroots critics" of the dominant neoliberal forms of economic development and economic globalization. Several key figures and organizations in this tradition are Vandana Shiva, Helena

Norberg-Hodge, Wolfgang Sachs, and *The Ecologist* magazine.[19] These grassroots critics share with the radical political economists a strong belief that capitalism is socially and ecologically destructive. They add an even stronger critique of consumerism, an emphasis on localization, and an appreciation for local/indigenous wisdom and for ecologically sensitive forms of spirituality. Criticizing the notion that the industrial capitalism of the First World nations represents an approach worth emulating, the grassroots critic Wolfgang Sachs provocatively asserts: "If all countries 'successfully' followed the industrial example, five or six planets would be needed to serve as mines and waste dumps. It is thus obvious that the 'advanced' societies are no model; rather they are most likely to be seen in the end as an aberration in the course of history."[20]

The radical political economists and grassroots critics both strongly challenge the assertions of the market liberals that further economic growth will solve ecological problems, or that technological innovations are primarily what is required for ecological sustainability. Rather, these critics assert the need for broader economic, political, cultural, and lifestyle changes. They argue that the theory of the "environmental Kuznets curve" (which, as mentioned above, contends that higher levels of economic growth will help solve ecological problems), is largely invalid. Although richer countries have successfully limited a few air and water pollutants, for example, they have not halted the growth in more systemic pollutants such as carbon dioxide and other greenhouse gases, which currently represent the gravest threat to humanity. Moreover, these critics assert that a significant factor in the limited ecological improvements that have taken place in wealthier countries has been the relocation of highly polluting industries to other parts of the world.[21]

With regard to the market liberals' stress on technological efficiency, these radical and grassroots critics point out that significant increases in overall efficiency in capitalist contexts have nonetheless generally been accompanied by increased rather than diminished overall resource use.[22] For example, in the United States energy use per dollar of Gross Domestic Product has been cut in half since 1975, yet overall energy use has nonetheless increased by more than 40 percent.[23] Similarly, vehicle fuel efficiency has increased over 30 percent since 1980, but overall fuel usage has continued to rise because of increased numbers of vehicles, more miles driven, and the increased popularity of larger vehicles such as SUVs.[24] Improvements in efficiency, these critics claim, are therefore not sufficient for attaining ecological sustainability, particularly in the context of an economic system devoted to ever-increasing expansion and the fostering of consumerism.

In addition to criticizing the general dynamics of capitalism and the nature of modern corporations, the grassroots critics and radical political economists issue specific, detailed criticisms of international institutions such as the World Bank, the International Monetary Fund (IMF), and the World Trade Organization (WTO). The IMF and World Bank, for example, are criticized for their commitment to neoliberal structural adjustment policies that critics claim prioritize the interests of the wealthy at the expense of the poor, workers, and the environment. The World Bank is criticized also for having invested heavily in fossil fuel projects, environmentally destructive dams, unsustainable and toxic industrial agriculture practices, and other projects with negative social and ecological consequences. The system of "free trade" overseen by the WTO is criticized for causing massive harm to small farmers, as well as harming small businesses, workers, and the environment. Critics also contend that free trade agreements undermine democratic governance by giving unelected international trade bureaucrats the ability to force changes in environmental, consumer protection, and other democratically enacted laws if these laws are found to interfere with free trade principles.[25]

Whereas market liberals are critical of environmental regulations that interfere significantly with economic growth, the radical political economists and grassroots critics claim that focusing on growth at the expense of the environment is misguided and myopic. "As the world was hurtling toward an ecological precipice of unfathomable dimensions," says the economist Juliet Schor, "the macroeconomic conversation [centered on the need for increased growth] was basically about how to get there faster."[26] In other words, an uncritical commitment to economic growth may contribute to further ecological degradation and undermine the possibility of a viable future for humanity and many of the world's other life-forms. "How can we assume," asks Lester Brown, "that the growth of an economic system that is shrinking the earth's forests, eroding its soils, depleting its aquifers, collapsing its fisheries, elevating its temperature, and melting its ice sheets can simply be projected into the long-term future?"[27] What proponents of current growth-centered policies fail to recognize, says Graeme Taylor, is the fundamental reality that "it is not possible to have a healthy economy on a dying planet."[28]

The grassroots critics stress that what is needed most is deep cultural transformation. Capitalism's emphases on consumerism, competition, self-interest, radical individualism, a devaluing of the common good, the role of the state in defending the common good, and an instrumental view of nature are all incompatible with what is needed for authentic human flourishing and the long-term survival of the human species. Many market liberals and some institutionalists offer the rejoinder that what is required is not cultural transformation but rather technological innovation. But grassroots critics remain unconvinced.

Although more environmentally benign technologies certainly have a major role to play in achieving sustainability, technology alone will not be sufficient to save us. Also direly needed are changes in lifestyles and in moral values, including a more humble relationship with nature and an embrace of sufficiency rather than the consumerist ideal of ever-expanding consumption. Only if these deeper issues are addressed can the ecological crisis truly be solved. Approaches that rely solely on technological fixes, Wolfgang Sachs asserts, "treat as a technical problem what in fact amounts to no less than a civilizational impasse."[29]

Catholic Social Teaching and Political Economy

In these debates concerning political economy and ecology, where does Catholic social teaching (CST) stand? With regard to capitalism, the views of CST are largely aligned with the radical and grassroots critics. Pope John Paul II, for example, expressed strong criticisms of existing forms of capitalism, in continuity with a long tradition of critique of capitalism within CST. "The Church, since Leo XIII's *Rerum Novarum* [in 1891]," says John Paul, "has always distanced herself from capitalist ideology, holding it responsible for grave social injustices. . . . I, myself, after the historical failure of communism, did not hesitate to raise serious doubts on the validity of capitalism."[30]

Speaking of neoliberal capitalist forms of globalization, John Paul II asserts:

> Various places are witnessing a resurgence of a certain capitalist neoliberalism that subordinates the human person to blind market forces. . . . From its centers of power, such neoliberalism often places unbearable burdens on less favored countries. . . . In the international community, we thus see a small number of countries growing exceedingly rich at the cost of the increasing impoverishment of a great number of other countries; as a result the wealthy grow ever wealthier, while the poor grow ever poorer.[31]

While expressing hope that economic globalization conducted according to ethical standards could have positive effects, the pope expresses deep concern about globalization that is guided primarily by market forces:

> If globalization is ruled merely by the laws of the market applied to suit the powerful, the consequences cannot but be negative. These are, for example, the absolutizing of the economy, unemployment, the reduction and deterioration of public services, the destruction of the environment and natural resources, the growing distance between rich and poor, unfair competition which puts the poor nations in a situation of ever increasing inferiority.[32]

What John Paul II and CST set forth is a vision of "integral development." Integral development rejects an overriding emphasis on economic growth as the proper goal of public policy, stressing instead the need to take into account factors such as the just distribution of resources, ecological sustainability, cultural preservation, and the fostering of community and of spiritual growth.[33]

Both Pope Benedict XVI and Pope Francis have reaffirmed the goal of integral development and have reiterated the critiques of capitalism expressed by previous popes. Most recently, Pope Francis issued a sharp critique of the "dictatorship" of the current global economic system. "The worship of the golden calf of old," Francis says, "has found a new and heartless image in the cult of money and the dictatorship of an economy which is faceless and lacking any truly humane goal." As a result of current policies, says Francis, a "new, invisible, and at times virtual, tyranny is established, one which unilaterally and irremediably imposes its own laws and rules." Highlighting the many negative effects of the ongoing worldwide financial and economic crisis, Francis ascribes blame to "ideologies which uphold the absolute autonomy of markets and financial speculation, and thus deny the right of control to States, which are themselves charged with providing for the common good."[34]

The critiques of capitalism contained within CST center especially on economic and social inequality, ecological degradation, lack of appreciation for the positive role of the state in protecting the common good, and a sharp critique of capitalism's vision of the human person, particularly its emphasis on consumption as a primary path to human happiness. Pope Francis, for example, speaks of "the gravely deficient human perspective" embodied in existing forms of capitalism, which "reduces man to one of his needs alone, namely consumption."[35]

The alternative economic vision that CST proposes can perhaps best be described as a vision of "economic democracy."[36] Key features of economic democracy include a more equal distribution of wealth and increased worker and community participation in economic decision making.[37] With regard to distribution, for example, Pope John Paul II declares: "It is the task of nations, their leaders, their economic powers and all people of goodwill to seek every opportunity for a more equitable sharing of resources."[38] In its most concentrated form economic democracy can be seen in worker-owned cooperatives, member-owned credit unions, and similar enterprises in which the workers or customers are themselves the owners. Support for these cooperative enterprises has deep roots in CST.[39] With regard to markets, CST appreciates their value, but emphasizes the need for these markets to be adequately regulated in order to protect the common good. "The market," John Paul II argues, must "be appropriately controlled by the forces of society and by the state, so that the basic needs of the whole of society are satisfied."[40]

CST repeatedly affirms the intimate connection between economic democracy and political democracy. If economic democracy is lacking and wealth is allowed to be concentrated in the hands of a few, the grave danger exists that political democracy will also be undermined as concentrated economic power gets translated into concentrated political power through practices such as lobbying, bribery, political contributions, corporate control of the media, and the ability of large holders of capital to threaten to move elsewhere if their political demands are not met. Pope Paul VI, for example, warns of the vast power of multinational corporations. These corporations "are largely independent of the national political powers and therefore not subject to control from the point of view of the common good." Their activities, he says, "can lead to a new and abusive form of economic domination on the social, cultural, and even political level."[41]

With regard to ecology, CST emphasizes that ecological problems are among the most important issues of our time. "Preservation of the environment, promotion of sustainable development and particular attention to climate change," asserts Benedict XVI, "are matters of grave concern for the entire human family."[42] Strong connections are highlighted in CST between ecological concern and social justice. "Proper ecological balance will not be found," says John Paul II, "without directly addressing the structural forms of poverty that exist throughout the world."[43] Along with structural change, the need for lifestyle change is also emphasized. "Modern society will find no solution to the ecological problem," John Paul II states, "unless it takes a serious look at its life style. . . . Simplicity, moderation and discipline, as well as a spirit of sacrifice, must become a part of everyday life, lest all suffer the negative consequences of the careless habits of a few."[44]

What Can Be Done?

If our world is to avoid ecological catastrophe and embark on a path of sustainability, numerous far-reaching changes are needed. Foremost among these are a shift to a new energy economy centered on renewable energy sources and a significant reduction in economic and social inequalities. Lester Brown, in his book *World at the Edge*, highlights a broad plan to transition to alternative energy sources, stabilize world population, eradicate poverty, and restore soils, forests, aquifers, and fisheries. A massive, rapid mobilization to implement such a plan, Brown argues, represents humanity's "only hope."[45] The estimated cost of this plan is about USD 200 billion per year. This is less than half of the current subsidies given worldwide to the fossil fuel industry, and less than one-eighth of current military spending.[46] Jeremy Rifkin similarly speaks of the need to rapidly transition to a "third industrial revolution." This new system would be based on decentralized energy production from renewable sources, along with accompanying technological, social, political, and economic changes that would foster sustainability and more equitably distribute wealth and power in society.[47]

Several of the main suggested policies for moving toward a sustainable future include implementing a carbon tax, ending the large subsidies that support the fossil fuel industry and other ecologically destructive industries, restricting new fossil fuel projects, and undertaking massive public and private investments in energy efficiency, renewable energy, public transportation, the creation of a decentralized smart grid for electricity transfer, and the education and empowerment of women. The latter is crucial for numerous reasons, including stabilizing population growth. Also crucial are transitions to ecologically sustainable forms of agriculture, new industrial practices that reduce energy usage and minimize or eliminate toxic wastes, and policies to foster greater economic democracy. Among these policies supportive of economic democracy would be debt relief, fairer rules of trade, and other forms of assistance to enable poorer nations to transition to more just and ecologically sustainable practices.[48]

Along with changes in public policy, individual lifestyle changes are also important, especially on the part of the world's wealthy. These could include, for example, eating less meat (according to a UN report, global livestock production is responsible for more greenhouse gas emissions than all forms of transportation combined),[49] using alternative modes of transportation, adapting homes for greater energy efficiency and alternative energy sources, engaging in socially responsible purchasing, and reducing overall consumption.

At the same time, it is important to recognize that there can be a danger of focusing too much on individual choices at the expense of systemic analysis and collective action. Overemphasizing individual responsibility can lead to paralyzing guilt, reinforce excessive individualism and consumerism (e.g., convincing people that they can shop their way to sustainability), and distract attention from the primary need of building mass movements for structural change. As Michael Maniates states, although it is important for people to appreciate the importance of their individual choices, it is also crucial to recognize "that their control over these choices is constrained, shaped, and framed by institutions and political forces that can be remade only through collective action, as opposed to individual consumer behavior."[50] For example, we cannot as consumers choose to travel by public transportation if reliable and affordable systems do not exist, nor can we as individual consumers choose to create the needed decentralized electrical smart grid. Collective political action is required to bring about these and many other needed changes.

Although the world has the resources and technological potential to create an ecologically sustainable future, major obstacles exist. Foremost among these obstacles is the extraordinary economic and political power of the fossil fuel industry and other wealthy corporations and individuals who profit from the current system, feel threatened by change, and are determined to undermine efforts at significant reform.[51] If the transformations to economic democracy, ecological sustainability, and integral development called for by CST are ever to become reality, massive grassroots mobilization will be required. One important task of the church in our age is to encourage the critical perspectives, alternative visions, and capacities for hope in difficult times that are needed to bring such transformative movements to life.[52]

Notes

1. For further writings by the author related to the themes of this chapter, see John Sniegocki, *Catholic Social Teaching and Economic Globalization: The Quest for Alternatives* (Milwaukee, WI: Marquette University Press, 1999); "Neoliberal Globalization: Critiques and Alternatives," *Theological Studies* 69, no. 2 (2008): 321–39.

2. Lester Brown, *World on the Edge: How to Prevent Environmental and Economic Collapse* (New York: W. W. Norton, 2011), xi.

3. For discussions of climate change, see Fred Pearce, *With Speed and Violence: Why Scientists Fear Tipping Points in Climate Change* (Boston: Beacon, 2008), and works by Joseph Romm, Michael Mann, and James Hansen.

4. Jeremy Rifkin, *The Third Industrial Revolution* (New York: Palgrave Macmillan, 2011), 27.

5. United Nations Development Programme, *Human Development Report* 2007/2008, http://hdr.undp.org/en/reports/global/hdr2007-2008.

6. For sources of data in this paragraph, see James Gustave Speth, *The Bridge at the Edge of the World: Capitalism, the Environment, and Crossing from Crisis to Sustainability* (New Haven, CT: Yale University Press, 2008), 31.

7. Rob Dietz and Dan O'Neill, *Enough Is Enough: Building a Sustainable Economy in a World of Finite Resources* (San Francisco: Berrett-Koehler, 2013), 21.

8. Graeme Taylor, *Evolution's Edge: The Coming Collapse and Transformation of Our World* (Gabriola Island, BC: New Society, 2008), 26.

9. Speth, *Bridge*, 40.

10. See http://www.worldbank.org/poverty; http://www. fao.org/hunger.

11. See http://inequality.org.

12. Martin Rees, *Our Final Hour: A Scientist's Warning* (New York: Basic Books, 2003), 8.

13. Taylor, *Evolution's Edge*, 112.

14. For a typology of perspectives on environmental issues, including the category of "market liberals," see Jennifer Clapp and Peter Dauvergne, *Paths to a Green World: The Political Economy of the Global Environment* (Cambridge, MA: MIT Press, 2005).

15. See ibid.

16. For discussion of radical political economy, see Charles Barone, *Radical Political Economy: A Concise Introduction* (Armonk, NY: M. E. Sharpe, 2004).

17. John Bellamy Foster, Brett Clark, and Richard York, *The Ecological Rift: Capitalism's War on the Earth* (New York: Monthly Review, 2010), 86.

18. Patrick Hossay, *Unsustainable: A Primer for Global Environmental and Social Justice* (London: Zed, 2006), 43.

19. For a work co-authored by many of the leading grassroots critics, see John Cavanagh and Jerry Mander, eds., *Alternatives to Economic Globalization: A Better World Is Possible*, 2nd ed. (San Francisco: Berrett-Koehler, 2004).

20. Wolfgang Sachs, Introduction to *The Development Dictionary* (London: Zed, 1992), 2.

21. For critiques of the "environmental Kuznets curve," see Clapp and Dauvergne, *Paths*, 106–7.

22. This combination of increased efficiency and increased resource use is commonly referred to as the "Jevons paradox." For discussion of this phenomenon, see Foster, Clark, and York, *Ecological Rift*, 177–81.

23. Juliet Schor, *Plenitude: The New Economics of True Wealth* (New York: Penguin, 2010), 89.

24. Foster, Clark, and York, *Ecological Rift*, 178.

25. For critiques of the policies of the World Bank, IMF, and World Trade Organization, see Hossay, *Unsustainable*, 82–117.

26. Schor, *Plenitude*, 9.

27. Brown, *World*, 9.

28. Taylor, *Evolution's Edge*, 221.

29. Sachs, *Development Dictionary*, 36.

30. John Paul II, "What Catholic Social Teaching Is and Is Not," *Origins* 23 (1993): 257. Further discussion of John Paul's views of capitalism can be found in John Sniegocki, "The Social Ethics of Pope John Paul II: A Critique of Neoconservative Interpretations," *Horizons* 33 (2006): 7–32.

31. John Paul II, "Homily in Havana, Cuba" (January 25, 1998), http://www.vatican.va.

32. John Paul II, *Ecclesia in America* (1999), http://www.vatican.va, no. 20.

33. For discussion of "integral development" in CST, see Sniegocki, *Catholic Social Teaching*, 126–28, 153–55.

34. All quotes in this paragraph are from Pope Francis, "Address to New Ambassadors to Holy See" (May 16, 2013), http://www.vatican.va.

35. Ibid.

36. See, for example, John Paul II, "Promote Real Economic Democracy: Address to the Central Institute of Cooperative Credit Banks of Italy" (June 26, 1998), http://www.vatican.va.

37. For discussion of CST's understanding of economic democracy, see John Sniegocki, "Catholic Social Teaching, Economic Rights, and Globalization," in *Christianity and Human Rights*, ed. Frederick Shepherd and Chris Metress (Lanham, MD: Lexington, 2009), 149–62.

38. John Paul II, "Address to World Food Summit" (November 13, 1996), http://www.vatican.va, no. 2.

39. For discussion of the history of CST on economic issues, see Sniegocki, *Catholic Social Teaching*, chap. 3.

40. John Paul II, *Centesimus Annus* (1991), http://www.vatican.va, no. 35.

41. Paul VI, *Octogesima Adveniens* (1971), http://www.vatican.va, no. 44.

42. Benedict XVI, "Letter to Bartholomew I, Ecumenical Patriarch of Constantinople" (September 1, 2007), http://www.vatican.va.

43. John Paul II, "The Ecological Crisis: A Common Responsibility" (1990), http://www.vatican.va, no. 11.

44. Ibid., no. 13.

45. Brown, *World*, 183.

46. Ibid., 17, 186.

47. See Rifkin, *Third Industrial Revolution*.

48. For discussion of policies for sustainability, in addition to the works highlighted above, see The WorldWatch Institute, *State of the World 2013: Is Sustainability Still Possible?* (Washington, DC: Island Press, 2013).

49. See Food and Agriculture Organization, *Livestock's Long Shadow* (2006), http://www. fao.org.

50. Michael Maniates, "Individualization: Plant a Tree, Buy a Bike, Save the World?," *Global Environmental Politics* 1, no. 3 (2001): 50.

51. For a case study of the powerful interests seeking to prevent action on climate change, see James Hoggan, *Climate Cover-up: The Crusade to Deny Global Warming* (Vancouver, BC: Greystone, 2009).

52. For discussion of the potential role of the churches in building transformative movements for change, see Cynthia Moe-Lobeda, *Resisting Structural Evil: Love as Ecological-Economic Vocation* (Minneapolis: Fortress, 2013); John Sniegocki, "Implementing Catholic Social Teaching," in *Faith in Public Life*, ed. William Collinge (Maryknoll, NY: Orbis, 2008), 39–61.

New Measures for Justice, Ecological Wisdom, and Integral Development

Dennis T. Gonzalez

In the instruction from Exodus for the first feast of the Passover, one reads the following:

> Tell the whole community of Israel that on the tenth day of this month each man is to take a lamb for the family, one for each household. If any household is too small for a whole lamb, they must share one with their nearest neighbor, having taken into account the number of people there are. . . . They are to eat the meat roasted over the fire. . . . Do not leave any of it till morning. (Exod. 12:3–10)

In ancient Israel, the process of slaughtering and consuming the Passover lamb communicated a complete sacrifice in which nothing went to waste or was thrown away. Thus, it was important to assess the number of people in each household and the amount of meat they could consume, so that small households would join together to ensure the complete consumption of the lamb.

The Passover celebrates God's liberation of a motley group of slaves and the unique initiation of their journey to become a holy people, a light to the nations, and an alternative society to the surrounding kingdoms and empires in which ruling groups in cities lived in comfort, complacency, and wasteful luxury even in times when the majority of their subjects in the countryside suffered from calamity and famine.

In their journey through the desert, when the chosen people craved for the crumbs and leftovers from the lavish tables of Egyptian lords and masters, the Lord gave them bread from heaven, the manna, and the wisdom of getting just enough on the basis of real need so that "he who gathered much did not have too much, and he who gathered little did not have too little" (Exod. 16:18).

The Lord was forming a people for, and leading them to, a land not bursting with silver and gold but flowing with milk and honey, a land not as rich in resources as other lands but rich enough for the people who would remember God's liberation constantly and celebrate Passover annually. Because "there should be no poor" in the promised land (Deut. 15:4), Moses commanded all the people to cancel debts periodically and thus prevent excessive and unwise concentration of goods and resources, or wasteful consumption of those goods and resources, among some persons and groups.

One major reason for the folly of wastage of goods and resources from ancient to contemporary times is the neglect or the inadequacy of measurement of the real needs and regular consumption of individuals, communities, and institutions. Today, in the midst of the oppressive poverty of many communities and the high risk of resource depletion and wars over diminishing resources for present and future generations of families, clans, and nations, recurrent or habitual wastage of goods and resources is a matter of human irresponsibility, an example of living in the state of sin, and thus a matter relevant to evangelization.

Periodic measurement of the development and welfare of people, including their production and consumption of goods and services, is widely recognized as a regular responsibility and practice of the contemporary state, whose will to measure and choice of measures belong to the realm of politics and public policy. This essay will use the Philippines as the locus for a sketch of what the Gospel and Catholic social teaching (CST) offer, and what CST needs to emphasize regarding the pursuit of human development and the role of politics in monitoring, measuring, and ensuring welfare in our age of pervasive poverty, ecological risk, and climate change.

Catholic Social Teaching and Integral Evangelization

CST affirms that the Gospel of Christ benefits the whole human person (body, mind, and spirit), all human practices (political, economic, ecological, cultural, educational, and spiritual) and the whole of creation, "which waits in eager expectation for the sons [and daughters] of God to be revealed" (Rom. 8:19). Thus, every field of human activity that affects ecological and social environments is a field of evangelization. When the Gospel is understood as a divine gift to the whole body of humankind with the whole of creation, evangelization becomes "integral evangelization."

In the Philippines, integral evangelization requires a church transformed into a "Church of the Poor," a church that is pro-poor for the sake of the common good and God's Reign. In such a renewed church, "the Church will not only evangelize the poor, . . . the poor in the Church will themselves become evangelizers. Pastors will learn to be with, work with and learn from the poor."[1]

A priority of evangelization is the realm of politics, because it can lead people to the common good or can dehumanize by entrapping them in practices and procedures that violate or degrade human dignity from one generation to the next. Politics should protect and not degrade human dignity, which flows from God's decision to create human beings in the divine "image" as co-creators who serve also as guardians "over the fish of the sea and the birds of the air and over every living creature that moves on the ground" (Gen. 1:27–28).

In the gospels, Christ fed and satisfied people in their hunger for food, wisdom, and compassion. He also declared that whatever we did, or failed to do, for the poor, the hungry, the sick, the abandoned, or the needy stranger, we did or failed to do for him (Matt. 25:31–46). In our time, believers are serving Christ the Lord himself, whose image or face is mysteriously present in the person in need, when they do any of the following: help generate good and steady jobs for the unemployed; raise the employment or the entrepreneurial skills of the poor; help the poor and the vulnerable to survive and adapt creatively to the effects of climate change and environmental degradation; and help them expand their ethical and scientific understanding of nature and wildlife.

Jesus said that "foxes have holes and birds of the air have nests" (Matt. 8:20), but many human beings are homeless, many involuntarily. And in our time, even the foxes are losing their holes and the birds their nests with the destruction of their habitats, owing to human greed and irresponsibility, which sustain involuntary and oppressive forms of poverty.

Politics and the Common Good

Noble and wise politics creates a stable environment of rules and regulations for livelihood and entrepreneurship, the creation and maintenance of decent jobs, the administration of justice, the protection of "the right of the people to a balanced and healthful ecology,"[2] and the development and application of technologies, which need to be energy efficient in light of climate change.

Those working in politics oversee local and national development planning, the preservation of a people's patrimony (ancestral lands and protected forests), and the administration of public resources (tax money, state buildings and equipment, and public land), which can include substantial and long-term investment in infrastructure for the creation of jobs and technologies in industries and sectors that enhance energy efficiency and produce or consume low-carbon energy.

Politics is the practice and art of governance of the citizens for the common good, which is what preserves or promotes the basic dignity of every person, whether one belongs to a minority or a majority group in society. Thus, for example, contemporary democratic states recognize the human right of equal protection of law for every citizen, whether poor or rich, man or woman, of whatever ethnic or religious group, especially in cases where life, liberty, or basic dignity is at stake. No person ought to be deprived by government of what is rightfully his or hers without due process. No innocent person ought to spend years in prison waiting for the wheels of justice to turn; in many weak states, they turn slowest for the financially poor and those with poor political connections.

The common good extends to the good of "future generations also," and thus implies in our time "the protection of the environment."[3] In light of climate change and the ecological crisis, CST has to emphasize this comprehensive understanding of the common good, which is a principle that usually is discussed and applied either to the present generation of a particular community or to all currently existing communities and nations of the earth.

For example, in his description of the common good in his last encyclical, *Caritas in Veritate* (2009), Benedict XVI wrote: "In an increasingly globalized society, the common good and the effort to obtain it cannot fail to assume the dimensions of the whole human family, that is to say, the community of peoples and nations" (*CV,* no. 7). Unfortunately, there is no mention of the future generations, and they would not likely be included in the average person's imagination of the community of nations.

The common good is not always easy to determine in practice, owing to the growing number of unique individuals and particular groups and associations globally and the dynamic complexity of their relationships and interests. But politics involves the art and science of resolving with fairness the conflicts of interests among groups in society. For example, there almost always tends to be a conflict between the interests of wage-workers who want higher wages or better benefits and the interests of investors who want a profitable or higher return on their investments. Another example is the desire of the landless to utilize or develop more land and natural resources, which can often conflict with the interest of indigenous groups who want to preserve their ancestral lands and resources. Politics is a reasonable means to resolve such conflicts without resorting to violence.

Politics and Climate Change

For a leading interdisciplinary sociologist, Anthony Giddens, politics is the field where long-term innovative thinking and action are most urgent in order to guide and empower the work of diverse groups, sectors, and institutions in seeking and pursuing an effective response to the threats and opportunities that climate change brings.

Giddens has published several works on social theory, human agency and structuration, modernity and globalization, and radical politics in our contemporary world. His concepts and insights can be useful especially for political and liberation theologians who are seeking to understand the forms and structures of domination, oppression, and legitimation, and the reproduction and alteration of such structures, in our dynamic and risky world.

"Political convergence" is one of the concepts that Giddens proposes in the formulation and pursuit of an effective politics to respond to climate change. It "refers to the degree to which policies relevant to mitigating climate change overlap positively with other areas of public policy" so that efforts in one area like "lifestyle politics" or "life politics" can be used to support climate change policies.[4]

The next sections present the ideas of Giddens with regard to the following: the significance of life politics to climate change mitigation and poverty reduction, the harmfulness of the ethos of productivism, and the phenomenon of overdevelopment.

Life Politics

For Giddens, "life politics" gives prominence to emotive and ethical concerns.[5] It is a politics of self-identity or self-actualization. It renders problematic both traditionalist and productivist beliefs about work, gender roles, sexuality, and other vital issues where personal choices are now possible. When life politics becomes central or prominent, it is less difficult to persuade citizens of affluent societies to prioritize the venture to seek and sustain expressive relationships over the venture to accumulate commodities or consume more goods. Thus a shift to low-carbon lifestyles would be more likely.

In the formulation of an alternative development program for the poor in developing nations, Giddens asserts that life politics should be made the vital center of the politics of emancipating people from the "shackles of the past" and from forms of "illegitimate domination" in the present.[6] Among the imperatives for such alternative development are the following: attend to "damage limitation" as regards the local culture and the environment; give prominence to life-political questions; distinguish the destructive ecological practices of the consumerist rich from those of the desperate poor;[7] help improve the position of women in the community; seek to sustain family ties but undermine patriarchy and child exploitation; and welcome critically the assistance of large organizations (states, businesses, and international agencies) as long as this assistance is sensitive to local sentiments and protective of the environment.[8]

For the affluent nations that are anxious about unemployment, Giddens supports the position of increasing employment through "public sector spending in six main areas: improving the energy efficiency of buildings; expanding public transport and freight; setting up smart electricity grids; building wind farms and solar power installations; and developing next-generation biofuels."[9]

Climate change, the ecological crisis, and global poverty and inequality set before the affluent the following challenges: to settle for moderate or less consumption, to live contently in frugal circumstances, to practice lifestyles that primarily satisfy emotionally, and to shun consumerism and wasteful luxury.

Productivism and Vital Enigmas

For Giddens, ecologically harmful consumerism is deeply rooted in the ethos of productivism, which stigmatizes, demoralizes, or embitters many homemakers and unemployed or underemployed persons who seek alternative identities or who experiment with lifestyles that demonstrate that there is much more to living than earning wages. Giddens writes:

> Productivism can be seen as an ethos in which "work," as paid employment, has been separated out in a clear-cut way from other domains of life. Work becomes a standard-bearer of moral meaning—it defines whether

> or not individuals feel worthwhile or socially valued; and the motivation to work is autonomous. Why one wishes, or feels compelled, to work is defined in terms of what work itself is—the need to work has its own dynamic.[10]

Pollution, deforestation, and the threat of extinction of many species are consequences of a productivist outlook, which regards nature and its resources as merely external and expedient. This outlook represses the existential contradiction of human life. Half of the contradiction, the inescapable fact and significance of being human as being part of nature, is put out of mind. The other half is retained and magnified. The fact of being "set off against nature," being able to oppose and modify nature,[11] becomes mesmerizing.

"Ecological problems disclose just how far modern civilization has come to rely on the expansion of control, and on economic progress as a means of repressing basic existential dilemmas of life."[12] A precursor of the ecological crisis is an extensive repression of existential and ethical enigmas. For Giddens, sources of existential anxiety such as deterioration and death, chronic sickness, madness, and eroticism got sequestered from day-to-day routines in the process of denaturing the environment and building modern urban locales.[13] These sources of anxiety and even breathless wonder indicate forcibly our being part of nature, its rhythms, and its contingencies.

In the process of building the surveilled environments of hospitals, asylums, and prison complexes, sources of existential anxiety and wonder became secluded from regular activities. The face-to-face presence of dying and death, the very smell of it, and the laughing and singing of the insane have become unusual phenomena to the average person, especially in affluent societies.

"In pre-modern societies chronic sickness was part of many people's lives and contact with death was a more or less commonplace feature of everyone's experience."[14] These critical yet familiar features of premodern life were often enveloped in traditional practices and rituals that offered meaning and solace. These practices and rituals were preserved and transmitted usually by religious communities and institutions. Deep immersion in tradition helped people appreciate the continuous intermingling of being and nonbeing in the world.

The sequestering of vital enigmas is interconnected with the modern disintegration of a comprehensive tradition and the dissolution of natural environments. These processes yielded the everyday life of pure economic compulsion. The sequestering of existential and ethical enigmas accommodated the ascendancy of productivism, the compulsive ethos in which single-minded work defines the social value of the individual.

Integral welfare or well-being cannot be sought by repressing, hiding, or burying under clumps of capital or consumer goods the human existential enigma of, on the one hand, being part of nature and its contingencies and, on the other hand, being able to wrestle with nature and domesticate or humanize it.

Overdevelopment and Gross Domestic Product

For Giddens, when integral welfare stagnates or deteriorates despite economic growth in affluent societies, this can be described as "over-development," which points to the narrowness of measuring a people's welfare by the magnitude and growth of their Gross Domestic Product (GDP). Giddens affirms:

> Activities that are environmentally damaging can appear to be wealth-generating in GDP measures, as many other harmful ones. GDP makes no distinction between industrial growth which acts to increase [carbon] emissions and that which does not. Nor does it factor in economic inequality—GDP can continue to rise even though only a small minority of the population is making any gains.[15]

Giddens sees great political convergence between climate change policy and a policy to measure welfare beyond GDP. Examples of alternative and apparently better measures of welfare are the Genuine Progress Indicator launched in 1995, the Index of Sustainable Economic Welfare, and the Sustainable Society Index (SSI) launched in 2006.[16] The SSI includes environmental measures like the levels of carbon emissions and depletion of nonrenewable raw materials. A better measure of welfare ought to guide national development planning and political decision making as regards public sector spending in infrastructure and long-term investment of the resources of the state.

In the next section, we return to CST to show points of convergence with Giddens's ideas.

Integral Development and Ecological Sensitivity

CST has emphasized constantly that authentic human welfare and development have to be integral and holistic. For example, Benedict XVI reiterates: "*Progress of a merely economic and technological kind is insufficient*. Development needs above all to be true and integral" (*CV*, no. 3). *Caritas in Veritate* recognizes also the uneven and distorted development of peoples globally, across and within nation-states:

> *The world's wealth is growing in absolute terms, but inequalities are on the increase*. In rich countries, new sectors of society are succumbing to poverty and new forms of poverty are emerging. In poorer areas some groups enjoy a sort of "superdevelopment" of a wasteful and consumerist kind which forms an unacceptable contrast with the ongoing situations of dehumanizing deprivation. (*CV*, no. 22)

In relating human development to God's creation and the natural environment, Benedict XVI affirmed our responsibility to the poor and to future generations and the necessity of "inter-generational justice" (*CV*, no. 48). He also recognized the link between the current ecological crisis and "the energy problem" in which poor countries not only lack access to nonrenewable energy sources but also have poor capability to develop renewable alternatives. In the name of solidarity, he asserted:

> The technologically advanced societies can and must lower their domestic energy consumption, either through an evolution in manufacturing methods or through greater ecological sensitivity among their citizens. It should be added that at present it is possible to achieve improved energy efficiency while at the same time encouraging research into alternative forms of energy. (*CV*, no. 49)

"Greater ecological sensitivity" among the citizenry is shown and sustained by examining current lifestyles, evaluating them, and embracing "new lifestyles" that seek and embody predominantly spiritual and moral values (*CV*, no. 51). Benedict XVI quotes his predecessor, John Paul II, who asserted the need "to create life-styles in which the quest for truth, beauty, goodness and communion with others for the sake of common growth are the factors which determine consumer choices, savings and investments" (*Centesimus Annus*, no. 36).

On the basis of Benedict XVI's statements, one of the ten "commandments" or principles for environmental concern can be formulated as follows: "Environmental protection requires a change in lifestyles that reflect moderation and self-control, on a personal and social level."[17] Under Benedict XVI, the Vatican did the following: it sponsored a two-day scientific conference on "Climate Change and Development" in 2007; it turned itself into the first carbon-neutral state in which its greenhouse gas emissions were offset by carbon credits and renewable energy consumption; it replaced the roof tiles of its Paul VI Auditorium with 2,400 solar panels; it embarked on other "green projects."[18] Also, "Vatican officials say the Vatican plans to have sufficient renewable energy sources to provide 20 percent of its needs by 2020."[19]

New Structure of Administration

In my humble opinion, for the institutional church to create and nurture lifestyles and practices that are energy efficient, ecologically sustainable, and equitable or fair to the present and the future generations, it may have to adopt and reproduce this structure or standard of operation and administration: *measure regularly and report transparently the communal or organizational usage of energy and other renewable and nonrenewable resources.*

In 2009, a large Philippine conglomerate of real estate, banking, electronics, water, and telecommunications firms issued its first "Sustainability Report," which was the first of its kind. In 2011, it issued another report; a third is expected to follow. The report included figures on carbon emissions and consumption of electricity and water of its diverse firms. The conglomerate's explicit goals for this initiative are as follows: measure its impact on communities and the environment, encourage good corporate behavior among its units, enhance its reputation, and attract investments from environmentally and socially responsible investors.[20]

According to a management adage, *what is not measured is not managed.* Measuring and evaluating periodically our activities and their impact, benefits, and costs are necessary steps toward making our deeds and efforts effective, efficient, and sustainable. Otherwise, they become wasteful or bear evanescent benefits, no matter how well-intentioned they happen to be. Those who are already committed to sharing and communicating God's love with their actions need to keep in mind that "deeds without knowledge are blind" (*CV,* no. 30).

Reporting regularly and transparently to the public or to a relevant body the measures and findings of the evaluation of activities and their impact is a reputable way to get feedback on the adequacy, accuracy, and relevance of the measures and findings and to validate, improve, or refine them.

As a teacher and learner, the Church as both institution and people must "listen to and distinguish the many voices of our times," including nonreligious voices from the fields of politics, public and business management, economics, ecology, and the natural sciences (*Gaudium et Spes*, no. 44).

The institutional Church can intensify the impact of its propositions on intergenerational justice, ecological sensitivity, and energy efficiency by urging and persuading its central bureaucracy, dioceses, universities, and institutes to adopt and integrate the structure to measure periodically and report transparently the collective consumption of energy, fossil fuels, water, and other renewable and nonrenewable resources.

To put the structure into practice, sufficient resources have to be allocated to the effort to measure, evaluate, and report. To improve the structure, benchmarking of the measures and results can be undertaken initially among similar Church units and organizations and afterward with similar entities in wider society.

The primary purpose to integrate the structure to measure and to disclose the consumption of resources by Church units and institutions has to be the intensification of the ecological sensitivity and the sense of justice of the leaders and members themselves of these units and institutions. The secondary purpose is to shine brighter as a model, and thus increase the impact, of CST on wider society.

In the Philippines, part of the vocation of Catholic educational institutions is to be "centers for the primary task of fostering critical and dynamic social consciences."[21] The structure to measure and to disclose both the consumption of resources and the efforts toward more efficient resource usage, in conjunction with learning activities on CST, can contribute to the formation of ecological and social consciences of educators, students, and their parents.

Missionary Aspect

Catholic education has to include and develop "the missionary aspect of the Church's social doctrine" (*CV*, no. 15). I believe that Catholic educators, learners, alumni, professionals, and citizens who understood this missionary aspect would try to proclaim their faith in Christ explicitly when there were opportune times in their professional, political, economic, educational, and civic activities.

Scripture says: "Always be prepared to give an answer to everyone who asks you to give the reason for the hope that you have. But do this with gentleness and respect" (1 Pet. 3:15). Thus every Catholic citizen, professional, politician, entrepreneur, blue-collar worker, white-collar worker, environmentalist, and social worker should be prepared to proclaim their faith with both conviction and humility, and with respect for the religious freedom of others, but not during inopportune times when faith proclamations may end up like pearls thrown to pigs (Matt. 7:6).

Ecology in the Social Action Apostolate

Since 1992, one task of Philippine bishops has been to set up an "ecology desk" in all social action centers.[22] In his research on what the Catholic Bishops Conference of the Philippines (CBCP) has done on this matter, Karl Gaspar says:

> The CBCP set up an Ecology Desk at the office of the National Secretariat of Social Action, Justice and Peace (NASSA) with one full-time staff person serving as Ecology Program Coordinator. From data provided by this Desk, some dioceses are engaged in ecological issues but with different priorities from waste management to anti-mining advocacy.[23]

The CBCP needs to mobilize more personnel and resources for this ecology desk, and to consider directing it to champion the integration of structures to measure and disclose resource consumption in Philippine dioceses and parishes.

In addition to integrating the proposed structure, the institutional Church ought to campaign against using the GDP as a predominant measure of the well-being of nations. On this matter, a specific Church pronouncement will be in convergence with what a growing number of social scientists and public policy experts are saying on the limitations and the misleading usage of GDP in national development planning and political decision making as regards public sector spending and investment. Catholic leaders, politicians, policymakers, and academics have to be more active and diligent in resisting the structure or standard to measure a people's development only or primarily through GDP and its growth.

Also, as mentioned above, CST needs to emphasize a comprehensive understanding of the concept of the common good, which includes and mentions specifically the welfare of future generations, and thus to link the common good closely with intergenerational justice.

Research on New Measures

Catholic universities and research centers have to be more active and prominent in the task of reviewing, refining, applying, and promoting alternative measures of human development such as the Sustainable Society Index. Furthermore, a Catholic institutional research agenda ought to include the creation of a data-based quantitative and qualitative measure of a people's spiritual development, which can integrate the degrees of intensity of the attitudes of all disparate communities toward nature, wildlife, and natural resources.

To guide local and national development planning and the decision making of political leaders and ordinary citizens, is it truly possible to formulate a reliable or respectable measure of integral human development that includes spiritual development and enduring liberation from greed, envy, and other harmful cravings? A systematic and adequate measure of a people's capability to create, sustain, and renew lifestyles "in which the quest for truth, beauty, goodness, and communion with others" predominates? A defensible index of a people's capability to creatively and sustainably respond to vital enigmas and the continuous intermingling of being and nonbeing in the world?

If such a research project were pursued diligently and its methods and findings were reported accurately and widely, even if it would in the last instance fail, it would have already constituted a milestone on the way toward ecological enlightenment, integral human development, and the formation of an alternative global community that embodies the liberative and enduring wisdom of using just enough resources on the basis of real needs.

Notes

1. Second Plenary Council of the Philippines (PCP II), *Conciliar Document* (Manila: PCP II, 1992), no. 132. PCP II (January 20 to February 17, 1991) was a major event in the history of the Philippine Church, which attempted to renew itself in light of the following: Vatican II and post–Vatican II documents, the 1983 Code of Canon Law, and the challenge of nation-building after the 1986 nonviolent "people power" liberation from a fourteen-year brutal dictatorship. PCP II was a milestone in lay participation and empowerment, as 156 lay leaders took active part in the discussions with 237 diocesan priests, major religious superiors, and 96 bishops. The bishops were the voting members of PCP II.

2. *Constitution of the Republic of the Philippines* (1987), art. II, sec. 16.

3. Pontifical Council for Justice and Peace, *Compendium of the Social Doctrine of the Church* (1994), 166.

4. Anthony Giddens, *The Politics of Climate Change* (Cambridge: Polity Press, 2009), 69. Another concept he proposes is "economic convergence," which "refers to the overlap

between low-carbon technologies, forms of business practice and lifestyles with economic competitiveness" (70).

5. Anthony Giddens, *Modernity and Self-Identity: Self and Society in the Late Modern Age* (Stanford, CA: Stanford University Press, 1991), 223.

6. Anthony Giddens, *Beyond Left and Right: The Future of Radical Politics* (Cambridge: Polity Press, 1994), 160.

7. In 1991, PCP II recognized the distinction, and declared: "Much environmental destruction may be attributed to the survival needs of the poor, as in slash and burn upland agriculture and dynamite fishing. But the greater sin against the integrity of God's creation must be placed at the doorsteps of those who with impunity cause the pollution of rivers, seas and lakes by industrial wastes, and who for profit systematically destroy our forest covers to the point of unrenewability." (*Conciliar Document*, no. 322).

8. The other imperatives for the alternative development program proposed by Giddens are: tap and encourage the existing activities that indigenous social movements and self-help groups are doing for community development; promote self-reliance and integrity; emphasize the importance of autonomous health care; emphasize not only rights but also responsibilities. For an elaboration of the imperatives, see Giddens, *Beyond Left and Right*, 159–63.

9. Giddens, *Politics of Climate Change*, 147.

10. Giddens, *Beyond Left and Right*, 175.

11. Anthony Giddens, *Central Problems in Social Theory: Action, Structure and Contradiction in Social Analysis* (Berkeley: University of California Press, 1979), 161.

12. Giddens, *Beyond Left and Right*, 212.

13. See Giddens, *Modernity and Self-Identity*, 159–64.

14. Giddens, *Modernity and Self-Identity*, 161.

15. Giddens, *Politics of Climate Change*, 65. In the case of poor nations, Giddens asserts the "development imperative" in which they "must have the right to develop economically, even if this process involves a significant growth in greenhouse gas emissions" (72).

16. Giddens, *Politics of Climate Change*, 65–67. Giddens considers "sustainability" a concept that is useful but difficult to define. For him, "sustainability in its simplest meaning implies that, in tackling environmental problems, we are looking for lasting solutions, not short-term fixes" (63).

17. Woodeene Koenig-Bricker, *Ten Commandments for the Environment: Pope Benedict XVI Speaks Out for Creation and Justice* (Pasay City: Paulines Publishing House, 2011), 23.

18. Ibid., 2–9.

19. Ibid., 10.

20. Felipe Salvosa II, "New Business 'Philosophy' for Ayala," *Business World*, November 5, 2009, S1/1, 3.

21. PCP II, *Decrees*, art. 106, no. 3.

22. Ibid., art. 31, no. 2.

23. Karl Gaspar, "To Speak with Boldness," in *Reimaging Christianity for a Green World*, ed. R. Odchigue and E. M. Genilo (Quezon City: St. Vincent School of Theology, 2011), 31. For Gaspar, the church in the Philippines has failed to speak and act boldly in responding to the ecological crisis because of the following: its opposition to pantheism to which panentheism is wrongly equated; the failure of its leaders to be updated on scientific and theological literature as regards ecology; their dependence on or close association with individuals and groups with vested interests in resource exploitation (35–38).

Toward Sustainability in Urban Planning

The Case of Kenya

Constansia Mumma-Martinon

The last few years have seen massive development in Kenya, particularly in the big cities. Huge offices, shopping malls, apartment complexes, and residential areas are being constructed at high speed. This construction has brought economic benefits at the same time as serious environmental damage. With Kenya's current forms of governance, it is clear that proper planning and creative change are required. This essay argues that efforts toward sustainable development, both urban and economic, must occur at both national and county levels in ways that are coherent and inclusive of all stakeholders.

This essay explains key aspects of contemporary sustainable planning theory and how it pertains to the development of several cities in Kenya. It also suggests concrete roles and activities that can be undertaken by planners, architects, landscape designers, engineers, developers, political leaders, church members and leadership, and the general public.

Defining Sustainable Development and Planning

The concept of "sustainability" in its modern sense emerged in the early 1970s in response to a dramatic growth in understanding that modern economic development practices were leading to worldwide environmental and social crises. The expression "sustainable development" quickly became a catchword for alternative development approaches that could be envisioned as continuing far into the future.[1] This expression appears to have been first used in 1972 by Donella Meadows and colleagues in *The Limits to Growth*, and by Edward Goldsmith et al. in *Blueprint for Survival* that same year.[2]

Meadows and other MIT researchers modeled trends in global population, resource consumption, and pollution and found that regardless of the range of assumptions they entered, the model showed the human system crashing in the mid-twenty-first century. But they argued that "it is possible to alter these growth trends and to establish a condition of ecological and economic stability that is sustainable far into the future."[3] Once introduced, the concept of sustainable development diffused rapidly not just through the networks of environmental activists but also among economists, ethicists, and spiritual leaders concerned about the course of global development. Thus, for example, a 1974 conference of the World Council of Churches issued a call for sustainable society, and an ethics book with the word "sustainable" in the title appeared in 1976, in a volume titled *The Sustainable Society: Ethics and Economic Growth,* by the Lutheran theologian Robert L. Stivers. With the release of the Brundtland Commission Report, *Our Common Future,* in 1987, and the United Nations Rio de Janeiro "Earth Summit" Conference in 1991, calls for sustainable development entered the mainstream internationally.

Since that time, many advocates of sustainable development have brought a number of different perspectives. These include environmentalists; economists (who use the language and tools of economics, a quasi-science that emphasizes monetary valuation of things and the goal of market efficiency); equity advocates (who often focus on the problem of inequality, exploitation, and First World over-consumption); and spiritually and ethically oriented writers. The idea of sustainable development does not mean the same thing to everyone.[4] For example, the term can mean "improving the quality of human life while living within the carrying capacity of supporting ecosystems,"[5] or "development that improves the long-term health of human and ecological systems."[6] More generally, some authors maintain that "sustainability implies that the overall level of diversity and overall productivity of components and relations in systems are maintained or enhanced,"[7] while others emphasize that sustainability entails "any form of positive change which does not erode the ecological, social, or political systems upon which society is dependent."[8] Moreover, sustainability can be viewed as "the ability of a system to sustain the livelihood of the people who depend on that system for an indefinite period," meaning that "sustainability, therefore, equals conservation plus stewardship plus restoration."[9] Entailments of sustainable development might include "five broad requirements: (1) integration of conservation and development, (2) satisfaction of basic human needs, (3) achievement of equity and social justice, (4) and provision of social self-determination and cultural diversity and the maintenance of ecological integrity."[10]

By far the most familiar definition of sustainable development is that provided in 1987 by the Brundtland Commission: "development that meets the needs of the present without compromising the ability of future generations to meet their own needs."[11] Since that time, sustainability has come to be seen as a core value and goal that is informed by an emerging ecological worldview, which weaves together scientific, cultural, and environmental contexts.

The Problem of Sustainability Planning in Kenya

At the most general level in Kenya, people share a multilayered principal concern about human societies' current uses of environmental resources, goods, and services. These uses—which include resource extraction, water consumption, pollution, and many more—are damaging key natural resources in ways that negatively influence people's quality of life in the present and that will persist into the future. Examples include air pollution and major economic development projects, such as the construction of large dams, which destroy valued landscapes, diminish biodiversity, and create environmental refugees.[12] And the beneficiaries of these processes are rarely the people whose daily lives are disrupted, whose water sources run dry or are polluted, or who must be relocated in order for a major building project to go forward. There is thus a disjuncture between who bears the burdens of development and who benefits.

Furthermore, Kenya has a rapidly growing population, but planners have not traditionally addressed population issues, which are often highly controversial. Population growth profoundly affects local growth management efforts and quality of life, as well as broader sustainability topics such as global resource use. Communities with excellent health, education, and family planning services can help address population pressures, especially when women are empowered with economic ability, education, and decision-making authority.

The issue of sustainable development rarely gets sufficient attention in Kenya, even when there are natural or human-caused environmental disasters, since these usually occur in slums or congested urban areas. More often than not, these calamities are due to inappropriate planning and construction, leaving the nonelites with a fragmented landscape of roads, with few sidewalks for pedestrians or bike paths for cyclists to use, big shopping malls and shopping centers without adequate parking, or else the few spaces are permanently reserved for office owners, with little or no parking places for visitors. In most cities, there is rising traffic congestion and overdependency on automobiles, which are too big to be accommodated on roads that have remained the same since colonial times. And, of course, the growing number of people driving in the cities has increased environmental pollution.

In a broader sense, phenomena such as global warming, resource depletion, and the loss of species are difficult or impossible to reverse. Moreover, there is a serious competition for scarce resources such as fossil fuels. To make matters worse, housing is frequently scarce, unaffordable, or inappropriately designed and located. Kenya also faces growing poverty and inequality; enormous numbers of people are left without access to decent-paying jobs, good schools, health care, or other necessities of life. And with the population becoming more individualistic and consumer oriented, the gap between the rich and the poor is widening, thereby reducing the sense of community, tradition, and extended families at an alarming rate.

As a result of these factors, planning for sustainability will be crucial in meeting the needs of future generations. Achieving sustainability for human communities will be one of the main challenges of the twenty-first century. In particular, urban planning has an important role to play. The economic development of the twentieth century brought some financial benefits, and much good has been done in terms of improving human welfare. Unfortunately, unsustainable development practices persist and must be tackled in far more comprehensive ways, especially within newly created counties in Kenya.

The Kenyan government mainly operates from a relatively short-term and small-scale perspective; planners have often had difficulties adopting a long-term viewpoint. Typically, planning documents address a five- to ten-year horizon, though occasionally plans emerge covering up to twenty years, as is the case with the Kenya Policy as stipulated in its "Vision 2030." This vision seeks to ensure that Kenya achieves and sustains an average economic growth rate of over 10 percent per annum over the next decade and a half; builds a just and cohesive society with equitable social development, and a clean and secure environment; and ensures a democratic political system that nurtures issue-based politics, and protects the rights and freedoms of every individual and of the whole society. If this vision is achieved, many of the unsustainable practices in this country would be done away with.

Local politicians often consider only a one- to four-year time frame until the next election. Cost-benefit analyses for large infrastructure projects focus at most on a twenty-year time frame. Since the day-to-day economic development keeps changing and is usually done mainly by private developers, it is difficult to consider costs and benefits more than thirty years into the future. All of these factors reinforce a relatively short-term viewpoint within local government planning.

Who Plans at Different Levels in Kenya?

In December 2005, following government reorganization, Kenya's Ministry of Housing was reconstituted as a full-fledged ministry. It was mandated to facilitate development and management of quality and affordable housing for Kenyans. Among many other responsibilities, the ministry rules and exercises general supervision and control over matters relating to housing and human settlement. Moreover, it facilitates access to adequate housing in sustainable human settlements; monitors and evaluates the effectiveness and equitability of the housing sector against set goals and objectives; and prescribes and sets standards for housing development, estate management, and maintenance.

Besides the Ministry of Housing there is also a Kenya Membership of Housing Board. This board consists of the ministry responsible for housing, finance, matters relating to the devolved government (where more powers are granted to local and regional governing bodies),[13] and lands; the attorney general; the Institution of Surveyors of Kenya; the Kenya Private Sector Alliance; the Institution of Engineers of Kenya; the Architectural Association of Kenya; the Kenya Institute of Planners; and the Civil Society caucus on housing. Despite being very inclusive, community members are not represented in this board. They should be included.

Reforms began in 2009 to review the outdated building code, which was singled out as a major impediment to realizing the dream of providing decent and affordable housing to all Kenyans. It is hoped that the new code will regulate and bring order to the construction industry, and will tame rogue developers who are used to building substandard houses that cause much damage in the booming real estate sector. It will also hopefully ensure that no developer shall commence any construction work unless all the plans and permits have been approved.

A committee with broad-based representation reviewed and analyzed the existing laws, policies, and regulations governing the chaotic building sectors and came up with a set of guidelines, regulations, and handbooks meant to guarantee that towns are developed in a controlled manner. In this framework a prospective house developer is required to seek approval from various relevant statutory authorities that have the mandate to ensure that any new house in their jurisdiction meets the standard set in the national building code as found in the above-mentioned documents. These enforced design standards concern zoning regulations, building structural stability, building occupancy, and design adequacy—all of which affect human health and well-being within the built environment. Thus every building is expected to pass through an intense process of approval by the municipal authority for authorization of every single element of construction according to its governing regulations. This is meant to address the problems plaguing the building industry, such as collapsing buildings, and to ensure that every building conforms to the building standards set out by the National Housing Authority (NHA).

The departments associated with the ministry responsible for housing, finance, matters relating to Kenya's devolved government, and lands are all involved in the approval processes within most of the municipal councils. These departments are on the board of the NHA and were part of the board that created the various housing bills. There are basic requirements for each concerning zoning requirements or building codes:

- *Physical planning department* deals with zoning and large-scale planning regulations, and ensures that a proposed development is in conformity with the allowable building types for an area, and also observes the relevant rules regarding building setbacks, road reserves, plot coverage, and plot ratios.
- *Roads and sewerage department* deals with civil-works-oriented types of approval, especially with regard to planning of roads and verification of sewer provisions in large estate developments and similar master plans.
- *Health department* deals with internal provisions relating to human comfort within habitable rooms. It scrutinizes provisions for house plans in Kenya for ventilation, room sizes, drainage systems, and similar components.
- *National Environment Management Authority (NEMA)* is a government organization established to exercise general supervision and coordination over all matters relating to the environment. The authority is the principal instrument of government in the implementation of all environmental policies.

- *Fire department* seeks conformity to fire safety provisions, especially regarding multiple dwelling units and office blocks.
- *Factories and industrial departments* are involved with approval of large industrial facilities such as factories, "godowns" (warehouses), and any buildings in which industrial and manufacturing processes are likely to be undertaken.

The process of approval of house plans in Kenya generally goes through these departments. Once satisfied, they append their certified stamps on the drawings and move the plans to the next stage until completion. Any developer who does not abide by the authorization process is punished. In this way, the authority should approve all building designs and plans, inspect all construction projects, issue occupation and maintenance certificates, and maintain a register of buildings. It has also the power to order evacuation, maintenance, stopping construction, or demolition if a structure fails to conform to the provisions of the law.

Seeking Sustainability: Housing Policy in a Devolved System and the 2007 National Land Policy

The new devolved system of government in Kenya may not result in any major change within the housing industry. Experts expect that policy formulation for the housing sector will be left to the central government, while the county governments will be charged with implementation. This will vary according to region, because counties have different environmental and climatic concerns, as well as limited resources. Through the Ministry of Housing, the central government will stipulate policies that will govern all counties while each county will adapt policies to their own particular situation depending on availability, environmental concerns, and other local considerations; this will include features such as the materials for housing and the building design. For the purposes of sustainability planning, both the national government and the different counties must play key roles in overseeing land use planning, transportation systems, environmental protection, equity, and the formation of municipal governments.

The overall objective of the 2007 National Land Policy (NLP) is to provide for sustainable growth and investment and the reduction of poverty, in line with the government's overall development objectives. It was formulated to address the critical issues of land administration, access to land, land use planning, restitution in cases of historical injustices, environmental degradation, conflicts in unplanned urban settlements, outdated legal frameworks, and information management, among others. This policy is a great opportunity for sustainable development to take place in Kenya.

Sustainable planning in Kenya requires reflection on an ecological viewpoint that respects and maintains various cultural perspectives. Quite obviously, sustainability planning seeks to bring about a society that will exist and thrive far into the future.[14] Sustainability planning is a holistic outlook that values the intertwined relationships between things and that embodies an ecological understanding of the world. This ecological worldview acknowledges cultural diversity but seeks to ground the development of society in fundamental values that we all share by virtue of being human and by living on the same planet. This perspective emphasizes interdependent, flexible, evolving systems that can learn and adapt.

What methods of sustainable planning, therefore, might be particularly useful to planners, political leaders, ecclesial bodies, citizens, and activists in Kenya? In light of the concepts of sustainability described above, it is important to hold several principles in mind. Sustainable planning must include a long-term assessment of costs and benefits; a participatory approach to decision making; an interdisciplinary, holistic outlook integrating various disciplines and analytic approaches; an awareness of ecological limits along with a questioning of traditional models of growth that ignore those limits; a new appreciation of the importance of place; and proactive involvement in healing societies and ecosystems. These principles can help reorient planning debates in constructive ways to address current development challenges in Kenya. The ultimate goal is to harmonize the varied activities of different actors at all levels to make planning sustainable in Kenya for the benefit of all Kenyans, present and future. Hence, we need to examine the role and responsibilities of the multiple moral agents described below.

The General Population

In Kenya, many people focus on their homes, neighborhoods, and daily lives without a sense of how these affect sustainability in the region and in the country. The impacts of personal actions on the daily environment are immediate; those affecting larger contexts are more remote and may occur far in the future. The Kenyan planning culture does not often encourage a connection between these personal concerns and national matters. Both the general population and private developers should become aware of the benefits and advantages of getting involved in sustainable planning because of its beneficial effects nationally. It is the responsibility of every citizen to make sustainability a nationally owned process and to realize the importance of one's contributions and participation, regardless of how insignificant these may seem to them. Therefore, any planning must be decentralized as much as possible. In this way, agents of sustainable planning in each community will be able to identify, and hopefully to address, the planning problems within their communities. The Kenyan Nobel Peace Prize-winner and environmentalist Wangari Maathai has agreed: "It's the little things citizens do. That's what will make the difference. My little thing is planting trees."[15] Furthermore, if you do not have local people who are committed to the process and willing to work with their communities, the projects will not survive.[16]

Women

The United Nations Security Council Resolution 1325 of October 2000 seeks to increase representation of women at all levels in national, regional, and international institutions. In Kenya, the current National Gender and Development Policy is intended to facilitate mainstreaming of the needs and concerns for men, women, girls, and boys in all sectors of development in the country's development policy. This would provide an opportunity for women at various levels to be more involved in the decision-making process, locally and nationally.

Women can use this opportunity to discourage unsustainable ways of planning and to encourage sustainable development at all levels, since "everything they lacked depended on the environment"[17] and "the world needed to address the realities of rural women, their poverty, the overall lack of development, and the state of environment that sustained them."[18] Wangari Maathai has advocated for planting trees since "the trees would provide a supply of wood that would enable women to cook nutritious food. They would also have wood for fencing and fodder for cattle and goats. The trees would offer shade for humans and animals, protect watersheds and bind the soil, and if they were fruit trees, provide food. They would also heal the land by bringing back birds and small animals and regenerate the vitality of the earth."[19]

The Youth

"Agenda 21," the action plan of the United Nations regarding sustainable development in the twenty-first century, calls for sustainable development through participation. Chapter 25, "Children and Youth in Sustainable Development," suggests that "it is imperative that youth from all parts of the world participate actively in all relevant levels of decision-making processes because it affects their lives today and has implications for their futures."[20]

In Kenya, the Kenya National Youth Policy was developed to deal with a myriad of challenges facing the youth today. This policy is aimed at ensuring that the youth play their role alongside adults in the development of Kenya, to promote youth participation in community and civic affairs, and to ensure that the youth programs are youth centered. It proposes guidelines and strategies that can facilitate youth participation and empowerment in developing the country by promoting employment opportunities, health, education and training, sports and recreation, environmental protection, art, culture, and media. All of these can be valuable avenues for sustainable development.

Higher Learning Institutions

Unsustainable development in Kenya will be inevitable if outdated policies are not upgraded. Higher learning institutions can play an important role in this process by becoming more efficient and responsive to sustainable development and planning interests. Concretely, they should welcome different students from all walks of life to allow openness. Ultimately, these students will contribute to finding solutions to sustainable planning problems.

In particular, these higher learning institutions should emphasize sustainable planning squarely in their curricula. Moreover, these institutions should collaborate with different social organizations to strengthen efforts toward sustainable planning in the country. They should also focus on research. Trained professionals should participate more actively and constructively in problem solving, in offering expert opinions and advice, in providing expert services where needed, and in helping to implement policies, especially when these concern conducting research facilitation and training. Finally, people from different countries, especially those where sustainable planning has been implemented successfully, ought to be encouraged to share their experiences. This sharing is important because sustainable development requires collaboration, and will only come about because of the dedicated work of many people, professionals, and researchers. As Maathai stated, "Education, if it means anything, should not take people away from the land, but instill in them even more respect for it, because educated people are in a position to understand what is being lost."[21]

The Government

The government should provide technical support and coordination between its existing levels, to better integrate the different contexts of planning. The term "governance" rightly describes a flexible, evolving, and mutually supportive interaction between various governmental agencies. It would lead to interdependence among the different stakeholders when planning for sustainability and would provide a valuable contrast to more rigid models of government institutions in the past. For example, the colonial government focused on developing infrastructures and social services in productive areas at the expense of the rest of the country. This inequality remained largely unaddressed during the successive governments and promoted many unsustainable practices all over the country.

Educational events and conferences could be organized to gather planners and activists. This would increase their mutual understanding and would facilitate the sharing of expertise and collaboration. Moreover, intergovernmental overview and coordination could be boosted, better integrating the different elements of planning. The government should fully understand the relationships between different levels of planning. Particular action should aim at giving voice to underrepresented voices—such as lower-income communities. Government officials should involve and invite spokespersons or advocacy groups from civil society to meetings and inform them about the planning process. In such a way, these groups could express their underrepresented perspectives to planners to foster participatory democracy and sustainability.

Policymakers and Politicians

Policymakers and politicians must work very closely with planners and developers. Policymakers are needed who can see the whole picture and integrate the different components of urban development. Urban design must be combined with public and economic policy; transportation planning should include land use and housing; quantitative methods need to rely on qualitative analysis. Other disciplines—such as architecture, landscape architecture, sociology, and environmental science—must contribute their expertise. Within the current devolved government, public policy modifications should be made to improve the future flexibility and sustainability of development. In the case of land use, for example, local officials at the county level may need to ask questions like who will clean up industrial land after it is used; how future options for parks, open spaces, and recreational corridors can be preserved within new developments; and how mechanisms can be put in place to encourage the recycling of strip developments, malls, and shopping centers to integrate them more in balanced ways within local communities.

Planners, Architects, and Engineers

Planners need a long-term assessment that would take into account the human and ecological well-being of future generations. To do this, planners should specifically evaluate how near-term actions can lead to long-term goals. They should figure out new ways to illustrate to the public how particular buildings, transportation systems, patterns of land use, and economic development programs help or hinder sustainability far into the future. Planners must understand the history and evolution of big cities like Nairobi, Mombasa, and Kisumu and how current problems arose. It is crucial to figure out critically how the planning of these cities evolved; what role was played by environmental, economic, social, political, and technological factors; how the land had been subdivided in Kenya; and how road systems were developed. A long-term perspective also means being able to propose small, incremental changes in the present to assess how they can interrelate and reinforce one another to build a more sustainable society in the future. The lack of this type of analysis leads to a fragmented and disjointed urban environment in which individual actions do not reinforce one another. Cultivating a multilevel mode of historical and spatial analysis can help planners organize otherwise isolated projects and initiatives so that they add up to a satisfactory whole.

Developers

In Kenya, most developers are private and usually design an inwardly oriented building, making maximum use of the little space available and not taking into consideration the value of beauty and attraction. Developers, whether private or governmental, should adopt a strategic vision in which individual construction projects work jointly with many other physical planning and economic development initiatives to create more vibrant estates and building spaces for pedestrians and cyclists within the cities. Developers should also embrace an economic development strategy to encourage locally owned small businesses while teaching them about and involving them in sustainability planning.

Ecclesial Groups

Religious institutions are both forces of reason and the critical conscience of Kenyan society. They include the Kenya Episcopal Conference (KEC), the Catholic Peace and Justice Commission, the National Council of Churches in Kenya, the Hindu Council, the Evangelical churches, and the Federation of Indigenous People. All these institutions can also play a very important role in providing education on sustainable planning and ecological advocacy, as well as act as watchdogs in ensuring that sustainable planning policies are implemented.

In particular, the Kenya Episcopal Conference covers the twenty-six Catholic jurisdictions in Kenya spread over four metropolitan provinces with their twenty dioceses, four archdioceses, one apostolic vicariate, and one military ordinariate. There are almost nine million Catholics in Kenya, with more than two thousand priests and almost eight hundred parishes. There are nearly nine thousand Catholic educational institutes, almost two thousand church-run hospitals, clinics, and charitable institutions. In all twenty-six Catholic dioceses, three major ecclesial associations are also present, gathering women, men, and the youth. These are strong grassroots groups that ensure community participation.

Regarding sustainable and environmentally sensitive development, the proposed long-term plan will be run by the KEC–Catholic Secretariat, based in Nairobi, and will be implemented within the church structure, from the Catholic family to the parish to the national level. Environmental care and sustainability are now given prominence in all pastoral projects implemented by the Catholic Church in Kenya. Representatives of the KEC are also involved in drawing up a toolkit on environmental education for use in all Kenyan Catholic schools.

Nonstate Actors and the Private Sector

Nonstate actors include private companies, development partners, civil societies, and charitable organizations. Among these are nongovernmental organizations, faith-based organizations, and civil-based organizations. These social agents should be involved in advocacy and resource mobilization to promote sustainable development both on the national level and in the counties, as well as in training, sensitization activities, and monitoring of ongoing development. If these activities are well coordinated, they can be the foundation on which sustainable development can take place in Kenya. Through joint business ventures, the activities of these multiple social agents can be beneficial in fostering sustainable development.

Within the private sector, property owners and developers can also lobby for support to initiate different development activities. Within civil society, grassroots activities to promote sustainable development can be organized and ensure that the local communities get involved in raising their issues and suggesting options to solve problems. This strategy will encourage a bottom-up approach. Nationally and locally, citizens—in particular youth, women, and opinion leaders—should find a common way of working together toward sustainable development.

Local and International Media

The media can highlight positive trends and foster sustainable development that is already taking place currently all over the country. They can also be instrumental in evaluating and monitoring sustainable activities locally, regionally, and nationally. Social media can reach people at the grass roots and respond to their specific needs. Reporters should also inform, educate, publish, document, investigate, and expose all sorts of unsustainable activities taking place in the country.

International Donors and Partners

The international community should influence the Kenyan government's policies and priorities to make sure the recommendations on sustainable development suggested by the experts are effected should the government display a laxity or reluctance at facilitating or carrying them out. Moreover, international agencies and economic partners should fund more activities geared toward sustainability and provide alternative mechanisms and shared experiences, especially in the case of countries already practicing sustainable development.

In conclusion, planning for sustainability is a crucial element in creating a viable future for Kenya. In the current governance system, this planning can help reorient debates in constructive ways to address development challenges that range from population pressures to pollution to climate change. The principles of sustainable urban planning encourage people to conceptualize problems in constructive ways and with long-term vision.

Notes

1. Stephen M. Wheeler, *Planning for Sustainability: Creating Livable, Equitable, and Ecological Communities* (London: Routledge, 2004), 1.

2. Donnella Meadows, Dennis L. Meadows, Jørgen Randers, and William Behrens III, *The Limits to Growth: A Report for the Club of Rome's Project on the Predicament of Mankind*

(London: Earth Island, 1972); Edward Goldsmith et al., *Blueprint for Survival* (Boston: Houghton Muffin, 1972).

3. Meadows et al., *Limits to rowth,* 24.

4. It is helpful to schematize some of the different ways to define sustainable development in light of different methods and by interest groups.

5. IUCN (the World Conservation Union), UNEP (United Nations Environment Programme), and WWF (World Wide Fund for Nature), *Caring for the Earth: A Strategy for Sustainable Living* (London: Earthscan, 1991).

6. Stephen M. Wheeler and Timothy Beatley, eds., *The Sustainable Urban Development Reader* (London: Routledge, 2004).

7. Richard Norgaard, *Development Betrayed: The End of Progress and a Coevolutionary Revisioning of the Future* (New York: Routledge, 1994).

8. William E. Rees, "Ecological Footprints and Appropriated Carrying Capacity: What Urban Economics Leaves Out," *Environment and Urbanization* 4, no. 2 (1992): 121–30.

9. Sim Van der Ryn and Peter Calthorpe, eds., *Sustainable Communities* (San Francisco: Sierra Club Books, 1984).

10. Wheeler and Beatley, *Sustainable Urban Development Reader.*

11. World Commission on Environment and Development (Brundtland Commission), *Our Common Future* (New York: Oxford University Press, 1987).

12. Paul Ekins, *Economic Growth and Environmental Sustainability: The Prospects for Green Growth* (London: Routledge, 2000).

13. The devolved system of government is a form of decentralization established by Chapter Eleven of the 2010 Kenyan Constitution. It establishes only two levels of government: national and county. The power of making legislation is assigned to the devolved entities.

14. Stephen M. Wheeler, *Planning for Sustainability: Creating Livable, Equitable, and Ecological Communities* (London: Routledge 2004), 34.

15. Dave Gilson, "'I Will Disappear into the Forest': An Interview with Wangari Maathai," *Mother Jones*, January 5, 2005, http://www.motherjones.com/.

16. See Wangari Muta Maathai, *Unbowed: A Memoir* (New York: Alfred A. Knopf, 2006).

17. Ibid., 124.

18. Ibid.

19. Ibid., 125.

20. W. M. Adams, *Green Development: Environment and Sustainability in the Third World* (London: Routledge, 2001).

21. Maathai, *Unbowed*, 138.

Of Empty Granaries, Stolen Harvests, and the Weapon of Grain

Applied Ethics in Search of Sustainable Food Security

Teresia Hinga

In his 1988 book, *My Faith as an African,* the late Jean-Marc Ela reflected on his pastoral experience among the impoverished peasants of Northern Cameroon, and spoke with prophetic urgency regarding the ethical challenge posed by chronic hunger, famine, and consequent massive loss of life in Africa.[1] Given the central Christian belief in a God who brings life and decries injustice, Ela considered it an ethical imperative for Christians to reject unjust "systems that produce empty granaries" and hence famine and death. He proposed the adoption of what he called a "Ministry of the Granary": a platform within the African Church through which to respond to the ethical challenges posed by acute food insecurity. Such a ministry would be based on prior analysis of underlying mechanisms and intersecting systems that cumulatively render the granaries empty, and its goal would be to enhance food sovereignty and to protect the masses from what Ela called the "weapon of grain."[2] This metaphor evokes both the lethal consequences of famine and the various ways that food is used by those in power as a means to economic profit and as a method of social control. Often the consequences are deadly. Moreover, Ela points out that behind many of the deadly and seemingly ubiquitous famines in Africa lie the cumulative effects of interlocking mechanisms and systems that block, derail, sabotage, or "hijack" food production and distribution, thereby effectively "stealing the harvest" and rendering granaries empty.[3]

In this essay, I first map the multiple dimensions of the phenomenon of hunger and allied concepts such as starvation, famine, and malnutrition. Second, I attempt a diagnosis of the root causes of chronic hunger and food insecurity on the African continent, using contextual examples where possible.[4] In so doing, I will test Ela's insight about interlocking, cumulative structures that forestall food security and sustainability; and I explore to what extent and in what ways "the weapon of grain" is wielded in Africa. Finally, I discuss promising analytical efforts on the problem of food sovereignty and security, focusing especially on the ethicists Peter Singer, Vandana Shiva, and Amartya Sen. I conclude that the notion of the "ministry of the granary," as envisioned by Ela, is vital for constructing and nurturing a sustainable prophylactic ethic, over and against the endemic and deadly food insecurity on the continent of Africa. Ultimately, the essay shows the importance of deliberate, strategic empowerment and partnership with the people in the Church's pews, particularly women and youth—indeed, those very same people who bear the brunt of the assault when grain is used as a weapon.

Defining Key Terms

Physiologically speaking, *hunger* is an uneasy, even painful sensation of being unsatisfied because of a lack of appropriate calorie intake in the body. At this level, hunger is rather indifferent to questions of quality of the food eaten. Some even seek to satisfy hunger pangs with food scavenged from garbage cans or dump sites. For many people, especially in the developed world, dealing with hunger pangs is easy since they have regular access to food. At times, people may even *voluntarily postpone* satisfying their hunger pangs as they await a suitable time to eat. Others may refrain from eating for reasons such as fasting to fulfill religious obligations, or while staging a hunger strike to make a political point. For millions of people in Africa, however, hunger is involuntary, acute, chronic, and often lethal.

Moreover, in millions of cases on the continent of Africa, the prolonged hunger and lack of food intake leads to *starvation*: a situation where the body is so hungry that it begins to feed on itself. Starvation is the most serious form of hunger and is usually the face of hunger that we see through media portrayals of marasmic children and adults during *famines*. These are situations where deprivation of food (on individual levels) or disappearance of food (on societal levels—i.e., empty granaries) persists on a large scale, in a given territory, and over a long period. Famine is thus a *quantitative* lack of food simultaneously affecting many people. Famines are often presented as *natural disasters*—the result of water scarcity or crop blight, for example. However, as more nuanced analyses of the phenomenon often reveal, many famines are politically instigated. Some are consequences of war, and in some cases famine can be generated and sustained to achieve political and other morally ambiguous ends. In such situations, food becomes a political ploy, a tool, or even a weapon used to manipulate people to pursue certain courses of action desired by those in power. It is in this context that Jean-Marc Ela speaks of the vulnerability of the masses in Africa to the weapon of grain.[5]

Malnutrition is another face of hunger that is no less deadly than famine, but that is much more hidden and prevalent. Most of the world's hungry are not at the point of starvation, and their suffering does not make the nightly news, though they are chronically hungry. Millions of people are *undernourished* (not getting enough energy and calories) and suffer from *malnutrition* (insufficient intake of micronutrients). The hidden hunger of malnutrition leads to developmental delays and diseases that are debilitating and even lethal, ranging from pellagra to kwashiorkor. Still more people die because of opportunistic diseases that take root because of stunted immune responses. Mothers living with constant hunger often give birth to underweight and weak babies who die at birth or soon after. In 2006, UNICEF reported that malnutrition is accountable for over three million deaths of children under the age of five each year, and iodine deficiency during pregnancy leads to babies born with irreversible brain damage.[6] In impoverished countries, malnutrition is primarily owing to the scant availability of good quality foodstuffs. In this context, it is important to note that relief and food aid that consist only of grains such as corn can only address *quantitative* hunger—that is, the basic demand for calories—but not the *qualitative* aspects of hunger that correlate to malnutrition. Dealing with food systems and the problem of hunger will require addressing both aspects simultaneously.

Every day, millions of people around the world *eat only the bare minimum* of food to keep themselves alive. Every night, they go to sleep uncertain of whether there will be food to eat the following day. This uncertainty is called *food insecurity* and is defined by the Food and Agriculture Organization:

> A situation in which people lack *secure access to sufficient amounts* of safe and nutritious food for normal growth and development and an active and healthy life. It is the *inability to acquire or consume an adequate quality or sufficient quantity* of food in *socially acceptable ways* (i.e., not by begging, scavenging or stealing) or *the uncertainty and worry that that one will be able to do so.*[7]

Hence, the goal is to facilitate *food security*. The phrase refers not only to quantitatively stocked up grain reserves but also to a social and economic situation that is characterized by the ready availability of adequate and safe foods, as well as the right of socially acceptable access by all people at all times to enough food for an active, healthy life. In many cases, food security is linked to *food sovereignty*, which is defined as "the right of peoples, communities, and countries to define their own agricultural, pastoral, fishing, food and land policies which are ecologically, socially, economically and culturally a*ppropriat*e to their unique circumstances."[8]

By all the above definitions, the continent of Africa is chronically food insecure. Acute hunger, starvation, and frequent and seemingly ubiquitous famines prevail. In recent years, Kenya is a case in point of this marked food insecurity and, as I have argued elsewhere, in order adequately to deal with the crisis of poverty and hunger, it is important to diagnose the root causes of this endemic crisis.[9] Moreover, sustainable food security is inseparable from *food sovereignty*. This means that development and relief approaches that emanate exclusively from elsewhere and which disregard or sidestep the sovereignty and empowerment of the people being targeted will at best be a partial solution.

Why is the granary *chronically empty* (or increasingly nonexistent)? What has led to the crisis of food and chronic hunger in Kenya and elsewhere on the continent, especially between 2007 and the present day?

Diagnosing Causes of Food Insecurity in Africa: Lessons from Kenya, 2007–2013

On one level, Kenya's crisis of hunger, starvation, and famine in the first decade of the twenty-first century can be explained as a result of negative climatic events—natural disasters. Kenya did indeed experience prolonged drought and consequent crop failure in these years. Additionally, crop failure occurred because too much rain came at the wrong times: while El Niño rains ended the crop-destroying drought, they also brought flooding and mudslides that destroyed human lives, crops, livestock, and farms. In this way, both drought and floods meant lost crops, empty granaries, and consequent hunger.

On the face of it, these were natural disasters. But as many scientists, scholars, and activists have pointed out, these drastic climactic disasters are not just natural happenstance. Rather, climate change—and its wayward patterns of drought and deluge—are linked to culpable human conduct and thus are subject to ethical scrutiny. Environmental reality has a human, and therefore ethical, dimension. In Kenya, the question of the relationship between drought and anthropogenic environmental degradation recently came to the fore in debates about the destruction of key water catchment areas.[10]

Moreover, it is noteworthy that while drought and flooding affected the supply of food by directly destroying the crops, it is also the case that there were social and economic factors at play. Due to the drought, in 2009 many farmers were given drought-resistant, fast-growing seeds, which they planted with enthusiasm. Indeed, the crops grew, but, unfortunately, the harvesting of the crop coincided with the onset of the severe rains. Harvesting in wet weather and lack of adequate storage or technology to dry the maize led to a strange and paradoxical situation where the granaries were full of corn but had to be emptied quickly and their contents destroyed, since the corn had become contaminated with aflatoxins. Consequently, the bumper harvest was deemed toxic and unworthy of human consumption, and thus, despite the bumper crop, Kenya's food supply was still highly vulnerable in 2010.

Although the immediate issue is clearly the need for proper storage and appropriate technologies for food preservation, the deeper issue is how societies effectively address such cascading negative consequences of unpredictable and complex weather patterns. Thus a response to the ethical and practical challenges of climate change and its connection with food security becomes a key dimension of the ministry of the granary proposed here.

Long-standing structural factors also contributed to the plight of Kenya regarding its food supply during this period. To describe these more subtle and systemic ways in which people are robbed of access to quality food, the scientist and ecological activist Vandana Shiva coined the phrase "stolen harvest," which highlights how the crisis of food security in the Third World is not just one of inadequate production but also one of ownership and distribution of food supply. In Kenya, both production and distribution have been subject to problematic structural constraints. First, granaries are empty because the production of cash crops has been prioritized over the production of food crops. Increased prioritization of such crops—cotton, for example, as well as tea and coffee—means that the best land is cultivated with such nonfood crops. The profits from these crops are often "stolen" since the peasants have little say regarding regional or global market prices and priorities.

In Kenya, this problem is also visible in Naivasha, for example, where decorative flowers are grown exclusively for export. Although this provides some boost to the Kenyan economy, it is also the case that the flowers are grown on large plantations, using the only freshwater lake for irrigation. As a result, Lake Naivasha has declined in volume and has become polluted. This situation has recently led to bloody conflicts as herders and peasant farmers around the lake fight over the water and land for productive uses.[11]

Often, even where people grow food crops such as wheat and maize (instead of obvious cash crops like flowers, cotton, or tea), the food crops can be turned into cash crops instead of sustenance crops. In this case, even when a bumper maize crop is harvested by hungry peasants, it is often sold to the last grain in order to meet other needs such as shelter and children's school fees. It is common therefore to have a bumper harvest in December and empty granaries in February, necessitating emergency food aid.

In a similar way, food insecurity is rampant even in the relatively lush areas of Kenya such as the Rift Valley or around Mount Kenya. Here, land from which people used to grow food sufficient for their needs is increasingly being leased out to grow foods for export that have little room in the culinary preferences of the locals (such as string beans and artichokes). What an irony that where plenty of food is grown, hunger and food insecurity persists.[12]

Finally, food insecurity in Kenya has been exacerbated by internal insecurity, corruption, and conflict. The marked insecurity and acute civil strife that resulted from the botched elections in 2007 and the consequent displacement of peoples affected food production and its distribution. Moreover, during the 2007–8 postelection violence, thousands of bags of corn in the field or in the granaries were vandalized as part of the vendetta that was going on in 2008. During this period, grain was also literally stolen from the national granaries and sold to the highest bidder.[13]

The cumulative results of all these factors mean that Kenya is highly food insecure and the threat of acute chronic hunger is real for millions of Kenyans.[14] It is against this complex background that a ministry of the granary becomes a matter of ethical urgency.

Ethical Resources for the Ministry of the Granary

What patterns of thought are available for constructing an ethics of the granary? Several prominent international ethicists have put forward important proposals that can inform this task. In response to the Bengal famine of 1971, the philosopher Peter Singer argued that affluent societies and individuals have a moral obligation to help the poor, even those who live in distant places. His contemporary work, as seen in his books *One World* and *The Life You Can Save,* continues to emphasize that this is a matter of ethical duty rather than mere charity (which is optional and depends on the individual's magnanimity).[15] From Singer, we see a moral claim about the duty to provide food—a claim that resonates in striking ways with the corporal works of mercy proposed by Jesus in Matthew 25.

The economist Amartya Sen, in his book *Development as Freedom,* offers another important insight when he suggests that hunger is palpably related to lack of political and economic freedoms, social opportunities, and other types of security.[16] Sen indicates that for the elimination of hunger and famine in the modern world to succeed, it is crucial to understand their *causation* in a broad way, rather than just in terms of some mechanical balance between food and population.[17] For him, what matters is "the substantive *freedom* of the individual and the family to establish *ownership* over an adequate amount of food by growing it or buying it"[18]—an insight that translates into food *sovereignty as well as food security.* Since this freedom can be subverted by unfavorable economic conditions or derailed by social instability, there is need to focus on how the overall economic or political situation might diminish these opportunities. Sen's work shows us the importance of social, economic fairness and justice as well as political stability in pursuit of food security and sovereignty.

Finally, Vandana Shiva augments Sen's insights with her trenchant analysis of the systems and mechanisms by which the poor are deprived of those fundamental freedoms. In *Stolen Harvest,* she carefully argues that the poor have been impoverished and pushed to starvation and death by structural injustices as well as the actions of others. For Shiva, a major cause of this situation is the fact that the global food supply is tethered to agribusiness and other multinational corporations. She concludes that a reclamation of "food democracy" is an imperative in this age of corporate-controlled, for-profit "food dictatorship," in which "a handful of global corporations control the global food supply and are reshaping it to maximize their profit and power."[19] Thus Shiva celebrates grassroots people's movements that seek democratic control over food systems by holding agribusiness and related corporations accountable (an example is the "*save the seed*" movement in India). She commends participants for exercising their sovereignty and actively seeking to replace "free trade" with "fair trade," in pursuit of "ecological and just systems of food production and distribution in which the earth, farmers and consumers are protected."[20]

Jean-Marc Ela's work resonates with key elements of these three theoretical approaches. Along with Sen and Shiva, he insists that regaining *food sovereignty* is the appropriate goal in light of the sustained crisis of hunger in Africa. He would further agree that hunger correlates to a *lack of fundamental freedoms*—indeed, this is a link he himself makes in his analysis of root causes of hunger and poverty in postcolonial Africa. Writing specifically of Cameroon, Ela laments the impact of the economic market's neocolonialism and criticizes what he calls "pseudo-pedagogies" through which peasants are persuaded to grow cotton instead of millet.[21] And finally, Ela would agree with Singer, who insists that the problem of hunger is a *moral problem for everyone*, not just for people in areas affected by food scarcity. He would push for effective interventions to protect peasants from vulnerability to the "weapon of grain." Like Shiva, he would urge for strategies to identify and subvert those systems that create hunger. It is in this kind of theoretical framework that a ministry of the granary might begin to take shape.

The Ministry of the Granary

In seeking theo-ethical precedents to handle the question of hunger and its overarching context of poverty, Christians do not have to look far for a mandate. Part of the good news that Jesus preached in word and deed revolved around feeding the masses. His parables, spoken and lived, suggest that Heaven will be a place or situation analogous to a banquet. Speaking to Peter at the end of the earthly stay, Jesus demands: "Do you love me? Then feed my sheep." In his well-known statements in Matthew 25, which forms the basis of the corporal works of mercy, Jesus reports how, "I was hungry and you fed me, . . . a stranger and you showed hospitality." Responding to hunger and destitution is thus an ethical imperative for Christians, and it is perfectly logical for Ela to call Christians to a ministry of the granary. The question remains: What kind of response best fulfills this mandate in our time?

Often, Christians provide relief though charity work.[22] But as contemporary theological ethicists like Maureen O'Connell as well as philosophers like Peter Singer point out, it is imperative to explore and respond to root causes of endemic problems, for the problem is one of justice.[23] I suggest that this quest for root causes must be a primary and defining feature of the ministry of the granary as envisioned here. Because of the complexity and diversity of contexts that complicate the hunger issue in Africa, however, the approaches to the implementation of the proposed ministry of the granary will necessarily be diverse. Despite this diversity of approaches, and while recognizing the importance of specific, context-driven incarnations of the ministry of the granary, I suggest that the ministry will incorporate at least five key features.

First, it will be a prophetic ministry. In the spirit of the prophets of old and the socially engaged scientists and ethicists of the present, it is imperative to *discern and name* ways in which the harvest is stolen and granaries rendered empty. No two places will be exactly alike, though common themes may be found—including the impact of multinational corporations, biotechnologies, and land and water ownership and use.[24] In some instances, the prophetic voice would challenge forces that amplify the instability caused by climate change, and thereby destabilize and displace whole communities into refugee situations (as in Somalia, the Democratic Republic of Congo, and Sudan).

Second, this ministry must play a role in *monitoring and evaluating proposed solutions* to the food crises in Africa and demand that sustainable food solutions include the participation of affected peoples. In light of various proposals to help Africa, ministers of the granary must ask: What version of sustainability is best for Africa? Granted that Africa needs to go green, what shade of green is most appropriate? Should Africa, for example, go with the Monsanto shade of green which has raised a lot of controversy and angst regarding its approaches to hunger by creating genetically modified organisms (GMOs) which seemingly exacerbate rather than alleviate the crisis of hunger? Or should Africa embrace the "New Green Revolution" proposed by Kofi Annan and funded by Bill Gates?[25] How do these proposals for greening Africa embrace both food security and food sovereignty in their decision-making processes? Or perhaps Africa should go with yet another version of greening Africa, the one proposed by the late Wangari Maathai, who envisioned people, particularly women and their agency, at the center of the quest for sustainable development.[26]

The prophetic ministry of the granary in its discernment, monitoring, and evaluation will likely discover that brand new shades of green are warranted, drawing on the strengths of other approaches while systematically raising questions of justice and sustainability. Thus a viable ministry of the granary would need to be *articulate and vigilant on behalf of the vulnerable*, both now and for future generations.

Third, a viable ministry of the granary would need to be *creative, resourceful, and entrepreneurial* by tapping the diverse resources in terms of *knowledge systems* available in Africa. Available knowledge includes but is not limited to Western science and technology.[27] However, the proposed ministry of the granary would be wary of the *overemphasis* on Western scientific knowledge while ignoring or demonizing local and indigenous knowledge systems. Such a priori dismissal of indigenous knowledge systems has not only been demeaning to Africans; it has also robbed them of much-needed resources in terms of practical, context-oriented knowledge. As Sambuli Mosha has persuasively argued, the dismissal and demonization of indigenous resources, knowledge, and ethical systems are a major factor in the multiple crises confronting Africa.[28] For example, infusing systems of food distribution with the indigenous ethics of Ubuntu solidarity and (distributive) justice would enhance the efforts to challenge unethical systems fueled by greed. In other words, the ministry of the granary would be innovative, creative, and entrepreneurial in reclaiming, nurturing, and applying pertinent knowledge and ethical systems conducive to just and sustainable solutions.

Fourth, the ministry would nurture a *prophylactic ethic and strategy*, responding in a proactive rather than the merely reactive way to the multiple inconvenient truths in our midst. It will raise questions, for example, about the unfair distribution of benefits and burdens that result from anthropogenic climate change, a phenomenon that is a major root cause of food insecurity in Africa and elsewhere. Moreover, since people can be manipulated through food scarcity, and considering that even famines can be manipulated for profit or other morally ambiguous ends (e.g., proselytization), this ministry will go beyond bringing relief to the victims of hunger. It will also ask hard questions about long-term root causes and investigate who gains and benefits from hunger and famine. Given the subtle causes and systems that exacerbate hunger, a ministry of the granary would proactively devise strategies for grappling with the complex structures of power and privilege in the twenty-first century.[29]

Finally, the ministry would function as a platform for *awakening, empowering, and mobilizing* the genius of the people—particularly those in the pew.[30] The global church, including the church in Africa, has talent in its pews. A great diversity of professionals, scientists, ethicists, and theologians are to be found among the laity. In Kenya, for example, the example of the late Dr. Wangari Maathai is a beacon: she coupled her scientific know-how with the ethical concern for the environment as well as the rights of women and their children, and thus her efforts became a major force in awakening global sustainability consciousness. She also realized that genius and agency is not exclusive to a chosen few like her, but that it is also to be found among people who may never have set foot in a university or a seminary. A viable ministry of the granary would similarly need to identify, nurture, and mobilize the wisdom in the pews. Moreover, this approach would also facilitate the reclamation of sovereignty and a sense of ownership on matters of food that Ela, Shiva, and Sen rightly prioritize.

The proposed ministry of the granary suggests that the problem of food shortages cannot merely be addressed exclusively from the halls of power. It suggests that profound insight and success can be achieved in partnership with the people in the pew who regain much-needed sovereignty by becoming ministers of the granary on their own behalf.

Notes

1. This essay is dedicated to the memory of Jean-Marc Ela. See Jean-Marc Ela, *My Faith as an African*, trans. John Pairman Brown and Susan Perry (Maryknoll, NY: Orbis Books, 1988).

2. Jean-Marc Ela, *African Cry*, trans. Robert Barr (Maryknoll, NY: Orbis Books, 1986), 87.

3. The phrase "stolen harvest" was coined by Vandana Shiva, and is the title of the book in which she discusses the multiple mechanisms and systems through which the global food supply has been hijacked and its access denied to the masses. For details, see Vandana Shiva, *Stolen Harvest: The Hijacking of the Global Food Supply* (Cambridge, MA: South End Press, 2000).

4. Jeffrey Sachs suggests that "clinical economics" is a process similar to a clinician diagnosing symptoms that a patient has before prescribing a cure. See Jeffrey Sachs, *The End of Poverty: Economic Possibilities for Our Time* (New York: Penguin, 2005), 74–89.

5. One example is the imposition of economic sanctions by withholding food aid, using food as a bargaining chip in efforts to bring about "regime change" in countries thought to be nondemocratic. For other well-documented examples of the instrumentaliza-

tion, militarization, and even "weaponization" of food, see Alex de Waal, *Famine Crimes: Politics and the Disaster Industry in Africa* (Bloomington: Indiana University Press, 1997), 117ff.

6. See World Food Programme website: https://www.wfp.org.

7. http://www.disabled-world.com. This definition of food security includes not only access to food as a measure of security but also an evaluation of the methods used to access the food. Thus begging or scavenging are clear marks of food insecurity.

8. By extension, this definition suggests that food sovereignty includes the right to safe, nutritious, and culturally appropriate food, the right of people to produce their own food (and therefore) the right to food-producing resources, particularly land. See http://family-farmers.org/.

9. See Teresia Hinga, "Becoming Better Samaritans: The Quest for New Models of Doing Social-Economic Justice in Africa," in *Applied Ethics in a World Church: The Padua Conference,* ed. Linda Hogan (Maryknoll, NY: Orbis Books, 2008), 85–97.

10. Recently, there have been heated debates linking food and water shortage in Kenya's Rift Valley region with the destruction of the Mau water catchment zone, resulting from the misappropriation, sale, and consequent abuse of this vital ecosystem. For details, see BBC columnist James Morgan's article, "Life Dries Up in Kenya's Mau Forest," *BBC News*, September 29, 2009, http://news.bbc.co.uk.

11. See http://documents.foodandwaterwatch.org.

12. The situation is even more scandalous since much of the food thus grown for export ends up being wasted when it is deemed not to measure up to the standards set by the importers. In response to this scandalous situation of food wastage, the United Nations Environment Programme (UNEP), on June 5, 2013, launched a new initiative, Soko Bila Waste. See http://www.unep.org.

13. For details of what came to be known as *the maize scandal*, and how it complicated the food crisis in Kenya in 2009, see the report by the African Center for Open Governance (Africog), http://www.africog.org.

14. This is not withstanding the emergency measures, such as fertilizer subsidy and enhanced school feeding programs, that the government enacted in the wake of this crisis. These measures were rather ad hoc and insufficient; in many instances they were "too little too late."

15. This is Singer's overall thesis in his book *One World: The Ethics of Globalization* (New Haven, CT: Yale University Press, 2002), 13. It is also a key proposal in his book *The Life You Can Save: How to Do Your Part to End World Poverty* (New York: Random House, 2009), 3.

16. Amartya Kumar Sen, *Development as Freedom* (New York: Random House, 1999), 10.

17. Ibid., 161.

18. Ibid.

19. Shiva, *Stolen Harvest*, 117.

20. Ibid.

21. Ela, *African Cry*.

22. For the most part, this has been the approach, for example, of Catholic Relief Services (CRS). Although providing urgent humanitarian aid to relieve hunger in situations of emergency continues to be a viable intervention as needed, increasingly there is awareness of the need for addressing root causes and developing prophylactic strategies. For details of ways CRS is embracing strategies beyond charity, see the CRS website: http://crs.org/.

23. See Maureen H. O'Connell, *Compassion: Love of Neighbor in an Age of Globalization* (Maryknoll, NY: Orbis Books, 2009), 183ff. She calls for transformation of the road to Jericho, beyond rescuing victims falling prey on that road!

24. As I write this paragraph, breaking news includes recent protests against the giant science and agribusiness corporation Monsanto as concerned thousands around the world took to the streets to protest the GMO approach to issues of hunger. See also http://viacampesina.org for a commentary on the struggle for food sovereignty by the international peasants movement "The Via Campesina."

25. http://www.agra.org/.

26. http://www.greenbeltmovement.org.

27. Some analysts of hunger in Africa have blamed Africans' failure to embrace modern science as a cause of hunger there. This blame, however, is not entirely justified since there is evidence that African farmers are ready to embrace science *when it enhances their welfare*. For an analysis that relates hunger in Africa to an alleged failure to embrace science, see Robert Paarlberg, *Starved for Science: How Biotechnology Is Being Kept Out of Africa* (Cambridge, MA: Harvard University Press, 2008).

28. See Sambuli R. Mosha, *Heartbeat of Indigenous Africa: A Study of the Chagga Educational System* (New York: Garland, 2000).

29. For a critique of the moral ambiguity of some of the prevailing humanitarian strategies in Africa, see de Waal, *Famine Crimes*. For an analysis of how ethical sensibilities embedded in religious traditions, including Indigenous African traditions, can be applied to challenge greed as a root cause of economic woes today, see Paul F. Knitter and Chandra Muzaffar, eds., *Subverting Greed: Religious Perspectives on the Global Economy* (Maryknoll, NY: Orbis Books, 2002), 15–37.

30. For an example of women's scientific genius at work in Kenya, see the story of Dr. Sheila Okoth and her efforts to find solutions to the aflatoxins menace, http://www.globalissues.org.

The Unsavory Gamble of Industrial Agriculture

Mark Graham

The industrialization of the agricultural sector through the introduction of manufacturing techniques and advanced technologies has been under way for quite some time. Given the world's almost complete dependency on industrialized agriculture to meet our food needs, it behooves us to pay careful attention to its performance and to the criteria by which we assess its performance. In what follows, I assess industrialized agriculture, focusing especially on sustainability issues and changing environmental contexts in this century that will almost assuredly exploit industrialized agriculture's vulnerabilities. In my estimation, industrialized agriculture will have a very difficult time weathering these threats, and the best course of action today is to begin constructing an alternative to "business as usual" in the agricultural sector. To this end, I outline a simple, inexpensive, and very accessible alternative as a way for individuals to begin opting out of industrialized agriculture and to begin constructing an agricultural system that is far more sustainable.

Contemporary Industrial Agriculture

Settled agriculture is a remarkably novel experiment. For 90 percent of human history, settled agriculture did not exist, and humans lived as nomadic hunter-gatherers, relying on memory and nature's uncultivated bounty to meet their food needs. Then, around 10,000 years ago, settled agriculture appeared in areas like the Fertile Crescent and began slowly and inexorably spreading outward.[1] The perceived benefits of settled agriculture proved too tantalizing for all but the most recalcitrant to resist, and over the intervening millennia this initial experiment became the norm as far as the human reach extended. Humans, for the first time in our existence, whether wittingly or unwittingly, had made a choice that would decisively alter the planet and chart a course toward "civilization" and its manifold consequences: food surpluses, organized militaries, centralized political systems, specialized trades and occupations, increasing technological sophistication, and growing populations.

The resounding embrace of settled agriculture, however, has turned out to be a Faustian bargain with the devil for many,[2] as the one billion chronically hungry people today would assuredly attest.[3] As Jared Diamond points out, over history some of the most scientifically and technologically advanced civilizations have collapsed, sometimes precipitously, because their agricultural systems failed.

Sometimes traditional culprits such as drought and pests were the catalysts; often though, as the historical record increasingly shows, it was anthropogenic causes that were the villains, with topsoil erosion, salinization, pollution, and a loss of natural fertility being the most common causes.[4] Human folly and ignorance, it turns out, were perhaps the greatest threats to settled agricultural systems, as unintended and unforeseeable consequences, poor agricultural practices, and a preference for short-term gains over long-term sustainability often undermined the natural resource base on which agricultural systems depended, thus effectively sealing their fate.

This note of caution is likely to fall on deaf ears today. The industrialized world is characterized by a type of agricultural triumphalism, which has touted the victories of modern science and technology over former natural limits and obstacles that seemed insurmountable. Especially in the United States, where being the "breadbasket to the world" is a source of national pride (among other delusions of grandeur), the ideology of agricultural triumphalism is so firmly entrenched psychologically that any naysaying is likely to be greeted by casual indifference. After all, the current world has been shaped by the Green Revolution, a movement that began shortly after the Second World War, which sought to raise agricultural production levels through intensive land-management practices, especially in the so-called developing world. If nothing else, the Green Revolution has consistently delivered on its promise to raise production levels, and its recipe for continued production gains is still in use.

Contemporary agricultural production follows a model marked by the following features: mechanization of farming; regional specialization; capital intensiveness; uniformity and monocultures; synthetic pesticides, herbicides, and fertilizers; hybrid seeds; high fossil fuel inputs; and technological sophistication. The Green Revolution's intensive form of agriculture engenders a remarkable degree of psychological acquiescence among the world's most materially fortunate, and it continues to make significant inroads among developing countries that are seeking to modernize along the lines of successful Western economies.[5]

Given the resounding success of the Green Revolution and the cheap, abundant food it has made available, it is difficult today to argue politically against this method of agricultural production, even in the throes of a global obesity epidemic brought about by chronic food overproduction: to take just one country as an example, three out of five Americans today are overweight, one out of five are obese, and the annual health care costs associated with these conditions are approaching USD 100 billion annually.[6]

The triumph of industrialized agriculture is a momentous gamble upon which the lives of billions of people depend. It can be considered a dangerous gamble for at least three reasons. First, from a historical perspective, industrial agriculture is still in its extreme infancy, and it is already showing signs of substantial structural fragility. Second, industrial agriculture is resource intensive, requiring massive amounts of land, water, and petrochemicals. But those inputs are finite, and, moreover, their use has led to some large-scale negative consequences, such as the pollution of water sources and the creation of aquatic "dead zones" due to excess runoff of nitrogen-based fertilizers. Third, patterns of food production and consumption are changing in the twenty-first century, owing primarily to forces of global climate change, growing global population, and changing diets.

Enough Food to Go Around?

From the emergence of modern humans roughly 100,000 years ago to the invention of agriculture 90,000 years later, approximately one million people lived on the planet. It took about another 10,000 years for the human population to reach one billion, around 1800, which coincided with the Industrial Revolution.[7] Since then, human population has taken off like a rocket: a mere 130 years later, it had doubled to two billion; the next billion was added in 1959, which was less than one-fourth of the time needed to reach the prior billion; the four-billion mark was eclipsed fifteen years later in 1974; thirteen years later the human population stood at five billion; only eleven years later, in 1998, the six billion mark was reached; in 2011, there were seven billion people on the planet; and the United Nations' Population Division predicts the following rises in human population: eight billion by 2025; nine billion by 2043; and ten billion by 2083,[8] which probably represents the absolute carrying capacity of humans on our planet. These trends demonstrate how the length of time needed to add one billion more people has shrunk to almost nothing.

The upshot of these population trends is that the twenty-first century will see roughly a 30 percent increase in human population, with most of this increase occurring in "developing" countries, which in many ways are less able structurally and technologically to navigate successfully the growing demand for additional calories compared to "industrialized" countries. Coupled with dietary changes and increased demand for biofuels, the United Nations estimates that net agricultural production "must increase by 70 percent" in the coming century in order to feed everyone![9] Nor is bringing more land into agricultural production a viable option for feeding these additional mouths; the vast majority of all arable land is already in production. Moreover, the two principal options for bringing new land into production—that is, converting marginal land to agricultural use or clear-cutting tropical rain forests—both result in only short-term gains or cause a profound decimation of biodiversity and soil health. None of these are ethically palatable or ecologically sustainable options. As a result, intensifying production on already existing agricultural lands seems to be the only viable option for responding to the population boom.

By most accounts, this is likely to be strenuous and the consequences perhaps quite dire. Some experts forecast that steady production gains in the recent past will start to decline in the immediate future.[10] It is estimated that 25 percent of arable land is already "highly degraded" and thus becoming marginal for agricultural use.[11] Desertification is a rapidly encroaching problem: Every year a quantity of land equivalent to three times the area of Switzerland is lost to desertification.[12] The depletion of aquifers and diversion of surface water likewise bodes poorly for water-intensive industrial agriculture. The well-known villains of topsoil erosion, compaction, salinization, and pesticide resistance, while showing some signs of improvement in some sectors, still remain intractable, long-term thorns in the side of farmers around the world.

Climate Change

In addition, global climate change is likely to interject a level of unpredictability hitherto unknown into the agricultural sector. In May 2013, scientists recorded levels of carbon dioxide at 400 parts per million (ppm) for a day in Hawaii—the highest level for that length of time in recorded history.[13] Furthermore, recent studies suggest that attempts to stabilize greenhouse gas (GHG) emissions in order not to exceed the consensus "safe" target of a two-degree Celsius average temperature rise is fanciful, at best, given the reserves of fossil fuels already located and ready to be extracted, refined, and burned—which constitute GHG emissions five times higher than we are currently planning to emit! If this scenario comes to fruition, we might be facing a temperature rise of six degrees Celsius (= eleven degrees Fahrenheit) instead of the two degrees Celsius target, which would almost assuredly wreak havoc with agricultural systems worldwide and engender unimaginable food shortages.[14]

Yet even if more conservative estimates of GHG emissions occur in this century, the defining hallmark of successful agricultural systems in the era of global climate change will be adaptability. Even if sufficient international political will were mustered to cap global GHG emissions at the levels specified by the Copenhagen Accord (2009), agricultural systems will still have to contend with a number of variables that increase structural fragility on agricultural systems worldwide: a shift geographically in optimal growing locales for many crops, and environments ill-suited for this relocation;[15] water stress; new pressures from invasive species; desertification of farmland; new plant diseases; changing rainfall patterns; and the increasing incidence of extreme weather events.[16] Beyond these relatively foreseeable changes, which in themselves represent considerable threats to agricultural systems worldwide, there looms an element of unpredictability that could turn out to be even more pernicious. Not only is it unknown whether GHG mitigation strategies will work, or what the concentration of GHGs in the atmosphere will be decades or centuries into the future, but the nonlinear nature of actual changes induced by global climate change means that different environments will respond differently to global climate change, with some getting hotter and drier and others getting colder and wetter, depending on the specific environment.[17]

In my opinion, this represents the most troubling aspect of global climate change: We know it is happening, and the best and brightest in the scientific community can predict general trends, but forecasting specific changes is an elusive enterprise at best—and specifics are what the agricultural sector most needs in order to prepare for the stresses that lie ahead. What this means, in a very practical sense, is that agriculture is entering a phase of unpredictability in which change, and maybe even rapid and multifaceted change, will become a regular mainstay.

Development and Dietary Demands

The third and final element to note is changing dietary preferences worldwide. One ironclad rule of economic development is that as per capita income increases, thereby making available a wider array of food choices, people consistently transition from a plant-based diet to a meat-based diet high in animal fats.[18] Given likely development trajectories, "global meat consumption is expected to double in the next 40 years."[19] This shift to a meat-based diet, however, requires vast quantities of land, energy, and water resources. It represents a highly inefficient and wasteful method for producing protein. Consider the United States, which has one of the highest meat-consumption rates in the world with a human population of 314 million. Roughly nine billion livestock animals are maintained to supply animal protein to US consumers. Yet these animals consume seven times the amount of grain consumed by Americans directly—an amount of grain sufficient to feed 840 million people if those grains were consumed by human beings instead of being fed to livestock for eventual meat production. In fact, for every one kilogram of animal protein produced, six kilograms of plant protein are expended, which represents a remarkable net loss of protein.

Moreover, meat is not resource neutral. In many ways, it is a highly inefficient and unsustainable food product. In terms of fossil energy input into this meat-based diet, it takes twenty-five kilocalories of fossil energy input to produce one kilocalorie of protein, an energy input that is more than eleven times higher than that for grain protein production.[20]

The story is also grim with regard to water consumption. The amount of water necessary to produce one kilogram of animal protein is one hundred times higher than that necessary to produce the same amount of plant protein![21] And from a moral perspective, the primary mechanism of meat production in the United States is through factory farms, which are tantamount to systematic cruelty to animals (as many recent reports and documentaries have made clear).[22] Overall, the meat-based diet that is the staple of US food preferences turns out to be one of the most wasteful, inefficient, environmentally damaging, and unsustainable enterprises we human beings have ever constructed.

The scene is set for the perfect storm for our agricultural experiment: international calls for unprecedented higher agricultural production levels to feed a burgeoning world population; limited options for increasing production other than intensifying existing agricultural spaces; a shrinking natural resource base of arable soil and water; hundreds of millions of people poised to embrace a meat-based diet and the higher levels of food and energy consumption associated with it; and global climate change, with the wide array of challenges and vicissitudes it will present. If ever there were a time to get agriculture right, now is that time. At stake are the lives of billions of people and the sustainability of human societies' relationship to the land.

Getting Agriculture Right

What difference can Christian thought and practice make in light of these massive global challenges to agricultural production and sustainability? From an ethical perspective, the Christian call of compassion, which is at the heart of the Gospel message, suggests that we strive to prevent unnecessary suffering as far as possible. From a theological perspective, creation and the gift of good land are intended for everyone—past, present, and future. As such, to tolerate knowingly or participate actively in an agricultural system that is unsustainable represents an abject failure to cooperate with God in tending our small piece of the universe. In order to act well in light of these considerations, three strategies are paramount: (1) insulating agriculture from a wide range of vicissitudes, and making it as adaptable and resilient as possible; (2) encouraging, supporting, and sometimes insisting on measures that make our agricultural system more sustainable; and (3) thinking small. Let me explain each of these briefly.

Adaptability and Resilience. Several elements are vital for ensuring a vibrant agricultural system capable of withstanding a number of different stresses and threats. First, topsoil is the lifeblood of any agricultural system, and abundant topsoil that is rich in organic matter, nutrient-dense, and holds good water absorption and retention abilities can not only support a wide variety of plant life, but it also makes it much easier to withstand successfully undesirable vicissitudes, whether they be natural or human in origin. Second, biodiversity within an agricultural system insulates against widespread loss, maximizes beneficial relationships between plants, and offers many possibilities for natural pest control. Third, inputs necessary to make the agricultural system function smoothly must be readily available and renewable. In most cases, this strongly favors reliance on local inputs that are abundant and acquired easily. Fourth, the use of solar energy must be maximized, and fossil energy minimized. The sun will be giving its bounty to us for the next five billion years, and the sooner we diminish the fossil fuel inputs for agriculture, the better.

Real Sustainability. The term "sustainable" has become quite fashionable today, and in such a climate it is often an adjective that can become elastic or amorphous, at worst rendering it virtually meaningless. The surest way to assess sustainability is to look at agricultural systems that have proven to be sustainable over long periods of time, and not simply use the label as a convenient and palatable adjective. Instead, we must look to the lessons of history. Fortunately for us, there are ample precedents of sustainable agricultural systems that have survived for millennia, and by comparing commonalities across these systems, we can begin to distill a general recipe for sustainability that has actually worked over time in a number of different environmental contexts. Some of these elements include: (1) a knowledge base located primarily in the farmer; (2) crop diversity; (3) minimal alteration of the physical environment; (4) multiple, complex recycling processes to augment soil fertility; (5) reliance on locally available, renewable inputs; (6) food production for the local community; and (7) a responsiveness to environmental changes and threats.[23] Although these criteria can be embodied via many different types of practices and systems, and many diverse types of agricultural systems can be, and have proven to be, sustainable, the ones that have withstood the test of time exhibit most, if not all, of these characteristics.

Small and Mighty. This leads to the most important message contained in this essay: thinking small. It may sound counterintuitive in an era characterized by global thinking and international food economies. But small-scale, local agriculture consistently emerges as an effective bulwark. Small-scale agriculture is not only more efficient than large-scale, industrialized agriculture; but acre for acre, it is also more productive![24] Indeed, small-scale agriculture offers the best possibility of inaugurating the march toward food sustainability, which is precisely why international organizations have begun favoring such approaches when it comes to policy decisions and funding opportunities.[25] Food sustainability and food security—the assurance that there is enough to go around—are increasingly linked. And there is an important element of individual agency in smaller-scale agriculture that is foreign to industrial agriculture: a farm can be made from a determined individual, a few simple tools, some seeds, a small plot of arable land, an enterprising attitude, and a willingness to learn and adapt.

To be sure, it might sound ridiculous to suggest gardening—yes, gardening!—as a viable piece of the food security puzzle. Yet in my mind there really is no potentially more loving, compassionate, and sustainable way to produce food than by doing it oneself. Indeed, the recent and meteoric ascent of urban community gardening has been a potent force in combating malnutrition in poor countries, amplifying civic engagement, and bringing fresh produce to low-income "food deserts" in many US cities.[26] Gardening offers a number of advantages: minimal startup costs; more nutritionally dense vegetables compared to their grocery store counterparts; the ability to grow food organically; easier topsoil erosion prevention; the mitigation, if not elimination, of pollution and GHG emissions associated with transportation, as well as of fossil fuel use;[27] the ability to compost household and yard waste to augment soil fertility, which also decreases landfill waste; increased biodiversity (beneficial for pest control and for our animal friends); and social benefits galore in both the tending the garden and sharing its bounty with others.[28]

In addition to these manifold benefits, as I mentioned earlier, gardening is far more productive than its large-scale, industrialized counterpart in terms of providing more food per acre directly to people. To give a visual representation of this comparative advantage of small-scale agriculture, consider, for instance, my backyard garden, which is 23' x 19', compared to an equally sized plot of farmland in Iowa, a state that epitomizes the large-scale, industrial model and that provides approximately 10 percent of the world's supply of corn—yes, the *world's* supply of corn, an astonishing amount. The corn on the Iowa plot of farmland is mostly used as animal feed, so let us just assume that the corn will be fed to cows. Given a conversion ratio of 16:1 (sixteen lbs. of grain to produce one lb. of beef), the plot of corn would produce approximately 5.5 lbs. of beef, which would probably fit into a standard-sized plastic bread bag. In contrast, my backyard garden produces the equivalent of two medium-sized garbage cans of a wide array of vegetables: tomatoes; potatoes; carrots; peas; spinach; several different types of lettuce; eggplants; broccoli; acorn, butternut, and summer squashes; cabbages; cucumbers; zucchinis; beets; radishes; green beans; edible soybeans, garlic; and herbs. The difference here is stark, not only in terms of sheer bulk, but also in terms of nutritional content! When done correctly, there is simply no better way of providing food for people more benignly and productively than gardening. In a moral framework, it is also a practice that facilitates a kind of attention to the ways in which our food is grown, distributed, and consumed.

Along with environmental thinkers like Bill McKibben and agricultural leaders like Wes Jackson, I am convinced that the future of sustainable agriculture lies securely in the hands of small-scale agricultural systems. Indeed, I think that one of the most important alterations that could occur to the Christian moral imagination is a warm embrace of agricultural bioregionalism, which gives a decided preference to food produced locally.

This is an opportunity for Christians to begin thinking creatively about ways in which our immediate environs can become hospitable environments for providing the food we need. Whether it be backyard gardening, urban gardening, community supported agriculture, farmers' markets, brownfield reclamation, the leasing of vacant lots to neighborhood organizations for growing food, edible landscaping, hydroponics, or the use of public parks and lands for agricultural production—the possibilities are virtually endless for producing healthy, safe, nutritious food on small parcels of land that simultaneously reduce our carbon footprint and the negative side effects associated with the industrial model of agriculture.

A Preliminary Ethics for Food Choices

Before closing, I want to articulate briefly some salient elements of a Christian food ethic, focusing especially on the level of individual choice and initiative. Given the virtual stranglehold of corporate agribusiness on agricultural policy, and given its robust preference for the dominant industrial model I have been criticizing throughout this essay, I have little hope that our political or economic leaders will be effective at encouraging the agricultural revolution that is sorely needed today. So if changes to our agricultural system are to occur in preparation for the perfect storm, it will be through the energies of dedicated, imaginative individuals and their grassroots initiatives. In that vein, here are a few points that I believe are vital for a Christian food ethic that contributes to food security and sustainability.

1. Grow as much of your own food as possible. For those who own a small plot of ground, turn over the dirt and plant some seeds. Keep things simple. No need for raised beds, expensive garden implements, or elaborate soil preparations. Experiment, pay attention, and grab a copy of *The Garden Primer* at your local public library.[29] You will discover what works and what does not, and over time you can customize your garden to produce the maximum amount of food that you like. Recycle household refuse by composting (especially worm composting), and use it as a soil additive. Capture grey water and use it to water your garden. Watch for signs of soil erosion. Share your bounty with your neighbors, and let children freely investigate the many fascinating critters who make your garden their abode. Healthy, nutritious, chemical-free food that significantly reduces waste, pollution, and GHG emissions—this is Christian environmental stewardship at its best.

2. Buy locally. The main benefit of local food production is responsiveness to individual demand. Walk into a chain grocery store, and you are simply one customer out of thousands—you mean very little, and truth be told, you simply take or leave what is offered. To a local farmer, a community supported agriculture operation, or a vendor at a farmers' market, however, your preferences matter. Ask questions, provide input, make requests, and support food providers whose operations best embody sustainable and compassionate food production.

3. Eat low on the food chain.[30] Become a vegetarian or vegan. Read *Dominion*[31] or *Eating Animals*[32] if your carnivorous tendencies prove stubborn, and you might think long and hard about supporting factory farms ever again. Most meat production is wasteful, inefficient, highly polluting, and brutal to animals. If you choose to eat meat, try to find an environmentally conscious farmer who allows his or her animals to live as natural a life as possible before death.[33]

4. Begin thinking about food in moral terms. Food selection among the world's economic elite (and if you are reading this essay, you are probably part of this group) is typically considered a matter of personal preference, and food choices are assessed on the basis of satisfying the individual consumer's desires. In this context, moral considerations are either absent altogether, and if they make an appearance at all, they are usually cast in terms of healthiness. In many ways, the latter is simply ethical individualism writ large: I buy a cheeseburger because that burst of fat in my mouth tastes so good to *me*; or I purchase low fat cheese because it is healthier for *me*; or I grab a microwaveable entrée because it is convenient for *me*. Resist this truncating tendency mightily, for it betrays the inherent relationality of eating food.

Eating is, first and foremost, a moral act whereby we affect creation, each other, the lives of animals, and God for better or worse.[34] Moreover, if, as I believe, the most formative things we do morally are those we do day after day, week after week, and year after year, then eating food is inescapably rife with moral meaning. In the end, the satisfaction of personal preferences is not what food is about. It is about extending the transforming possibilities of love and compassion outward through something as pedestrian as choosing food that sustains human beings and the natural resources upon which all life depends.

Notes

1. Jared Diamond, *Guns, Germs, and Steel* (New York: W. W. Norton, 2005), 85–92; Clive Ponting, *A Green History of the World: The Environment and the Collapse of Great Civilizations* (New York: Penguin Books, 1991), 37–67.

2. For criticisms of the dominant industrial model of agriculture, see Wendell Berry, *The Unsettling of America: Culture and Agriculture* (San Francisco: Sierra Club Books, 1977); Wendell Berry, *The Gift of Good Land: Further Essays, Cultural and Agricultural* (San Francisco: North Point Press, 1981); Wes Jackson, *New Roots for Agriculture* (Lincoln: University of Nebraska Press, 1980); Wes Jackson, *Altars of Unhewn Stone* (San Francisco: North Point Press, 1987); Wes Jackson, *Becoming Native to This Place* (Lexington: University Press of Kentucky, 1994); Christopher Cook, *Diet for a Dead Planet: How the Food Industry Is Killing Us* (New York: New Press, 2006); Judith D. Soule and Jon K. Piper, *Farming in Nature's Image: An Ecological Approach to Agriculture* (Washington, DC: Island Press, 1992); Gene Logsdon, *At Nature's Pace: Farming and the American Dream* (New York: Pantheon Books, 1994); Jules Pretty, *Agri-Culture: Reconnecting People, Land, and Nature* (London: Earthscan, 2002); Helena Norberg-Hodge, Peter Goering, and John Page, *From the Ground Up: Rethinking Industrial Agriculture* (New York: Zed Books, 2001); Marty Strange, *Family Farming: A New Economic Vision* (Lincoln: University of Nebraska Press, 1988).

3. Commission on Sustainable Agriculture and Climate Change, "Achieving Food Security in the Face of Climate Change" (Copenhagen: CGIAR Research Program on Climate Change, Agriculture, and Food Security, 2012), 8.

4. Jared Diamond, *Collapse: How Societies Choose to Fail or Succeed* (New York: Viking, 2005); Daniel Hillel, *Out of the Earth: Civilization and the Life of the Soil* (Berkeley: University of California Press, 1992).

5. Paul Roberts, *The End of Food* (Boston: Mariner Books, 2009).

6. Michael Pollan, *The Omnivore's Dilemma: A Natural History of Four Meals* (New York: Penguin Press, 2006), 102.

7. Laurence C. Smith, *The World in 2050: Four Forces Shaping Civilization's Northern Future* (New York: Penguin Group, 2011), 9–10.

8. United Nations, Department of Economic and Social Affairs, Population Division, *World Population Prospects, 2010 Revision*, http://esa.un.org .

9. United Nations, Food and Agriculture Organization, Executive Summary of "How to Feed the World in 2050," 2.

10. Food and Agriculture Organization of the United Nations, *The State of Food and Agriculture, 2012* (Rome: FAO, 2012): 104.

11. Ibid.

12. United Nations Convention to Combat Desertification, *World Day to Combat Desertification*. http://www.unccd.int.

13. Elizabeth Landau, "CO2 Levels Hit New Peak at Key Observatory" (2013), http://www.cnn.com.

14. Bill McKibben, "Global Warming's Terrifying New Math," *Rolling Stone*, July 19, 2012, http://www.rollingstone.com.

15. The general rule of thumb is that for every increase of one degree Fahrenheit in the average annual temperature, the optimal temperature for a particular plant's growth will move forty miles northward (in the northern hemisphere; in the southern hemisphere, forty miles southward). This poses stark challenges for the agricultural sector, since conditions for many crops makes it virtually impossible to grow them commercially either farther north or south.

16. Commission on Sustainable Agriculture and Climate Change, "Achieving Food Security," 11.

17. Gerald Braun, Monika Hellwig, and W. Malcolm Byrnes, "Global Climate Change and Catholic Responsibility: Facts and Faith Response," *Journal of Catholic Social Thought* 4, no. 2 (2007): 374–76.

18. Commission on Sustainable Agriculture and Climate Change, "Achieving Food Security," 14.

19. Mark Bittman, *Food Matters: A Conscious Guide to Eating, with More Than 75 Recipes* (New York: Simon and Schuster, 2008), 9.

20. David Pimental and Marcia Pimental, "Sustainability of Meat-Based and Plant-Based Diets and the Environment," *American Journal of Clinical Nutrition* 78 (2003): 661–62.

21. Ibid., 662.

22. *Death on a Factory Farm* (Teale-Edwards Productions, 2009); *A River of Waste* (Cinema Libre Studio, 2009); *Fresh* (Ripple Effect Films, 2009); *Eating Mercifully* (Humane Society of the United States, 2008); *Peaceable Kingdom* (Tribe of Heart Films, 2004); *Food, Inc.* (Magnolia Pictures, 2008).

23. This synopsis is taken from Miguel Alteri, "Why Study Traditional Agriculture?," in *Agroecology*, ed. C. Ronald Carroll, John H. Vandermeer, and Peter Rosset (New York: McGraw-Hill, 1990), 551–64.

24. For a practical illustration of the adaptability of small farms compared to large farms, see Mark Graham, *Sustainable Agriculture: A Christian Ethic of Gratitude* (Cleveland, OH: Pilgrim Press, 2005), 174–83.

25. Food and Agriculture Organization of the United Nations, *The State of Food and Agriculture, 2012.*

26. Annu Ratta and Jac Smith, "Urban Agriculture: It's About Much More Than Food," *WHY Magazine* 13 (1993): 26–29; Catherine Murphy, *Cultivating Havana: Urban Agriculture and Food Security in the Years of Crisis* (Oakland, CA: Food First, 1999), 1–4; Lauren Baker and Jin Huh, "Rich Harvest," *Alternatives Journal* 29 (2003): 21–25.

27. The average agricultural product travels an average of 1,500 miles between producer and consumer.

28. For a fuller description of the many benefits of gardening, see Graham, *Sustainable Agriculture*, 157–64.

29. Barbara Damrosch, *The Garden Primer* (Emmaus, PA: Rodale Press, 2003).

30. Julie Hanlon Rubio, "Toward a Just Way of Eating," in *Green Discipleship: Catholic Theological Ethics and the Environment*, ed. Tobias Winright (Winona, MN: Anselm Academic, 2011), 372–76.

31. Matthew Scully, *Dominion: The Power of Man, the Suffering of Animals, and the Call to Mercy* (New York: St. Martin's Griffin, 2002).

32. Jonathan Safran Foer, *Eating Animals* (New York: Little, Brown, 2009).

33. For an illustration of what meat farming ought to be like, read about Joel Salatin's Polyface Farm in Pollan, *The Omnivore's Dilemma*, 123–33, 185–273.

34. For treatments of food ethics, see Norman Wirzba, *Food and Faith: A Theology of Eating* (New York: Cambridge University Press, 2011); Fred Bahnson and Norman Wirzba, *Making Peace with the Land* (Downers Grove, IL: Inter Varsity Press, 2012); James E. McWilliams, *Just Food* (New York: Back Bay Books, 2010); Graham, *Sustainable Agriculture*; Peter Singer and Jim Mason, *The Ethics of What We Eat* (Melbourne: Text Publishing, 2006); Paul B. Thompson, *The Agrarian Vision: Sustainability and Environmental Ethics* (Lexington: University Press of Kentucky, 2010); Gregory E. Pence, ed., *The Ethics of Food: A Reader for the Twenty-First Century* (Lanham, MD: Rowman and Littlefield, 2002); Paul Pojman, ed., *Food Ethics* (Boston: Cengage Learning, 2011); Robert L. Zimdahl, *Agriculture's Ethical Horizon*, 2nd ed. (New York: Elsevier Science, 2012).

Sustainable Mining in South Africa

A Concept in Search of a Theory

Peter Knox, SJ

In *Africae Munus*, Pope Benedict XVI identified a significant ecological threat in Africa and appealed for the sustainable extraction of resources in order to preserve life and peace:

> Some business men and women, governments and financial groups are involved in programmes of exploitation which pollute the environment and cause unprecedented desertification. Serious damage is done to nature, to the forests, to flora and fauna, and countless species risk extinction. All of this threatens the entire ecosystem and consequently the survival of humanity. I call upon the Church in Africa to encourage political leaders to protect such fundamental goods as land and water for the human life of present and future generations and for peace between peoples.[1]

Not a naïve eco-warrior, Benedict XVI was reflecting what he had heard at the Second African Synod in 2009, from participants reporting their experiences from all over the continent. The synod displayed an ecological awareness unprecedented in African church teaching.[2] Here the then-pope makes a focused appeal for sustainable economic and environmental practices. He identifies land, water, forests, fauna, and flora as fundamental goods necessary for sustaining human life and peace, which are under threat from unprincipled exploitation. And he insists that such solidarity must extend across countries in the present (a prerequisite for peace) as well as benefiting future generations.

Mining is an aspect of resource extraction that endangers both the environment and peace in Africa.[3] Yet the concept of "sustainable mining" presents an inherent paradox. The resources mined constitute limited matter that agglomerated when the earth formed billions of years ago, or when decaying organic matter formed into deposits millions of years ago. How is it possible to mine these resources sustainably, since they are neither in infinite supply nor constantly being renewed? Moreover, industries that support mineral extraction have sustainability issues of their own (for example, mining consumes inordinate amounts of water and electricity, the provision of which is a major issue in resource-poor countries). This essay seeks an adequate understanding of sustainability that acknowledges these realities.

I will focus on formal mining and metallurgical operations in South Africa. Much of what appears here can be applied mutatis mutandis to mining in other contexts. This essay examines the utility of two different models of sustainability. First, it addresses the Brundtland Report, which was seminal in analyzing, applying, and popularizing sustainability as intergenerational solidarity and international equity.[4] The Brundtland Report states principles and makes recommendations, but its applicability to mining is limited. Our attention thus turns to a second model, the Five Capitals Model, as a tool with which to examine sustainability in mining. Although it also has limitations, the model promises a potential framework on which to structure an assessment of mining sustainability. Still, neither Brundtland nor Five Capitals addresses who actually *owns* the minerals being mined. This consideration allows a Christian light to be thrown on the matter from the perspective of Catholic social teaching.

Sustainable Mining in the Brundtland Report

Operating from 1963 to 1987, the United Nations World Commission on Environment and Development[5] (UNWCED) issued a moral clarion call to the world in its final report, which is often referred to as the Brundtland Report. It is not an exaggeration to say that it redefined the way many people conceptualize our being in the world and our use of limited resources. It popularized the ethical principle of sustainability premised on intergenerational solidarity and international equity, with the famous aphorism that "sustainable development is development that meets the needs of the present without compromising the ability of future generations to meet their own needs."[6]

Sustainable Use of Limited Resources

Although the report optimistically posits the necessity of economic growth to lift millions of the world's poor out of poverty,[7] it also recognizes that we must come to terms with "limitations imposed by the present state of technology and social organization on environmental resources and by the ability of the biosphere to absorb the effects of human activities."[8] It is imperative that decision makers in the mining and allied industries take seriously both of these limitations.

Paragraph 12 of the introductory section, titled "From One Earth to One World," speaks of sustainability of supply of nonrenewable resources, such as fossil fuels and minerals, recognizing the obvious fact that "their use reduces the stock available for future generations. But this does not mean that such resources should not be used." In an attempt to get around this paradox, the report advises that "in general the rate of depletion should take into account the criticality of that resource, the availability of technologies for minimizing depletion, and the likelihood of substitutes being available." But in the middle of the paragraph, the following detail slips in almost imperceptibly: "Thus land should not be degraded beyond reasonable recovery." The meaning of this sentence is opaque, since while many underground mining operations might not interfere with the fertility of land, such land is useless if the water supply to the land is contaminated.

The paragraph continues about the depletion and consumption of mineral resources: "With minerals and fossil fuels, the rate of depletion and the emphasis on recycling and economy of use should be calibrated to ensure that the resource does not run out before acceptable substitutes are available. Sustainable development requires that the rate of depletion of non-renewable resources should foreclose as few future options as possible." This sentence conveys a presumption of eventual discovery of acceptable substitutes (which is contingent on scientific advances), as well as a mechanism to govern the rate of use of nonrenewable resources (which depends on the political will to set a pace for the consumption, recycling, and use of the resources). However, it is not evident that either of these presumptions is warranted. For example, the world has an insatiable appetite for fossil fuels, and is neither on the point of finding viable alternatives nor of regulating its consumption. Although great strides are being made in terms of the deployment of alternative and renewable energy sources, in most parts of the "developed" world oil remains an indispensable fuel. However, a time is approaching when it is not possible to extract oil any faster—the so-called moment of "peak oil." Other types of fossil fuels like natural gas are increasingly being sought, but they too are nonrenewable energy sources. The problem of renewability is deferred.

Instead, the Brundtland Report deals with the continuing dilemma of the use of fossil fuels under the heading of "managing climate change, reducing urban-industrial air pollution and damage from the long-range transport of air pollution."[9] As conventional sources of oil dry up, more and more hazardous means are employed in the transportation and extraction of fossil fuels.[10] These certainly do not honor the principle noted above, that "the land should not be degraded beyond reasonable recovery." Indeed, lives and livelihoods of thousands of people are affected by contamination, as is evident in many parts of Africa and the world today.[11]

What of nonfuel mineral resources? The Brundtland Report is more sanguine about this type of extraction. It maintains that growing demand is unlikely to become problematic[12] and that "industry can adjust to scarcity through greater efficiency in use, recycling and substitution." Ultimately, it recommends greater international equity so that the world trade in minerals be modified "to allow exporters a higher share in the value added from mineral use, and improving the access of developing countries to mineral supplies, as their demands increase."[13]

Along the same line, the report points out how a few transnational corporations control entire industries associated with one or two metals.[14] Therefore, it encourages greater beneficiation (that is, the refining of ores) in the "Third World" countries that mine these minerals for export. This is an obvious strategy to strengthen local economies' share in the final value of their mined goods. My concern, which is addressed in the following paragraph of the report, is that increasing industrialization is inevitably accompanied by increased pollution. Will developing countries learn from the mistakes of developed countries to avoid the pitfalls of environmental damage and costly cleanup?

Thus, overall, the UNWCED report comprehensively addresses a range of technical challenges posed by the apparent incompatibility between environment and development. It makes no attempt to sugarcoat the bitter pill of overconsumption and unsustainable use of resources. It is optimistic in its assumptions about the possibility (and desirability) of future growth, as well as in its belief in international solidarity and goodwill around common challenges. (In case this optimism is not met, it has an annex of proposed legislation.) The report importantly addresses material aspirations of people in countries with growing populations and that want to "develop" in order to provide for their needs. As a pragmatic survey of the world situation from the 1960s to the 1980s, it is masterly. But it has a weak theoretical background, which presumes twin imperatives of industrialization and growth. Ultimately, it does not say very much about the mining industry. We turn thus to another model for a more structured framework with which to examine sustainability in the mining industry.

The "Five Capitals Model" of Sustainability

The Five Capitals Model of Sustainability was devised in the 1990s by the Forum for the Future to evaluate an organization's sustainability and to guide its spread of capital investment.[15] The five capitals of the title of the model are explained:

- "Natural capital is the basis for production and for life itself."
- "Human capital consists of people's health, knowledge, skills, and motivation."
- "Social capital concerns the institutions that help us maintain and develop human capital."
- "Manufactured capital comprises material goods or fixed assets which contribute to the production process rather than being the output itself."
- "Financial capital . . . enabling the other types of capital to be owned and traded . . . has no real value in itself but is representative of natural, human, social, or manufactured capital."[16]

There are flows and trade-offs between the various capitals as value is transferred from one to another. For example, as gold is mined and used in technology or as an economic reserve, natural capital is converted to manufactured or financial capital, respectively. Financial capital can in turn be converted to social capital by spending the gold on education, health care, or infrastructure. This then has spin-offs for human capital.

Although the available literature from the Forum for the Future offers scant theoretical background for the model, the forum's website refers interested readers to Jonathon Porritt's *Capitalism as if the World Matters*. Part 2 of the book develops the Five Capitals as a framework for sustainable capitalism.[17] Porritt professes no ideological commitment to capitalism but takes the pragmatic view that we have to deal with it as the prevailing economic model. His blog article on the book explains: "Whether capitalism really is capable of delivering a genuinely sustainable, equitable economy is by no means clear. But it had better be. It is the only game in town, and will be for many years to come."[18]

For the purposes of this essay, the important contribution of the Five Capitals Model is its "twelve features of a sustainable society." It is possible to assess how the mining industry in South Africa measures up against these twelve features.[19] We focus only on the first two types of capital—natural and human, that is, the environment and the workers—as two important features of mining in South Africa. This treatment will of necessity be at the level of generalization but will nonetheless identify important considerations in the industry.

A Prior Question: Ownership of Natural Capital

Who owns valuable subterranean minerals? This is not addressed by the Forum for the Future or the Brundtland Report, but it is a vital question, especially for mining in Africa. Patterns of ownership often follow patterns of colonial conquest and privilege. During the colonial and apartheid eras the state intervened heavily to subsidize and maintain the economic domination of white people. Perhaps the greatest injustice of this crony capitalism of the ancien régime was to award ownership of mineral rights to landowners, and cede only 13 percent of the land to black people.[20] Thus, large mining companies were established that exploited the minerals and the workers and enriched a very small portion of the population. After the discovery of diamonds and gold in South Africa in the late nineteenth century, the names of Rhodes, Oppenheimer, De Beers, Barnato, Robinson, and others became synonymous with conspicuous wealth and political influence, while millions of anonymous workers have toiled in the mines for over 130 years. On the linkage between economic globalization and human and ecological degradation, a Jesuit decree describes the situation in a nutshell: "Transnational interests, unconstrained by national laws and often abetted by corruption, frequently exploit the natural resources of the poor."[21]

This situation sits uneasily with biblically based reflection on the world's resources, which take the creation narratives in Genesis 1 and 2 as indicative of God's intention regarding our use of the earth. In neither narrative does God give *ownership* to the humans. Human beings are entrusted with the goods of the earth, to consume as they need, but as stewards, not as owners. Arguably owners might do as they like with their effects. But in Genesis, God retains the ownership of all that has been created. Humans are simply allowed to utilize them for their own good, and recent scholarship has pointed out how stewardship is a better interpretation of these passages than "domination."

In a similar way, Catholic social teaching informs us that God destined the goods of creation for all people. *Gaudium et Spes* says: "God destined the earth and all it contains for all men and all peoples," and "we must never lose sight of this universal destination of earthly goods."[22] The constitution cites both Pope Leo XIII's encyclical *Rerum Novarum* on capital and labor, and *Mater et Magistra*, Pope John XXIII's encyclical letter on Christianity and social progress.[23] In *Mater et Magistra*, John XXIII quotes the Pentecost radio discourse of Pius XII, restating the right of everyone to make use of the goods of the earth, and the duty of the state to control private and public use: "the first and fundamental right which concedes their use to all."[24]

In addition, in his encyclical on human work, Pope John Paul II enunciates the principle of the priority of labor over capital, teaching that the ownership of assets is for the good of the workers and not an absolute value in itself.[25] Ownership is always subordinate to the right of common use. Ideally, there is a mutuality between owners and workers, rather than antagonistic competition. In sum, the teaching of the church is that the goods of the earth are a universal patrimony, and the state's duty is to protect private ownership, which is a human right, but at the same time to ensure that the exercise of this right does not force some to remain in poverty.

This means that the people and corporations to whom mineral rights have been granted only control them in the name of a wider community. Of course, they invest heavily in order to make natural capital accessible and ultimately profitable for the larger community, and they merit some incentive for risking financial capital. However, their investment does not entitle them to take home tens of millions in profit while workers struggle to make a living. Even less does it permit them to transfer vast financial capital offshore to enrich people in other countries at the expense of local citizens.

This problem is evident in South Africa's mining industry. To assert national sovereignty and to restore the patrimony of the poor, the Congress of the People addressed this fundamental economic factor directly. Under the heading "The People Shall Share the Country's Wealth," the Freedom Charter states that "the mineral wealth beneath the soil [and] the banks and monopoly industries shall be transferred to the ownership of the people as a whole."[26] This is in line with a more traditional, perhaps now romanticized, precolonial African sense of communal ownership of land.[27] As part of its selective implementation of the charter, the present government enacted legislation in 2002 to redress structures of ownership of mineral rights. But it runs the risk of simply reproducing previous structures, with different faces at the top of new mining corporations, still leaving the majority of the country in poverty.[28]

Sustainable Natural Capital in the Mining Industry: An Oxymoron?

Mining is essentially the extraction of natural capital—mostly nonrenewable mineral deposits—for conversion into other forms of capital. Main considerations include that, in their extraction, manufacture, and use, substances taken from the earth and artificial substances "do not exceed the environment's capacity to disperse, absorb, recycle or otherwise neutralize their harmful effects (to humans and/or the environment)." The Five Capitals model also points out that a feature of sustainability is when "the capacity of the environment to provide ecological system integrity, biological diversity and productivity is protected or enhanced."[29] We will take each of these considerations in turn.

Substances Taken from the Earth

In terms of these features, mining in South Africa is decidedly unsustainable. It is associated with acid water seepage, contamination of aquifers and rivers, and airborne pollutants near population centers. The point here is not that resources will inevitably and eventually be depleted; rather, the industry is destructive of other natural environmental capital. It is dangerous to regard undeveloped land as a sink that absorbs many harmful substances. Many people think of oceans in a similar way, turning them into vast international rubbish dumps. If the environment cannot reabsorb, recycle, disperse, or otherwise neutralize the potential harm of mined or manufactured goods, then damage builds up, affecting this and many future generations. A few examples will illuminate the point. The release of asbestos dust around mining operations has caused untold suffering for miners and their communities, causing lung cancer, asbestosis, and mesothelioma. This situation persists despite the fact that mining companies have long known the dangers of airborne asbestos dust.[30]

Asbestos dust is a solid, so its dispersal and danger are relatively localized. This is not the case for gaseous products of extraction and combustion of fossil fuels,[31] which can disperse for thousands of kilometers. The harmful effect of one of them, carbon dioxide (CO_2), is global. The earth is not able "to absorb, recycle or otherwise neutralise" all the CO_2 being produced by the combustion of mined fossil fuels that had been sequestered in the earth for eons. Along with other gases, CO_2 accumulates in the atmosphere, retaining solar heat, and gradually raising the temperature of the earth's surface (the "greenhouse effect"). There is near unanimity among scientific communities that this effect contributes to extreme weather events, and to the warming of the oceans, and will eventually raise sea levels as polar ice melts.

Manufactured Products

Similar considerations apply to the manufactured products of the mining industry. Many of the most troublesome nonbiodegradable pollutants are either manufactured from refined ores—such as heavy metals or radioactive isotopes—or from other material that was originally mined. Example of this are the hundreds of different types of plastics that end up strewn all over the globe. In South Africa, there is an enormous industry of manufacturing polymers using coal as the raw material. During the apartheid years, when international economic sanctions were biting, the government spent billions on an industrial process of "cracking" locally mined coal to manufacture smaller-moleculed liquid and gas fuels.[32] The industry has since diversified into the production of waxes, plastics, solvents, and other chemicals.[33] It is possible to recycle most of these plastics, but they remain among the most visible pollutants all over South Africa; many plastic products are not recycled but downcycled and put in trash dumps, partly because they are so cheap and easily available. This is an example of a manufactured mineral by-product exceeding "the environment's capacity to disperse, absorb, recycle or otherwise neutralise" them, and they end up in rivers or landfills, scattered across the countryside, in the stomachs of animals, or floating in the oceans.

Ecological System Integrity and Biodiversity

It is difficult to think of any mining activity that actually enhances or even protects the integrity or biological diversity of natural systems. Indeed, much opposition to mining is based on the justifiable perception that their activity degrades and even destroys ecological systems.

Examples abound in South Africa. Consider Richards Bay Minerals (RBM), which in 1989 proposed mining titanium in the ecologically sensitive coastal dunes of the (then) Natal Province. The company claimed that they could rehabilitate the centuries-old apex coastal forest within thirty years.[34] After a national and international outcry, in 1995 the postapartheid government decided that the wetland area was too precious to destroy, and would benefit more from ecotourism than from mining, and in 1999 the 3,280 square kilometers iSimangaliso Wetland Park was declared South Africa's first World Heritage Site.[35] However, in a 2003 workshop RBM organized for natural scientists, the company claimed that ecotourism had not delivered development for local communities, and that the area should therefore be mined.[36] In 2007, similar arguments were being heard about proposed titanium mining of coastal dunes in Pondoland. Even though ecotourism is not a panacea for poor local communities, it offers more lasting jobs than mining does, and is less destructive of intact natural systems on which people depend for their sustenance.

Asbestos, carbon dioxide, and the coal derivatives are but three indicators of the unsustainability of the mining industry, as the earth simply cannot "neutralise their harmful effects (to humans and/or the environment)." One needs only to visit any mining operation in the country to observe the destruction of biological diversity and natural systems. Thus, in light of the three features of sustainable use of natural capital proposed by the Forum for the Future, mining in South Africa cannot be considered to be sustainable.

Sustainability of Human Capital

It is in the interest of any organization to invest in the people who work for it. However, this is not always self-evident in an industry with an annual turnover of hundreds of billions of dollars of revenue,[37] and in which the cost of any stoppages is measured in millions, even when these stoppages are related to health and safety issues. Certainly, at some level, economic decisions are made relating to expenditure on human capital, and sustainability isn't always the first priority: "Unprofitable" mines are closed; workers are laid off in the thousands; foreign migrant workers are repatriated.

The Forum for the Future proposes three features of sustainable organizations with respect to human capital. The first is beguilingly simple: "At all ages, individuals enjoy a high standard of health." The second feature is that "individuals are adept at relationships and social participation, and throughout life set and achieve high personal standards of their development and learning." The third requires "access to varied and satisfying opportunities for work, personal creativity, and recreation." (Oddly, just remuneration is not listed among the sustainability features of human capital. Perhaps it is included under the rubric of sustainable *social* capital, the first feature of which is: "there are trusted and accessible systems of governance and justice.")

A High Standard of Health

Mining is an inherently dangerous activity. In addition to the ubiquitous dust causing a range of lung diseases, mining involves exposure to heavy machinery and explosives, as well as to industrial-strength chemicals in the metallurgical operations—all of which pose their own hazards. The underground working environment is hostile to human physiology, with poor lighting, extremes of noise and temperature combined with poor ventilation and potential gas buildup, geological instability, and the ever-present danger of rockfalls.[38] These risks are all known, and reasonable precautions are deemed to be in place.[39] Indeed, to compel employers to fulfill responsibilities toward employees, the post-1994 government has passed much progressive legislation to protect workers' rights in terms of occupational diseases and injuries, basic conditions of employment, and more.

Generally, the mines go beyond these strict requirements of the law: the hospitals and health care facilities run by the mining companies in South Africa rate among the best in the country. They treat employees who suffer work-related illnesses and injuries, as well as other illnesses.[40] They are the envy of many provinces and cities.[41] In fact, in the interest of retaining their workforce, mines were the first employers in South Africa routinely to provide antiretroviral treatment to HIV-positive employees (a provision that has recently been extended to their dependents).[42]

However, in 2011 there were 123 on-duty fatalities out of 513,211 people employed in the mining sector.[43] Moreover, labor disputes can lead to the loss of life, which was seen tragically on August 16, 2012, when the police shot and killed thirty-four striking miners at Lonmin's platinum mine in Marikana. Personal hostilities may also result in violence, and it is not unheard of for miners to be dispatched in industrial "accidents." Thus, not all the deaths recorded in the industry are necessarily related to the inherent physical dangers of mining.

Human Development, Variety, and Satisfaction

Many mining houses attract prospective employees or retain existing employees with offers of funds for study at the undergraduate level. This arrangement works to the advantage of the company and the student and ensures a supply of new graduates to keep the wheels of industry turning. To keep the work interesting, mining companies might make the work as varied as possible—by rotating an employee among jobs within his or her range of skills. But there is a limit to the number of ways one can access ore, bring it to the surface, and process it into a saleable end product. When the industry operates on such a large scale, it is difficult to be responsive to the creative urges of individuals.

The recreational and living conditions on mines are far from optimal. Traditionally, the industry is labor intensive and relies on a migrant labor force. Often thousands of men live together in cramped single-sex hostels, with the chance to go home to their families only once a year. In many regions the mines are the main providers of recreational facilities, the character of which can either make or break a community. Focusing on sport and alcohol, the social facilities provided by the mines go only so far to relieve boredom. It is common for men to take a "wife" (either male or female), or to have a second "mine" family while they are employed in the mines. Because of this social situation, HIV/AIDS remains widespread in mining communities despite education programs. When the mines are better established or are close to towns, the living conditions are better. Some mines subsidize workers to take accommodations off the mine premises so that miners' families can live in the town, with children attending local schools. Social networks thus exist independent of the mines.

On balance, the mines still have a way to go in terms of sustainability of human capital. Spurred on by strong labor unions and by labor-friendly legislation, they have improved almost beyond recognition since the age of colonization and apartheid. In a hazardous industry, mining corporations do try to keep their workforce healthy, stimulated, and socially integrated.

Perhaps the idea of "sustainable mining" is a paradox, since the resources being mined will not last ad infinitum. The inspirational Brundtland Report expands on the principle that a sustainable activity is one that meets the needs of the present without compromising the ability of future generations to meet their own needs, but its treatment of mining is vague. The main guideline is that consumption be calibrated so that resources are not depleted before suitable alternatives are found. Besides the ambiguity of such a statement, it is not evident that the presumption of substitutability is warranted.

The Five Capitals model of sustainability describes twelve features that characterize a sustainable organization. This essay considered only those features relating to natural and human capital and concluded that, from this perspective, the mining industry in South Africa cannot be considered sustainable: the products and manufactured goods of the industry cause harm to humans and the environment. However, especially in the realm of human capital, the industry does appear to be moving in the right direction.

Many questions remain at the interface of mining, sustainability, and natural and human capital. For example: How does one appropriately quantify the satisfaction and health of a mining workforce alongside destruction of ecological system integrity or diminishment of biodiversity? What limits to extraction and consumption are best suited for nonrenewable mineral resources, some of which have negative consequences for the environment? And who owns and benefits from the extractive industries? In the course of exploring the Brundtland and Five Capitals Model theories of sustainability, we considered the question of ownership of—and access to—the natural capital on which all mining is based. A biblical interpretation, as well as clear stipulations from Catholic social teaching, insists that the "goods of Creation"—in this case, nonrenewable minerals—belong to all people, and it is the state's duty to ensure that the benefits are evenly distributed.

Notes

1. Benedict XVI, *Africae Munus: Postsynodal Apostolic Exhortation of the Church in Africa in Service to Reconciliation, Justice and Peace* (Vatican City: Libreria Editrice Vaticana, 2011), no. 80.

2. See Peter Knox, "Theology, Ecology and Africa: No Longer Strange Bedfellows," in *Reconciliation, Justice and Peace: The Second African Synod*, ed. Agbonkhianmeghe E. Orobator (Maryknoll, NY: Orbis Books, 2011), 159–70.

3. The question of Africa's notorious "conflict diamonds" and "resource wars," such as international competition over coltan in the eastern Democratic Republic of Congo, warrants an entire chapter of its own. Apart from mentioning it in passing here, this present chapter does not deal specifically with the *threat to peace* posed by mining.

4. Influenced by the Brundtland Report, sustainability has become a new popular moral touchstone, understood as a cross-generational application of Kant's famous categorical imperative.

5. The commission is eponymously referred to as the "Brundtland Commission" and its report the "Brundtland Report," after its chairperson, Gro Brundtland.

6. United Nations World Commission on Environment and Development, *Our Common Future* (Oslo: United Nations, 1987), chap. 2, para. 1ff. There appears to be no standard pagination in the various versions of the report that are available—even on the UN website. So for reference purposes I use chapter number or section title and the paragraph within that chapter.

7. Ibid., "From One Earth to One World," para. 3. "We see instead the possibility of a new era of economic growth, one that must be based on policies that sustain and expand the

environmental resource base. And we believe such growth to be absolutely essential to relieve the great poverty that is deepening in much of the developing world."

8. Ibid., para. 27.

9. Ibid., chap. 7.

10. I refer here to the 2010 Deepwater Horizon disaster, as well as to the tar sands projects in Alberta with their destruction of swathes of boreal forests and their toxic effects on groundwater. Closer to home, the South African government is seriously considering permitting the use of hydraulic fracturing ("fracking") technology for the extraction of shale gas in the sparsely populated and water-scarce Karoo, despite irrefutable evidence that such technology poisons groundwater. Lacking cheap alternative fuels, Poland and "clean, green" Germany continue to expand open-cast mining of lignite ("brown coal").

11. Historically, the transportation of oil has been a major source of pollution. Two notorious examples are the leaking pipelines in the Niger Delta and the Exxon Valdez spill in Alaska. Despite corporate assurances, the cleanup of such spills is never complete, and the land, seafloor, and coastline are never restored to their pre-spill state.

12. UNWCED, *Our Common Future*, chap. 2, para. 63.

13. Ibid.

14. Ibid., chap. 8, para. 30.

15. Forum for the Future, *The Five Capitals Model: A Framework for Sustainability*. See http://www.forumforthefuture.org.

16. Ibid.

17. Jonathon Porritt, *Capitalism as if the World Matters* (London: Earthscan, 2007), chaps. 6–11, 137–211.

18. Jonathon Porritt, *Capitalism as if the World Matters* (blog).

19. Although the mining industry is not an "organization" or "society" in the sense envisaged by the Forum for the Future, it is not stretching the model beyond its limits to apply the features to an entire industry. In March 2013, the Forum for the Future published a "Sustainable Economy Framework" that "sets out parameters for a suitable future economy that can help today's investments and business decisions deliver sustainable value over the long term." This framework considers some *thirty* basic needs, necessary social and political factors, and environmental boundaries. Although this is a more recent tool, offering greater refinement, it has too many factors to take into account in this present chapter. See Forum for the Future, *Sustainable Economy Framework*.

20. With the infamous Natives Land Act 27 of 1913.

21. Society of Jesus, *General Congregation 35* (Rome: Society of Jesus, 2008), decree 3, no. 26.

22. "*Gaudium et Spes*, 69.

23. Leo XIII, *Rerum Novarum, Acta Apostolicae Sedis* 23 (1891): 651; John XXIII, *Mater et Magistra, Acta Apostolicae Sedis* 53 (1961): 411. *Rerum Novarum* was the first Catholic teaching to say, "For God has granted the earth to humankind in general, . . . no part of it was assigned to anyone in particular, and the limits of private possession have been left to be fixed by our own industry and by the laws of individual races."

24. Pius XII, *Nuntius Radiophonicus, Acta Apostolicae Sedis* 33 (1941): 199.

25. John Paul II, *Laborem Exercens, Acta Apostolicae Sedis* 73 (1981): 12, 19.

26. Congress of the People, *The Freedom Charter* (Kliptown: June 26, 1955).

27. Cousins makes the point that "'communal' or 'customary' land tenure regimes are not static and tradition-bound, . . . but dynamic and evolving." Ben Cousins, "Potential

and Pitfalls of 'Communal' Land Tenure Reform: Experience in Africa and Implications for South Africa," *World Bank Conference on 'Land Governance in Support of the MDGs: Responding to New Challenges'* (Washington, DC: World Bank, 2009).

28. In 2008, South Africa had a Gini coefficient of 0.7 for household income and 0.63 for expenditure. This indicates great inequality in the country, which appears to be increasing. See Sudhanshu Sharma, "Rising Inequality in South Africa: Drivers, Trends and Policy Responses," in *Consultancy Africa Intelligence*, http://www.consultancyafrica.com.

29. Forum for the Future, *Five Capitals Model.*

30. After the collapse of the asbestos mining industry and after almost a decade of litigation, Cape PLC, a British mining firm eventually had to compensate some 7,500 victims of its negligence. See Anthony Coombs, "End of Struggle for Cape Asbestos Victims," John Pickering & Partners, http://www.johnpickering.co.uk.

31. South Africa exploits reserves of natural gas off the Southern Cape coast.

32. Although the SASOL oil-from-coal process gave the country a measure of independence from volatile oil markets since the 1950s, it never accounted for more than about one-third of the country's liquid fuel use.

33. See http://www.sasol.com.

34. One can understand the Jews' incredulity when Jesus said: "Destroy this temple and in three days I will build it up" (John 2:19).

35. Legal action comes too late once mines have already destroyed the integrity of ecological systems. For example, in the Wassa district of Ghana, environmental destruction from cyanide spills has occurred downstream of Gold Fields mines, depriving people and animals of potable water and rendering crops inedible. See Earthworks No Dirty Gold, "Wassa District, Ghana," http://www.nodirtygold.org. Mining has consequences for soils, forests, and water. See chapter 5 of Solo Maninga Kiabilua, and Paul Mabolia Yenga, *La problématique des exploitations du diamant en RDC: La pipeline du diamant et le développement durable*, ed. CEPAS (Kinshasa: Médiaspaul, 2009), 97–103. In Costa Rica, mining companies challenged the constitutionality of legislation to ban new open-pit mining in the long-term interests of a tourist-driven green economy. See Dorothy Kosich, "Costa Rican Mining Chamber Sues to Overturn Open-pit Mining Ban," *Mineweb*, http://www.mineweb.com. Lest I convey the impression that it is only in the "developing" world that the mining industry has a reputation of being cavalier toward natural capital, I refer the reader to the plans of two gold mining companies in Alaska. They proposed dumping waste into pristine Lower Slate Lake and the headwaters of Bristol Bay, in contravention of the US Clean Water Act of 1972. See Earthworks No Dirty Gold, "Berners Bay, Alaska," http://www.nodirtygold.org.

36. See Keith Ross, "We Were Naïve, Says Dune Mining Activist," http://www.iol.co.za.

37. See Chamber of Mines, *Facts and Figures 2012* (Johannesburg: Chamber of Mines of South Africa, 2012), 3.

38. South African mines are the deepest in the world, with one going to four thousand meters underground.

39. Despite extensive safety education given to all employees, these measures are only as good as the people who effect them. Despite the availability of cumbersome safety equipment, my colleagues and I would routinely use our mouths to suck acid solutions of uranium oxide into pipettes, and with our naked hands collect samples from a flow.

40. And thereby conform with the health care principle enunciated in *Laborem Exercens,* 19.

41. When residents of the area need medical care, they try to receive it at the mine hospitals. This applies a fortiori to other African countries. See *Le forum de la societé civile de la RDC, Révision des contrats miniers en RDC: Rapport sur 12 contrats miniers*, ed. CEPAS (Kinshasa: Médiaspaul, 2007), 130.

42. See Anglo American, "HIV/AIDS," http://www.angloamerican.com. It is also reported in Creamer Media's Mining Weekly, "Gold Fields to Provide Workers with HIV/AIDS Treament," http://www.miningweekly.com.

43. This amounts to one death per 4,172 employees, which is one-third of the rate of one death per 1,434 employees in 2002. See Chamber of Mines, *Facts and Figures 2012*, 10–12.

Health Systems Challenges, National HIV/AIDS Response, and Public Health Policy in Chad

Ethical and Efficiency Requirements for Sustainable Health Systems

Jacquineau Azétsop, SJ

Health systems (HS) consist of all organizations, people, and actions whose primary intent is to promote, restore, or maintain health. This includes efforts to influence determinants of health as well as more direct health-improving activities.[1] Most strategies used for sustaining HS over time are mainly technical. These strategies have been unsuccessful because health systems sustainability (HSS) involves value-laden choices. Focusing essentially on technical solutions does not equip decision makers with the moral compass needed to address a broader range of relevant values including social justice, public accountability, competence, and community participation. The absence of these values negatively shapes the general environment of health systems and reduces odds for better organizational and managerial capacity.

Relying on the evaluation of the national HIV and AIDS program performance in Chad, this essay seeks to highlight the potential contribution of ethics to HSS and policy. The central thesis of this essay is that the limited success of the AIDS program is, at least partly, due to the fragmentation of HS and the lack of health promotion ethics. Ethics should be part of the process of elaboration and implementation of health policy because critical reflection can improve public health intervention outcomes through the integration of values and principles that promote a just society. This essay will highlight the importance of ethics in a country where normative reflection does not produce institutional change through public health policy.

Health Systems Sustainability: Definition and Analytic Framework

The most widely cited definition of sustainability emphasizes the aim "to meet the needs of the present without compromising the ability of future generations to meet their own needs."[2] This widespread definition focuses essentially on inequities that fuel the urban and rural divides in the world. Other definitions emphasize self-sufficiency and capacity-building generated by a project or program as outcomes of the long-term economic commitment by donors.[3]

The implications of "sustainability" in health are difficult to describe in a comprehensive way, and this has consequences for both the practice and the ethics of HSS. Moreover, sustainability is not a static condition, but a process that presupposes an ongoing input-output interplay that involves a multitude of social agents. Most approaches to sustainability include moral or intergenerational equity, efficiency, capacity-building, self-sufficiency, ownership, and continuity.[4]

HS, rather than health care systems (HCS), are the focus of this essay because our approach to sustainability emphasizes the ultimate outcome of promoting public and individual health, and not only the performance of the formal system of care designed primarily to treat illness. HCS performance focuses on service provision, while HS denotes a much wider range of institutions and actors beyond the traditional so-called health sector, including actors who directly or indirectly influence and affect health. The strength of HS depends essentially on the justice of social institutions.

Since health care needs are not static, to remain viable and sustainable, the HCS must respond adaptively to new diseases, changing demographics, scientific discoveries, technological advances, changing social systems, and competing political claims.[5] Responses to some of these challenges are formulated within HS to which the HCS belongs. Good medical care is certainly vital to people's well-being, but improved clinical care is not enough to overcome HIV/AIDS in Chad. Structural factors that shape or constrain HS need to be addressed. However, this makes the discussion of HSS difficult because it is hard to know whether we should focus only on activities strictly defined as HSS or whether we should also include all activities that influence HSS. Furthermore, the boundaries between HSS and the rest of public health are unclear. The scope of this study does not permit us to address this problem. Instead, I present an analytic framework within which HSS can be discussed, both as a practice and as a normative endeavor.

Unlike those who emphasize project- or program-based approaches and those who value sustained primary health care as an ultimate objective of sustainability initiatives, I defend a systems approach and consider the entire health sector (not only primary health care) as an interrelated system that needs to be strengthened through policy change and structural interventions.[6] As a systemic endeavor, HSS depends on the social and political context and investment decisions. Investment strategies are reflected by process variables including program strategy, design, and management.[7] Contextual factors include the political and economic environment within which the health care system operates. Contextual factors also include the interests and actions of main actors.

Hence, health systems are considered sustainable when operated within a health-promoting environment by an organized system of actors and institutions with the long-term ability to mobilize and allocate sufficient resources for activities that meet individual or public health needs.[8] Consequently, the HSS framework should include, first, contextual factors that outline the task and general environment of the services; second, an activity profile that describes the services delivered and the activities carried out to deliver them; and, third, an organizational capacity that shows the country's ability to sustain all the components of a health system.[9] Relying on all the elements of this definition, we examine the capacity of HS to sustain the fight against HIV and AIDS over time.

Why Is Sustainability Important for Health Systems?

There are at least five reasons why sustainability concerns HS decision making and research. First, sustained HS can maintain their effects over a long period, allowing for the study of long-term effects and providing an empirical basis for a sound evaluation. Second, sustainable HS favor the realization of health interventions over time. Third, sustainable HS are beneficial for people's health because they possess the organization, resources, and well-integrated services needed to carry on ordinary interventions over time. Fourth, an absence of sustainability often leads to an investment loss for the funding agencies or the state, as well as for the beneficiaries, due to the discontinuation of programs. Fifth, sustainability provides a framework for analyzing HSS performance.

HS should address the social determinants of health and generate equitable health outcomes through their health care delivery system.[10] Sustainable HS are endowed with values and means to achieve the overarching and specific goals of health promotion. These values and means are safeguards for health justice, intersectoral collaboration, and professional ethics. The overarching goal, which is that of health promotion, is to help ensure sufficient well-being, in all its dimensions, for everyone.[11] The specific goal of sustainability is to set standards for performance and efficiency over time and to avoid the fragmentation of HS. It also includes the need for defining the shape of each component of HS and how those components intermingle.

Sustainability is not only a technical concept but also an ethical one. Hence, the promotion of HSS requires both a moral deliberation about the values operative in society and a critical examination of the efficiency of practices used for such a venture. The practice of sustainability refers to concrete solutions used to sustain organic and efficient HS over time. The normative ideal of HSS is the aspect of public health practice that is particularly concerned with the justice of social arrangements. Since HS are part of social systems, interventions that alter social arrangements can be beneficial to everyone no matter their health risks. These systemic interventions require governmental commitment to citizens' welfare and the active support of individuals and local communities.

Critical Evaluation of the National Health System in Chad

Based on the framework suggested here, I will evaluate the performance of the Chadian HSS based on the successes and failures of the national AIDS program.

The Successes and Failures of the National AIDS Program

The 2005 national sero-prevalence survey showed that people living with HIV represent 3.3 percent of the entire population in Chad. The prevalence was higher in urban (7 percent) compared to rural (2.3 percent) areas. Women were more frequently infected (4.0 percent) than men (2.65 percent).[12] Since 2007, antiretroviral drugs (ARVs) are given for free to eligible individuals in Chad. This has allowed some of these affected people to access ARVs. Universal access to antiretroviral treatment (ART) in Chad was officially declared in December 2006 and is funded by the country's budget and external donors. This initiative is led by the National AIDS Council with the technical support of the United Nations Development Programme (UNDP) and the financial support of the Global Fund.

The most at-risk population groups are identified as a priority target for the HIV/AIDS response. They include women, children, sex workers, young people, and refugees. Many nonbehavioral factors have triggered the spread of HIV/AIDS.[13] Despite efforts by the government and its partners to contain the AIDS pandemic, the success rate of both preventive and clinical efforts remains quite low. The number of patients on ARVs increased from 7,215 in 2007 to 32,832 in 2010, against 97,196 infected individuals who actually need to be on ARVs.[14]

Access to ART is unevenly distributed from one region to another and between rural and urban areas. The proportion of women (above fifteen years old) infected increased significantly from 2006 to 2009, from 63 to 65 percent with a peak of 69 percent in 2007.[15] Children's access to ARVs is low.[16] In 2007, 0.82 percent of infected children were on ARVs. This situation has not improved significantly, since only 9 percent of children were on ARVs in 2009 versus 4 percent in 2008. The situation will worsen, since the estimated number of new cases of pediatric HIV in 2010 was 656, and the number of children living with HIV was 11,965.[17] Pregnant women's access to antenatal care has been proven to reduce significantly incident cases of pediatric HIV. Unfortunately, access to antenatal care is constrained by many social factors, and the integration of prevention of mother-to-child transmission in antenatal care is still in an early stage.[18] The weaknesses and fragmentation of the health system is one of the reasons for the limited success of the national HIV/AIDS program.

Environmental Factors, a Challenge to Sustainability

Contextual factors refer to those conditions that influence HS and cannot be addressed within an overall concern for sustainability. These factors highly influence HSS because they are connected to politics, economy, physical environment, and culture. Acting on those conditions can yield important gains for human health and improve the health system.

The postcolonial era was determined by sociopolitical tensions and wars that severely damaged the health system in Chad. The sociopolitical turmoil facing the country since the early 1960s contributed to the collapse of the embryonic sustainable conditions that were set up during the colonial era. Postindependence tensions disrupted the internal dynamics of Chadian society. The quality of health services was severely compromised. After a long period of war, the country has achieved a certain level of social stability since the early 1990s, but still has not yet completed its structural adjustment. Despite efforts by the government to improve the living conditions of the population, the country has not yet reached a level of development that can generate conditions conducive to social well-being.

Economic disparities between individuals, population groups, and regions are growing tremendously. These disparities influence ART access. ART access differentials also exist between rural and urban populations because ART clinics are concentrated in major cities.[19] This reveals that the distribution of public health facilities and resources across the country is not driven by needs. Health systems are affected by all the evils that diminish the quality of life in society. These evils increase the deficit of dialogue between health actors and decision makers.

The lack of democratic accountability that prevails in the country also creates an atmosphere within which structural violence not only curtails HS organization and access to care, but also increases risks for infection. Structural violence occurs when harmful or untenable structural conditions and forces persist and result in the undue suffering of groups of people who often are already vulnerable to marginalization.[20] These forces are violent because they cause injury to people, and typically not those who are responsible for perpetuating such inequalities. Infections and health crises pervasively make their way in places where the rule of law remains alien to public values.

The physical environment affects access to ART and to HS in many ways. Chad is a large country (1,284,000 square kilometers). More than 60 percent of it is covered by hard-to-reach desert. Chad is a poor country where more than half of its population (55 percent) is mainly rural and lives below the poverty threshold.[21] The country's size and absence of coastline raise problems of communication, transportation, and access both inside and outside. Most roads, especially rural ones, are largely impassable during the rainy season. Seven out of the twenty-two regions are partially isolated during the rainy season.[22] Environmental factors make access to care and medical supply a real challenge. Despite multiple efforts to strengthen HS, intended sustainable improvements in health outcomes have not been seen. Population access to health services remains limited. Patients travel an average of about 14.4 kilometers to access care,[23] and one patient in ten makes use of traditional healers because access to health facilities is difficult.[24]

Unfulfilled Activity Profile

The Minimum Package of Activities (MPA) and the Complementary Package of Activities (PCA) are two important strategies for effective primary health care (PHC) delivery in Chad.[25] They are also effective channels of AIDS care and HIV prevention. The MPA is the set of PHC services covered by a health care center for the well-being of people. It often happens that the MPA is not fully realized in rural centers. This failure deprives a portion of the population of PHC coverage. A health care center is led by a state registered nurse or sanitary technical agent who does not have the right to prescribe ARVs but can, at least, treat opportunistic diseases, treatment of which is part of the MPA. Apart from routine immunization and nutrition recuperation activities for children, the workload prevents the centers' personnel from fulfilling other outreach programs, including HIV prevention.

In addition to the lack of qualified personnel, the lack of adequate equipment or a consistent drug supply system prevents effective access to PHC. This technical conditionality is extremely worrisome because people living in rural areas and with no other place for treatment than the local health care center are marginalized. Similarly, district hospitals are confronted with the lack of equipment and poor drug supply. It is not, then, surprising to realize that nearly a third of these hospitals did not fulfill the entire PCA in 2008. The PCA includes services that exceed the technical capabilities of a health care center, such as referral consultation, complicated deliveries, medical and surgical emergencies, hospitalization, laboratory diagnosis, and medical imaging.[26]

In most district hospitals, biomedical equipment has not been renewed for several years. The obsolescence of this equipment reduces the performance of health services. Most of these hospitals may be able to manage AIDS care but do not have CD4 counters (to measure white blood cells that fight infection).[27] Despite improvement in HIV infrastructure, the number of ARV-providing institutions remains low compared to the workload. From twenty-two in 2007, there was an increase to sixty-four in 2009.[28] Another area of concern is the prevention of mother-to-child transmission; such prevention efforts are not widespread still because human resources are insufficient, and the use of antenatal care is quite low (48.05 percent in 2009).[29] Thirteen districts implemented this prevention in 2007, and they increased to twenty-two in 2008, while the thirty-seven sites offering prevention in 2007 increased to eighty-one in 2009. These efforts are largely insufficient, taking into account the extent of the national territory. So far, ARV and prevention of mother-to-child transmission are mostly available in hospitals and selected clinics. In addition, the ability to diagnose viral load and to measure CD4 counts remains low. Most laboratories in district hospitals are poorly equipped. There is also a lack of quality control.

Finally, the HS are confronted with all sorts of organizational challenges at all levels of the health care pyramid. The lack of dialogue between levels of the pyramid and poor supervision by higher levels reduces the performance of the whole health care system.

Health Information System and Epidemiologic Surveillance

A lack of data also deprives policymakers of empirical and evidentiary proofs needed for improving the health system's performance. This lack of data is not owing to the absence of tools or platforms for information, but to the glaring lack of national capacity to implement and maintain these tools. In Chad, epidemiological surveillance is essentially passive. It is limited to the reporting of cases of diseases under surveillance from the district to the region and then to the Ministry of Public Health. Using the existing community system to prevent epidemic diseases by training community workers to identify their early signs, based on simple observational techniques, may improve community involvement in health promotion. Under the leadership of the senior nurse, the community system can overcome the shortcomings of the current surveillance system.

Operational research activities are rare, and their results are flawed. Such negative results cannot be used to inform practice and design genuine policy. The methodology and the quality of data collection are infected with biases and confounding factors. Biased data are of limited use for strategic planning and decision making, program implementation, and monitoring. The improvement of health information system should be a priority of the Ministry of Public Health, because sound data are definitely important for evidence-based decisions. The ministry needs to enhance the regional health delegations' capacity in data collection and analysis by providing resources to produce sound data.

The Lack of Human and Financial Resources

The governmental contribution to the national response against HIV and AIDS is important but remains insufficient compared to the challenges faced by the affected populations. To reduce financial barriers to treatment and testing, the head of state reiterated the policy of free care for sexually transmitted infections (STI) and people living with HIV—without, however, increasing the state's financial support to the program.[30] So far, instead of the 15 percent required by the Abuja declaration,[31] Chad has committed less than 6 percent of its annual budget to the health care sector.[32]

Human resources are important in enabling and ensuring quality health care. Although the health sector is recognized as a priority by the Chadian government,[33] the extent of the weakness in human resources in the health sector is deplorable. There was one doctor for 31,481 inhabitants in 2009 against a ratio of one doctor per 27,471 in 2008. The World Health Organization (WHO) recommends a doctor for every 10,000. There is one nurse for every 6,453 people against 1/5,000, a midwife for 9,074 women of childbearing age against 1/5,000 according to WHO standards.[34] This significant decline in numbers and the lack of human resources could be explained by the departure of physicians from the public to the private sector and by population growth.[35] The shortage of trained health care workers is a major impediment to HIV prevention and AIDS treatment access, and alleviating this shortage needs short-term action linked to long-term measures. Proper training for health care providers and staff is important but not sufficient. The Chadian health care system is faced with a crisis of an ever-increasing patient volume that has a strong tendency to overwhelm the available human resources and infrastructure. Policymakers should ensure that trained personnel and infrastructure are appropriately proportionate to the patient load. The sustainability of the HS is at stake.

Health Systems Sustainability, Public Health Policy, and Ethics

HS in Chad are weak because they operate within an environment managed by a poorly organized system of actors and institutions that do not have the ability to mobilize and allocate enough resources for activities that meet public health needs. Technical solutions are but one element needed to improve the sustainability of these systems. Beyond technical solutions, ethics can play an important role, because the conceptual tools that shape public health practice and discourse are determined by public and personal values that define social systems.[36] Ethics can be understood as an organizational, development-oriented force that provides both methodological and motivational support to public-health practitioners and policymakers.[37]

The normative ideal of HSS has three main characteristics. The first is its vision of society as a place for mutual support where government plays its welfare-enhancing role by providing people with public institutions and social services that sustain their well-being. The second emphasizes individual and community participation in service delivery and health promotion through grassroots mobilization. It also highlights the need for a democratic process that would ensure effective participation of citizens and public accountability. The third stresses the quest for efficiency not as a technical question but as an ethical one.

Structural Justice, Effective Access to Care, and Prevention

The normative ideal of HSS is grounded in a vision of what it means to be a just society. All the WHO documents on HS and PHC strongly assert the importance of equity and the need to care for the worse off of society as means for development. These ideals resonate well with the traditions that emphasize civic and institutional solidarity, particularly with Catholic social teaching—as it is indicated by many authors in this volume. However, the integration of values in HS should not be taken for granted, since ideals do not always shape practices in real life. When adequately designed and managed, these systems can deliver general population gains and close unfair socioeconomic disparities in health.[38] The goals of health systems are ethical in nature, since they refer to all activities that sustain the promotion, restoration, and maintenance of people's health.[39]

Social justice requires that all persons are entitled equally to key ends such as health protection[40] and satisfaction of basic needs as means to promote one's well-being. Used as a rhetorical device, the concept of social justice expands our language and our circles of interlocutors, and enriches our moral discourse. It places the quest for human flourishing at the heart of HSS.[41] The egalitarian ends of a public health vision can, indeed, take the national HIV/AIDS program to another level, the structural one. To improve the performance of HS and to remedy existing inequalities, structural interventions are needed. Tackling both the lack of democracy that prevents a serious debate on social policy and other social evils cannot be understood as inimical to HSS. A deeper reflection on structural issues, as they relate to the AIDS crisis, necessarily leads to the importance of universal coverage as a means for health promotion.[42]

The insufficiency of prevention programs raises issues of justice. Prevention initiatives are not carried out due to the lack of human and financial resources as well as community mobilization. In rural areas, for instance, workload often outweighs the health care personnel. The goal of prevention is to intervene in the causal pathways of diseases. The ethical endeavor of prevention is to reduce the burden of disability and disease.[43] Poor people—those who do not have the economic power to become patients or those who live in high-risk neighborhoods or unstable conditions—should be the primary beneficiaries of preventive interventions where they have been empowered to participate. Disease and harm prevention carry a special moral weight. Prevention aims at promoting social equity.[44] When service delivery is reduced to clinical work because of financial constraints and a lack of health care professionals, the entire health system misses opportunities to address both the pandemic's fundamental causes and the structural barriers to treatment access.

As a whole, the health sector should work with other sectors because most barriers to ART are socially located. Intersectoral collaboration can be instrumental in addressing nonclinical determinants of poor health and in promoting access to care. Through such collaborative efforts, HS can deliver gains to the general population. They can also close unfair social and economic differentials in health, promoting overall health equity.[45] These systems can achieve these goals when they specifically address the needs of socially disadvantaged and marginalized populations.

Intersectoral actions might also help address food and transport challenges that people living with HIV in hard-to-reach areas have identified as major barriers to accessing and adhering to HIV care. It has long been established that location, distance, and particular geographical features obstructing access continue to affect people's willingness and ability to use services. For example, the probability of visiting a care provider decreases with the distance the person has to travel to the provider. People with limited mobility, due to low income, age, or poor access to transport, are more sensitive to distance and thus more likely to use the nearest health care provider, often to the detriment of quality of care.

Accountability, Leadership, and Democratic Governance

Leadership is critical to the success of HIV prevention and AIDS treatment because it can provide guidance toward clear ways of doing research, managing available resources, and monitoring interventions. The ability to scale up a sound national response requires more than the provision of ART, but also community, institutional, and individual preparation and education in order to manage health care and social services appropriately so as to support good health outcomes. Investment decisions here face a trade-off between highly focused versus broader and longer-term investments. An explicit diagnosis of the context of the systems is critical for finding the right balance in targeted versus broader investments.

One area where this is clear is in the shortage of ARVs and reagents for testing, a shortage that is often due to problems with the supply system and with a lack of professionalism; this is simply unacceptable. ARV supply shortage increases the risk of developing drug-resistant strains of HIV. Stock managers should be held accountable. However, individuals engaged in acts of corruption often go unpunished. Supervision and leadership of the Ministry of Public Health is needed. The ministry should provide public and private health care facilities with guidelines to regulate performance and provide deontological rules. It is shocking to discover that interpersonal struggles often influence the quality of care and the functioning of health services in major public hospitals.

Democracy requires effective civil participation, which is still lacking in Chad. For an effective national response to HIV/AIDS, the private and public sectors need to collaborate in providing ART. Cost-sharing and insurance schemes will make this collaboration sustainable. Civil society and affected communities should participate in designing and implementing policies that will address the social determinants of health. Social participation is key in redistributing power, by engaging decision makers to listen and respond to the demands of excluded communities.

The government should take actions that ensure transparency and accountability at all levels. Moreover, the principle of responsibility assures that the government will comply with or will be forced to guarantee social rights and that citizens are protected from encroachment on those rights. It is also necessary to develop specific regulatory and legal policies that will facilitate citizens' demands to respect their rights.

As they attend to people living with HIV, health professionals are rediscovering the role of the community system. The bedrock of most community initiatives is made up of volunteers, men and women who willingly take care of destitute sick and vulnerable people at home or in the neighborhood. Community responses have proven to be vital in rural and urban areas, whether or not adequate medical infrastructure is available. These initiatives often spring from religious values or from the spirit of togetherness that shapes social interaction in African communities.[46] Unfortunately, the lack of home-based care weakens the national response to AIDS in Chad. Even though trained social communicators, social agents, and peer educators have been addressing HIV/AIDS from the grassroots perspective,[47] community response to this pandemic remains weak.

Unlike faith-based health care institutions, the public health care system does not always include local communities as stakeholders in service delivery. Local communities can play an important role in reducing the loss of follow-up patients, improving access to information with regard to prevention and ART, and facilitate a long-term adherence to assuming antiretroviral drugs. Local communities can also initiate income-generating activities and support actions aimed at caring for HIV-affected orphans and elderly people. In rural settings, an adequate response should include home-based and community care, especially in areas not covered by public health services. Through home-based care, patient compliance can be ensured and improved. Even when antiretroviral drugs and related services may be free for the poor, paying transportation to access them may be difficult to afford on a regular basis.[48]

Efficiency, Ownership, and the AIDS Program

A fragmented health system cannot integrate gains from the AIDS program or sustain adequate health care delivery. The best measure of this system's performance is its impact on health outcomes. Because such a system is highly context-specific, there is no single set of best practices that can be put forward as a model for improved performance. But a health system that functions well will have certain shared characteristics. Importantly, improving its performance and efficiency requires well-organized PHC and the ability to integrate vertical (i.e., aimed at addressing a particular disease) programs into the overall health care system at an appropriate and effective pace.

The need for an urgent response to AIDS led to vertical programming to meet short-term demands. Vertical programs are appropriate if a service is urgently needed, especially in a country where the national health system is too weak and the resources are routinely too limited to be able to confront the burden of HIV and AIDS through the regular channels. However, if such vertical approaches are allowed to proliferate, they are likely to result in a patchwork of uncoordinated services. Simultaneous and concerted strengthening of the overall health system needs to occur to avoid such a situation. Vertical programs can hinder the development of comprehensive approaches, which are needed to tackle social inequities and to address the wider determinants of health, thereby negatively affecting the development process of the whole health system. Vertical programs will only sustain the long-term delivery of ARTs if they are included within such a system. If AIDS care is not incorporated within the local health system, it may fail to create the synergies often generated by integrated services and will instead drain funds and human resources, thereby undermining the long-term sustainability of the health system.[49]

In the case of major epidemics, however, more focused vertical interventions are often unavoidable. Moreover, what medical professionals have learned from AIDS care should be immediately integrated into health care practices so as to strengthen the overall health system—in what can be defined as a horizontal approach.[50] Unnecessary polarization between vertical and horizontal programming can lead to the neglect of the diagonal approach developed by Gorik Ooms and colleagues.[51] This approach consists in targeting specific disease results through improvements of the health system. Such a diagonal approach is now implemented and/or supported by the President's Emergency Plan for AIDS Relief, the Global Fund, and the International Treatment Preparedness Coalition.[52]

It is now common knowledge that well-integrated HS can produce great public health and social gains. These systems should be shaped by values and practices that seek to promote health. Even though there is a growing awareness of the role of ethics in shaping HS among policymakers and health practitioners, ethics remains either nonexistent or peripheral in the health policy domain in Chad. This lack affects the success of the AIDS program. A stronger health system, with a health policy that promotes solidarity and care for the poor and the needy, will make the AIDS program successful and eventually will foster a sustainable health system.

Notes

1. World Health Organization, *World Health Report 2000: Health Systems: Improving Performance* (Geneva: World Health Organization, 2000), 1.
2. The World Commission on Environment and Development, *Our Common Future*, http://www.un-documents.net.
3. Eric R. De Winter, "Which Way to Sustainability? External Support to Health Projects in Developing Countries," *Health Policy and Planning* 8, no. 2 (1993): 150–56.
4. Paul Hawken, *The Ecology of Commerce: A Declaration of Sustainability* (New York: Harper Business, 1994), 2; Lincoln Chen and Sagari Singh, *Sustainability of the Children Summit Goals: Concepts and Strategies* (Boston: Harvard Center for Population and Development Studies and the Harvard School of Public Health, 1995), 17.
5. Harvey Fineberg, "A Successful and Sustainable Health System—How to Get There from Here," *New England Journal of Medicine* 366, no. 11 (2012): 1020–27.
6. Anne K. LaFond, *Sustaining Primary Health Care* (London: Earthscan, 1995), 17.
7. Ibid.
8. Ingvar T. Olsen, "Sustainability of Healthcare: A Framework for Analysis," *Health Policy and Planning* 13, no. 3 (1998): 287–95.
9. Ibid.

10. Lucy Gilson et al., *Challenging Inequity through Health Systems* (2007), http://www.who.int.

11. Madison Power and Ruth Faden, *Social Justice: The Moral Foundations of Public Health and Health Policy* (New York: Oxford University Press, 2006), 5.

12. UNAIDS, *Rapport de la Situation Nationale à l'Intention de l'UNGASS* (N'Djamena: ONUSIDA, 2009), 14.

13. UNAIDS, *Cartographie et Etude Sérologique chez les Travailleuses de Sexe au Tchad: Rapport Provisoire* (N'Djamena: ONUSIDA, 2009), 6.

14. ONUSIDA, *Rapport d'Activités sur la Riposte au Sida 2010–2011* (N'Djamena: ONUSIDA, 2012), 10.

15. Ibid., 1, 22.

16. Ibid.

17. Ibid.

18. Ibid., 20.

19. Jacquineau Azétsop and Blondin A. Diop, "Access to Antiretroviral Treatment, Issues of Well-being and Public Health Governance in Chad: What Justifies the Limited Success of the Universal Access Policy?," *Philosophy, Ethics, and Humanities in Medicine* 8, no. 8 (2013), http://www.peh-med.com.

20. Paul Farmer, *Pathologies of Power: Health, Human Rights, and the New War on the Poor* (Berkeley: University of California Press, 2003), 40.

21. Ministère de la Santé Publique, *Plan National de Développement des Ressources Humaines pour la Santé au Tchad 2010–2020* (N'Djaména: Ministère de la Santé Publique, 2010), 9.

22. Ibid.

23. Ministère de la Santé Publique, *Draft de l'Annuaire des Statistiques Sanitaires* (N'Djamena: Ministère de la Santé Publique, 2009), 2.

24. Ibid., 3.

25. Ibid., annex 14.

26. Ibid.

27. Programme National de Lutte contre le SIDA, *Cadre Stratégique National de Lutte contre le VIH/SIDA et les IST 2007–2011* (N'Djamena: Programme National de Lutte contre le SIDA, 2007), 30.

28. Ibid., 12, 37.

29. Ibid., 23, annex 16.

30. Ibid.

31. African Union, *Abuja Declaration*, http://www.un.org.

32. Ministère de la Santé Publique, *Profil Pays en Ressources Humaines pour la Santé au Tchad* (N'Djaména: Ministère de la Santé Publique, 2010), 13.

33. Ibid., 9.

34. Ibid., 22.

35. Ibid.

36. Adnan Hyder et al., "Integrating Ethics, Health Policy and Health Systems in Low- and Middle-Income Countries: Case Studies from Malaysia and Pakistan," *Bulletin of the World Health Organization* 86, no. 8 (2008): 606–11.

37. Ibid.

38. Ibid., 10.

39. Ibid., 1, 5.

40. Dan E. Beauchamp, "Public Health as Social Justice," *New Ethics for the Public's Health*, ed. Dan E. Beauchamp and Bonnie Steinbock (New York: Oxford University Press, 1999), 101–9.

41. Ibid.

42. James F. Keenan, "Developing HIV/AIDS Discourse in Africa and Advancing the Argument for Universal Health Care," in *AIDS 30 Years Down the Line: Faith-based Reflections about the Epidemic in Africa*, ed. Paterne A. Mombé, Agbonkhianmeghe E. Orobator, and Danielle Vella (Nairobi: Paulines Publications Africa, 2013), 63–82.

43. Ibid., 40.

44. Ibid.

45. Ibid., 10.

46. Maria M. Rossi, "The Community Responses to the Scourge of HIV/AIDS in Sub-Saharan Africa: An Example From Zambia," in *AIDS 30 Years Down the Line*, 419–35.

47. ONUSIDA, *Accès Universel pour la Prévention, le Traitement, la Prise en Charge et l'Appui dans le Cadre de la Lutte contre le VIH/SIDA et les IST au Tchad: Rapport de Suivi 2008* (N'Djamena: ONUSIDA, 2009), 28.

48. Michael J. Kelly, *HIV and AIDS: A Social Justice Perspective* (Nairobi: Paulines Publication Africa, 2010), 39–42.

49. Ravi Rannan-Eliya, "Addressing the Funding Gap—Strengthening Health Financing Strategies in Partner Developing Countries," G8 Task Force on Health Systems Strengthening, Paper presented at the International Conference on Global Action for Health Systems Strengthening, Tokyo, November 3–4, 2008.

50. Helen Schneider et al., "Health Systems and Access to Antiretroviral Drugs for HIV in Southern Africa: Service Delivery and Human Resources Challenges," *Reproductive Health Matters* 14, no. 27 (2006): 12–23.

51. Gorik Ooms et al., "The 'Diagonal' Approach to Global Fund Financing: A Cure for the Broader Malaise of Health Systems?," *Globalization and Health* 4, no. 6 (2008), http://www.globalizationandhealth.com.

52. Rick Rowden, *The Deadly Idea of Neoliberalism: How the IMF Has Undermined Public Health and the Fight Against AIDS* (London: Zed Books, 2009), 39.

Technology, Ecology, and the Divine

A Critical Look at New Technologies through a Theology of Gratuitousness

Celia Deane-Drummond

This essay addresses structural problems implicit in global application of new technologies and their particular significance for the livelihood of the most vulnerable human societies. The cases I have chosen to focus on have direct relevance to sustainability, inclusive of ecological flourishing as well as economic and social relationships. Mindful of the problems with the misuse of the word "sustainability," I nonetheless use this term because there are to my mind no other readily available alternatives. Sustainability, as I understand it, is about human flourishing both now and for future generations set in a context of flourishing of other life-forms, rather than narrowly conceived in terms of economic stability. Therefore, the question of ecological impact is not so much an afterthought but is instead the basis from which long-term economic and social flourishing can be maintained.

This essay presents three case studies, each of which poses important challenges that must be thought through carefully. I begin with genetic modification of food and assess its growth in recent decades, particularly in the developing world. What might account for the shift toward the developing world as major sites of use of genetically modified (GM) crops in agriculture? What stances are appropriate to adopt when considering the impact of this genetic technology? The next case study explores the historical and present use of pesticides, herbicides, and toxic wastes, many of which are associated with industrial agriculture in the developed world, especially the United States, where the historical proliferation of toxic chemicals in the food chain—including hormone disruptors—affects human and ecological health. The final case study is nano-products, the effects of which are almost undetectable since they mimic molecular biological processes. As such, the health and environmental impacts of nano-products are often poorly understood; yet the dynamics of the global market economy and weak international regulation shape political decision making about the permissibility and use of such products.

In light of concerns raised within each of these contexts, I draw on Benedict XVI's encyclical *Caritas in Veritate*, and argue that the fundamental relation between human beings and the created order needs to be one of gift, so that an economy of gratuitousness reforms the structural economy of the market. The encyclical did not aim to fill out what gratuitous might mean in specific cases;

so this essay seeks to begin to address that lacuna. I also argue that gratuitousness then informs other relevant virtues—including charity, mercy, prudence, and temperance—which are crucial for establishing appropriate and just structural relationships amid the ever-rising tide of advancing technologies. The advantage of taking this approach is that it provides an ethical framework for a way to mediate between institutional reform at the level of governance and individual responsibility to act. It is also, in my view, preferential to alternative starting points focusing on individuals that tend to be more confrontational, such as the use of rights language, or collective institutional approaches that can seem abstracted from local considerations.

Genetically Modified Food

Controversy over genetic modification of food is not particularly new, in that this topic has been discussed for well over three decades. As someone who was working as a scientist when the first GM crops were being developed, I witnessed firsthand the enthusiasm of researchers developing the technology and its anticipated benefits for food production. Yet the desire to solve the problems of global hunger or malnutrition was perhaps less prominent in the mind of those scientists when compared with the more immediate acquisition of support from multinational companies, which were interested in development of solutions to perceived problems in production. These corporations would profit from sales of patented seeds, and, indeed, profit to such corporations has been readily forthcoming. Often, the promise of social benefits was used to persuade people to trust and adopt this new technology. As the history of GM crops has demonstrated, the most successful genetically modified crops had far less to do with world hunger, and more to do with persuasion of farmers to adopt GM crop seed.

GM Crops: Have They Delivered on Their Promise?

Proponents of GM crops have suggested that engineered seeds could accomplish many desirable goals. GM crops could be resistant to herbicide sprays, or they could produce insecticide internally, thus purportedly leading to insect resistance. In truth, there have been acute difficulties with implementation of even these limited promises. For example, so-called insect-resistant crops are not always resistant to the specific insects that are prevalent in the local area, leading to increase in use of insecticides in some cases.[1] Much the same applies to arguments in favor of GM crops for nutritional purposes; one example is the development of vitamin A rice, where the actual vitamin A content seems to be less readily available than naturally occurring alternatives such as curry leaves or coriander leaves.

In a similar way, the scientist and activist Vandana Shiva argues against claims that crops can become more resilient to climate impacts through GM methods, since monocultures are always more vulnerable than diversified, traditional crops, and since industrialized agriculture contributes to climate change through its energy use and buildup of methane through intensive feeding lots.[2] Other features of the economy of GM crops, such as hybrid seeds that force farmers to buy new seeds every year from the same producer, lead to an overall strong suspicion that the major beneficiaries of these crops are the multinational companies rather than farmers. Therefore, GM food is rarely an appropriate technological solution to world hunger but represents particular vested interests.

Since 2002, the majority of growth in the use of GM crops has been in the developing world, especially Africa, China, and Latin America. The United States, parts of Asia, and India are also heavy users of GM crops. Recent figures suggest that nineteen out of the thirty countries using GM crops are developing rather than industrialized nations.[3] There are various reasons for this trend. My suggestion is that this expansion in GM crop use is a result of structural weakness in governance that has failed to control aggressive marketing by multinational companies and has also failed to regulate the market.[4]

In Europe, there has been a strong public suspicion of interference in agricultural processes, fueled by memories of bovine spongiform encephalopathy disease (mad cow disease), which was eventually traced to prion products in cattle feed. This event fueled fears of "artificial" means of production and incited a lack of trust in government regulation, spurred by further grim memories of recurrent waves of foot-and-mouth disease in sheep and cattle. In fact, the latter led to widespread slaughter of animals along with the sight of burning carcasses in relatively close proximity to large conurbations. It is, therefore, hardly surprising that when the UK government conducted a nationwide public survey on the acceptability of genetically modified crops, the prospect was generally met with suspicion and strong public resistance.[5] Similar resistance in the rest of Europe meant that the outlet for GM crops was not as lucrative in Europe as the developers had hoped. And although the regulation of GM food is established in Europe, regulation is almost nonexistent in North America and in the developing world.

In the United States there is virtually no regulation of the use of GM crops, and GM products, especially GM soya, can be found in virtually all processed food. There is little incentive to label products and inform the consumer. Yet alongside this activity, there is a growing movement of those in the United States who have been influenced by environmentalists such as Wes Jackson, or pioneers in the land ethic, such as Wendell Berry, who are starting to campaign for public resistance to the consumption of food whose origins are unknown or undeclared. Farmers' markets are escalating in numbers, alongside a push toward eating food that has been grown without the use of pesticides and herbicides.[6]

GM Livestock

Even so, the development of GM animals for agricultural purposes does seem to have slipped into place in the European Union, including the United Kingdom, with less public discussion and outcry when compared with earlier hostile reactions to the introduction of GM crops. Animals bred to withstand crowded conditions means that the intensification of agriculture is continuing apace, reinforced by genetic modification. The sociologist Richard Twine gives a number of examples of genetic enhancement of domesticated animals, and those most significant for our present context are related to agricultural use, rather than for production of medicines in "pharming." Such enhancement is achieved through targeting of particular genomes, or in some cases genetic modification.[7]

Precision animal breeding shares with GM crops a fervent rhetoric of agricultural promise, which is used in order to promote the use of this technology, and which is also narrowly conceived in terms of specific economic gain.[8] As the developing world experiences an exponential increase in livestock production, many countries (including China) opt for intensive methods based on the Western factory-farming model, with cruel practices of confinement for utilitarian ends abounding (such as cutting off chicken beaks without anesthetic in order to prevent pecking from overcrowded factory-farm conditions).[9] Unfortunately, those people and communities that are most impoverished in the United States cannot often afford the kind of food that is both ethical in terms of animal practice and more sustainable.

Toxic Bodies

The second case I wish to highlight is of the saturation of the environment with products that are known to be toxic to human health.[10] Some of these products are historical relics that have been banned from use, such as DDT. However, it takes what amounts to a public experiment to find out the impacts of other chemical products that are currently still on the market. It is highly likely that these poisons have also affected the well-being of other creatures in the ecosystem, but much more of the research to date has focused particularly on human health. A primary example has to do with synthetic hormones. After World War II, pharmaceuticals such as synthetic estrogens became very popular in the United States, and even though scientists warned of the danger, there was very little regulation of their use. These chemicals were suspected even as early as 1940s of being responsible for causing cancer and disrupting sexual development, but little was done because building up conclusive evidence for these impacts was difficult. Science, not uncommonly, cannot always provide proof of causative agents, and this uncertainty was exploited by those wishing to develop the products for financial gain.

Consider how in the 1940s millions of women in the United States were treated with Diethystilbestrol (DES), an estrogen substitute, to combat the side effects of menopause and to reduce the risk of miscarriage. It was also widely used in cattle and poultry in order to promote growth. Industrialized feedlots for cattle were only really possible through the widespread use of DES in the 1950s. In the early 1970s young women whose mothers had been exposed to DES suffered a much higher rate of a very rare vaginal cancer, eventually forcing a ban on its use. Ninety-five percent of those exposed to DES prenatally have suffered from reproductive problems, infertility, and a higher rate of reproductive cancers. When DES was used in the feedlots, millions of people were exposed to it indirectly through consuming meat from cattle laden with DES chemicals.

Nancy Langston asks why the federal government still approved the drug, even though it was known to have likely impacts on cancer rates.[11] Although they initially adopted a precautionary principle to prove the drug was safe, eventually the pressure for readily available cheap food and pressure from the industry caused them to adopt a failure-to-prove-harm approach, allowing for permissive legislation. Hence, although the regulatory structures were in place, pressure from the industry and its demand for growth allowed serious errors of judgment. Langston suggests that part of the reason for such a mistake was because there was scientific uncertainty about the toxicity of very low levels of synthetic chemicals, and the fact that natural hormones, also present in the ecosystem, seemed to be harmless, while the artificial chemical compounds were not. The regulators as well as those in the industry presupposed that human beings should control the natural world through technological inventions, which means that they were already inclined to support their position. Finally, the primary impact on women raises questions of whether there were cultural and gender issues around the relative seriousness of such impacts, making regulators dismissive of reports of harm.

Although DES is now banned in the United States, livestock continue to be treated with steroids, and pesticides proliferate. And what of other chemical hormone disruptors? In the United States, in the 1960s, polychlorinated biphenols (PCBs) used in industrial settings to coat copy paper made their way into river systems and accumulated in fatty tissue of fish that were then consumed by the local inhabitants. These chemicals had disrupting impacts on sexual and fetal development. PCBs have since been known to alter brain and immune development as well as thyroid function. Although these substances are now banned, they have left a toxic legacy in the local environment. This is but one example of synthetic chemicals known to disrupt hormone function, but there are many others used in the development of plastics, pharmaceuticals, and pesticides that are known to damage reproductive health and ecological function. Thus even today, plastics such as biphenol A leach chemicals that have hormonal potency into drinking water.[12]

This experience shows that although in the United States there is legislation in place designed to curb the release of harmful substances into the environment through the Toxic Substances Control Act of 1976 (TSCA), it is largely ineffective. The Environmental Protection Agency has used the act to restrict only five substances since its inception, largely because the substances have to be proven to cause harm. In July 2010 the regulatory weaknesses in the TSCA was addressed through a bill titled the Toxic Chemicals Safety Act, which adopts a precautionary principle and asks the industry to prove safety, rather than prove harm. There has been much opposition to such an act, arguing that it would stifle innovation and profits. Industry advocates consistently press for lighter regulation in the name of progress. Environmentalists are more wary of a living experiment to test such properties.

Nanotechnologies

My final case is a newly emerging technology for which there has been relatively little historical opportunity to evaluate its potential impacts. Nanotechnology is engineering at the molecular scale. Fueled by the desire for new and innovative products, nanotechnology is arguably set to facilitate the next major breakthroughs in technology. On an ethical level, however, risks of nanotechnology run largely parallel with those associated with GM crops and toxic chemicals: Namely, how far are such technologies likely to disrupt human and ecological health? Should the precautionary principle be adopted in this case or not?

The technology is so new that specific health and environmental impacts are not clearly understood.[13] For example, while nanoparticles used in sunscreen appear unable to penetrate the skin, when inhaled they can lead to inflammatory responses. The nano-coating on the outside of artificial joints can degrade and lead to further bone loss. There is even less certainty about the environmental impacts of nano-materials, including their relative persistence. In most cases there has been no meaningful risk assessment. Furthermore, the industry is largely unregulated, so that in the United States for example, any regulation of nano-chemicals falls under the premise of the relatively ineffectual Toxic Chemicals Act.

One aspect of nanotechnology that is far more complex compared with genetically modified food and toxins is the sheer range of possible application of nanotechnology, from precision medicine to water treatment options. In the latter case the promise of nanotechnology to support the provision of clean water by nano-filtration mechanisms holds out a positive prospect for an application that seems, on the surface at least, to be advantageous in terms of positive environmental impact. For these sorts of reasons, the philosopher Peter Singer believes that nanotechnology can be harnessed to solve global problems.[14] Others are far more cautious. For example, the attorney George Kimbrell comments that not only are nano-materials let loose into the environment in a way that is untested and unmanaged, but, moreover, existing environmental protection laws in the United States and globally are not set up in order to deal with nano-materials. Hence, environmental agencies

> lack cost-effective mechanisms of detecting, monitoring, measuring or controlling manufactured nanomaterials, let alone removing them from the environment once they are released. The regulatory frameworks are data-driven and with nanotechnologies there is a general dearth of data; company-created data are considered confidential business information and so are not released.[15]

Overall, then, the regulatory measures, such as they exist, are wholly inadequate to the task when it comes to nano-materials. In addition, given the diversity of nano-products, it would be essential to design regulatory mechanisms for each process, which makes regulatory instruments particularly complex to achieve. Initiation and implementation of adequate global regulation of nanotechnology looks particularly grim. In 2006, under pressure from the US government, the World Trade Organization filed a ruling that the European Union had no grounds to restrict import of GM crops, as it had no proof of lack of safety. It is possible that this precedent may affect attempts by other nations to restrict proliferation of nano-materials.[16]

There are, nonetheless, calls by the US Environmental Protection Agency for tighter monitoring of environmental impact. Others have funded research that is designed to make the development of nano-materials more responsible in terms of its life cycle and ensuring equitable deployment. Structurally, however, it is extremely hard to regulate nano-material development and use on both a national and global scale.

Toward a Political Economy of Gratuitousness

In all the cases discussed so far, one of the underlying social issues influencing the development of these new technologies is the reign of a free-market economy that fosters innovation but also proliferates from a lack of adequate regulatory mechanisms. Such regulation is viewed as an infringement on the liberty to develop new products and exploit particular markets. One way forward, therefore, is to tackle not simply the technologies themselves in terms of finding ways to regulate the processes of their development, but to introduce different ways of conceiving of the economy. Such a transformation can then, ideally, be used to good effect in transforming the ethos and social responsibility of all citizens involved in the development of new technologies. One such approach comes from the theological notion of gratuitousness.

In his 2009 encyclical *Caritas in Veritate*, Pope Benedict XVI introduced the idea of gratuitousness as that which was relevant to promoting what he termed the "earthly city," understood to mean the witness to the way the reign of God needs to find expression on Earth. Here he claims that "relationships of gratuitousness, mercy and communion" are more "fundamental" than "relationships of rights and duties."[17] I am sympathetic to this sentiment that suggests going back to a primary critique of how we relate to one another, rather than trying to fix the problems once they have arisen through what might be termed a secondary order of duties. In the present example, positive *fundamental relationships* need to be established first before we begin to work out what might be our duties in applications of new technology. It is also noteworthy that gratuitousness, or what might be termed a sense of giftedness of relationship, is paired with mercy and communion. Receiving the gift of creation as our own depends on God's mercy, and the goal is full communion.

It is therefore fitting and relevant that the next time gratuitousness appears in *Caritas in Veritate* is in the chapter on fraternity, economic development, and civil society. Gratuitousness, which I interpret as a strong sense that all is a gift from God, is countercultural; it is contrary to the "consumerist and utilitarian view of life."[18] Here Benedict XVI suggests that inasmuch as the human being is "made for gift," so it is not an optional extra, but a fundamental aspect of what being human means. Further, such giftedness of humankind makes present the "transcendent dimension."[19] In this way Benedict traces the original sin of Adam to a refusal to acknowledge gift as fundamental relation; but he pushes this further than individual fault by pointing to social relationships in the area of economics as needing reform: the unbridled use of economics, like the original sin of Adam, promises a form of autonomy that is ultimately destructive. In a self-enclosed social world, the human spirit seems to be deprived of that hope that is given to us through a kind of superabundant life in God. Other fundamental gifts are truth, including the truth about ourselves. But it is the gift of charity, which reaches out to others in building solidarity and ultimately a universal community, that is called into being by God. In other words, the human worlds of economic, social, and political development are not simply human inventions, but, in order to be fully and authentically human, have to embrace "the principle of gratuitousness as an expression of fraternity."[20]

Using the example of the economic crisis in 2009, Benedict urges a principle of gratuitousness as an expression of solidarity to inform normal economic activity and support the ethical social principles of honesty, transparency, and responsibility.[21] In other words, he seems to be urging that in our economic dealings with others, we need to express virtues of solidarity and care for those with whom we are dealing, including commercial relationships. Drawing on Pope John Paul II's encyclical *Centesimus Annus*, he argues that the most natural settings for such renewed economic relationships are in the structures of market, state, and civil society.[22] It is the application of such a principle to market and state that is most relevant in terms of structural reform, even though gratuitousness and solidarity are more easily envisaged in civil society. For him, it is also an expression of the way democracy must work to allow "economic democracy" by being fully representational and in solidarity with the diverse social groups in a nation-state.[23] Justice, according to this model, makes no sense without a prior principle of gratuitousness.

In the market sphere, Benedict opts not so much for completely overturning a market economy, but for the existence of "commercial entities based on mutualist principles and pursuing social ends" to exist alongside profit-oriented private enterprise.[24] This eventually leads to reform of the economy oriented toward social and cultural needs.[25]

Gratuitousness in the Application of Biotechnology

It is easy to envisage how Pope Benedict XVI's insistence on gratuitousness is relevant to the modern growth in technology of all kinds. In the case of GM crops, instead of having commercial gain as the primary goal, such an approach would envisage food technologies being tailored to suit the needs of the community. There are very rare examples of this in practice, where genetic modification of, for example, GM potato plants (incorporating rice cystacin gene) has allowed poor Bolivian farmers to grow nematode-free crops that once relied on heavy pesticide usage.[26] In the case of development of plastics or other commercially produced products with associated harmful by-products, such products would need to fulfill the demand to be considered safe first of all, rather than retrospectively proving harmful. This gives the interests of consumers and users a much higher ethical stake than current arrangements. Moreover, and importantly, structural reform needs to lead to much tighter regulation at local and national levels. Much the same could be said for new nano-materials, that civic society needs to be energized to make this a priority for governmental reform.

Pope Benedict XVI also suggests, controversially perhaps, that an affirmation of subsidiarity, which respects governance at the most local level possible, will prevent any dangerous tyrannical global governance.[27] This applies not just to economic growth but also to the bewitching power of new technologies—these need always to be at the service of authentic human development and building a covenantal relationship between human beings and their natural environment, mirroring God's love for creation.[28] Although he does not use the language of gratuitousness here, it is a logical extension of this idea, for all creation is gift. A creeping tendency of technology to usurp its rightful place needs to be resisted. But it is Pope Benedict XVI's suggestion that key political players at the local, national, and international levels should come into existence that are capable of steering the globalization process. As such, gratuitousness implies solidarity among those of different nations facing similar global questions. Inasmuch as regulatory devices exist in Europe, for example, these need to become models for those nations that do not yet have such structures in place.

Approaching Advanced Technologies through Virtue Ethics

If gratuitousness sets up what might be termed the fundamental right relation between human beings in a way that is inclusive of the natural world, then human relationships with each other and with creaturely beings are relations of solidarity and kinship, rather than mastery and control. It is through this lens that new developments in technology need to be viewed, since it is a reminder that our responsibilities toward the natural world include a primary right relation rather than a manipulative attitude toward it. This is also what Pope John Paul II had in mind when he suggested that

> The word and the concept of "mercy" seem to cause uneasiness in man, who, thanks to the enormous development of science and technology, never before known in history, has become the master of the earth and

> has subdued and dominated it. This dominion over the earth, sometimes understood in a one-sided and superficial way, seems to leave no room for mercy.[29]

As well as gratuitousness and mercy, there are other virtues that are relevant here, including temperance (not taking more than we need) and prudence (practical wisdom). The structural and regulatory reforms that have to be put in place need to be developed with temperance and prudence in mind, where prudential decision making points to the common good.[30] Of course, finding agreement at an international level on what that good entails is very difficult, but as a bare minimum the Christian hope is that some overlapping consensus will be reached. Certainly, in the case of new technologies it is hard to envisage a collective argument in favor of destructive chemicals being released into the environment. In solidarity with those nations that have weak governance, it is important to inform and provide alternatives to poor farmers who are being manipulated by aggressive campaigns to adopt GM crops. The levels of toxic waste in many parts of the world and their health impacts are unknown.

Developing nations are particularly vulnerable to the overgrowth of new technologies that are not properly regulated. It seems to me that it is important and essential to put some regulatory processes in place, even if they are not ideal solutions. European regulatory models that have adopted a precautionary principle have not stifled growth in the way feared by antiregulatory proponents. There is therefore reason to hope that structural changes can and will take place, but only by increasing public pressure for reform in democratic societies and taking steps toward forms of global governance that enable the needs of the most vulnerable members of the global economy to be recognized.

Notes

1. As documented by Vandana Shiva, who has written prolifically and passionately on this and other matters related to food security. See, for example, Vandana Shiva, *Stolen Harvest: The Hijacking of the Global Food Supply* (Cambridge, MA: South End Press, 2000), 95–116.

2. Vandana Shiva has been a champion in this cause, targeting the multinational company that has sought to dominate the field, Monsanto. She is well educated, a passionate activist, and a prolific writer. She points out the damaging impact of GM crops on the lives of subsistence farmers. See Vandana Shiva, "Climate Change and Agriculture," http://www.vandanashiva.org.

3. See summary of the report *Global Status of Commercial Biotech/GM Crops,* chaired by director of International Service for the Acquisition of Agribiotech Applications, Clive James, http://bic.searca.org.

4. The environmentalist James Speth argues that capitalism's fixation on economic growth is disastrous in terms of sustainability. He presses for stronger regulatory measures. See James Speth, *Bridge at the End of the World: Capitalism, the Environment, and Crossing from Crisis to Sustainability* (New Haven, CT: Yale University Press, 2008).

5. I have discussed this elsewhere in, for example, "Biotechnology," in *God, Humanity and the Cosmos*, ed. Christopher Southgate, 3rd ed. (London: Continuum, 2011).

6. Farmers' markets have grown by 17 percent between 2010 and 2011, and latest figures represent 7,175 in total. For data see http://www.ams.usda.gov.

7. I would agree with Twine that to assume that selective breeding is benign from an ethical point of view is problematic. Transgenetic modification speeds up the process of genetic transfer and allows for bizarre incentives, such as attempting to solve diseases caused by industrial, biotechnological agriculture through genetic enhancement. See Richard Twine, *Animals as Biotechnology* (London: Earthscan, 2010), 53–55. Twine also raises the disturbing prospect of the slippery slope, that enhancement of domestic animals makes human experimentation more likely, with social groups deemed less rational likely to be specifically targeted.

8. Twine, *Animals as Biotechnology*, 124–25.

9. For this account and other excellent examples of the cruel practices toward domesticated animals rampant in intensive farming, see Charles Camosy, *Peter Singer and Christian Ethics* (Oxford: Oxford University Press, 2012), 86–90.

10. I am drawing on a book by Nancy Langston, *Toxic Bodies: Hormone Disruptors and the Legacy of DES* (New Haven, CT: Yale University Press, 2010).

11. Ibid., x.

12. Further graphic examples of the way current government regulation in the United States has failed to protect the environment and health are given in more detail in Kristin Shrader-Frechette, *Taking Action and Saving Lives: Our Duties to Protect Environmental and Public Health* (Oxford: Oxford University Press, 2007).

13. For discussion of environmental impacts, see Deb Bennett-Woods, *Nanotechnology, Ethics and Society* (Boca Raton, FL: CRC Press, 2008), 155–78.

14. Peter A. Singer, Fabio Salamanca-Buentello, and Abdallah S. Darr, "Harnessing Nanotechnology to Improve Global Equity," *Issues in Science and Technology* (Summer 2005): 57–64.

15. George Kimbrell, "Commentary," in Bennett-Woods, *Nanotechnology*, 166.

16. James Hughes, "Global Technology Regulation and Potentially Apocalyptic Technological Threats," in *Nanoethics: The Ethical and Social Implications of Nanotechnology*, ed. Fritz Allhoff, Patrick Lin, James Moor, and John Weckert (Hoboken, NJ: John Wiley, 2007), 207.

17. Benedict XVI, *Caritas in Veritate* (2009), http://www.vatican.va, no. 7.

18. Ibid., no. 34.

19. This refers to humankind, and "man" in this translation is gender inclusive.

20. Ibid.

21. Ibid., no. 36.

22. Ibid., no. 38.

23. Ibid.

24. Ibid.

25. He argues here that state plus market in the traditional structural model are "corrosive" elements in society and must give way to forms of solidarity that are generated from activities within civil society. Ibid., no. 39.

26. For discussion of this and other examples, see C. Deane-Drummond, "Biotechnology: A New Challenge to Theology and Ethics," in Southgate, *God, Humanity and the Cosmos*, 390–419.

27. Benedict XVI, *Caritas in Veritate*, no. 57.

28. Ibid., no. 70.

29. John Paul II, *Dives in Misericordia: On the Mercy of God* (1980), no. 2. Official translations of papal documents generally use the term "man" to stand for "humankind" where inclusivity is intended.

30. I have discussed prudence or practical wisdom in more detail in relation to a range of ethical issues, including biotechnology, in C. Deane-Drummond, *The Ethics of Nature* (Oxford: Wiley-Blackwell, 2004).

Part III

Theological Stances and Sustainable Relations

Humans and Other Creatures

Creation, Original Grace, and Original Sin

Denis Edwards

What theological stances will promote human flourishing within an ecologically sustainable community of life on Earth? I focus here on two such theological stances. The first arises from theology's engagement with ecology, where Christianity is commonly perceived as extremely anthropocentric. I suggest a biblical/theological stance, which is neither anthropocentric nor biocentric, but one that centers on God and understands human beings within the community of God's creatures. The second theological stance I explore arises from the Christian engagement with evolutionary biology, where it is sometimes assumed that an evolutionary view of the world undermines the Christian doctrine of original sin. I propose, on the contrary, that the concepts of original grace and original sin are essential to the promotion of human flourishing within an ecologically sustainable community of life. Furthermore, I suggest that recent scientific work on the evolution of cooperation can offer new insights into the nature of original sin.

Human Beings and Other Creatures

In 1967, the Presbyterian medieval historian Lynn White published an article in the journal *Science* titled "The Historical Roots of Our Ecologic Crisis."[1] In his analysis, Christianity's biblical faith embodies a linear notion of time, which implies faith in continual progress and encourages a concept of endless growth. Furthermore, he says, Christian faith rests on a creation account in which human beings are made in the divine image, and the rest of creation is to serve the human. Famously, White found Western Christianity to be anthropocentric in the extreme:

> Especially in its Western form, Christianity is the most anthropocentric religion the world has seen. As early as the 2nd century both Tertullian and St. Irenaeus of Lyons were insisting that when God shaped Adam he was foreshadowing the image of the incarnate Christ, the Second Adam. Man shares, in great measure, God's transcendence of nature. Christianity, in absolute contrast to ancient paganism and Asia's religions (except, perhaps, Zoroastrianism), not only established a dualism of man and nature but also insisted that it is God's will that man exploit nature for his proper ends.[2]

White argues that Christianity demystifies nature, allowing it to be exploited with indifference. He adds that Christian interest in natural theology supports the eventual dominance of science and technology.[3] Combined with Christianity's conviction of the rightness of human mastery over nature, factors such as these have led to the current ecological crisis. Thus White finds that "Christianity bears a huge burden of guilt"[4] for the fact that human exploitation of the natural world is out of control.

Many have questioned aspects of White's historical argument. (Ernst Conradie has tracked the discussion and provides a helpful bibliography.[5]) For example, the historian of science Peter Harrison accepts that some biblical texts have been used as resources for Western exploitation, but he denies that this played a major role before the rise of modern science in the seventeenth century.[6] Certainly in the history of Western philosophy there are key figures, such as Francis Bacon (1561–1626), for whom scientific progress implements the vision of a God-given mandate of human dominion over creation, a "mandate" that is usually traced to Genesis 1:28. On Bacon's interpretation, the human capacity for such dominance has been partly lost by sin but is to be restored in the great enterprise of scientific achievement.[7]

The dominion text has undoubtedly been invoked to justify exploitation of the environment by human beings. But I am not convinced that the biblical and Christian tradition is simply, or necessarily, anthropocentric. Although it is true that some nineteenth- and twentieth-century theology has focused emphatically on the human-God relationship, it is also the case that pre-Reformation Christianity—especially in its biblical, patristic, and medieval expressions—always revolved around three realities: God, humans, and the rest of the natural world. Of course, there are instances when Christian thinkers have taken strongly anthropocentric positions, as when Aquinas sees animals and plants as existing only for the use of human beings.[8] Still, it is important to recall that such views coexisted in Aquinas and others, with a broad theology of God's good creation, with the Benedictine theology of care for creation, and with the long tradition of such saints as Cuthbert (of Celtic tradition) and Francis of Assisi, who treated animals as fellow creatures before God and saw creation as the expression of God the Creator.

In more recent years, some theologians and philosophers have striven to eradicate vestiges of anthropocentrism, so far as is possible. A prominent example is the late Passionist priest and historian of world religions, Thomas Berry. A prophetic figure in the ecological movement, he argued that we need consciously to shift from an anthropocentric to a biocentric norm of reference.[9] Human beings must come to see ourselves as part of the community of life on the planet, and this will involve "the change from an exploitative anthropocentrism to a participative biocentrism."[10] We will need to learn to go beyond our cultural coding, shaped by anthropocentric traditions that determine language, intellectual insights, educational programs, spiritual ideals, imaginative power, and emotional sensitivities. We will need to go deeper to live from our genetic coding, where we are an integral part of the universe and the community of life on Earth.[11]

I am not convinced that the remedy for human arrogance is to move from an anthropocentric approach to a biocentric one. Theologically, I think that what is needed is neither the extreme anthropocentrism that offers no respect for the dignity of other creatures nor the biocentrism that would seem to reject the unique dignity of the human person, but a position more nuanced than either anthropocentrism or biocentrism, which is explicitly theocentric. The biblical/theological position is not necessarily anthropocentric, and it is not simply biocentric. Instead, an explicitly theocentric approach sees human beings and the whole creation in relation to God. It contains the resources for a broader and more inclusive understanding of the relation between the human being and the rest of God's creation. In what follows, I build on insights offered by the biblical scholar Richard Bauckham to develop a constructive theology of the human in relation to the wider creation.[12] This involves three interconnected and complementary dimensions of the biblical/theological tradition: humans as called to serve and protect the wider creation; humans as called to cosmic humility before God and God's creation; humans as part of the community of creation on Earth before God.

Called to Serve and Protect Creation

Although opposing exploitative anthropocentrism, I see little sense in attempting to minimize the uniqueness of the human. From a scientific perspective it is clear that something extraordinary happens with the emergence of the human—for the human brain is by far the most complex thing we know of in the whole universe. From an ethical perspective, it seems fundamental to require of human beings that they take responsibility for the damage they have done to Earth and its other creatures, and begin to act for Earth's healing. And from a theological perspective, it is clear that Christianity's commitment to the incarnation involves a unique view of the human vocation, even as it also demands a clear-eyed view of human sin. Unfortunately, as noted previously, Christianity's concept of the human is often simply identified with an uncritical reading of Genesis 1:26–28, where human beings are commanded to have "dominion" over and "subdue" other creatures. "Dominion" over other creatures can easily become domination and exploitation. "Subduing" is extremely harsh language that needs to be interpreted as time conditioned and as dangerously inappropriate when used unthinkingly in today's ecological context. But above all, it is important to remember that these words need to be understood in their context of Genesis, where God celebrates the goodness of the whole creation and blesses its fruitfulness, and in the context of the wider biblical view of God's love and care for all creatures.

Nonetheless, I hold to the enduring importance of the idea found in this same text of Genesis that human beings are made in the image of God. But unlike my colleague Norman Habel, I think that the idea of being made in the image of God can be freed from its connection with the language of subduing.[13] With Claus Westermann, I take it to mean that humans are creatures with whom God can speak

(Gen. 1:28–30), creatures to whom God relates personally.[14] On my Thomistic reading, God relates to all creatures in terms of their own proper nature and integrity; for humans, this is as interpersonal beings with the capacity for analysis and reflection. The teaching that humans are made in the image of God can mean, then, that human beings are called to share in the divine feeling for other creatures, called to relate to them as God does, with something like divine love and respect. Humans, in the divine image, have a responsibility for creation as humble servants of God and should use our powers rightly.

The relationship of humans to other creatures receives positive expression in the second creation account in Genesis, where God takes the newly created human to the Garden of Eden in order "to till it and keep it" (2:15). Habel points out that the Hebrew word usually translated as "till" (*abad)* has the basic meaning of "serve." Human beings are thus called to "serve and preserve" the land, and in doing so they contribute to the greening and completion of creation. Habel notes that, in the gospels, we find Jesus rejecting all domination, and replacing it with loving service of others (Mark 10:42–45). Habel rightly proposes that we need to apply this not only to other humans but also to the other creatures that make up the community of life.[15] This attitude finds expression today when human beings protect the habitats of other creatures at some cost to themselves.

On March 19, 2013, the feast of St. Joseph, Pope Francis began his Petrine ministry as bishop of Rome with a Eucharist in St. Peter's Square. In his homily he reflected on Joseph's vocation as protector of Jesus and of Mary, and went on to speak of the vocation to be protectors of creation and of human beings, above all of the poorest:

> The vocation of being a "protector," however, is not just something involving us Christians alone; it also has a prior dimension which is simply human, involving everyone. It means protecting all creation, the beauty of the created world, as the Book of Genesis tells us and as Saint Francis of Assisi showed us. It means respecting each of God's creatures and respecting the environment in which we live. It means protecting people, showing loving concern for each and every person, especially children, the elderly, those in need, who are often the last we think about.[16]

What Francis calls the human vocation to be a protector of the natural world is closely related to the long tradition, particularly strong in Protestant ecological theology, of speaking of the human vocation to be faithful "stewards" of creation. This theology of stewardship supports a great deal of ecological commitment. It is important, I believe, to recognize that the language of stewardship, like the language I am using of the call to serve and protect the creation, is part of the picture in ecological theology and not the whole. To make all of ecological theology into a debate about stewardship is to slip again into distorted anthropocentrism that fails to recognize God's direct relationships with other creatures. It fails to take account of the larger context of the call to cosmic humility, and the fuller picture of the human as part of the community of creation.

Called to Cosmic Humility

Alongside the affirmation of the unique dignity and responsibility of humans, there is a biblical/theological tradition that puts humans in their place and challenges them to cosmic humility, not only before God but also before God's other creatures. These creatures are seen as having their own unique relationship to the living God. I will point briefly to the way these ideas appear in two of the major treatments of creation in the Bible: the book of Job and Psalm 104.

In Job we find the longest passage in the Bible about nonhuman creation. It comes after thirty-five chapters in which Job's friends offer unsatisfactory explanations for the evil that has befallen Job, and Job accuses God of being unjust. Finally, at the beginning of chapter 38, God answers Job from the whirlwind. The divine response is not an explanation, but a challenge to Job to look at the universe that God has created. As Bauckham describes it, God invites Job "into a vast panorama of the cosmos, taking Job on a sort of imaginative tour of his creation, all the time buffeting Job with questions."[17] God's questions challenge Job's worldview and call him to a new way of seeing. The first question immediately puts Job in his place and sets the tone:

> Where were you when I laid the foundation of the earth?
> Tell me if you have understanding.
> Who determined its measurements—surely you know!
> Or who stretched the line upon it?
> On what were its bases sunk, or who laid its cornerstone
> when the morning stars sang together
> and all the heavenly beings shouted for joy?
>
> (Job 38:4–7)

God then lays out before Job the immensity and wonderful order of the physical universe. Job is challenged to humility before God's creation of the land, the sky, the sea, the snow, the rain, the clouds, and the constellations of the night sky. The emphasis then turns from the physical universe to the biological, as God asks Job: "Can you hunt the prey for the lion, or satisfy the appetite of the young lions?" To emphasize the point, God puts before Job the raven, the mountain goat, the deer, the wild ass, the wild ox, the ostrich, the horse, the hawk, and the eagle. Each of the ten animals or birds mentioned is wild, independent of human beings. Each stands in relationship to God in its own right. There is no human mediation. Each creature is described in detail, in species-specific ways. Job is challenged not only to humility but also, it seems, to share God's joy in them, in all their distinctive otherness from the human.

The same interest in the unique and independent relationship of other species with the Creator and the same invitation to humans to share God's delight in their diversity are found in the great biblical song of creation, Psalm 104, which hymns:

> The trees of the Lord are watered abundantly,
> the cedars of Lebanon that he planted.
> In them the birds build their nests;
> the stork has its home in the fir trees.
> The high mountains are for the wild goats;
> the rocks are a refuge for the coneys.
> You have made the moon to mark the seasons;
> the sun knows its time for setting.
> You make darkness, and it is night,
> when all the animals of the forest come creeping out.
> The young lions roar for their prey,
> seeking their food from God.
> When the sun rises, they withdraw
> and lie down in their dens.
> People go out to their work
> and to their labour until the evening.
> O Lord, how manifold are your works!
> In wisdom you have made them all;
> the earth is full of your creatures.
>
> (Ps. 104:16–24)

In this presentation, human beings are fellow creatures with other animals before God. All are related among the "manifold works" of God, all of them made in divine wisdom. God breathes into each the breath of life (v. 30).

Pondering Job and Psalm 104 today can lead us into a humble stance before the mystery of the universe, of the quantum depths of reality, of the evolution of life. We are led to a deeper respect for other species in their distinctive difference from our own, as having their own direct relationship to God their Creator, and as having their own God-given integrity. These texts not only bring human beings to cosmic humility but point to humanity's place before God within the one community of creation.

The Community of Creation

In the rich biblical tradition, humans are seen as united with other creatures in one community of praise. This is the theme of many of the psalms. Psalm 148 is a beautiful example:

> Praise him, sun and moon;
> praise him, all you shining stars!

Praise him, you highest heavens,
and you waters above the heavens!
Let them praise the name of the Lord,
for he commanded and they were created.
He established them forever and ever;
he fixed their bounds, which cannot be passed.
Praise the Lord from the earth,
you sea monsters and all deeps,
fire and hail, snow and frost,
stormy wind fulfilling his command!
Mountains and all hills,
fruit trees and all cedars!
Wild animals and all cattle,
creeping things and flying birds!
Kings of the earth and all peoples,
princes and all rulers of the earth!
Young men and women alike,
old and young together!

(Ps. 148:3–12)

More than thirty categories of creatures are addressed in this psalm.[18] Each praises God in its own unique way. A similar theme is found in the Book of Daniel, sung regularly in the Morning Prayer of the Church on Sundays and feast days: "Bless the Lord, you whales. . . . Bless the lord, all birds of the air. . . . Bless the Lord, all wild animals" (Dan. 3:79–81). And one of the most appealing developments of this theological vision is found in St. Francis of Assisi's *Canticle of Creation,* in which other creatures are addressed as brother and sister to us before God. With Francis the relationship with other creatures is that of kinship.

Finally, there is a liturgical perspective on the community of praise. Liturgically, the Eucharist is the primary event where our location within the community of creation is often explicit: Immediately after the Sanctus, in the third Eucharist Prayer used in many parishes on Sundays, we explicitly praise God in union with all other creatures: "And all you have created rightly gives you praise." To think of a great Sequoia tree, or a laughing kookaburra, or a dolphin riding the surf, as praising God, is to enter a biblical way of thought in which we see ourselves as fellow creatures with others in the one communion of creation, all of which is to be transformed in Christ (Rom. 8:18–25).

Original Grace and Original Sin in an Evolutionary World

A second major issue in theological anthropology considered here is that of original sin. It is a doctrine that some Christians today are inclined to abandon as meaningless or as an oppressive relic of the past. They name a variety of reasons:

they hold to an evolutionary view of life on Earth and see biological death as a cost of evolution rather than as the result of human sin; they interpret Genesis contextually, figuratively, and theologically rather than literally; they oppose the way some have linked original sin to a negative view of human sexuality and have used Eve's part in the story to justify misogyny; they reject the idea, held until recently by many in the Catholic Church, that because of original sin, unbaptized children do not find eternal life in God. Each of these critical positions is justified, but what is needed, I believe, is not an abandonment of original sin, but a renewed and deepened theology that can take these critical positions into account.

The real theological question remains: Is there a wisdom at the heart of the doctrine of original sin that we need, a wisdom that our world needs? When the question is asked in this way, I think an answer starts to emerge. Original sin brings a strongly critical note to the theological view of the human person. It reminds us that human beings are not only wonderfully graced, but also have the capacity for terrible evil. The theology of original sin challenges all romantic views of humanity, all uncritical views of evolutionary progress, all idealistic visions of the future, all naïve revolutionary utopias, with radical realism about humanity. Such a critical note is not opposed to vision and hope, I believe, but grounds them in truth.

What I am arguing, then, is that the first theological stance I have advanced, of the human being as a responsible member of the community of life on our planet, needs to be fully grounded in the second stance offered by a theology of grace and original sin. Becoming part of one community of life on Earth means facing the tendency we have to make other human beings into outsiders and enemies whom we can exploit or kill. And it means dealing with our tendency to see ourselves as so other to the rest of the natural world that we can dominate, exploit, and manipulate it with no regard for consequences for other creatures or for human beings now and into the future. Original sin, I am suggesting, is deeply implicated in the accelerating ecological devastation we face. Dealing with it demands facing the pull to evil in us.

Original Grace, Original Sin, and the Evolution of Cooperation

A renewed theology of original sin needs to be situated within a theology of original grace. One of the great advances in Christian theology during the twentieth century is the new clarity with which Christian churches teach that God's saving grace is not limited to Christians, but is universal in its reach, to people of all places and ages.[19] How might we think about this universal presence of the Spirit in the light of human evolutionary history? What can be said, I believe, is that when human beings evolved on Earth, they emerged into a grace-filled world. They emerged into the presence of the Spirit, Love directed to them, freely offered to them. We do not know precisely when humans became capable of religious experience and of some form of human response to Love's offer. But the theological claim is that when this occurred they were in a graced world.

How do we think of original sin in this context? I will attempt only a partial answer, pointing to the tendency to make others into scapegoats and enemies. Children gang up on a vulnerable child; adolescents bully one another; adults build connections with one another by gossip that demeans, excludes, and damages others; politicians seek to bond with voters by attacking "outsiders" like asylum seekers. Television screens are filled with war, with the killing of noncombatants, rape, torture, the maiming of children, and of the terrible loss of life and limbs suffered by combatants. We live with the horrors of the two World Wars, and the extreme of human violence, the Shoah. It has been estimated that the conflicts and wars of the twentieth century killed 231 million people.[20]

The anthropologist René Girard has analyzed the human tendency to violence in terms of the "scapegoat mechanism."[21] He sees this as grounded in rivalry that flows from our imitation (*mimesis*) of others—we want what others want. Violence can erupt from a conflict of desires, but it is contained by rivals uniting against a common enemy: "Suddenly the opposition of everyone against everyone else is replaced by the opposition of all against one. Where previously there had been a chaotic ensemble of particular conflicts, there is now the simplicity of a single conflict: the entire community on one side, and on the other, the victim."[22] Raymund Schwager and other theologians have taken up the idea of the scapegoat mechanism as a central theme in a renewed theology of original sin and salvation. Before his death, Schwager had begun to explore scapegoating in relation to our evolutionary inheritance, seeing sin as "woven into the natural tendencies of human life" through the course of evolutionary history.[23] I will seek to take up some of these ideas, exploring what recent work on the evolution of cooperation might suggest about grace and sin.

The psychologist Michael Tomasello is the co-director of the Max Planck Institute for Evolutionary Anthropology in Leipzig. He has sought to understand cooperation through a series of comparative experiments that involve young children, on the one hand, and chimpanzees, on the other. These experiments have shown the surprising degree to which very young children help, inform, and share with others.[24] Young children are prepared to participate with others in a common goal that creates an "us."[25] In Tomasello's view, altruism and culture are born from the human capacity for cooperation that is already evident in very young children. Humans have evolved a species-specific capacity for social relationships and for shared intentionality. They have a natural tendency to cooperate and to work together to a common goal. But, Tomasello notes, human cooperation tends to be inside the group, while heinous crimes can be committed against those who are outside the group.[26]

Martin Nowak is a theoretical biologist, professor of biology and mathematics at Harvard University, and director of the Program for Evolutionary Mathematics. He points to the important role played by group selection (groups that cooperate can outcompete others) in evolutionary history.[27] Group selection functions together with other mechanisms of cooperation, particularly direct reciprocity (you scratch my back and I will scratch yours) and indirect reciprocity (doing the right thing earns me a better reputation). Groups that cooperate tend to survive, flourish, and reproduce better than their competitors. The result is what the biologist Edward O. Wilson calls our human "tribalism." Wilson sees tribalism, the human tendency to form groups and to defend them against other groups, as among the "absolute universals" of human nature.[28]

The work of Tomasello, Nowak, and Wilson is recent and still controversial, but it suggests that theology might recognize that although there is a tendency in human beings toward self-interest, explainable through natural selection, there is also a tendency toward cooperation. This tendency is innate, part of our genetic as well as our cultural heritage. Cooperation is intrinsic to human evolution, to human nature, and to human culture. Our earliest human ancestors evolved by cooperating with insiders over against outsiders, and this was a successful evolutionary strategy. My argument is that the innate tendency toward making others into outsiders, not just other humans but also the rest of the natural world, is a central dimension of what the Christian tradition calls original sin.

Insiders and Outsiders

It would be an easy step in Christian theology to celebrate our innate tendency to cooperate as an unalloyed good; it would be a simple step, too, to see the evolutionary tendency toward self-interest as evil. Cooperation would then be aligned with grace, self-interest with sin. I think, however, that this would be a major theological mistake. We can cooperate in torture or in economic exploitation of the poor. Cooperation can easily become irresponsible conformity. And self-interest is not necessarily to be associated with evil. At a fundamental level, it is the tendency we inherit, by way of natural selection, which directs us toward seeking our own survival and generativity. Theologically, this tendency, too, can be seen as part of God's good creation, a tendency open to grace, which can become virtue, as it can also become evil. For Christian theology, other-orientation and self-affirmation together can be seen to be a fundamental way in which the human being is made in the image of God. The God whose image we reflect in our limited human way is communion-in-love.

The emergence of ethical behavior that extends love, compassion, or help to outsiders is not favored by our evolutionary heritage. The tendency that we inherit is for cooperative and altruistic behavior toward insiders. But a genuine ethics has to reach beyond insiders. As the evolutionary biologist Ernst Mayr says, real ethical behavior requires a *transformation* of our evolutionary inheritance, "a redirecting of our inborn cultural tendencies toward a new target: outsiders."[29] A new cultural factor is required for such an ethical transformation toward outsiders. Mayr suggests that we need something like the teaching of a great philosopher or the preaching of a great prophet to move us to include outsiders within the range of our ethical concerns and actions. Christians see this cultural factor in God's self-revelation in Israel, and its culmination in Jesus Christ. It finds expression in Jesus' prioritizing the poor, his healing ministry, his celebratory meals with outsiders, and above all in his radical teaching of love for the enemy: "Love your enemies, do good to those who hate you, bless those who curse you, pray for those who abuse you" (Luke 6:27; Matt. 5:44). It finds expression in his love for creation, for seed growing quietly, for yeast at work in the making of bread, for the wild flowers of Galilee and for sparrows—"Not one of them is forgotten in God's sight" (Luke 12:6).

Notes

1. Lynn White, "The Historical Roots of Our Ecologic Crisis" appeared in *Science* 155 (March 10, 1967): 1203–7. My references to it are from *This Sacred Earth: Religion, Nature, Environment,* ed. Roger Gottlieb (New York: Routledge, 1996), 184–93.

2. White, "Historical Roots," in Gottlieb, *This Sacred Earth*, 189.

3. Ibid.

4. Ibid., 191.

5. Ernst Conradie, *Christianity and Ecological Theology: Resources for Further Research* (Stellenbosch, South Africa: Sun Press, 2006), 61–67.

6. Peter Harrison, "Having Dominion: Genesis and the Mastery of Nature," in *Environmental Stewardship: Critical Perspectives, Past and Present,* ed. Robert J. Berry (London: T&T Clark, 2006), 17–31.

7. On this history see Richard Bauckham, *Living with Other Creatures: Green Exegesis and Theology* (Waco, TX: Baylor University Press, 2011), 14–62.

8. Thomas Aquinas, *Summa Theologiae*, II–II, q. 64, a. 1.

9. Thomas Berry, *The Dream of the Earth* (San Francisco: Sierra Club Books, 1988), 21, 30, 165–66, 202–10.

10. Ibid., 169.

11. This approach has been taken up for a new generation by some of Berry's former students, Mary Evelyn Tucker and Brian Swimme, in their book *The Journey of the Universe* (New Haven, CT: Yale University Press, 2011).

12. Richard Bauckham, *Bible and Ecology: Rediscovering the Community of Creation* (London: Darton, Longman & Todd, 2010). This chapter is a development of some material already discussed in Denis Edwards, *Jesus and the Natural World* (Mulgrave, Victoria: Garratt, 2012); *Partaking of God: Trinity in Evolutionary and Ecological Context* (Collegeville, MN: Liturgical Press, 2014); and David Kirchhoffer, Robyn Horner, and Patrick McHardle, *Being Human: Groundwork for a Theological Anthropology for the 21st Century* (Preston, Victoria: Mosaic Press, 2013).

13. Norman Habel, *An Inconvenient Text: Is a Green Reading of the Bible Possible?* (Adelaide: ATF Press, 2009), 1–10.

14. Claus Westermann, *Creation* (Philadelphia: Fortress Press, 1974), 58.

15. Habel, *Inconvenient Text*, 68–77.

16. http://www.vatican.va.

17. Bauckham, *Bible and Ecology*, 39.

18. Ibid., 77.

19. *Lumen Gentium*, 16; *Gaudium et Spes,* 22.

20. Milton Leitenberg, "Deaths in Wars and Conflicts in the 20th Century," http://www.cissm.umd.edu.

21. René Girard, "Violence, Scapegoating and the Cross," in *The Evolution of Evil*, ed. Gaymond Bennett, Martinez J. Hewlett, Ted Peters, and Robert John Russell (Göttingen: Vandenhoeck & Ruprecht, 2008), 334–48; *The Scapegoat* (London: Athlone Press, 1986); *I See Satan Fall Like Lightning* (Maryknoll, NY: Orbis, 2001).

22. Girard, *Things Hidden*, 24.

23. Raymond Schwager, *Banished from Eden: Original Sin and Evolutionary Theory in the Drama of Salvation* (Herefordshire, UK: Gracewing, 2006), 55.

24. Michael Tomasello, with Carol Dweck, Joan Silk, Brian Skyrms, and Elizabeth Spelks, *Why We Cooperate* (Cambridge, MA: MIT Press, 2009), 37.

25. Ibid., 40–41.

26. Ibid., 99–100.

27. Martin A. Nowak, with Roger Highfield, *Supercooperators: Altruism, Evolution, and Why We Need Each Other to Succeed* (New York: Free Press, 2011), 21–111.

28. Edward O. Wilson, *The Social Conquest of Earth* (New York: Liveright, 2012), 57.

29. Ernst Mayr, *What Evolution Is* (London: Weidenfeld & Nicolson, 2002), 259.

The Ecclesial Contribution to Sustainable Communities

Randy J. C. Odchigue

The question of sustainability is a matter of socioeconomic and environmental justice. It is becoming clear that contemporary arrangements of political economy too frequently ignore how economic growth is dependent on environmental resources. But when we begin to look more carefully, we find—as the international policy figure Timothy Wirth declares—that "the economy is a wholly owned subsidiary of the environment."[1] Without the raw materials and "natural resource capital" provided by the environment, there is no such thing as production or economic growth. In this way, biophysical conditions of the planet limit the economy's ultimate growth potential; indeed, infinite growth is rendered impossible in a finite environment. In an ethical framework, such growth is only desirable when it factors in the costs of drawdown of ecological capital, and the resource-opportunity lost for the future generations. This issue of intergenerational sustainability is related to the question of intragenerational justice.

Inter- and Intragenerational Justice: A Case in Point

A brief look at the mining industry in the Philippines provides an illustration of this point. Widespread mining for natural resources brings economic benefit to the country, but it is blamed by environmental advocates for ravaging the small island ecosystems of the archipelago. Furthermore, it is not clear that the country as a whole is benefiting in a way proportionate to the benefits of private corporations; one study reveals that while the production value in mining rose from USD 568.7 million in 2001 to USD 912.4 million in 2005, the government revenue within this duration averaged only 4.64 percent of the gross production value—an example of gross disparity between wealth generation and wealth sharing.[2]

From a conservation perspective, several key species of national wildlife of cultural heritage are threatened. A foundation for the protection of endangered bird species revealed that in 2011 about 60 percent of key biodiversity areas and approximately one-third of the ancestral domains of indigenous peoples overlap with the twenty-three mining projects in the country.[3] Critics argue that not only does mining development threaten biodiversity areas in the Philippines but it also disenfranchises the indigenous peoples—who are the poorest of the poor—of their traditional livelihood, identity, and culture, which are based on their native lands. The mining industry of the Philippines has yet to show an example of a community that justly and sustainably thrives after its resources are extracted and exported to other countries in the world.

This example reveals how degradation of the environment is directly proportional with the exploitation of the poor.[4] Pursuit of a sustainable and equitable future requires us to problematize concentrations of economic, state, and transnational corporate power, and to focus on the welfare of less powerful individuals and communities.[5] And in addition to the problem that people living in poverty tend to bear the worst effects of environmental degradation, there is also the theological question of the integrity of creation—the claim that there is intrinsic value in the environment and the species in it. Integrity of creation denotes "the value of all creatures in themselves, for one another, and for God, and their interconnectedness in a diverse whole that has unique value for God."[6]

In this essay, I propose a framework of being church—empowered by the Holy Spirit—that lives out its mission by becoming communities of justice and love, creatively engaged in a praxis of ecological sustainability. This contribution has three main divisions: it begins with a sort of a cartographic description of the broad lines of theological reflections on environment. It next articulates a theological appeal to pneumatology as a foundation of the framework of creativity and generativity, on which the proposal of a church giving birth to just and sustainable communities is ultimately hinged. The last part of the essay is a proposal of a performative-ethical ecclesiology that synthesizes sacramental and communal-contextual practices as resources for concrete response to ecological challenges of our time.

Mapping Responses and Resources

What are broad lines of affiliation between theological reflection and environmental ethics? The scholars Laurel Kearns and Willis Jenkins have outlined a series of connections that illuminate this nexus. These can mark important insights in various narratives, or as Jenkins calls it, "ecologies of grace."[7] Three categories are ecojustice, Christian stewardship, and creation spirituality.[8] We will consider each in turn before reflecting on the significance of these approaches for seeking sustainability in a Catholic, ecclesial context.

The strategy of *ecojustice* is a practical-ethical approach that utilizes the secular strategy of emphasizing nature's intrinsic value, although in religious contexts such value is understood to derive from God. Transgressive policies and actions that destroy and disrespect the integrity of creation and that negatively affect human and ecosystem communities are acts of injustice.[9] Ethicists who employ this strategy must respond to the thorny question of how to account for experiences of natural catastrophes and suffering: Are tsunamis and hurricanes, earthquakes and predation rightly considered "justice" issues? Most scholars would hesitate to affirm that, but it remains to be seen how "natural" dynamics and human actions coalesce to cause profound suffering.

The next theme is *Christian stewardship*,[10] which emphasizes responsibility of the human person as a good steward entrusted by God with the goods of the earth. This framework has been criticized as having failed to rid itself of the vestiges of anthropocentrism, yet it emphasizes the strength of the narrative in Genesis 2, which exhorts humankind to "till and keep" the earth.[11] Stewardship thus defined is not equivalent to domination or reckless use. Rather, it is intimately linked with discipleship: it invites the human person to follow the precepts of God by his or her responsible use of human freedom to become accountable for the well-being of the environment.

Stewardship theologians emphasize key distinctions between God and creation. The fulcrum on which the framework of stewardship stands is the affirmation that only human persons bear the *imago Dei*. Because of this, humans are understood as uniquely capable and responsible, patterned after Christ who was obedient to the will of the Father unto death.[12]

The third strategy, *ecological spirituality*, addresses the embodied, earthly, and intimate relationships among self, social community, ecosystems, and God. This strategy tries to connect environmental quality with human dignity and with God. Such an approach is sometimes criticized for failing to distinguish real differences between humanity and the rest of creation.[13] That criticism, however, can be deflected by articulating the cosmic scope of God's communion with Creation. In other words, it is precisely through the capacity for creativity—a trait that is, in significant ways, unique to humans—that humans participate in God's grace. Theologians such as Pierre Teilhard de Chardin, Ian Barbour, Catherine Keller, and John Haught emphasize this vital, creative element in which humans have a role to play. Often, this approach draws on process philosophy and connects to pneumatology, or the theology of the Spirit.[14]

The preceding cartographic approach helps us locate our own framework, one that allows for a possible integration between the key issues being tackled in the three ethico-theological schemes enumerated above. In the succeeding sections, the questions of justice for the environment and the responsibility of the human steward as the *imago Dei* (central concerns for the ecojustice and Christian stewardship themes, respectively) will be framed within the eco-spiritual-theological concerns of creativity and generativity, with its attendant issues of the freedom of God, the responsibility of the human, and the integrity of creation. This will be made possible through an appeal to pneumatology.

Spirit Birthing Communion

Generativity and creativity are important terms for the approach to ecotheology mentioned above. The nonrivalrous creativity among humans, creation, and God is described by some systematic theologians as a feature of the power of the

Holy Spirit. For example, Peter Scott contends that the Spirit mutually orients creatures toward each other, renews their communion, sustains their being, and elicits diverse gifts toward creativity.[15] Jürgen Moltmann and Catherine Keller recover images of the womb as living space for generativity and creativity. (Moltmann's use of *Lebensraum* particularly draws parallels between wildlife habitat and the space for life that the Spirit vivifies.[16]) Denis Edwards associates the Spirit with creative love:

> The power of the Creator Spirit is a power defined by love, a power the makes room for creatures to be their finite creaturely selves. It makes room for human freedom and the integrity of the laws of nature. It is a power that is self-limited because, in the freedom of love, it respects the otherness and autonomy of both human freedom and physical processes.[17]

As Edwards observes, creation therefore has an ongoing aspect, but still there remains "otherness and autonomy" for biological, earthly realities. In a slightly different nuance to how God interacts with a world characterized by autonomous processes, the Lutheran theologian Ted Peters, extending the insights of Wolfhart Pannenberg, contends that we can construe cosmic history as a single act of God with several "sub-acts."[18] This means that there is room for creativity and generativity, which for Peters is determined by "mutual reciprocity" between the finite and the overarching divine plan.[19] The role of the Spirit is an enabler of generativity and creativity while respecting creation's integrity and freedom.

Furthermore, theologians express the generativity of nature by appealing to the imagery of Paul in Romans 8 where the latter sees the sufferings and struggles of childbirth: "For we know that the entire creation has been groaning together in the pangs of childbirth up till now."[20] Joseph Fitzmyer, SJ, points out that this groaning conveys the eschatological possibility of creation, and thus that the text is relevant in our context of ecological crisis.[21] Edwards suggests that the Spirit is more than a midwife who enables the process of birthing; rather, the Spirit empowers creation from within to bring into birth a future that is "ultimately the unimaginable transfiguration of creatures as they participate in the divine Communion in their own specific and differentiated ways."[22] On this view, the Spirit not only secures the nonrivalrous creativity but also actively vivifies the cosmos as evolving within the divine, trinitarian communion.

This trinitarian aspect is important. In recent theological and ecclesiological reflections, authors from diverse backgrounds have come to a common understanding that if God's being is constituted by relationality and communion, then this fact has consequences in our ethical practice. If the Trinity is a model of noncompetitive relationships, what does that mean for human action? The Orthodox theologian John Zizioulas famously contends: "It is communion that makes things be: nothing exists without it, not even God."[23] This mode of existence is absolute and irreplaceable.[24] He asserts that through *hypostasis* and *ekstasis*, "God is freed from the necessity of ontological monism and is acknowledged to act in radical freedom in relation to creation and the cosmos. God is, therefore, essentially a *koinonia* in love."[25]

In Zizioulas's mind, God's hypostatic and ekstatic *koinonia* is both descriptive and prescriptive of the being of the church, that is, ecclesial existence. The being of the church takes after the being of God, who is communion. The human person participates in this communion but is not the center of it. In Zizioulas's framework, although the human is displaced as the sole referent of existence, she or he now becomes situated in a vast web of interrelations;[26] she or he retains the singular responsibility of having received the *imago Dei* through baptism, which is both descriptive and prescriptive of his or her vocation in relation to the whole of creation.

The foregoing assessment of some theologians' perspectives on the pneumatological foundation for creativity, generativity, and communion provides a possible platform whence an ecospiritual praxis for ecclesial communities may be launched. I argue that the reflections of theologians coming from different Christian traditions enrich, criticize, and help articulate a more relevant Catholic theological ethics (and vice versa).[27] The pneumatological reflections of Zizioulas (which resonate with Edwards's approach) complement and better articulate the Christological (and seemingly stewardship-directed) slant of Roman Catholic ecological engagement. Moreover, Pannenberg's idea of the "sub-acts" within the single cosmic creative act of God makes it possible for the nonrivalrous activity between creative stewardship with the freedom of God and creation's integrity.[28]

With this integrative gambit, I am now in a position to argue that the three approaches (ecojustice, Christian stewardship, and ecospirituality) can complement each other in order to give way to a new articulation of a Catholic ecclesiological perspective that is at once oriented toward the ecological praxis of creative justice and sustainability, but which is also essentially rooted in the theology and spirituality of the Holy Spirit. Concretely, and in the context of ecclesiology, what might this mean?

Church Birthing Just Communities

In relation to the exploitation of the environment, what can the church as the sacrament of communion offer? This essay affirms the framework of relationality and communion described above. In particular, Eucharistic reflection on the Filipino ecclesiological and cultural context can help reveal important insights about proper ecological and social relationships.

Zizioulas's regard of creation stems from what he calls a "liturgical" vision of the world. The term "liturgical" is here used according to the Orthodox tradition, in which Eucharistic liturgy is the iconic "re-presentation" of God's irruption into, and interruption of, history.[29] Existence and transcendence are united: "There is no longer a dualism which separates the secular and the sacred because creation and her gifts, in and through the liturgy, are offered to God as Eucharist and thanksgiving symbolizing the cosmic communion with humanity and creation."[30]

Zizioulas affirms that the Eucharist is simultaneously the icon of the eschatological banquet and the action where this banquet proleptically irrupts into history—empowering its participants to an engagement in the world following God's vision of the future.[31]

This same notion is paraphrased by Cavanaugh, who describes the Eucharist as "God's imagination of the church; we participate in that imagination insofar as we are imagined by God, incorporated into the body of Christ through grace."[32] This point can serve as a good signpost as to how human and Christian communities play their role in the nonrivalrous creativity and generativity among God, human, and environment. In a related way, David Power describes how Eucharist is "the communion of the diverse members of the church in the elements of bread and wine, around a common table, sharing in the things of earth."[33] What does this iconic re-presentation of sharing imply in the concrete life of the church?

What is necessary is a performative understanding of the Eucharist. What relationships can be transformed through it? Historically, the ancient church looked at the Eucharist in terms of "doing" (*eucharistiam facere*) or "performing" the mysteries (*mysteria telein*).[34] This is a view of Eucharist as action—not a self-satisfied securing of salvation, but rather an initiative to go out and transform the world. The Eucharist becomes a sacrament of communion with the whole of creation—indeed, a performance of ecological communion.

The performative character of the Eucharist is very much connected with the Filipino meal experience as a central aspect of family communion. The *Catechism for Filipino Catholics* correctly points out in its section on the identity of the Filipino Catholic that Filipinos are meal-oriented:

> Because Filipinos consider almost everyone as part of their family (*parang pamilya*), we are known for being gracious hosts and grateful guests. Serving the guests with the best we have is an inborn value to Filipinos, rich and poor alike. We love to celebrate any and all events with a special meal. Even with unexpected guests, we Filipinos try our best to offer something, meager as it may be, with the traditional greetings: "Come and eat with us" (*Tuloy po kayo at kumain muna tayo*).[35]

The section then connects the Eucharist with the experience of the meal in which Jesus is simultaneously the host (of the new Paschal meal, 1 Cor. 11:23–26), the food (as the bread of life, John 6:48–58), and the guest (Matt. 18:20; Rev. 3:20). As the New Testament reference of eating together in table fellowship with the risen Christ (1 Cor. 10:17) reminds us, meals are indeed privileged actions of connection among the early Eucharistic communities.[36] "So Filipinos feel naturally 'at home' in breaking bread together with Jesus."[37]

What is more, our catechism looks at the Eucharist not only as a ritual performance; it also refers to the Second Plenary Council of the Philippines (PCP II) on social transformation, and in so doing, the catechism explicitly connects the Eucharist with the work of liberation:

> A spirituality of transformation . . . is a spirituality that listens to and heeds God's word, discerns and follows the Spirit in the Scriptures, in the Church and in history, in the voices of the voiceless and powerless and finds in the Eucharist not only its full nourishment but also its total prayerful communion with the Lord of salvation and liberation.[38]

Although this section in PCP does not explicitly mention ecology, it provides for a methodology that connects the Eucharist with the concrete praxis and work for justice. Moreover, other documents from the Filipino bishops indicate the importance of ecological awareness in light of justice and liberation. As early as 1988, the Catholic Bishops' Conference of the Philippines issued a pastoral letter titled "What Is Happening to Our Beautiful Land?" denouncing the exploitative mentality behind ecological degradation. In this document, the Filipino bishops connect intergenerational equality with intragenerational justice: "The attack on the natural world which benefits very few Filipinos is rapidly whittling away at the very base of our living world and endangering its fruitfulness for future generations."[39]

Gustavo Gutiérrez stated: "By preaching the Gospel message, by its sacraments, and by the charity of its members, the church proclaims and shelters the gift of the Kingdom of God in the heart of human history."[40] In light of the preceding arguments, perhaps a practice of meal sharing can provide a framework for a Christian "politics" of noncompetitive resource sharing. Here, Gutiérrez's idea of charity stands against environmental apartheid and injustice. The earth's resources cannot be exploited in order to serve the wants of the few. Appropriated into the context of sustainability and justice, the Eucharist as a sacramental event of resource sharing becomes a moment where critical engagement and dialogical questioning occurs.

Becoming an ecclesial body through the Eucharist has an important ethical dimension: we cannot share the Eucharistic bread without also sharing our daily bread.[41] Therefore, every Eucharistic meal is, and becomes, an event of interrogation as to why some of God's children have large portions in their daily bread while others languish in deprivation and abject poverty. It is an event of inquiry why there is a hellish division between the "haves" and the "have nots." It becomes a ritual of inquest as to why the body of God's creation that is sanctified in the Eucharist is exploited and made to serve the caprice of the few.[42]

In this way, according to William Cavanaugh, the "simultaneity of past and future in the present, which characterizes the Christian eschatological imagination of time," is experienced in the Eucharist—and it opens up a space of protest and resistance.[43] As many liberation theologians have pointed out, the Eucharistic performance of the dangerous memory of Jesus having life-changing meal fellowships (Luke 19:1–10) two millennia ago effects a transformation of historical time into eschatology. Through the iconic Eucharist, the eschatological banquet interrupts the historical time and opens up spaces for critique against social and economic inequalities.[44]

The Eucharist experienced this way empowers the participants to respond "to the hunger for justice and peace" as "there are no distinctions around the Table of the Lord."[45] The partakers of the Eucharist are thereby given the task of what Zizioulas calls a Eucharistic ethos, indeed leading even to an ecological asceticism whereby people are made aware of the effects on the environment of their excesses and of the need for personal and communal conversion.[46]

The cultural characteristic of the Filipino celebration and fondness for eating together, which is brought into the meal sharing of the Eucharist, becomes also the icon of God's vision for the heavenly banquet. It becomes an icon of tactical resistance for the poor. The celebratory character of the Eucharist becomes an event where the poor and those who witness injustice can resist unjust socioeconomic and cultural configurations, through their "memory of the future" in which economic and material disparities are banished, and which gives rise to the healing of fractured relations with other human beings and with the biosphere.[47]

This liberative vision of empowerment, healing, and justice becomes an interpretative key for a better, inclusive, sustainable, and just future even while we stand in the pain and suffering of history. Such a theology is neither an interim sedative nor a comforting fantasy but rather an expression of a hope that determines the ecological praxis of the present. Thus, the value of the Eucharist lies in no small part in its potential to be an event of resistance of the unjust setup of the present "in its refusal to forget what can be," in the words of Herbert Marcuse.[48]

This memory of the future—of what can be—opens up spaces in order to re-create various possibilities of liberation and concrete praxis.[49] It is a kind of a "stubborn hope" that cannot be extinguished by the despair of the present degradation of the environment. By plumbing the potential of the iconic function of the Eucharist we are able to propose, in a nonanthropocentric and nonrivalrous way, an "ecclesiological birthing" of human agency intrinsically connected to, and empowered by, a just vision of the whole of creation.

In Place of a Conclusion: "Oikopraxial" Ecclesiology

It seems that sustainability as the "capacity of natural and social systems to survive and thrive together indefinitely" can be theologically fortified with the framework of generativity-creativity in communion.[50] What possibly can give birth to these practices and attitudes, and provide a context and structure for these practices and attitudes to develop and thrive? One answer is an "oikopraxial" ecclesiology. At its very basic meaning, *oikos* means "home." As Larry Rasmussen has pointed out, "*Oikos*—earth as a vast but single household of life—means the capacity for survival, that is, sustainable habitat. It means space and the means for the living of all living things."[51] (Indeed, the word "ecology" comes from *oikos* and *logos,* which literally means the structure of the house.[52])

"Praxis" is a word associated with the practical. The root meaning of praxis seems to be associated with virtuous action or practice. *Oikopraxial* can then refer to the virtuous practices in a habitat. This meaning has both descriptive and prescriptive aspects. Descriptively, it means the systems of processes and practices that happen in the household of life. Prescriptively, it means the constant challenge of virtuous action that brings about, nurtures, and respects the creative and generative capacity of the habitat. The dwellers of the *oikos* are tasked with the mutual upbuilding of the community.[53]

Oikopraxial ecclesiology is therefore a proposal of a church community that discerns and incarnates generative and creative practices within the panentheistic household of life. Through a participative global network of communions and local communities, oikopraxial ecclesiology enacts its identity both as a prophetic voice of just sustainability and as a mother who gives birth and nurtures life so that God may be all in all (1 Cor. 15:28).

Notes

1. Timothy Wirth, Undersecretary of State for Global Affairs, at National Press Club, July 12, 1994 as quoted in Daniel Maguire, "More People: Less Earth: The Shadow of Mankind," in *Ethics for a Small Planet: New Horizons on Population, Consumption, and Ecology*, ed. Daniel Maguire and Larry Rassmusen (Albany: State University of New York Press, 1998), 2.

2. Christian Aid UK, *A Rich Seam: Who Benefits from the Rising Commodity Prices?* (London: Christian Aid, 2007), 28–29.

3. Birdlife International, Haribon Foundation, and Philippines Association for Intercultural Development, 2011 as quoted in *Alyansang Tigil Mina*, Position Paper on the Continued Adoption of the Aquino Government of the Revitalization of the Philippine Mining Industry Policy, 2011.

4. See Sean McDonagh, *Passion for the Earth: The Christian Vocation to Promote Justice, Peace, and Integrity of Creation* (Quezon City: Claretian Publications, 1995); Sean McDonagh, *The Greening of the Church* (Quezon City: Claretian Publications, 1990).

5. Cynthia Moe-Lobeda and Daniel Spencer, "Free Trade Agreements and the Neoliberal Economic Paradigm: Economic, Ecological, and Moral Consequences," *Political Theology* 10, no. 4 (2009): 714.

6. Jay McDaniel, "'Where Is the Holy Spirit Anyway?' Response to a Skeptical Environmentalist," *Ecumenical Review* 42, no. 2 (1990): 165. See also Maguire, "More People: Less Earth," 21.

7. Willis Jenkins, *Ecologies of Grace: Environmental Ethics and Christian Theology* (New York: Oxford University Press, 2008), 245n4.

8. See Laurel Diane Kearns, "Saving the Creation: Religious Environmentalism," (PhD diss., Emory University, 1994), 3; Laurel Diane Kearns, "The Context of Eco-Theology," in *The Blackwell Companion to Modern Theology*, ed. Gareth Jones (Malden, MA: Blackwell, 2004): 465–84.

9. See McDaniel, "'Where Is the Holy Spirit Anyway?,'" 165.

10. See Jenkins, *Ecologies of Grace*, 77–92.

11. See Randy J. C. Odchigue, "Recasting Christian and Cultural Resources for Environment and Sustainability," *Asian Horizons: Dharmaram Journal of Theology* 6, no. 2 (2012): 274–76.

12. The radicalization of the role of the steward pushes this strategy from being a caretaker of the earth's household to the edges of martyrdom. Jenkins correctly observes though that stewardship ethicists do not focus on narratives and stories about people being martyred for the sake of the environment. Jenkins mentions the martyred Filipino priest Fr. Nerelito Satur, who was brutally murdered after having tirelessly fought against illegal logging. Jenkins, *Ecologies of Grace*, 86–87.

13. Sally McFague, *The Body of God* (Minneapolis: Fortress Press, 1993), 69–73.

14. See Jenkins, *Ecologies of Grace,* 98; Ian Barbour, *Nature, Human Nature, and God* (Minneapolis: Fortress Press, 2002), 104–17; Catherine Keller, *Face of the Deep: A Theology of Becoming* (New York: Routledge, 2003), 117.

15. Peter Scott, *A Political Theology of Nature* (Cambridge: Cambridge University Press, 2003), 204–6.

16. Jürgen Moltmann, *The Spirit of Life: A Universal Affirmation* (Minneapolis: Fortress Press, 1992), 95, 157, 176–79.

17. Denis Edwards, *Breath of Life: A Theology of the Creator Spirit* (Maryknoll, NY: Orbis Books, 2004), 109.

18. See Wolfhart Pannenberg, *Systematic Theology* (Grand Rapids, MI: Eerdmans, 1991).

19. Ted Peters, "God as Future of Cosmic Creativity," in *Science, Theology, and Ethics* (Burlington, VT: Ashgate, 2003), 89–90.

20. Romans 8:22.

21. Joseph Fitzmyer, *Romans: A New Translation with Introduction and Commentary*, Anchor Bible 33 (New York: Doubleday, 1993), 505.

22. Edwards, *Breath of Life*, 112.

23. John Zizioulas, *Being as Communion* (Crestwood, NY: St. Vladimir's Seminary Press, 1993), 17.

24. John Zizioulas, "Human Capacity and Incapacity," *Scottish Journal of Theology* 28 (1975): 427.

25. Odchigue, "Recasting Christian and Cultural Resources," 278.

26. See John Zizioulas, "Preserving God's Creation," *Sourozh* 39 (1990): 8–9.

27. Catholic theology seems to be labeled often as oriented toward the institutional and political. Orthodox theology, in contrast, seems to be slanted toward the pneumatological and eschatological. Our integration here helps recuperate the theological balance that is needed for ethical praxis not to fall toward secular social activism and for the pneumatological-eschatological spirituality and liturgy to have concrete consequences in the flesh-and-blood struggles of human persons.

28. Walter Kasper succinctly puts the relationship between the Creator and the steward in the following axiomatic terms: autonomy is directly, not inversely, proportionate to theonomy. Walter Kasper, *The God of Jesus Christ*, trans. Matthew O'Connell (New York: Crossroad, 2005), 284.

29. John Zizioulas, "Church as Communion," *St. Vladimir's Theological Quarterly* 38 (1994): 15.

30. Randy J. C. Odchigue, "Sacramental Relationality: Eco-Theological Possibilities," *Hapag* 8, no. 1 (2011): 121.

31. Cavanaugh quotes Zizioulas's idea of the memory of future in the Eucharist as the converging point between the past, the engagement of the present, and eschatological church of all times. See William T. Cavanaugh, *Torture and Eucharist: Theology, Politics and the Body of Christ* (Malden, MA: Blackwell, 1998), 234; Zizioulas, *Being as Communion*, 180.

32. Cavanaugh, *Torture and Eucharist*, 272–73.

33. David Power, "Eucharistic Justice," *Theological Studies* 67 (2006): 860.

34. Dom Gregory Dix, *The Shape of the Liturgy* (1945; New York: Seabury Press, 1982), 599.

35. Catholic Bishops' Conference of the Philippines, *Catechism for Filipino Catholics* (Manila: Episcopal Commission on Catechesis and Catholic Education, 2005), no. 37. Hereafter *CFC*.

36. Ibid., no. 38.

37. Ibid.

38. *Acts and Decrees of the Second Plenary Council of the Philippines* (Manila: St. Paul, 1992), no. 281; *CFC*, no. 38.

39. Catholic Bishops' Conference of the Philippines, "What Is Happening to Our Beautiful Land? A Pastoral Letter on Ecology," *Pastoral Letters (1945–1995)*, ed. Pedro C. Quitorio III (Manila: Peimon, 1996), 663–73.

40. Gustavo Gutiérrez, *A Theology of Liberation* (London: SCM, 1974), 11.

41. Walter Kasper, *That They May All Be One* (London: Burns and Oates, 2004), 58.

42. See Sallie McFague, "Imagine a Theology of Nature," in *Liberating Life: Contemporary Approaches to Ecological Theology*, ed. Charles Birch, William Eakin, and Jay B. McDaniel (Maryknoll, NY: Orbis Books, 1991), 217.

43. Cavanaugh, *Torture and Eucharist*, 277.

44. For a parallel point on the critical potential of the Eucharist against torture, see ibid.

45. *CFC*, no. 171.

46. John Zizioulas, "Ecological Asceticism: A Cultural Revolution," *Sourozh* 67 (1997): 23.

47. The eschatological celebration impinging on the present through the iconic function of the Eucharist becomes the strength of the weak in order for them to articulate an ethical engagement toward policies that are exploitative of their social, cultural, and ecological space.

48. Herbert Marcuse, *Eros and Civilization: A Philosophical Inquiry into Freud* (Boston: Beacon Press, 1974), 148.

49. See John Kekes, "Moral Imagination, Freedom and the Humanities," *American Philosophical Quarterly* 28, no. 2 (1991): 101–11.

50. Larry Rasmussen, "Next Journey: Sustainability for Six Billion and More," in Maguire and Rosmussen, *Ethics for a Small Planet*, 67.

51. Larry Rasmussen, *Earth Community, Earth Ethics* (Maryknoll, NY: Orbis Books, 1998), 91.

52. John Cobb, *Sustainability: Economics, Ecology and Justice* (Maryknoll, NY: Orbis Books, 1992), 56.

53. Rasmussen, *Earth Community*, 93. See also Konrad Kaiser, *Ecumenism in Transition* (Geneva: World Council of Churches Publications, 1991), 84–91.

Feminism and Ecology

Ann Marie Mealey

There have been many new developments in the area of Catholic theology in recent decades. Perhaps one of the most notable has been an increasing interest in adopting a "green agenda" and attending to pressing issues such as climate change, sustainable development, water shortages, or the spread of disease and its connection with care for the environment. The ways in which scholars have approached these issues are varied and oftentimes complex.

Despite competing claims about which method to use when discussing environmental ethics (such as virtue theory or utilitarianism, for example), one can say with some degree of certainty that significant strides have been made in Catholic environmental thought. For instance, scholars are now using terms such as "sacramental universe" to indicate a new or renewed relationship between the human community and the earth.[1] Such developments in language are important because theologically salient concepts make the call for care and cooperation with the earth's natural rhythms more urgent and personal for Catholics.

The concept of stewardship has been criticized and refined. Increasingly, it is interpreted to express how being a Christian entails a responsibility to care for God's creation.[2] In this and related endeavors, scholars have reread key texts from the biblical tradition and tried to balance the seemingly anthropocentric thrust with ecologically attentive exegesis. Others have looked to the texts of Vatican II and sought to draw attention to the need for an ecological consciousness when interpreting concepts such as the common good. Still others qualify historical church texts that express, in no uncertain terms, that "humankind can and should increasingly consolidate its control over creation," since statements of this sort often allude to biblical texts that stipulate the need for humans to have dominion over the earth (*Gaudium et Spes*, no. 12). The incorporation of scientific and especially ecological paradigms has, in turn, caused another shift in method, toward a more relational model of understanding the interconnectivity of humans and the entire ecosystem.[3]

In addition to these developments, work is also being carried out on the links between environmental degradation and poverty. People are increasingly aware that, for instance, an environmental policy that might be viable in the First World might not be so in the Third World. Many scholars are keen to communicate how environmental concerns are linked with structures of injustice that force many people to eke out a living in ways that destroy natural habitats and their own immediate environment.

All of the preceding developments signal positive advances in Catholic ecological awareness. However, there are other pressing areas that also need attention and are sometimes forgotten or merely mentioned in passing. One such area is the relationship between women and the environment. Christian feminist theology includes a wide variety of views and approaches and can often be a complex field of perspectives. And when one adds consideration of the earth into the equation, things might seem even more complex. Nevertheless, by sketching briefly what we mean by feminism in the area of theology, we can then outline what a feminist ecological ethics might look like, referring to some leading voices in the field.

After outlining what ecofeminism entails, this article will emphasize the need to deconstruct patterns of behavior and theological thinking that perpetuate structures of inequality between women and men that are subsequently reflected in the ways in which we relate to the environment. It will argue that the Catholic tradition must reconsider the ways in which currently it refers to and uses key theological concepts, in order to challenge rather than perpetuate issues of sexism, class, gender, and power. Using the Appalachian Bishops' *At Home in the Web of Life: A Pastoral Message on Sustainable Communities in Appalachia Celebrating the 20th Anniversary of "This Land Is Home to Me"* as an illustrative example, the article will show how an attentive, listening magisterium at the local level can help address ecological issues from the grass roots as well as liberate women from the range of contexts that keep them in positions of inferiority and oppression.

Ecology and Women in the Christian Tradition

Christian feminist theology is a complex field that, generally speaking, involves a concern that Christian theology has been written in a way that privileges male experience and patriarchal patterns of thought as well as social and ecclesial systems. Indeed, God is often considered to be male if only in an implicit way through traditional language such as "Father"; so the question becomes, "Is there room for women in this model of theology?" Feminist theologians insist that theological formulations and epistemological baselines need to be addressed if women are to be given full consideration in all areas of theology and social life. Thus a major emphasis in most theological writings of our time includes the need to consider women's experience and theological formulations within, as Celia Deane-Drummond puts it, "egalitarian social arrangements."[4] This approach indicates that feminist consciousness is not simply a question of replacing patriarchy with matriarchy but with replacing patriarchy with more just and egalitarian arrangements that benefit the full scope of humanity.[5] Feminist theologians argue that this is both a practical and an epistemological issue, for traditional models of society and the methods of theology must be expanded.

Of course, what counts as "women's experience" is a thorny issue. As Deane-Drummond points out, "A sharp critique by conservative women and men is that feminists do not recognize the experience and views of ordinary women who are quite content to be part of social structures where males take responsibility and are dominant."[6] Whatever one's view on the matter, it is clear that women's voices and experiences ought to be heard and considered in theological matters. Taken seriously, this will affect how we see and interpret theological concepts.

For example, if we are to take feminist theology seriously, we will need to think of Trinity in egalitarian and inclusive terms. We will need to stress the feminine images of God as well as the male so that the entire human community sees itself as bound up with the unending love of God. We will also need to reread the biblical texts with a view to unearthing more inclusive models that can assist our theological understanding and our search for truth. These endeavors have been taken up by many feminist theologians because, to put it simply, they are concerned that "Western culture has been dominated by male social structures and male values which encourage detachment and separation, rather than involvement and integration."[7]

Concern about domination and separation has led many writers to link the oppression of women with that of the earth. Many feminist writers maintain that the dominance in society of men over women is similar to the dominance of humanity over creation. The contention, therefore, is that in order to address the ecological crisis, we need also to address the inequality that exists between men and women. Many believe that attention to women's experience can not only help create a more just society but can also provide a vital starting point for egalitarian responses to the ecological crisis.

In concrete terms, for example, in many countries around the globe, it is frequently women who farm the land but yet who lack input or control over environmental policies or strategies that affect their working life or on the ways in which they make a living from the land. Overcoming sexist attitudes toward women in society can help correct an overly narrow method of addressing environmental issues. The work of Rosemary Radford Ruether gives us much to think about in this regard.

Catholic Voices on Women and the Environment: Rosemary Radford Ruether

Rosemary Radford Ruether is a prolific scholar who has become known as an ecofeminist, the title affirmed and given to those who study the interconnectedness between the role and status of women and that of the environment. Central to ecofeminist concerns are four claims:

1. the oppression of women and the oppression of nature are interconnected;
2. these connections must be uncovered in order to understand both the oppression of women and the oppression of nature;
3. feminist analysis must include ecological insights; and
4. a feminist perspective must be part of any proposed ecological solutions.[8]

Radford Ruether develops an account of how women's roles have traditionally been to serve the needs of men, and she widens this concern to include a critique of deep ecology and other approaches to environmental consciousness.[9] For Radford Ruether, ecofeminism is connected to the basic inequality that exists between men and women in patriarchal culture. Inequality exists on cultural, symbolic, and socioeconomic levels and is mirrored in the ways in which the environment has been considered and treated.[10]

The connection between the status of women and the status of the environment is made first and foremost on a *cultural symbolic level*. For Radford Ruether, patriarchal culture has painted a picture of women as being more intrinsically connected to nature or as being on the "nature" side of the nature/culture binary.[11] This is shown, she says, "in the way in which women have been identified with the body, earth, sex, the flesh in its mortality, weakness and 'sin-proneness,' vis-à-vis a construction of masculinity identified with spirit, mind, and sovereign power over both women and nature."[12]

The second level of ecofeminist considerations goes beyond the cultural symbolic level to include *socioeconomic considerations*. Domination of women's bodies and work is believed to be interconnected with the exploitation of land, water, and animals: If societies justify the exploitation of women and their work, so too do they justify exploitation of land and the environment.[13] Thus, these two become interiorized, and exploitation of women, animals, land, water, and resources becomes a normal part of patriarchal society and its "cosmovision."[14] As such, Radford Ruether believes that we ought not to maintain that "anthropocentricism" is a universalizable term. Instead, she maintains that the extent to which we may or may not be promoting anthropocentrism in our dealings with the cosmos depends to a large extent on questions of class, gender, race, and culture.

Put simply, "All humans do not dominate nature equally, view themselves as over nature or benefit from such domination."[15] Rather, what tends to happen in society is that elite men dominate women and the environment in diverse ways and create hierarchies in different contexts depending on the circumstances. The result is that we find systems of domination in various parts of the world wherein whites are dominating blacks, landowners are dominating tenants, ruling classes are dominating slaves, men are dominating women, human nature is dominating nonhuman nature.[16] This is the point at which ecofeminism begins to take shape. Hence, Radford Ruether argues strongly that ecofeminist analysis needs to be integrated with considerations of gender, class, race, and socioeconomic issues.

But there is a distinction to be made between feminists and how they link their agendas with ecology. According to Radford Ruether, there are two main branches of ecofeminism: social ecofeminists and essentialist ecofeminists. The former group maintains that the link between the status of women and the earth is the result of a social ideology constructed by patriarchal culture that justifies and corroborates the oppression of women and the earth. Both are seen as property or as something that is owned in some respect.[17] The central aim and concern of ecofeminism, therefore, is to deconstruct this dualism along with the tendency to treat women and the earth as property. For Radford Ruether, this view needs to be overcome not by separating women and the earth from men, but by calling "men as much as women to overcome the myth of separation and learn to commune with nature as our common biotic community."[18]

The second branch of ecofeminism identified by Radford Ruether is essentialist ecofeminism. This group maintains that there is a deep truth about women that must be recognized in society: namely, that women are life givers, birth givers, and sustainers of life. Some essentialist ecofeminists hold that the "sacred female," the Goddess, must be revered; similarly, women are encouraged to connect with their innate, life-giving powers.[19] Some feminists are skeptical of essentializing claims made in this manner, suggesting that maintaining a male/female binary does not mitigate the fundamental problems posed by dualistic ways of thinking.

Several insights can nonetheless be attributed to ecofeminist thought. First, it is clear that ecofeminism must be characterized by reflection not just on gender and sex but also with regard to class, social arrangements, and the poor. Second, there is also a need to recognize that there might be plural spiritualities at play in various concepts of ecofeminism. Furthermore, other traditions and methods of study need to be included in our ecological reflections so that a common response to the ecological crisis might be found, albeit using differing methodologies or pathways of analysis. Moreover, Radford Ruether points out how a central concern of ecofeminism must be the poor and the status of women in poorer regions of the globe—for ecofeminist considerations are not simply limited to Western conceptualizations. As she puts it,

> The challenge of ecological theology and ethics is to knit together, in the light of both earth knowledge and the crisis of human history, a vision of divine presence that underlies and sustains natural processes and struggles against the excesses of the powerful while reaching out to the victimized to create communities of mutual flourishing.[20]

Still, finding this vision of divine presence will require careful analysis and consideration of how Catholic theology conceptualizes the divine being, spirituality, and Trinity. As Radford Ruether puts it, "Instead of modeling God after male ruling-class consciousness, outside of and ruling over nature as its controlling immortal projection, God in ecofeminist spirituality is the immanent source of life and the renewal of life that sustains the whole planetary and cosmic community."[21] In this sense, "God is neither male nor anthropomorphic."[22]

Rather, God should be seen as an everlasting divine being from which diversity and coexistence flow. God is the great sustainer and life giver who shows us what life in communion is all about: interdependency, coexistence, mutual respect, and love. To use Radford Ruether's words, God is the one that "enables us to overcome the distortions that threaten healthy relations."[23] Such an understanding of God has led some ecofeminist theologians to reconsider how we view the Trinity as the eternal life-sustaining model of interdependence and relationality. Radford Ruether cites Ivone Gebara as a leading voice in this regard.

Unity, Diversity, and Trinity: Ivone Gebara

Although many Christians associate the Trinity with oneness, perfect harmony, and collaboration, the theologian and philosopher Ivone Gebara argues that our notions of Trinity have become hazy and distant. She suggests that we need to locate trinitarian thought more closely with our human experiences and existence. In other words, we need to see the Trinity as "diversity and unity, existing and interrelating in a unique and single movement of continual creativity."[24]

Gebara does not wish to deny the mystery of the Trinity but to bring it closer to our own experiences in the created world. For example, if we see ourselves as Trinity, we note that we are made up of the complexities of our individual stories and lives but we are also one with the created order: the earth. This is why ecological consciousness is so important. We exist within ourselves, but we also exist in relationship to the universe: plants, rivers, mountains, animals, and life processes. For Gebara, "This vision gives us a new worldview and a different anthropology, on the basis of which we see ourselves as persons who are *of* the earth and *of* the cosmos, participants in the extraordinary process of life's evolution."[25] Such points have been echoed by ecological theologians and scholars of theology and science, including John Haught, Ilia Delio, and Elizabeth Johnson.

Furthermore, if we see the diversity in unity aspect of the Trinity as being an integral part of our lives and of our existence, we can also see that the subjugation of the earth, the poor, women, slaves, and those who are suffering in some way can no longer be justified because their experiences are part and parcel of the makeup of our shared human existence. In addition, we come to the view that the frailty of our human condition is also included in our struggle to be human in the fullest sense of the word. Gebara encourages us to look beyond a view of the Trinity that sees God as distant or remote, and instead to turn toward an image of God that is located within the very stuff of life and its complexities.

As a result, viewing the Trinity as part of our earthly relationships and experiences initiates an ethic that is aware of oppression and seeks to entice us along a path of faith to leave behind crude and highly patriarchal, hierarchical, materialistic, class-biased understandings of God.[26] It locates the Trinity in the very fabric of society and refutes any attempt to make one set of experiences the norm for all of humanity. In this sense, dualisms that set women, the earth, or the poor apart from our ethical deliberations are not considered to be a part of faith in God or of the trinitarian vision of the world.

Critics might object that Gebara's approach de-deifies the Trinity; to the contrary, Gebara's approach is to bring us closer to the divine creativity and diversity in unity that is reflected within the trinitarian life in order to promote an ecological ethic that challenges the structures that keep various groups, including women, in positions of inferiority or subjugation. Of course, listening to the stories of all oppressed groups in society makes the search for truth all the more difficult, but such listening enables a creativity that lies at the heart of the Trinity and at the heart of our human existence, which brings forth a fountain of knowledge about who we are and how we should live in harmony with all that exists. And this can only be a positive step forward in the search for what is truly human and just.

Similarly to the Trinity, therefore, our lives are made up of a shared nature that is often experienced differently depending on sex, social class, and other factors. This foundational complexity and diversity of experience explains why ecofeminism is so important: it seeks to relate the subjugation of women with that of the earth in order to create a dialogue that is based on equity, fairness, and justice in the fullest sense of the word—irrespective of, yet attentive to, the intricacies of social position, gender, class, and race.

Engaging Ecofeminism within the Catholic Church

Inclusive theological formulations are important for deconstructing the dualisms that are at play in our ecological consciousness. An additional, major concern for the continuation and potential success of ecofeminism is the need to integrate its agenda into the Church. How might this be possible, given the diversity of feminist ecological methods and approaches? Whose approach do we take as normative? Which approach represents women in a universalist sense? Who should compromise and, perhaps, change their approach? Is the Western model superior to that of the global South? These are important questions for discernment. Nevertheless, we can make some suggestions of how the Church might proceed to take ecofeminism seriously.

The first point to note is perhaps the need to move away from attempts to find a universalizable approach to ecofeminism or ecofeminist principles. The complexities and diversities of women's experience and of course of ecological concerns are such that the task of finding a "one size fits all" principle is impossible. Instead, since ecofeminism focuses on the task of liberating women and the earth in specific contexts where oppression is experienced, we could begin by adopting a "hermeneutic of difference."[27]

Many feminist and liberation theologians have adopted an approach that does not rely merely on a theoretical epistemological base but rather incorporates theory into a praxis-based methodology. The advantage is that deliberations about women can be understood in relation to the actual experience of women in their specific historical contexts, while remaining open to the critique that traditional theories provide. In this way, many feminist theologians have succeeded in shifting theological considerations from an imperialist approach or a universalist approach toward a more experienced-based approach, where the actual lives and experiences of women can be considered in diverse ways.

A theology that is based on experience and praxis must learn to value difference. This means that, for example, in terms of feminist theology, exclusively white feminist accounts cannot become the norm for understanding women's experience. As Linda Hogan explains, "White women's experience and praxis has [been] 'honored' with the badge of normativity, while women of colour have been further marginalized, in the name of justice. Such a whitewashing of experience has not gone unchallenged. Womanists have demanded that white feminists own this history of oppression."[28] Ecofeminism, including its social and essentialist formulations, must of necessity be a capacious endeavor.

Calling for a "hermeneutic of difference" need not necessarily threaten orthodoxy or objectivity, but such an approach values difference: it encourages people to begin to reflect morally from where they are, from the grass roots of their own experience. This approach cannot and does not begin with the assumption of sameness or uniformity. Instead, it embraces the complexities of diverse views and experiences of oppression, and it must respond to a plethora of diverging experiences.[29] Ecclesially, one might ask, what would this look like within the church in practice? And where might such practices currently be found?

The Appalachian Bishops: An Example of Working from the Grass Roots

In 1995, the Bishops of Appalachia in the United States issued *At Home in the Web of Life: A Pastoral Message on Sustainable Communities in Appalachia Celebrating the 20th Anniversary of "This Land Is Home to Me."*[30] It is an example of how the ordinary magisterium has enabled the story of a community to be told and has then set about addressing some of its most pressing ecological, social, and political issues. Some of the most notable features of the document include its stress on viewing Appalachia—an area rich in coal deposits—not simply as a "deposit of resources" but as a community that is called to sustainable living in sacred cooperation with "land and forest and water and air, indeed with all Earth's holy creatures."[31]

The bishops note in particular that they wish to address the "culture of death" that appears to be prevalent in Appalachia. They argue that industrialization and exploitation of their coal mines and natural resources have brought about a mentality that needs to be changed from a culture of death to a culture of life. The bishops outline how this transformation must take place at every level of their community, including ecological, political, social, and relational levels. In particular, they emphasize the need to address how social inequalities and the exploitation of land affects women and their intimate relationships, stating:

> This same struggle of all society between a culture of death and a culture of life is also played out at the intimate level in personal relationships. Here the culture of death invades our very souls through addictions and co-dependencies, often leading to abuse and violence, especially against women and children.[32]

The Appalachian bishops point out that in many cases the practical wisdom that women possess in relation to farming the land and fostering the local economy must be harnessed and disseminated locally in order to protect the dignity of women and that of the environment from oppression and exploitation. By telling the story of Appalachia and drawing principled conclusions, the bishops put forward a compelling case. The text is worth citing in its entirety here:

> In the judgment of many people, a sustainable society would build primarily on the rooted local informal economy, all in communion with the local ecosystem.
>
> Often this is called the "social economy," in contrast to the global "market economy," though the local economy is itself a market. Traditionally in most cultures, this local social market has been rooted in women's economic activities.
>
> There is a need, we believe, for various regions within Appalachia, perhaps on the county level, to begin exploring the alternative development of sustainable communities with emphasis on the social economy of women.[33]

In light of the stories and experiences of women in Appalachia, the bishops outline some of the ways in which the economy, land, and women can be liberated and encouraged to continue working in a sustainable and life-giving way. They stress the need for sustainable agriculture, forestry, ownership paradigms, technologies, cultures, families, and churches.[34] In addition, they advocate microfinancing as a way of empowering local businesses that demonstrate ecological responsibility; and they note that many of these businesses are run locally by women who are poor.[35]

This document shows us that teachings from the ordinary magisterium need not be focused solely on finding universal, timeless, essentialized principles that might make us more attuned to the needs of women and the environment. Rather, it demonstrates that listening and reflecting on local wisdom and experiences can provide us with a source of knowledge from which we can proceed to live thoughtfully—and perhaps even sustainably—in a plethora of contexts. This enables a diversity of views and experiences to be considered so that our ecological awareness and our treatment of women are attuned to the specific contexts in which women live and work.

The final sections of the document are also interesting, for the bishops thank all those who "took part in the listening sessions in preparation for the writing of the pastoral document," and they underline the fact that this listening experience has led them to hope and to believe in the "spiritual depth and creativity of the people of Appalachia."[36] This process of listening at a local level is a prime example of ecofeminist epistemology. It is vital to achieving the kind of theological and ecological awareness that can concretely benefit communities. We need to foster dialogue and reciprocal exchange at the level of the local Church. We need, of course, also to make judgments and recommendations for action. But, as Kevin Kelly suggests, "They must be the best we can do at the time," even if they are only provisional and "open to further dialogue and refinement."[37]

A key point here is that having an open mind and an awareness of the status of women and that of the environment does not mean a blank mind devoid of convictions, nor does it mean relativism. But, as Kelly notes, "we do need to see ourselves involved in an ongoing search for truth."[38] In his view, that "does not mean jettisoning the truth as we currently see it but it might mean re-examining and re-thinking the truth so that we can appreciate its richness even more fully in the light of where we stand today in the ongoing story of human culture and civilization."[39] This is what is needed in the Church if we are to respond to and adequately consider the issues surrounding the degradation of the environment and the situations of women worldwide.

Of course, part of such an endeavor will be seen by some as a threat to the universal Church. Although in principle the Church acknowledges that the local Church is an expression of the universal Church, there continues to be a concern that when a local Church takes up local issues and addresses them under the supervision of ordinary magisterium that it might wish to become completely "self-sufficient."[40] There might also be concern that such an epistemology challenges the teachings on conscience contained in *Veritatis Splendor*.[41] However, in spite of these concerns, it is clear that the diversity of women's experience is such that only a "creative hermeneutic" can adequately address the problem. This does not necessarily mean a rejection of principles; rather, it requires us to uncover in local domains a source of wisdom that can be used to liberate women and the earth from the destructive forces that keep both in positions of inferiority and subjugation.

We must also bear in mind that norms or principles formulated at the universal level within the Church will be general: their application requires imagination and creativity in order to be applied to and make sense in specific contexts, regions, geographical spheres, and locations. It is more accurate, therefore, to see ecofeminism not so much as a threat to orthodoxy or objectivity but to see it as an exercise of practical reason in the Thomistic sense: an attempt to locate connections between universal truths and local contexts.

What we aim to find, then, is not absolute truth but the best estimation of what is required in the situation given the context-specific information that we have. The content of the ethical criteria will subsequently be a constant dialogue between scripture, tradition, reason, theological interpretations, and experiences at all levels of society and in all disciplines.[42] This makes the search for truth all the more difficult, of course, but it also makes it all the more authentic.

What we need now, however, is to convince Christians that ecofeminism is indeed a field worthy of our consideration and reflections and to enable the local Church to attempt to listen to the voices that are living within its domain in order to appreciate the connection between feminism and ecology more fully. We need to allow the creative Spirit of the Trinity to flow freely within our Church so that the marginalization of women and the earth can be adequately addressed and considered. If we attempt this, we might then be empowered to respond to the unanswered needs of the human and nonhuman communities of our time.

Notes

1. John Hart, *What Are They Saying about Environmental Theology?* (Mahwah, NJ: Paulist Press, 2004), 100.

2. See Clare Palmer, "Stewardship: A Case Study in Environmental Ethics," in *The Earth Beneath: A Critical Guide to Green Theology*, ed. Ian Ball, Margaret Goodall, Clare Palmer, and John Reader (London: SPCK, 1992), 68ff. Palmer argues that the term "stewardship" does not feature consistently throughout the biblical texts. She also points out that where it is used in the Book of Daniel 1:11, for example, it gives us a less than benevolent view of the term "steward." Here the term "steward" means "man over the household," who answers only to his superior. Palmer argues that there is a problem here in the sense that anthropocentricism and male dominion seem to reemerge. See also Patrick Curry, *Ecological Ethics* (London: Polity Press, 2005), 28. Curry argues that "stewardship" implies that the earth needs humans to look after it.

3. Hart, *What Are They Saying about Environmental Theology?* 100.

4. Celia Deane-Drummond, *A Handbook in Theology and Ecology* (London: SCM Press, 1996), 53.

5. Ibid.

6. Ibid., 54.

7. Ibid., 55.

8. Lois K. Daly, "Ecofeminism, Reverence for Life, and Feminist Theological Ethics," in *Feminist Theological Ethics: A Reader*, ed. Lois K. Daly (Louisville, KY: Westminster John Knox Press, 1994), 296.

9. She claims that "the critique by ecofeminists that deep ecologists have been oblivious to the sexist structures of domination over nature seems . . . correct." Rosemary Radford Ruether, "Deep Ecology, Ecofeminism, and the Bible," in *Deep Ecology and World Religions: New Essays on Sacred Grounds*, ed. David Landis Barnhill and Roger S. Gottlieb (Albany: State University of New York Press, 2001), 229.

10. Ibid.

11. Ibid.

12. Ibid., 230.

13. Ibid.

14. Ibid.

15. Ibid.

16. Ibid.

17. Ibid., 237.

18. Ibid.

19. Ibid. Even within this genre of feminism there are those who emphasize the need to worship the Goddess as the sacred female and those who maintain that men need also to embrace the Goddess as "Divine Feminine." The central goal of the latter view is that men need to seek and to find the lost Goddess within themselves.

20. Rosemary Radford Ruether, "Ecofeminism: The Challenge to Theology," in *Christianity and Ecology: Seeking the Well-Being of Earth and Humans*, ed. Dieter T. Hessel and Rosemary Radford Ruether (Cambridge, MA: Harvard University Press, 2000), 110.

21. Ibid., 106.

22. Ibid.

23. Ibid.

24. Ivone Gebara, "The Trinity and Human Experience," in *Women Healing Earth: Third World Women on Ecology, Feminism, and Religion*, ed. Rosemary Radford Ruether (Maryknoll, NY: Orbis Books, 1996), 17.

25. Ibid., 18.

26. Ibid., 20.

27. Linda Hogan, *From Women's Experience to Feminist Theology* (Sheffield, UK: Sheffield Academic Press, 1995), 162ff.

28. Linda Hogan, "A Theology for the Future," in *Readings in Church Authority: Gifts and Challenges for Contemporary Catholicism*, ed. Gerard Mannion, Richard Gaillardetz, Jan Kerkhofs, and Kenneth Wilson (Aldershot,UK: Ashgate, 2003), 432.

29. Ibid., 433.

30. The Appalachian Bishops, *At Home in the Web of Life: A Pastoral Message on Sustainable Communities in Appalachia Celebrating the 20th Anniversary of "This Land Is Home to Me,"* (Webster Springs, WV: Catholic Committee of Appalachia, 1995).

31. Ibid.

32. Ibid.

33. Ibid.

34. Ibid.

35. Ibid.

36. Ibid., conclusion.

37. Kevin Kelly, *50 Years Receiving Vatican II: A Personal Odyssey* (Dublin: Columba Press, 2012), 133.

38. Ibid.

39. Ibid.

40. Congregation for the Doctrine of the Faith, *Letter to the Bishops of the Catholic Church on Some Aspects of the Church Understood as Communion: Universal Church and Particular Churches* (1992), http://www.vatican.va, no. 37.

41. John Paul II, (1993), http://www.vatican.va, no. 55. The teachings on conscience contained in this document claim that a "creative hermeneutic" can lead to a rejection of negative precepts set out by the hierarchy of the Church.

42. See Lisa Sowle Cahill, "Feminist Ethics in a Christian Perspective," *Theological Studies* 51, no. 1 (1990): 49–64, esp. 64.

A Catholic Virtues Ecology

Nancy M. Rourke

Who and what are we? Many religious and moral problems raise this fundamental question. Theology addresses it with a description of *whose* we are. Environmental ethics also addresses this question but answers it with a description of *where* we are. Yet if we are created beings, existing within God's creation, then these two sets of answers will share similarities. If this is the case, then good environmental ethics and good theology must need one another. Many theologians, environmentalists, and philosophers have already arrived at this conclusion.[1]

A common denominator shared by theology and environmental ethics is ecological awareness, which helps us (humans) notice our interdependence on one another and on all of creation. It makes clear our vulnerabilities and the ways in which our finitude and fragility are complemented by other forms of life, physically and in other ways. Our physical interdependencies in creation are interwoven with our social, mental, and spiritual interdependencies. To forget this is to forget that the nature of our createdness, of our creation, is that we are inextricably embedded within complex webs of interdependencies. In this chapter, I describe an ecology of virtues for theological anthropology. A Catholic ecology of virtues, or a virtues ecology, uses Catholic virtue ethics to help Catholic theological anthropologies incorporate ecological awareness.

Virtue ethics argues that a person shapes his or her own moral character by shaping the virtues that make up that character. She does this by choosing actions and practices that form moral habits: the virtues. Catholic virtue ethics visualizes a person's moral character as a dynamic web of relationships between his or her will, intellect, passions, vices, and virtues. These components or participants in a moral character interact continually, and the ways in which they interact are an important focus of virtue ethics thought. This emphasis on interdependence and complex interactions tends to resonate with ecological sensibilities. Developing this strand of thought, Catholic virtue ethics can offer a theological anthropology that relies on and enhances ecological awareness.

In this essay, first I rearticulate four environmentally significant virtues: integrity, wonder, temperance, and prudence. Next, I describe a Catholic virtues ecology as a type of interdependent, indeed "ecological," structure to show how these rearticulated virtues interact with the rest of a moral agent's character. Finally, I look at what happens when theological descriptions of who, what, whose, and where we are proceed with deliberate ecological awareness.

Integrity

Definitions of integrity often focus on those integrations "*within* the individual of beliefs, statements, and actions."[2] Here, a person of integrity acts in ways that are consistent with her beliefs. This usually means that her actions are shaped by her beliefs, but it rarely means that her beliefs are influenced by her actions. It locates integrity exclusively within the moral agent's character, imagining an outward emanation from that internal world to the world "outside" the agent. In other words, integrity means that an agent's beliefs shape her actions,[3] and it implies that integrity holds a moral agent's self still and constant over time.[4] It finds no merit in a moral agent whose beliefs change in response to her external worlds. If this is integrity, then a moral agent's context ought not influence her character, and her character ought never change.

By contrast, virtue ethics assumes that one's actions (practices, habits) shape one's moral character. Integrity as a virtue must mean more than stasis and self-sufficiency. The components of an agent's moral character (beliefs, intellect, virtues, etc.) and her external worlds (her environmental, social, and economic contexts) necessarily influence one another. Integrity, then, is best conceived as a trait that allows and encourages a productive mutual responsiveness. An ecologically attuned view of integrity is the habit of integrating one's life and self into one's physical, social, economic, and ecological contexts by working to adjust one's intellect, beliefs, virtues, as well as the environments, cultures, economic practices, and so on, within which one participates.

Catholic social teaching and liberation theologies demonstrate this kind of integrity when they describe the ways that our social, political, and economic contexts and participations relate to our spiritual health, our moral lives, and even to our ability to perceive God. In other words, integrity is not merely a tendency to act in accordance with one's own beliefs. It is also a tendency to grow in belief in response to others' actions; for example, it can mean a tendency to adjust one's understanding of God's justice when one learns of local effects of global trade structures, or to find that this adjusted vision of justice in turn changes one's way of participating in one's political contexts.

Leonardo Boff is an example of a liberation theologian who values the integration of our many-layered life. He admires "ecological knowledge" for its way of relating "laterally (ecological community), frontward (future), backward (past), and inwardly (complexity) all experiences and all forms of comprehension."[5] For Boff, this habit of acknowledging our many levels of complex interrelationality should also take root in our spiritual lives.[6]

But how is one to know what practices and beliefs to adjust—and what to hold firm, and when? In virtue ethics, a virtue is understood as a trait in balance. Excesses and deficiencies of traits are vices. An agent who exercises courage in every single situation demonstrates foolhardiness, or brashness, or recklessness—all vices—but not courage. Therefore, an uncritical or limitless "integrity" would not be a virtue.

The internal worlds of an agent with integrity would strive to fit her environments well in some respects and to alter them in others. From conscience to cosmos, her layers of existence would mutually inform one another. Integrity is not a self-sufficient virtue; its (previously described) vices of deficiency and excess can be known only in relationship with the other virtues, as will become clear when we examine the structure of a virtues ecology.

How resilient is this notion of integrity in light of Christian doctrine? One potential critique of this rearticulation of integrity is that it conflicts with the Christian understanding of original sin. If sin has infected the world, then integrating ourselves into that world might not be a good idea! But Christian integrity as a virtue asks for something more difficult than either a rejection of this world or an unquestioning acceptance of it. Rather, it asks for integrity and fluidity between wholes and parts, from moral character to local bioregions to globe—to *eschaton*.

Indeed, among the contexts to which our moral character must adjust is the Christian eschatological frame of our lives. A Christian moral character with integrity will shape itself and its contexts with an eye to Christian eschatological limits and hopes. This kind of integrity will cause dissonance. For example, the Christian theologian and environmental virtue ethicist Steven Bouma-Prediger describes just such a dissonance when he speaks of the Christ event as an event of the "good future . . . breaking into the not-so-good present."[7] Dissonance results when we integrate ourselves toward that radically different sacred reality, that "good future, " which may not be evident in the present time.

On this interpretation, integrity does not and should not produce only placid landscapes and an unruffled life. Instead, it brings a struggle to acknowledge our many layers of participation and to continually align them and ourselves with the eschatological frame within which a Christian lives. Ultimately, this is the kind of integrity that a Catholic virtues ecology requires.

Wonder

Catholic virtue traditions identify infused virtues as those virtues that are not earned but are given as grace by God. The theological virtues of faith, hope, and love are primary examples. The moral virtues, however, are acquired: that is, they are traits and habits that we cultivate. I would argue that wonder is a moral virtue, and hence something we attain by practicing it. But how do we practice "wonder" before we have it? Are we to fake wonderment until it becomes real?

The Christian ecofeminist theologian Sallie McFague offers an interesting response to this question. She notes, as an example, that wonder can result from the study of different species.[8] This is a pragmatic approach to cultivating an attitude of wonder: study a thing carefully, and you may well come to wonder at it. If it is worth the wonder, then the wonder will appear. This approach is evident in many environmental writers' work. Even when they aim only to describe or to observe, their descriptions eventually become something more: admiration, enjoyment, ecstasy: in short, wonder.[9] If this is the way to cultivate wonder, then many possibilities emerge. For example, even in urban environments, learning about our neighboring species may bring us to wonder at the life-systems into which we are embedded. So wonder arises from knowledge, from observation of our world.

But why does this work? Theologically, the reason is that these lives and ecosystems are wondrous, generative examples of divine creativity.[10] In a way, then, wonder as a moral virtue appears to be acquirable only because it is *already infused into our environments*. Naming wonder as a moral virtue brings us to recognize that objects of wonder are everywhere. Studying them will nurture wonder at God. We could even say that they *compel* our attention to a degree, inspiring our inner wonder from without. This makes wonder a virtue that is easily nurtured. We have only to look, listen, pay attention, and learn.

Temperance

Temperance seems an obvious environmental virtue. We often affiliate temperance with restraint, or a saying "No" to excessive enjoyment or even to enjoyment at all. Temperance then encourages us to lessen the burden our enjoyments levy onto our environments. But in fact temperance is not about deprivations. It is about enjoyment in its truest and fullest sense.[11] Temperance is about desires for pleasures for what they can actually give, not for what they suppress or deny.[12] Temperance is about being "rightly pleased."[13] How are we to know what constitutes being *rightly* pleased? The object of such pleasure is that which enables continued life,[14] but what is too much or too little of these kinds of pleasures?

In virtue ethics, as noted above, the right amount is neither too much nor too little. Our reason helps us know the limits, and for this it needs a good understanding of the full context within which our enjoyments take place. (Reason is assisted here by the virtue of prudence, which I will discuss next.) We need awareness and a good understanding of all the layers of our lives, such as our social and political structures and the bioregions within which our lives are lived. Any version of pleasure that will eliminate the source of that pleasure or that will work against continual life is vicious.

Temperance in a virtues ecology moderates our passions with an awareness of the rightful pleasure capacity of our social, geographical, economic, and ecological contexts. Temperance, then, enables right enjoyment of our many layers of existence. Balanced between extremes of excess and deprivation, temperance emphasizes enjoyments that are attuned to all these layers taken together, not absolutizing any one (like that of individual or domestic or economic layers) over other aspects.

Prudence

Prudence is central to Catholic virtue ethics. As the cardinal moral virtue, it harmonizes various other constituents of a moral agent's character. Prudence perceives and maintains the balance points of virtues with their corresponding vices—the "golden mean," as Aristotle had it. As a result, when rightly practiced, prudence is attentive in multiple directions: to the agent's contexts, to her theological virtues, and to the will, all in the effort of continually shaping that agent's moral character. For example, prudence attunes the moral agent's way of carrying out a decision in accordance with the situation within which the agent will act and thus is often called "practical wisdom" (because it is skilled at perceiving, interpreting, and adjusting to situations).[15] In other words, prudence overlaps and coordinates an agent's intellect and moral life.

Prudence's role in decision making, then, is to balance a moral agent's responsiveness to God with her responsiveness to each evolving, layered situation of her contexts.[16] When prudence is viewed like this, it reminds us of moral agents' intrinsic interrelationalities with one another and with all our spatial, temporal, political, social, spiritual, and economic environments. In these ways, prudence nurtures moral growth.

An Ecology of Virtues: Developing the Metaphor

Now that I have rearticulated four ecologically significant moral virtues we can see the beginnings of a structure for a Catholic virtues ecology, augmented by help from ecological studies. To this end, the next section of this essay describes three doctrines of ecology. First: ecosystems are open systems. Second: nestedness is a quintessential trait of ecosystems. Third: ecosystems' inhabitants universally demonstrate individuality.

The term "ecosystem" refers to the interrelationalities at work within a bioregion. Any place can be considered a bioregion. Bioregions comprise living beings, earth, rock and stone, water, and air. All these interact continually, forming systems, and the patterns of these systems of interactions are that bioregion's ecosystem. Studying an ecosystem—in other words, doing ecology—means examining the systems of interrelationality *between*, *among*, and *within* the living beings, earth, rock, water, and air.[17] So ecosystems are webs of systems of interaction, of interrelationalities. Whereas "bioregion" refers to an area, the location, an "ecosystem" refers to the interacting systems that are found there, to the functions performed, and to the near-infinite responses that can and sometimes do result.[18]

The first ecological doctrine that I import into Catholic virtues ecology is that all ecosystems and subsidiary functions are open systems.[19] Boundaries between systems are porous and imprecise because each ecosystem influences and is influenced by its neighboring ecosystems. (This description is true of geographic regions but also can be thought of in terms of an individual human being. Ecologically speaking, we are entities, we are systems, and we *contain* systems of bacteria, metabolic exchange, and more.) Furthermore, each ecosystem is also a participant in a larger region's ecosystems. In other words: "What is a system, and what is a subsystem is an arbitrary characteristic of one's point of view. One person's system is another person's subsystem."[20] More than this, ecologists have also seen that "there are apparently similar laws of function and mechanism operating at all levels of scale and size."[21] This is our second ecological doctrine: *nestedness* is a fundamental trait of ecosystems and their participants. The difference between subsystem and system is a matter of scale of observation, and that is a matter of the observer's point of view. An ecologist chooses a scale of observation: an individual living thing, an individual species, one habitat within a bioregion, or the energy system or water system of an entire bioregion.[22]

Universal individuation is the third doctrine. Each individual within an ecosystem is unique. Universal individuation appears among participants in ecosystems in large part because each participant *fits* among the others (spatially as well as functionally) and adapts responsively. Interrelationality shapes each being. This shaping is constant, mutual, and takes place on multiple scales, including within and between organisms and within and between species, through adaptation, cooperation, exploitation, and competition (to name a few).

Implications of Ecological Doctrines for an Ecology of Virtues

These doctrines have interesting implications for a Catholic virtues ecology. As organisms with porous and imprecise boundaries, we are not entirely distinguishable from our environments. A person's environment *becomes* his or her self as she or he eats and breathes. Similarly, a moral agent's character is not isolated from the moral character of the societies she inhabits. All these systems are open: persons absorb and reinforce the virtues of our societies, internalize the values of surrounding social structures, experience these values within our bodies physically (in the form of healthy teeth or cancerous skin, for example), and in other ways.

In our discussion of wonder, we noted that this acquired virtue is possible only because of the infusion of wonder-worthy lives, relationships, species, and phenomena in our environments. But this means that the difference between infused and acquired elements of our moral character (and of our world) becomes less clear. This is appropriate—in Catholic tradition, the border between human agency and God's agency is porous and imprecise. Creation and divine agency are conceptualized as open systems.

Open systems offer an important corrective to much traditional reflection on Catholic virtue ethics, where the individual human person has been the focal unit to such an extreme that some scholars have accused virtue ethics of lacking social justice awareness altogether.[23] As critics point out, societies also have virtues, and the virtues of individuals and of societies are mutually causally related. Part of what a virtues ecology makes clear is that a moral agent is not isolated: the boundaries around her are porous and permeable. She is nested within societies and lives out the dynamic of her internal moral worlds' interactions.

Integrity is an important concept in environmental ethics, but there it is more often seen as a characteristic of ecosystems than of human persons.[24] As proposed above, a Catholic virtues ecology can take a further step. If moral virtues like integrity are nested within human persons, they are therefore also nested within environments.[25] The *broader* scales of integrity (within ecosystems) are met and continued by the *smaller* scales within a moral agent's character. As a moral virtue, then, integrity would mean the habit of *participating* in ecological integrity, both without and within. It would signal a moral agent whose practiced responses, abilities, and impulses are responsive to her inner worlds, to her local bioregion's needs, to her family's values and traditions, to her religious commitments, to her gender's burdens and expectations, and so on. Integrity entails recognition of dynamism and prompts a response. In an ecology of virtues, integrity is a nested responsiveness.

An "ecology of virtues" model also benefits from the idea that various virtues inform and relate to one another, while also always being expressed in the context of an individual person's life. Although we can generalize to some extent what specific virtues entail, the way each virtue looks and functions within each moral agent differs. For example, one moral agent's temperance might be so heavily informed by his enjoyment of organically grown foods that he practices great care in his food shopping, traveling farther to find appropriate produce when these foods are unavailable and drawing on patience and fortitude to maintain his standards. This specific practice is probably not a part of the virtue of temperance for most other moral agents; his practices may be challenged when he learns of the ecological significance of locally grown foods. Each virtue looks and behaves differently in each moral agent yet is identifiable by the function it manifests in relationship with the other virtues.[26]

Objections to the Virtues Ecology Metaphor

One objection to this ecology of virtues metaphor is that human persons have moral agency, whereas ecosystems do not.[27] Moral agents pursue goals and make decisions, and have intention and will. Ecosystems produce by-products and demonstrate responsiveness, but not in a conscious, moral way. This is a fair observation. Still, perhaps there is room for some flexibility here, in at least two directions.

The "agency" of ecosystems has been discussed in environmental ethics,[28] and the question of whether human persons truly make fully free, volitional decisions has been questioned in light of developments in cognitive psychology. Although both of these realms of inquiry need further attention, the fact remains that the complexity attributed to moral agency in ecological discourse can help Catholic virtue ethics and moral theology in general to consider the category of agency with more subtlety. Notions of causality in ecological studies differ from those of Catholic ethics.[29] Given ecology's heightened awareness of complex interrelations, a weaker and more widespread causality is acknowledged. This is summarized in the ecological truism that one can never do *only* one thing. How might this broader, weaker, and more complex causality help our virtues ecology?

Consider the example of invasive species. A single set of living beings introduced into a bioregion can dramatically and permanently alter its ecosystem. Invasive species' roles in an ecosystem are too many and too minute for us to perceive, much less to control. But when we account for broad and weak causality, we can trace many more changes back to the arrival of an invasive species. Similarly, a single event can begin unpredictable chain reactions of consequences within the moral character of a human person. Consider an instance of violence. It can appear from outside a person's agency to wreak havoc on that person's internal world. Physical, emotional, spiritual, and structural forms of violence can overwhelm on impact. Causality is easy to recognize then. But such events can also appear quietly, seeding their effects to sprout later. Victims of violence may find that their moral character has difficulty recovering its balance, and they may not even be able to recognize why this is. Considered in this way, a virtues ecology offers even more reasons to address violence in all its forms (including poverty). It can help us remember to think of the nature of causality in moral development in a way that remembers the subtleties and systemic changes that are the result of broad, wide, and even diffuse networks of causes.

In conclusion, a virtues ecology helps us recognize the limits of moral agents' own powers of self-determination. We play significant roles in each other's character formation, and, as we saw in our discussion of the virtue of wonder, God plays a significant role in a Catholic virtues ecology. This approach may help us recognize the nestedness, the openness, the interrelations, the sacred, and, in short, the wildness that is our continual moral growth and invitation.

Notes

1. See Lynn White, "The Historical Roots of Our Ecologic Crisis," *Science* 155, no. 3767 (March 10, 1967): 1203–7; Leonardo Boff, *Cry of the Earth, Cry of the Poor* (Maryknoll, NY: Orbis Books, 1997), 63; Roger S. Gottlieb, *A Greener Faith: Religious Environmentalism and Our Planet's Future* (Oxford: Oxford University Press, 2006), 36; Dieter Hessel and Larry Rasmussen, eds., *Earth Habitat: Eco-Injustice and the Church's Response* (Minneapolis: Fortress Press, 2001), 187–89; Willis Jenkins, *Ecologies of Grace: Environmental Ethics and Christian Theology* (Oxford: Oxford University Press, 2008), esp. 3–18; Luke Timothy Johnson, "Caring for the Earth: Why Environmentalism Needs Theology," *Commonweal* 132, no. 13 (July 15, 2005): 16–20; Catherine Keller, "The Energy We Are: A Meditation in Seven Pulsations," in *Cosmology, Ecology, and the Energy of God,* ed. Donna Bowman and Clayton Crockett (New York: Fordham University Press, 2011), 12; James A. Nash, "Ecological Integrity and Christian Political Responsibility," *Theology and Public Policy* 1 (Fall 1989): 32–48; Nancy M. Rourke, "Prudence Gone Wild: Catholic Environmental Virtue Ethics," *Environmental Ethics* 33, no. 3 (September 1, 2011): 249; and Rosemary Radford Ruether, *Gaia & God: An Ecofeminist Theology of Earth Healing* (San Francisco: HarperSanFrancisco, 1992).

2. For example, see Jan Tullberg, "Integrity: Clarifying and Upgrading an Important Concept for Business Ethics," *Business and Society Review* 117, no. 1 (March 1, 2012): 89 (emphasis mine). The popularity of this sort of definition is demonstrated in Wikipedia's page defining integrity, which says (in its seventh paragraph as of September 27, 2013): "In discussions of behavior and morality, an individual is said to possess the virtue of integrity if the individual's actions are based on an internally consistent framework of principles."

3. William Werpehowski's 2007 presidential address to the Society of Christian Ethics offers a definition of integrity that describes this inside-outwards directedness: "integrity or wholeness of the moral life, taken here to be a truthful self-understanding that is embodied in one's acts and relations in the world." William Werpehowski, "Practical Wisdom and the Integrity of Christian Life," *Journal of the Society of Christian Ethics* 27, no. 2 (Fall–Winter 2007): 55–56.

4. For example, see Werpehowski, "Practical Wisdom and the Integrity of Christian Life," 56, where he notes: "I imagine integrity to consist of a kind of self-renewing perseverance."

5. Boff, *Cry of the Earth, Cry of the Poor*, 4.

6. Leonardo Boff, *Ecology and Liberation: A New Paradigm* (Maryknoll, NY: Orbis Books, 1995), 38.

7. Steven Bouma-Prediger, "Creation Care and Salvation," *Vision* 9, no. 1 (Spring 2008): 18.

8. Sallie McFague, *The Body of God: An Ecological Theology* (Minneapolis: Augsburg Fortress, 1993), 121.

9. Louke van Wensveen has noticed this. See Louke Van Wensveen, *Dirty Virtues: The Emergence of Ecological Virtue Ethics* (New York: Humanity Books, 1999), 5. See, for example, the writings of Rachel Carson—particularly the earlier sections of *The Edge of the Sea* (Boston: Houghton Mifflin, 1955), and those of Aldo Leopold, Henry David Thoreau, and John Muir. This is even true of ethicists who are careful *not* to write as virtue ethicists! For example, see Laura Westra and Willis Jenkins (whose book specifically avoids promoting any particular approach in order to present the broader discourse more fairly). Laura Westra, *Living in Integrity: A Global Ethic to Restore a Fragmented Earth* (Lanham, MD: Rowman and Littlefield, 1998) and Jenkins, *Ecologies of Grace*, esp. 12.

10. One could also name other virtues whose strengthening would enhance our capacity for wonder (such as attentiveness and awe).

11. Diana Fritz Cates, "The Virtue of Temperance," in *The Ethics of Aquinas,* ed. Stephen J. Pope (Washington, DC: Georgetown University Press, 2002), 322.

12. Thomas Aquinas, *Summa Theologiae*, II-II, q. 141, aa. 4–5.

13. Cates, "Virtue of Temperance," 324.

14. Aquinas, *Summa Theologiae* II-II, q. 141.

15. Aquinas, *Summa Theologiae*, I-II, q. 57, a. 5.

16. This is not to say that this moral agent determines exclusively where God and world meet—only where they meet uniquely in her own actualization or locatedness.

17. "Ecology studies interactions among organisms and between organisms and their environment in nature and is also concerned with the effects that organisms have on the inanimate environment." Lawrence B. Slobodkin, *A Citizen's Guide to Ecology* (New York: Oxford University Press, 2003), 3. Examples of such systems of interrelationality include systems of energy exchange, of nutrient cycles, of succession of organisms, of carbon, of chemical cycles

and of power. For more on these, see Howard T. Odum, *Environment, Power, and Society for the Twenty-First Century: The Hierarchy of Energy* (New York: Columbia University Press, 2007) and Holmes Rolston III, *Environmental Ethics: Duties and to and Values in the Natural World* (Philadelphia: Temple University Press, 1988), esp. 180.

18. This section draws on observations and conclusions of ecologists, particularly Howard T. Odum, a pioneer in ecological studies. Other useful resources for this section are Douglas W. Larson, *Cliff Ecology: Pattern and Process in Cliff Ecosystems*, Cambridge Studies in Ecology (Cambridge: Cambridge University Press, 2000); Edward T. Wimberley, *Nested Ecology: The Place of Humans in the Ecological Hierarchy* (Baltimore: Johns Hopkins University Press, 2009); Lawrence B. Slobodkin, *A Citizen's Guide to Ecology* (New York: Oxford University Press, 2003); Richard Karban, *How to Do Ecology: A Concise Handbook* (Princeton, NJ: Princeton University Press, 2006); and Frank R. Spellman, *Ecology for Nonecologists* (Lanham, MD: Government Institutes, 2008).

19. Howard T. Odum, *Environment, Power and Society for the Twenty-First Century: The Hierarchy of Energy* (New York: Columbia University Press, 2007), 59. Systems "such as seas, cities and savannahs have structures and processes that blend into adjacent nature, often without discontinuities and only rarely with distinct boundaries."

20. Howard T. Odum, *Systems Ecology: An Introduction* (New York: Wiley-Interscience, 1983), 3.

21. Ibid., 17. This observation is at the foundation of systems ecology. For the purposes of our use of this ecosystem metaphor, it will be important not to concede that chosen points of view are "arbitrary." In ethics decisions about points of view are anything but arbitrary.

22. As Kevin O'Brien has pointed out, this choice is one moralists also make, and it involves a trade-off between scale and resolution. For more, see his excellent chapter on scale (chap. 4) in Kevin O'Brien, *An Ethics of Biodiversity: Christianity, Ecology, and the Variety of Life* (Washington, DC: Georgetown University Press, 2010), 79ff. For a useful discussion of problems involved in this choice among ecologists, see also Larson, *Cliff Ecology,* 1–17.

23. See, for example, Daryl Trimiew, "Presidential Address," Annual Meeting of the Society of Christian Ethics (January 8–11, 2009).

24. For example, Laura Westra does not claim that protecting ecosystems' integrity is likely to help individual humans cultivate the virtue of integrity. She wants us to respect integrity, but she does not say she wants us to have it. Westra, *Living in Integrity*, 240, 244.

25. Louke van Wensveen has made this argument as a critique of Westra's work. See Louke Van Wensveen, "Ecosystem Sustainability as a Criterion for Genuine Virtue," *Environmental Ethics* 23, no. 3 (September 1, 2001): 239–40.

26. This point touches on debates about the unity of the virtues, which time and space prevent engaging here.

27. See Rolston's discussion in *Environmental Ethics*: "The organism is one kind of survival unit, as the liver is not. The ecosystem is another: a comprehensive, critical survival unit without which organisms cannot survive. The patterns (energy flow, nutrient cycles, succession, historical trends) to which an organism must 'tune in' are set 'upstairs,' though there are feedback and feedforward loops, and system-level patterns are altered by creativity arising from individual level mutations and innovations. . . . The community forces are prolific, though they are also stressful forces from the perspective of the individual." Rolston, *Environmental Ethics*, 180.

28. This is touched on in Lawrence Johnson, "Toward the Moral Considerability of Species and Ecosystems," *Environmental Ethics* 14 (Summer 1992): 145–57, and Harley Cahen, "Against the Moral Considerability of Ecosystems," *Environmental Ethics* 10 (Fall 1998): 195–216.

29. Note: I speak here of causality, not of intention, which is a separate problem.

Unleashing Catholicism's Stranded Assets in the Fight for Just Sustainability

Christine Firer Hinze

In our fractious contemporary world, ecology and economy connect with each other and connect us as never before.[1] Even in today's highly technologized and financialized global markets, economy's originating, material relationship to ecology remains foundational.[2] "We live," writes E. O. Wilson, "by both a market economy—necessary for our welfare on a day-to-day basis—and by a natural economy, necessary for our welfare (indeed, our very existence) in the longterm."[3] Given this, economic understanding and responsibility require ecological understanding and responsibility, and vice versa, a fact that mainstream economics is only beginning to take into account.[4]

Writ small, economy and ecology permeate and shape the concrete conditions and possibilities of people's daily lives. Writ large, they constitute huge, interacting metasystems, complex and difficult to comprehend. Both exert enormous influence over human lives; human activity influences both. Both systems are subject to changes and can produce effects that elude human prediction or intention. And given how tightly the two have become intertwined, shifts and effects in the economic sphere reverberate in the ecological sphere, and vice versa.[5] This essay first delineates central notions of economy and ecology, with attention to the notions of risk, vulnerability, and moral hazard. It then presents Catholic social teaching on sustainability and argues that this tradition is underutilized, asking why this is so and what can be done about it. The final section explores what conversion and solidarity have to do with just sustainability.

Economies and Ecologies at Risk

The connections between economy and ecology extend also to their vulnerabilities.[6] Few experts today disagree that modern economies are leveraging, contaminating, and depleting basic natural resources at rates that threaten to undermine the conditions for future economic activity. Evidence for mounting ecological degradation in the modern era is virtually indisputable.[7] And evidence is accumulating that humanly generated or exacerbated *environmental scarcity*—the endangerment or extinction of animal and plant species, the depletion of mineral and fossil fuel resources, and climate degradation and destabilization—is approaching crisis levels that, unless reversed or remediated, threaten earth's habitats and species' survival.[8]

As for the global economy, despite the continual ratcheting up of worker productivity and Gross Domestic Product outputs, lingering effects of the recent financial meltdown, rising inequality, and high rates of poverty all suggest dysfunction. In the United States, trends in average household wealth and income between 2003 and 2013 reveal stunning disparities of economic gain and pain. Millions in the lowest 20 percent of the population lost, on average, 75 percent of their net worth. Incomes also suffered. "Between 2007 to 2011, the average real income of households in the bottom four income deciles declined by 9 percent," while averages in the top 5 percent held steady.[9] Global statistics tell an even bleaker story. "Using market exchange rates, the richest population quintile gets 83 percent of global income with just a single percentage point for those in the poorest quintile." Progress is occurring, but at current rates "it would take more than 800 years for the bottom billion to achieve 10 percent of global income." Children and youth suffer disproportionately, with approximately 50 percent worldwide below the USD 2.00/day international poverty line. The worst recession-related effects—in areas such as employment, price, and food security—accrue to those already least able to survive them.[10]

Economic and ecological problems, moreover, are embedded in huge, intertwining systems of enormous complexity. The "nonlinear behavior"[11] to which such complex systems are prone exhibits "uncertainty, intermittently long time lags between perturbation and response, and the potential to 'flip' abruptly from one state to another."[12] Ironically, absent a blatant crisis, these features make it easy for leaders to ignore evidence of dysfunction and to forestall policy responses.[13]

We can see the mutually destabilizing impacts of complex economic and ecological systems in current global dynamics surrounding carbon and water. In 2013, researchers led by the Nobel-laureate economist Andrew Stern warned of a "carbon bubble" threatening global financial markets.[14] Despite accumulating risk, investors continued to bet that countries would not adhere to carbon emissions targets. Expanding energy markets were heading into a dangerous double bind between economy-degrading "financial overshoot" caused by overvaluing oil, coal, and gas reserves held by fossil-fuel companies, and climate-degrading "ecological overshoot" should these reserves actually be used. Driving this perilous behavior is the narrowly focused profit seeking that financial markets incentivize, and an ethos of "short-termism," exemplified by analysts' dictum that investors "should ride the train until just before it goes off the cliff." The problem is that everyone "thinks they are smart enough to get off in time, but not everyone can get out of the door at the same time. That is why you get bubbles and crashes."[15] Unless this pattern is altered, warns John Fullerton, "Civilization is facing our $20 trillion big choice—our investments or our planet."[16]

Potentially more serious is a crisis of scarcity looming for the freshwater (increasingly drawn from nonrenewable, deep-earth aquifers) needed for global food production. Countries including Mexico, Pakistan, and Iran are already suffering water-driven declines in grain harvests. Now, "aquifer depletion also threatens harvests in the big three grain producers—China, India and the United States—that together produce half of the world's grain. The question is not whether water shortages will affect future harvests in these countries, but rather when they will do so."[17]

Three Meta-Level Responses

The theme of this book, "just sustainability," asserts a bold imperative: to build ecologically sustainable economies that provide economic sufficiency for all members. Among contemporary efforts in this direction, three broad approaches stand out.[18]

1. Change economic policy and practice. This policy-oriented line of approach advocates requiring businesses to calculate, disclose, and take appropriate responsibility for the social and ecological risks, impacts, and costs of economic activity. "Full cost accounting" aims to monetize and internalize as costs, so-called "externalities"—impacts on community, society, and the environment.[19] One popular example of this approach is the "triple bottom line"—"profits, people, and the planet"—approach to business.[20]

Transparency and disclosure of risk in financial regulation are similarly targeted. Disclosure, advocates contend, "should also include environmental risks such as physical damage from the changing environment, regulatory risks from implementing costly environmental regulations or fines, or legal liability issues related to a firm's environmental performance."[21] Combating corruption and exploitation in poorer nations by requiring corporate and governmental transparency concerning resource extraction is another pressing agenda.[22] Repeated economic crises and growing ecological concerns have heightened calls for "integrating environmental risk disclosure more directly into official national and international financial standards and regulations," and for more effective enforcement. Such strategies aim to provide a buffer against future financial crises, while "reorienting financial markets towards a more environmentally sustainable future."[23]

To be effective, policies must respect the complex workings of both economic and ecological systems. Addressing complex system behavior through public policy and governance is tricky work, especially in polarized political situations, particularly when there are no clear "silver bullet" solutions to most ecological problems. But complexity does not abrogate the responsibility to act. "When uncertainty, unpredictability and lags shroud future outcomes . . . policy makers should generally adopt a precautionary or prudential approach to system governance."[24] Catholic social teaching, discussed below, advocates the "precautionary principle" as a means to take active, but provisional, steps that can be revised in light of new data.[25]

Policy reforms also must control for moral hazard. In the years preceding the recent financial crisis, inadequate regulation, short-termism, compounding product complexity, and system opacity helped create enormous moral hazard.[26] Many individuals and institutions succumbed to optimistic market forecasts and unsustainable rates of profit seeking. The destructive results of foolish private risk taking were eventually visited upon, and largely paid for by, the public. In effect, "The taxpayers of many countries are the unwilling insurers for markets," writes Andrew Beattie. Yet although "insurers profit by selling policies, taxpayers gain little or nothing for footing the bill on the policies and bailouts."[27] Incentivizing compliance and deterring corruption requires vigilant attention to moral hazard in all areas of regulation and practice.

2. Change the economic paradigm. This second response goes further, calling for a paradigm shift from an economics of growth to an economics of sufficiency and sustainability.[28] Ecological economics, which employs a sustainability paradigm, attempts to address a classic economic problem—scarcity—in its full ramifications. Neoclassical economists prioritize efficient resource allocation among producers to promote growth, and deal with distribution by assuming that "a rising tide lifts all boats."[29] But neoclassical economics, argues Eric Zencey, insufficiently accounts for the fact that "the creation of wealth has physical constraints, set by ecosystem limits, physical laws, and the limits of the technology we currently employ."[30]

Technology can improve efficiency. Borrowing can add virtual space for growth. But eventually, a debt-inflated "infinite growth economy runs into the limits of a finite world."[31] Economies that allow debt—financial or environmental[32]—to grow faster than wealth can be created or renewed are subject to crises and destructive breakdowns, for which nonelites inevitably pay the steepest price. To prevent this, "we must balance claims on future production of wealth with the economy's power to produce that wealth."[33] To that end, ecological economists squarely face limits to growth by attending to the scale, or size, of the economy—and its capacity to provide for all members—relative to its containing, sustaining ecosystem.[34]

3. Change the power equation. Rebecca Todd Peters criticizes the "social development" model of globalization that dominates both United Nations and Catholic social discourse, which, she argues, lacks adequate emphasis on ecological sustainability or the democratic redistribution of power.[35] Peters's call for a "democratizing" and "earthist" redirection of global development jibes with recent movement toward making an "option for the poor and option for the earth" central to Catholic thought and practice.[36] For advocates of this third, more radical approach, enacting a just-sustainability paradigm requires changed relations and priorities in at least four fundamental areas.

New Ways of Assigning Value. A just sustainability model reorients assumptions about economic and ecological value. Kevin Gibson, for example, interrogates quantitative and Western-cultural assumptions underlying the "triple bottom line" (known as 3BL) metric. 3BL's monetizing strategy, Gibson argues, inevitably undervalues "intangible assets or deeply held values" like beauty, the sacred, indigenous customs, relations with nature, public goods, natural nonmarket goods, and unpaid care work. 3BL supporters' confidence that more sophisticated accounting techniques can resolve these difficulties bespeaks the limits of a paradigm entrenched in "Western notions of property, ownership and the primacy of the market."[37] Gibson advocates inverting 3BL's starting point, "so sustainability discussions begin by establishing shared values (fungible and not) among all stakeholders," and then creating rules for analysis and action that reflect these values.

New Political Strategies. Most US scholars and activists, observe Gar Alperovitz and Steve Dubb, conceive of political change as either "reformist" or "revolutionary." Alperovitz and Dubb advocate an alternative model, "*evolutionary reconstruction*—systemic institutional transformation of the political economy that unfolds over time."[38] In the face of the "longer-term challenges being created by issues of political stalemate, of scale, and of ecological, resource and climate change," Alperovitz and Dubb champion diverse community experiments geared toward building a different political economy, one that "emphasizes sustainable, economically and democratically healthy local communities that are anchored by wealth-democratizing strategies, policies and institutions."[39] Their envisaged "pluralistic commonwealth" or "community-sustaining system" rests on four axioms: democratization of wealth; community as a guiding theme; decentralization; and democratic planning to support community and longer-term economic, democracy-building, and ecological goals.[40] In the quest for this renovated polity, "state and local experimentation . . . may suggest new democratizing approaches for larger-scale system-defining institutions when the appropriate political moment occurs."[41]

New Energies for Transformative Action. Despite a variety of attempts to address complex problems through both governmental and nongovernmental means, many US citizens today are demoralized and unconvinced that such efforts have any lasting impact.[42] Unless people can envisage what veteran community organizer Marshall Ganz calls "the plausibility of the possible rather than the inevitability of the probable,"[43] ecological and economic problems can overwhelm, paralyze, and evoke strong desires to be distracted or soothed.[44] Catering to those desires, consumerist culture drains energies for civic engagement with great efficiency, monopolizing people's time and attention with all that the "work-spend cycle" promises and demands.[45]

What counteracts civic stasis? Psychologists and community organizers highlight two "essential psychological building blocks": "individual self-respect" and "collective self-confidence." These traits enable people to believe they deserve empowerment and that, together, they can succeed in procuring it.[46] In this vein, the political theorist Jeffrey Stout illumines broad-based, democratic community organizations' capacity to generate renewable energies for long-haul transformative work.[47] Ganz highlights grassroots leaders' responsibility to "mobilize the emotions that make agency possible."[48] To overcome "action barriers" like inertia, apathy, fear, isolation, and self-doubt, good leaders cultivate emotions that are "action catalysts": urgency, indignation at injustice, hope (fed by "direct experiences of credible solutions," small successes and victories, and people able to inspire hope in others), solidarity (fed by community connections and an ethos of "belovedness"), and efficacy, a sense that "you can make a difference," fed by focusing on "what we can do," and by recognizing and celebrating accomplishment and accountability.[49]

New Priorities and Resource Allocations. At present, richer communities' refusal to undertake their share of the burdens of ecological and economic interdependence exerts enormous drag on progress toward change. (This is a problem about which the Catholic social teaching has strong words for industrialized nations, as will be shown in the next section.) Given current global economic and ecological trajectories, continuing business—and consumption—as usual will only spell more disruption, especially for the poor, and exacerbate threats to everyone's future survival. We thus face, Homer-Dixon contends, this urgent question:

> How do we design our economies to provide what we need, without increasing our throughput? We don't have a clue. We need social science research on how to restructure our economies, both nationally and globally. We need an energy research program. These should be Manhattan Project–scale research programs, and we're not doing it.[50]

This frustrating impasse evokes Martin Luther King Jr.'s 1964 observation:

> There is a sort of poverty of the spirit which stands in glaring contrast to our scientific and technological abundance. . . . If we are to survive today, our moral and spiritual "lag" must be eliminated. Enlarged material powers spell enlarged peril if there is not proportionate growth of the soul.[51]

To address this lag, we must find ways to bring ethical and religious wisdom into more fruitful contact with scientific knowledge and technological know-how, in order to generate and sustain urgently needed action for change.

Mining and Mobilizing the Catholic Social Teaching

What can Catholicism in particular contribute to the formidable struggle for just sustainability? One significant resource is the modern Catholic social teaching (CST),[52] the body of Catholic teaching, writing, and action that since the later nineteenth century has championed "an integral and solidary humanism capable of creating a new social, economic and political order, founded on the dignity and freedom of every human person, to be brought about in peace, justice and solidarity."[53] A hallmark of CST is its conviction that the work of economic and ecological justice is entrusted to all humanity and therefore demands dialogue and collaboration among "all people of good will."[54] One thus finds many contact points between CST and the secular economic and ecological discourse and movements discussed in this chapter.

Grounded in a God-centered, sacramental vision of reality, and drawing on scripture, tradition, and careful analysis of "the signs of the times,"[55] modern Catholic social teaching encompasses a set of principles intended to promote and protect the life and dignity of persons within their social and natural contexts and communities.[56] Central themes of CST include *reverence for human dignity, respect for human life*, and commitment to ensuring the material and social conditions for its flourishing; a relational view of reality that emphasizes global interdependence and the *common good;* a multi-associational vision of political life that stresses both *subsidiarity*—that is, the value of locating power and decision making at local levels of organization—and an active role for *governmental authority* in ensuring the well-being of citizens and communities; an understanding of *the universal purpose of created goods* that requires equitable use of and access to the world's resources; a conception of *authentic, integral development* that sets directions for human progress that promote the human dignity of each and all, and respect the integrity of creation; and a focus on *solidarity* and a *preferential option for the poor and vulnerable* as the keys to combating social patterns or *structures of sin* that corrupt or thwart authentic, sustainable development.[57]

Since the 1960s, CST has increasingly emphasized ecology and the dangers posed to vulnerable peoples and to "the small delicate biosphere of the whole complex of all life on earth" by current patterns of global development.[58] Successive popes have affirmed the right to economic development for all. But because economy and ecology are meant to provide sustenance for *all* God's children, the fact that environmental scarcity precludes universal access to the types of development rich nations now enjoy makes current patterns of development illegitimate.[59] Bluntly, "development" that is available only to some is not development but a kind of exploitation, both of the earth's resources and of all those left out of the development loop.[60] Traditional exhortations to generosity by the rich are now joined with calls for changes in affluent nations' lifestyles, and for redistributing political and economic power to marginalized peoples.[61] As Pope Francis has repeatedly stated, an economy that benefits the few at the expense of the many and the earth is simply unacceptable.

Recent Catholic teaching, in short, eloquently supports a just-sustainability agenda. Yet US Catholics' inertia in the face of its challenges mirrors that of their fellow citizens. Although recent popes have explicitly linked pursuing just economies and sustainability to the life of faith, many Catholics either do not know about the rich teachings contained within CST or consider church social teachings to be epiphenomenal to their religious and moral lives.[62] Even for those who take them seriously, Catholic social principles often remain disconnected from either robust economic and ecological analysis or concrete strategies for change. As a result, for most Catholics, the treasures of the their social tradition remain stranded assets, and the discourse of CST risks becoming an exercise in futility—rearranging words on a melting ice floe. To remedy this, more people need to know about CST's critical insights concerning economic and environmental exploitation, and more work must be done to connect CST to astute economic and ecological understanding, and to positive strategies for change.

Unleashing CST's Assets: Conversion as Catalyst

To catalyze action for just sustainability, Catholic social principles must move from ideas to embodied dispositions and practices of *solidarity.*[63] Pope John Paul II elaborated solidarity as a prime antidote to "structures of sin" that humanly produced ecological degradation and economic injustice represent. He described solidarity as a social virtue: a firm commitment to serving an inclusive, common good. Solidarity entails *seeing* the interdependency of all peoples within earth's habitats, *judging* that embraces intelligent responsibility for those connections, and *acting* collaboratively for the shared good of people and the planet.[64] In a world of radically unequal power and opportunities, he notes, enacting inclusive solidarity further requires a deliberate, *preferential option for the poor and vulnerable,* including the vulnerable earth.[65]

But how do we, personally and collectively, make the move from ignorance, powerlessness, and inertia to intelligent, effective economic and ecological solidarity? Though less well known than CST, Catholic wisdom concerning *conversion* can help show the way. Whether the issue is climate change, feeding poor populations, or the depletion of freshwater aquifers, pursuing just sustainability is as much about reorienting people's awareness, values, and behaviors—about transforming ourselves—as it is about scientific, technical, and policy issues. An especially rich account of these processes of reorientation, or conversion, is the analysis of the dynamics of human thought, love, and action by the philosopher and theologian Bernard Lonergan, SJ.[66] Popularly conceived as a dramatic, often sudden, and thoroughgoing turnaround in one's life, conversion for Lonergan is a transformation of worldview or "horizon": a positive, qualitative shift in the perceptual, moral, and affective framework of one's knowing, valuing, and deciding. A powerful antidote to ignorance, bias, and sin, conversion for most people, writes Robert Doran, "is in fact . . . a continual, slow, and unobtrusive movement beyond the isolation of the subject, beyond a constantly self-referential horizon, to self-transcendence. And for almost all of us it has to be continually renewed."[67] Lonergan's reflections on our human capacities for (and tendencies to resist) conversion offer another set of tools for sparking and guiding work toward just sustainability.

Human authenticity and progress versus bias and decline. Christians, Lonergan notes, view human beings as built to know, value, love, and act in ways reflective of their deepest identity in the divine image—an identity that comes to fruition in truthful, loving, and life-giving relationships to self, others, nature, and God. Authentic human living, therefore, is marked by patterns of *self-transcendence* and sustained by ongoing dynamics of *conversion.* Thriving communities and institutions depend on the self-correcting processes that typify any well-functioning human endeavor: engaging in social practices yields data and raises questions about how to do things better; attentive persons pursue those questions; this leads to insights into possible improvements, and actions that modify previous ways of doing things—leading to further data, questions, and insights, and so forth.[68] The process by which persons come to see bottled water as an ecological and economic problem, and change their buying and consumption accordingly, is one simple example of this.[69] When complex human systems are informed by intelligent, continually self-correcting insights into the relationships involved, patterns of responsible decisions form, which support social and environmental well-being. Over time, economic and ecological decisions oriented toward authentic value help sustain progress, while hedging against opposing, destructive patterns that accumulate to become "cycles of decline." Decline, like progress, is "a dynamic that builds on itself," but one "yielding conditions that seem more and more opaque and impenetrable to understanding, much less to repair."[70]

What represses or thwarts the self-correcting dynamics that foster personal and social vitality and authentic development? A major culprit, Lonergan proposes, is *bias*: individual and collective "blind spots" that, over time, distort living into dysfunctional constellations.[71] Bias invariably operates "by ignoring the reflective processes of asking and answering all the questions that are raised by complex situations."[72] By evading relevant questions and intelligent self-correction, biased courses of action breed patterns that degrade psyches, communities, institutions, and natural environments. The resulting decline follows a "logic of vicious cycles that can lead to great destruction, unless something acts to reverse their downward trends."[73]

Biased logics riddled behavior leading up to the recent global financial crisis and were clearly implicated in the 2013 carbon bubble.[74] Bias is also detectible in public and private sector reactions to hydraulic-fracturing ("fracking") methods for extracting gas and oil from deep below the earth's surface, which have created a bubble of dubious optimism concerning the availability of fossil fuel while dissipating interest and investments in energy conservation.[75] Here, focus on short-term gains and inattention to relevant, further questions bespeak an "overconfident shortsightedness of common sense,"[76] compounded by individual and group bias among those who profit from fracking industries. These examples of decline testify to the compounding harms wrought when "the self-correcting potential of intelligence, inquiry, and insight" is repressed or abandoned.[77] Over time, effects of habitual failures to seek and do what is reasonable and valuable become entrenched in social patterns that recent CST calls "structures of sin."[78]

Thankfully, two other dynamics counter bias and decline: the creative power of intelligent self-correction and the avenues of reconciliation and growth opened by authentic love.[79] Here economic and social life connect to deeper energies and motivations located in human capacities for self-giving. Seen in Christian perspective, the infrastructure for human action is sustained and ultimately fulfilled by the enabling, healing, energizing, and guiding grace of God.[80] For Christians, "the reversal of sin and its devastating social consequences is by God's grace."[81] But this grace works in and through human minds, hearts, and action.[82] To combat bias and cycles of economic or ecological decline, therefore, persons and communities must dedicate themselves to the hard, ongoing work of cultivating their capacities for authentic knowing, valuing, and acting; in other words, they must cultivate their capacities for ongoing conversion.[83]

Conversion, an engine of solidarity. Lonergan's analysis of conversion illumines a promising pathway between Catholic economic and ecological principles, and concrete action toward just sustainability. Authentic living, for Lonergan, is marked by conversion in three, interrelated forms. *Intellectual conversion* moves one from incurious, superficial habits of looking at reality to attentively entertaining and investigating, in any particular situation, relevant questions as they arise.[84] *Moral conversion* transforms "the criteria of one's decisions from egoistic satisfactions to love of authentic values." Finally *religious,* or *affective,* conversion involves "recognizing that one is loved unconditionally by God, and responding to that radical gift by cooperating in the process whereby one's own loving becomes unconditional."[85] This level of conversion liberates one from self-enclosure, reorienting one's desires "from obsession with self-needs to concern for the needs of others."[86] It involves the whole person in "the decision of commitment to love in action."[87] It frees persons to engage in generous self-giving that "heals hatred and bias, and offsets the corrosive effects of stupidity and wickedness."[88]

Understood in this multifaceted way, conversion names the intellectual, moral, and spiritual infrastructure that makes solidarity "tick" by animating the commitments and practices that translate Catholic social principles into real life. Receptivity to conversion empowers people for the intellectual labor, ethical judgment, and responsible action that just sustainability demands.[89] It helps them muster hope and spread confidence that making positive change for a better world is possible.

Tapping energies of conversion also helps people connect clear-eyed assessments of current problems with what Pope Paul VI called "the revolutionary power of a 'forward-looking imagination' that can perceive the possibilities inscribed in the present and guide people towards a new future."[90] Fueling intelligent creativity, responsible course corrections, reconciliation, and forward movement in social relations and institutions, conversion, it turns out, is one of humanity's most valuable renewable resources.

Conversion, Solidarity, and the Work of Just Sustainability

Moving the economic-ecological agenda limned in Catholic teaching from page to practice requires a living bridge: women and men whose capacities for self-transcendence have been unleashed, whose personal and communal lives embody habits of intellectual, moral, and affective-religious conversion. Only such people can cultivate the inclusive solidarity—a solidarity that embraces both vulnerable peoples and vulnerable ecosystems—on which a culture capable of supporting just sustainability depends. This approach invites people to reenvision "conversion" beyond a personal stance toward the divine, and toward a recognition that love of God is inherently linked to love of neighbor. In a context of economic globalization, this also entails attention to, and amelioration of, a variety of structural sins.

Conversion-propelled work for just sustainability has room and need for every actor, every talent, and contributions at every level. Reshaping policies and practices demands dogged effort at countless business, civic, and consumer sites. Transforming the dominant economic paradigm depends on the multiplying effects of changed beliefs, values, and practices among individuals, local communities, businesses, and governments. And redistributing democratic power to create inclusive, sustainable polities requires people of all classes who will undertake what Jacques Maritain called "the sufferings due to solidarity," and Jon Sobrino, "the heavy light burden" of solidarity with the poor and marginalized.[91]

This multifocal approach reflects CST's principle of subsidiarity, which champions both smaller organizational units' ability to provide for their own flourishing and to contribute to society, and the need for larger structures of governance to facilitate and protect these functions. In line with conversion's exploratory, self-correcting temperament, subsidiarity fosters diversity, innovation, and experimentation. Pope Benedict's praise of alternative economic organizations and business practices reflects this.[92] So do Dorothy Day's personalist localism, the work of Catholic Relief Services and the Campaign for Human Development, and the community organizations described by Ganz and Stout. Subsidiarity also warrants efforts to build new forms of international governance and regulation to ensure that globalization serves and supports not only powerful elites but also all communities.[93] Theologically, subsidiarity evinces a predilection to make room for a God at work in history amid messiness and trial and error, and at frontiers.[94] "Cultures of dialogue and encounter," attentiveness to experience, and practices of discernment further equip communities for the arduous work of conversion of minds, hearts, and structures.[95]

Crucial to this work are leaders: women and men able to propose, model, and incite others to participate in transformative action. Amy Larkin speaks of "waiting for an American president to ask the country to lower our energy use by 20 percent within the year." Where are leaders of Catholic institutions issuing, and rising to, this same challenge? Leadership is also a democratically distributed charism, conferred by baptism or citizenship. So, writes Larkin, "the individual sector [a.k.a. each person and household] *can* eliminate every bit of wasted and unnecessary energy." Civic, work, and family spheres all provide opportunities for local, creative initiatives for just sustainability. Pope Francis's choices of simple clothing, lodging, transportation, and boundary-breaking forms of communication model other potent, replicable ways of leading by practicing solidarity in everyday life.

Engaging their self-transcending capabilities empowers individuals to disrupt patterns of blindness, selfishness, and irresponsibility that Pope Francis decries as

> the culture of well-being that makes us think of ourselves; that makes us insensitive to the cries of others; that makes us live in soap bubbles that are beautiful but are nothing, are illusions . . . of the transient; that brings indifference to others. . . . We have fallen into a globalization of indifference. We are accustomed to the suffering of others, it doesn't concern us, it's none of our business.[96]

But people animated by conversion burst bubbles of indifference to respond to their neighbors' suffering, and the earth's, with attention and care. They heed Pope Benedict's urging that society "take a serious look at its life style," and commit to "simplicity, moderation and discipline, as well as a spirit of sacrifice . . . [as] a part of everyday life."[97] Moved by what Pope Francis calls large-heartedness or magnanimity, they take risks to serve the poor, to protect the earth, and to advance a common good from which no one is excluded.[98] By providing ongoing, practice-oriented formation in this *habitus* of conversion, Catholic communities can prepare their members to be the bridges between their church's rhetoric and on-the-ground action for a just, sustainable world. The task does not end with the individual: it is also a collective task that must be taken up in the Church at large, in civic groups and local governments, and at state, national, and transnational levels.

Intelligent people and societies, Lonergan writes, will not "consistently undertake initiatives that destroy their underlying conditions, including natural ecological conditions."[99] Current trajectories suggest that we humans may prove ourselves, in the end, stupid rather than intelligent, doomed to dysfunction, conflict, misery, and likely extinction. Yet our species' remarkable capacities for beginning and building anew, undergirded for Christians by trust in the power of God's mercy and grace to overcome ignorance, sin, and evil against all odds, offer hope.[100] Harnessing hope is crucial for narrowing the dangerous gap, decried by King, between material-technical and spiritual-moral development. Where persons and communities embrace the joys and sufferings of economic and ecological solidarity, God's Spirit finds spaces to work and nurtures power to carry on. Drawing on conversion's deep aquifers, Catholics with their neighbors must ply the urgent work before us: to construct economies that will sustain us and our families, our sisters and brothers present and future, and our planetary home.

Notes

1. Eugene Odum and Gary Barrett, *Fundamentals of Ecology*, 5th ed. (Belmont, CA: Thomson/Brooks-Cole, 2005), 1–2.

2. Amy Larkin, "No Nature, No Business: The Costs of Climate Change and the Financial Crises," posted May 27, 2013, http://www.csrwire.com. See also Amy Larkin, *Environmental Debt: The Hidden Costs of the Global Economy* (New York: Palgrave Macmillan, 2013).

3. E. O. Wilson, "Foreword," in Odum and Barrett, *Fundamentals of Ecology,* xiii–xiv.

4. Odum and Barrett, *Fundamentals of Ecology*, 2.

5. See, e.g., Damian Carrington, "Carbon Bubble Will Plunge the World into Another Financial Crisis," *Guardian,* April 18, 2013; Charles A. McDaniel Jr., "Theology of the 'Real Economy': Christian Economic Ethics in an Age of Financialization," *Journal of Religion and Business Ethics* 2, no. 2 (2011), http://via.library.depaul.edu; Eric Zencey, "The Financial Crisis Is the Environmental Crisis," Center for the Advancement of the Steady State Economy, January 6, 2011, http://steadystate.org.

6. Sarah Steingraber, "On Ecology, Economy, and Human Health," *Orion Magazine* (May/June 2009), http://www.orionmagazine.org.

7. See, e.g., United Nations Global Environment Program (GEP) and Global Environmental Outlook website, http://www.unep.org; Elizabeth Kolbert, "The Anthropocene Debate: Marking Humanity's Impact," *Yale Environment 360* (May 17, 2010), http://e360.yale.edu. Cf. Pontifical Academy of Sciences Working Group Report, *Fate of Mountain Glaciers in the Anthropocene* (Vatican City: Pontifical Academy of Sciences, 2011).

8. On "environmental scarcity," see Thomas Homer-Dixon, *Environment, Scarcity, and Violence* (Princeton, NJ: Princeton University Press, 1997), 8.

9. Fabian Pfeffer, Sheldon Danziger, and Robert Schoeni, "Wealth Disparities before and after the Great Recession" (University of Michigan), April 1, 2013, 13–14. https://www.russellsage.org; cf. Larry Bartels, "Power to (Altruists concerned with) the Poor?" Posted August 13, 2013, http://themonkeycage.org; cf. Phillip Swagel, "The Cost of the Financial Crisis: The Impact of the September 2008 Economic Collapse," Pew Financial Reform Project, Briefing Paper #18, April 28, 2010, 18, http://www.pewtrusts.org.

10. Isabel Ortiz and Matthew Cummins, "Global Inequality: Beyond the Bottom Billion—A Rapid Review of Income Distribution in 141 Countries," Working Paper, United Nations Children's Fund (UNICEF), New York, April 2011, vii–viii. Cf. Isabel Ortiz and Matthew Cummins, *A Recovery for All: Rethinking Socio-Economic Policies for Children and Poor Households* (New York: UNICEF, 2012), http://ssrn.com or http://dx.doi.org.

11. Thomas F. Homer-Dixon, "Complex Lessons of the Financial Crisis," in *Environmental Sustainability and the Financial Crisis: Linkages and Policy Recommendations,* ed. Eric Helleiner et al. (Waterloo, ON: Center for International Governance Innovation, 2009), 31–34.

12. "Uncertainty arises from our incomplete knowledge of climate feedbacks, especially of self-reinforcing positive feedbacks in the global carbon cycle. . . . Lags arise from inertia in the climate system—owing to, for instance, the oceans' absorption of heat—that slows the climate's response to our carbon emissions. They also arise from the slow turnover of our carbon-emitting energy infrastructure. Flips appear in the paleo-climatological record, which shows occasional sharp discontinuities in ancient climate regimes." Homer-Dixon, "Complex Lessons," 33.

13. Ibid.. Critics argue that lags in global average temperature rise disprove scientists' consensus on global warming. See Larry Bell, "The New York Times' Global Warming Hysteria Ignores 17 Years of Flat Global Temperatures," *Forbes*, August 21, 2013, http://www.forbes.com; versus Alister Doyle, "Global Warming 'Hiatus' Unlikely to Last," *Scientific American*, September 20, 2013, http://www.scientificamerican.com.

14. Carrington, "Carbon Bubble," reporting on the "Stern Review: The Economics of Climate Change," http://webarchive.nationalarchives.gov.uk.

15. Carrington, "Carbon Bubble," quoting James Leaton.

16. Larkin, *Environmental Debt,* 150–51. Cf. Jeremy Grantham in Carrington, "Carbon Bubble."

17. Lester Brown, "The Real Threat to Our Future Is Peak Water," *Observer,* July 6, 2013, http://www.guardian.co.uk. Cf. Christiana Z. Peppard, *Just Water: Theology, Ethics, and the Global Water Crisis* (Maryknoll, NY: Orbis Books, 2014); Pontifical Council on Justice and Peace, *Compendium of the Social Doctrine of the Church* (Washington, DC: United States Conference of Catholic Bishops, 2004), nos. 485–86 on water as a universal right.

18. See, e.g., Larkin, *Environmental Debt,* 132–34, 147–48.

19. Herman Daly and Joshua Farley, *Ecological Economics: Principles and Applications,* 2nd ed. (Washington, DC: Island Press, 2010), 1–3, 461. Cf. Dennis King and Marissa Mazzotta, "Eco-System Valuation" (2000), http://www.ecosystemvaluation.org.

20. John Elkington "proposed that the conceptual language of sustainable development ought to include not only traditional economic terms of profit and loss (first bottom line), but it also has to look at its total impact on the planet, including both its environmental and social effects (the second and third bottom lines)." Kevin Gibson, "The Fungible and the Sacred: Reimagining the Triple Bottom Line for Sustainability," *International Journal of Environmental, Cultural, Economic and Social Sustainability* 7, no. 4 (2011): 133.

21. Eric Helleiner and Jason Thistlethwaite, "The Greening of International Financial Regulation," in Helleiner et al., *Environmental Sustainability and the Financial Crisis,* 10–12.

22. See, e.g., Tom Bamat, Aaron Chassy, and Rees Warne, eds., *Extractives and Equity: An Introductory Overview and Case Studies from Peru, Angola, and Nigeria* (Baltimore: Catholic Relief Services, 2011).

23. Helleiner and Thistlethwaite, "Greening of International Financial Regulation," 12. See also Joshua Farley, Matthew Burke, et al., "Monetary and Fiscal Policies for a Finite Planet," *Sustainability* 5, no. 6 (2013): 2802–26; Dodo J. Thampapillai, "Economic Fixes Should Not Worsen Environmental Crisis," *Yale Global Online Magazine,* October 19, 2011, http://yaleglobal.yale.edu; Michael Konczal, ed., *Will It Work? How Will We Know? The Future of Financial Reform* (New York: Roosevelt Institute Project on Financial Reform, 2010).

24. Homer-Dixon, "Complex Lessons," 34.

25. See *Compendium,* no. 469; European Union website, http://europa.eu.

26. See, e.g., Richard Nielsen, "High-Leverage Finance Capitalism, the Economic Crisis, Structurally Related Ethics Issues, and Potential Reforms," *Business Ethics Quarterly* 20, no. 2 (2010): 299–330.

27. Andrew Beattie, "What Is Moral Hazard?," *Investopedia* (2009), http://www.investopedia.com.

28. See, e.g., Daly and Farley, *Ecological Economics.*

29. Brian Czech, "Ecological Economics," in *Animal and Plant Productivity,* ed. Robert J. Hudson, in *Encyclopedia of Life Support Systems* (Oxford: EOLSS Publishers, 2009), 1.

30. Zencey, "Financial Crisis, Environmental Crisis."

31. Ibid.

32. Larkin, *Environmental Debt,* 151.

33. Zencey, "Financial Crisis, Environmental Crisis." Cf. Tim Jackson, *Prosperity without Growth: Economics for a Finite Planet* (New York: Earthscan, 2009), who notes that

markets for new, resource-conserving technologies and products will yield real, but sustainable, growth.

34. Czech, "Ecological Economics," 10; Daly and Farley, *Ecological Economics*, 59–124.

35. Rebecca Todd Peters, *In Search of the Good Life: The Ethics of Globalization* (New York: Continuum, 2004).

36. The third edition of Donal Dorr's widely read CST commentary, *Option for the Poor,* first published in 1983, was renamed to reflect this development: Donal Dorr, *Option for the Poor and for the Earth: Modern Catholic Social Teaching* (Maryknoll, NY: Orbis Books, 2012).

37. Gibson, "Fungibility," citing Vandana Shiva, *Monocultures of the Mind: Biodiversity, Biotechnology and Agriculture* (New Delhi: Zed Press, 1993), 265. See also Marjorie Kelly, "The Architecture of Enterprise: Redesigning Ownership for a Great Transition," *Good Society* 22, no. 1 (2013): 61–73.

38. Gar Alperovitz and Steve Dubb, "The Possibility of a Pluralist Commonwealth and a Community-Sustaining Economy," *Good Society* 22, no. 1 (2013): 8.

39. Ibid., 9–10.

40. Ibid., 12.

41. Ibid., 11. Pope Paul VI's *Octogesima Adveniens* (1971) and Pope Benedict XVI's *Caritas in Veritate* (2009) both encourage diverse experiments with alternative, power-sharing forms of market and polity.

42. Bruce E. Levine, "Three Things That Must Happen for Us to Rise up and Defeat the Corporatocracy," *Alternet*, August 25, 2011, http://www.alternet.org. Cf. Levine, *Get Up, Stand Up: Uniting Populists, Energizing the Defeated and Battling the Corporate Elites* (White River Junction, VT: Chelsea Green, 2011).

43. Marshall Ganz, "Leading Change: Leadership, Organization, and Social Movements," in *Handbook of Leadership Theory and Practice: A Harvard Business School Centennial Colloquium,* ed. Nitin Nohria and Rakesh Khurana (Boston: Harvard Business Press, 2010), 11.

44. On public resistance to acknowledging complex systemic problems, see Ted Nordhaus and Michael Shellenberger, "Apocalypse Fatigue: Losing the Public on Climate Change," posted November 16, 2009, *Yale Environment 360,* http://e360.yale.edu.

45. See, e.g., Kenneth R. Himes, OFM, "Consumerism in Christian Ethics," *Theological Studies* 68 (2007): 132–53; Juliet Schor, *The Overspent American* (New York: Basic Books, 1998).

46. Levine, *Get Up, Stand Up,* 140–45, 161–65.

47. Jeffrey Stout, *Blessed Are the Organized: Grassroots Democracy in America* (Princeton, NJ: Princeton University Press, 2010).

48. Ganz, "Leading Change," 10–11.

49. Ibid. Moreover, notes Jeffrey Stout, nonelites' apathy, inaction, and ineptitude are a boon to elites who benefit from the status quo. Stout, *Blessed Are the Organized*, 278. Cf. Stanley Aronowitz, *How Class Works: Power and Social Movement* (New Haven, CT: Yale University Press, 2005), 174.

50. Thomas Homer-Dixon, "Exploring the Climate 'Mindscape'" (interview), *Bulletin of the Atomic Scientists* 68, no. 3 (2012): 7. Cf. Anthony Giddens, "The Politics of Climate Change," Breakthrough Institute, February 23, 2010, http://www.youtube.com.

51. Martin Luther King Jr. "Acceptance Speech," December 10, 1964, http://www.nobelprize.org.

52. See David O'Brien and Thomas Shannon, eds., *Modern Catholic Social Teaching: The Documentary Heritage* (Maryknoll, NY: Orbis, 1992); *Compendium;* Dorr, *Option for the Poor and for the Earth*. A useful, current digital resource on CST is http://www.catholicsocialteaching.org.uk.

53. *Compendium*, no.19; cf. *Gaudium et Spes*, no. 30.

54. See, e.g., *Compendium*, nos. 1, 3, 4, 53, 84, 104.

55. *Gaudium et Spes,* no. 4.

56. An early effort to connect church social and ecological teaching is US Catholic Bishops, "Renewing the Earth" (Washington, DC: US Catholic Conference, 1991), 5–6.

57. Cf. *Compendium*, chaps. 3, 4.

58. Dorr, *Option for the Poor and the Earth,* 207, quoting Synod of Bishops, *Justice in the World*, 1971, no. 8.

59. Dorr, *Option for the Poor and the Earth*, 208.

60. Ibid.

61. See, e.g., *Justice in the World*, nos. 9–10; *Compendium*, nos. 52, 55.

62. See Tobias Winright and Jame Schaefer, eds., *Environmental Justice and Climate Change: Assessing Pope Benedict XVI's Ecological Vision for the Church in the United States* (Lanham, MD: Lexington, 2013).

63. On solidarity, see Pope John Paul II, *Sollicitudo Rei Socialis* (*SRS*), nos. 36–40; Christine Firer Hinze, "*Gaudium et spes* 'Forty Years After': Straining toward Solidarity in a Suffering World," in *Vatican II Forty Years Later,* ed. William Madges, ed. (Maryknoll, NY: Orbis Books, 2006), 165–95.

64. John Paul II, *SRS,* nos. 36–40.

65. *Compendium,* nos. 182, 449, 451–87.

66. Bernard J. F. Lonergan, *Insight: A Study of Human Understanding*, 5th ed., ed. Frederick E. Crowe and Robert M. Doran (Toronto: University of Toronto, [1957] 1992); Lonergan, *Method in Theology* (New York: Herder & Herder, 1972).

67. Robert M. Doran, "What Does Bernard Lonergan Mean by 'Conversion'?" (Typescript, 20 pages, c. 2011), 4, http://www.lonerganresource.com.

68. Patrick H. Byrne, "Ecology, Economy and Redemption as Dynamic: The Contributions of Jane Jacobs and Bernard Lonergan," *Worldviews* 7, nos. 1–2 (2003): 12.

69. Cf. Peppard, *Just Water*; also Christiana Z. Peppard, "Seven Reasons to Never Drink Bottled Water Again," *MindBodyGreen* (October 3, 2013), http://www.mindbodygreen.com. Another example of "education for ecological conversion" is the work of Annie Leonard and the "Story of Stuff" project, http://www.storyofstuff.org.

70. Kenneth Melchin, interview, Lonergan Web site, n.d. (ca. 1997), http://lonergan.concordia.ca; see also Melchin, *Living with Other People* (Ottawa: Novalis, 1998); Lonergan, *Insight,* 8, 256–57.

71. Tad Dunne summarizes the forms of bias Lonergan highlights: (1) Neurosis—dramatic bias—resists insight into one's psyche. (2) Egoism—individual bias—resists insight into what benefits others. (3) Loyalism—group bias—resists insights into the good of other groups. (4) Anti-intellectualism—general bias, or the bias of common sense—resists insights that require any thorough investigation, theory-based analyses, long-range planning, and broad implementation. Tad Dunne, "Bernard Lonergan (1904–1984)," *Internet Dictionary of Philosophy* (2005), http://www.iep.utm.edu.

72. Patrick H. Byrne, "Ecology, Economy and Redemption as Dynamic: The Contributions of Jane Jacobs and Bernard Lonergan," paper presented at the conference "Ecology,

Theology, and Judeo-Christian Environmental Ethics," University of Notre Dame, February 21–24, 2002, http://www3.nd.edu, 7.

73. Ibid., 8, citing Lonergan, *Insight,* 214–23, 242–63. Cf. Byrne, "Ecology, Economy and Redemption as Dynamic" (2003), 13.

74. See Carrington, "Carbon Bubble," and discussion of Stern report in the first section of this essay.

75. Homer-Dixon, "Mindscape," notes that in Canada, climate change conversations are increasingly identified "as unpatriotic, because the Canadian economy [along with the federal government] is now so closely tied to energy resource extraction [fracking]." Peppard, *Just Water,* chap. 8 treats hydraulic fracturing from the perspective of CST.

76. Bernard Lonergan, "Healing and Creating in History," and "Misson and the Spirit," in *A Third Collection*, ed. Frederick Crowe (Mahwah, NJ: Paulist Press, 1985), 100–109, 23–24.

77. Byrne, "Ecology, Economy and Redemption as Dynamic" (2002), 7.

78. Cf. John Paul II, *SRS,* nos. 36–40; *Compendium,* nos. 119, 193, 332, 446, 566.

79. Byrne, "Ecology, Economy and Redemption as Dynamic" (2003), 14–15; cf. Lonergan, *Insight,* 718–25, 741; Lonergan, "The Human Good as Object," in *Topics in Education*, ed. Frederick E. Crowe and Robert M. Doran (New York: Herder and Herder, 1971).

80. Byrne, "Ecology, Economy and Redemption as Dynamic" (2002), 7–8; Byrne, "Ecology, Economy and Redemption as Dynamic" (2003), 14–15.

81. Byrne, "Ecology, Economy and Redemption as Dynamic" (2002), 7; cf. Bernard Lonergan, *Method in Theology* (New York: Herder and Herder, 1972), 102.

82. Byrne, "Ecology, Economy and Redemption as Dynamic" (2002), 15.

83. Doran, "Conversion," 2.

84. By opening that horizon of questions, intellectual conversion combats bias and reorients one's cognitional life "so that questions regarding meaning and truth are pursued for their own sake, and not for utilitarian and narrowly pragmatic purposes." Doran, "Conversion," 8.

85. See Lonergan, *A Third Collection*, 29–30, 176, 179–80. See also Walter Conn, "Affective Conversion: The Transformation of Desire," in *Religion and Culture: Essays in Honor of Bernard Lonergan, S.J.,* ed. Timothy Fallon and Philip Reilly (Albany: State University of New York Press, 1987), 161–76.

86. This is, for Christians, the experience of "God's love poured into our hearts through the Holy Spirit" (Rom. 5:5); for others, it is "as if a room were filled with music though one can have no sure knowledge of its source. There is in the world, as it were, a charged field of love and meaning; here and there it reaches a notable intensity; but it is ever unobtrusive, hidden, inviting each of us to join." Lonergan, *Method in Theology,* 290.

87. Conn, "Affective Conversion," 170. The essence of affective conversion "is 'signed' in the other-centered transformation of feelings effected by symbols and guided by reflection, 'sealed' in the deliberate decision of commitment to love, and 'delivered' in the action of loving service."

88. Byrne, "Ecology, Economy and Redemption as Dynamic" (2002), 8. "The power of God's love brings forth a new energy and efficacy" that in particular, calls people "to the higher authenticity that overcomes evil with good." Doran, "Conversion," 10, 11.

89. In *Caritas in Veritate* (2009), no. 19, Pope Benedict XVI traces failures of human development efforts to breakdowns in thinking, in valuing, and in "brotherly love,"

suggesting the connections among and need for the three types of conversion Lonergan describes.

90. Pontifical Council for Justice and Peace, "Towards Reforming the International Financial and Monetary Systems in the Context of Global Public Authority," Vatican City, October 2011, no. 22, citing Pope Paul VI, *Octogesima Adveniens* (1971), no. 37.

91. Jacques Maritain, *Man and the State* (Chicago: University of Chicago Press, 1951, 1998), 207; Jon Sobrino, SJ, "Communion, Conflict, and Ecclesial Solidarity," in *Mysterium Liberationis,* ed. Ignacio Ellacuría and Jon Sobrino (Maryknoll, NY: Orbis, 1993), 632–33.

92. Benedict XVI, *Caritas in Veritate*, nos. 46–47.

93. The work of the sociologist Elinor Ostrom echoes this emphasis. See, e.g., Elinor Ostrom, "A Polycentric Approach for Coping with Climate Change," World Bank Policy Research Working Paper No. 5095 (Washington, DC: World Bank, 2009).

94. Cf. *Compendium*, no. 53: "The transformation of social relationships that responds to the demands of the Kingdom of God is not fixed within concrete boundaries once and for all. . . . [The] Spirit of the Lord, leading the people of God while simultaneously permeating the universe, . . . from time to time inspires new and appropriate ways for humanity to exercise its creative responsibility."

95. *Compendium*, no. 552; "Pope Urges Culture of Dialogue and 'Social Humility,'" *America*, July 27, 2013, http://americamagazine.org.

96. "Pope on Lampedusa: 'The Globalization of Indifference,'" *Vatican News*, July 8, 2013, 4, http://www.news.va.

97. Benedict XVI, "World Day of Peace Message" (2010), http://www.vatican.va, no. 13.

98. On magnanimity, see "Pope Francis Address to Students of Jesuit Schools of Italy and Albania," June 7, 2013, *Catholic Culture*, http://www.catholicculture.org.

99. Lonergan, *Insight*, 629, quoted in Byrne, "Ecology, Economy and Redemption as Dynamic" (2002), 6.

100. Cf. *Compendium,* no. 579. "Christian hope lends great energy to commitment in the social field, because it generates confidence in the possibility of building a better world, even if there will never exist 'a paradise on earth.'"

THE EXPLOITATION OF NATURAL RESOURCES

Reconfiguring Economic Relations toward a Community-of-Interests Perspective

Edward Osang Obi, MSP

Natural resources, precisely because they are natural and occur where they do completely independently of human agency, are constantly a source of political, economic, and social tension. This tension arises for a variety of reasons, including the uncertainty and apprehension associated with the inevitable fact of resource scarcity and finitude. Because some geographical locations are better endowed than others, resource-rich areas can be theaters of political, social, and ecological strife, and communities that inhabit these locations are often at the center of this strife, quite inadvertently. Good and strong social and political institutions are required to determine the most economic way to extract natural resources without upsetting the ecological balance, so that present as well as future generations can benefit from these resources. But this is easier said than done, because human beings have, historically, demonstrated a remarkable lack of prudence in their exploitation and use of natural resources.[1]

The rapacious exploitation of these environmental goods in the last century alone has placed a major strain on the well-being of the planet, in large part because of our understandings of economic growth. Now more than ever before, humanity is threatened with the imminent collapse of the support structures of the ecosystems that supply the stability required to sustain all earth's inhabitants. Required, therefore, is a conscious reconfiguration of our geographies of sustainability, and the economic relations that undergird them. We can do this by interrogating previous understandings of sustainability that overemphasized generational equity at the expense of generational justice. Syndromes like the so-called "resource curse" in developing countries are the result of entrenched global asymmetry of power relations—economic, political, and otherwise. Our current ecological straits require a new relationship framework in which our common interests, if nothing else, persuade us to act more like a community than as atomized individual persons or nations.

The "Resource Curse" and the Illusion of Growth

When the political economist Mancur Olson mused in the 1980s about the "mysterious decline or collapse of great empires or civilizations" and compared it with "the remarkable rise to wealth, power, or cultural achievement of previously peripheral or obscure peoples," it was in an effort to make sense of a recurrent phenomenon that defies easy explanation. Olson insisted that "if the causes of the collapse of various ancient empires had been straightforwardly explained . . . there would be no 'mysterious' decay to attract continuous speculation."[2] Numerous books since then have sought to illuminate the causes of civilizational collapse. In this realm, econometric analysis has tended to attribute the collapse of empires to persistent failures of economic development in resource-rich, developing nations. Economists have wondered over the inverse association between economic growth and resource abundance, and queried why huge incomes from oil and other mineral resources, for instance, have consistently failed to lead to a reduction in poverty or to the improvement in the lives of the people as a whole.

The answer, I believe, is not far-fetched if the example of Nigeria is anything to go by. This country has so far failed to lift itself out of poverty because, among other policy mishaps, there is the well-acknowledged fact that the military and political elite of that country have squandered successive oil boom intakes since the 1970s.[3] By some estimates, nearly half a trillion US dollars have been frittered away from the system, with no clear accountability in sight.[4] One need not speculate that the line between inordinate rent-seeking behavior and outright corruption is very thin indeed.

In contrast, resource-poor countries have been found to be less prone to the kind of policy failures that resource-abundant countries experience.[5] The comparison is usually made between the resource-rich countries of Sub-Saharan Africa and South America, on the one hand, and the resource-poor ones of Southeast Asia, on the other. Whereas the former tend to yield to the incentive to spend more on luxuries, the latter "appreciate the need to invest efficiently from a very low per capita income and they are less likely to pursue policies that cause the economy to diverge from its long-term comparative advantage."[6] The basic econometric irony is that one would have expected that resource-rich developing nations would seize the opportunity that the scarcity and consequent high demand for these goods brings, and thereby to use their mineral wealth to lift themselves out of poverty. Indeed, one would also expect that the abundance of natural resources in these nations holds the promise of sustained economic growth and development, but for many of them this has not been the case.

Weak sociopolitical institutions in these countries further generated conditions for what has been described as "voracity effects," whereby "interest groups devote their energies to captur [ing] . . . economic rents"[7] more than anything else. These effects are usually "characterised by a struggle for control . . . accompanied by distrust, inadequate information flows, a lack of transparency, and uncertain accountability."[8] The cumulative impact of the ever-present possibility of conflict within this prevailing political and economic disjuncture literally lays "siege" to their future economic development.[9]

Since the 1990s, the economist Herman E. Daly has questioned the conception of economic growth that discounts nature or considers it as merely one out of many other factors of growth. He contends that nature is not just one factor, but "an envelope containing, provisioning and sustaining the economy."[10] Natural capital, therefore, together with humanmade capital, is the source of welfare. Thus, "natural capital is transformed into manmade capital. More manmade capital results in a greater flow of services from that source. Reduced natural capital results in a smaller flow of services from that source. Moreover, as growth of the economy continues, the services from the economy grow to a decreasing rate."[11] But this is precisely what policymakers fail to see, relying rather on what William Rees describes as a mythic construct based on the "demonstrably flawed assumption that human well-being derives from perpetual income growth."[12] Thus, in the standard interpretation, the "resource curse" is believed to persuade governments and people inadvertently to act irrationally, because the most obvious economic measures get discounted in favor of boom-directed ones. Apparently, in the haste to exploit more and more of the resources, a certain recklessness creeps in with regard to the environment and the supporting ecology. These become negotiable and dispensable in favor of perceived economic growth. Unfortunately, says Rees, this myth knows no ecological bounds.

Intragenerational Justice Assures Sustainability

In the nearly thirty years since the publication of the Brundtland Report, "Our Common Future" (1987), there has been an overwhelming focus on *inter*-generational justice. Many a writer has urged caution in the exploitation of natural resources because future generations have to have at least as much environmental capital as we have now. But not a lot has been said, comparatively, about the unjust economic structures existing among and between those human beings now alive, who inescapably live on the resources of this one planet, here and now. This *intra*-generational justice has become more urgent now because of the overconsumption and obvious extension of the ecological footprint of certain regions of the world, and the unfair burdens that others have to bear as a result. There is no gainsaying the fact that "in this highly interconnected dynamic global system, cumulative or sudden ecological failure in one region can threaten human sustainability in other regions and the entire global system."[13] The intricate connections between ecology and economics are no longer in doubt.

For this reason, it would be foolhardy for some regions to carry on as if economy and ecology do not matter. In a globalizing era, their continued progress might very well be dependent on the continued productivity and sustainability of other regions.[14] It is therefore in the interest of all to denounce the lip service often paid to issues that concern the poor: issues of trade imbalance, unfair competition, and outright economic arm-twisting of poorer countries. People now see the numerous failures of the international community in meeting targets and attaining agreed-upon developmental goals as due to the absence of political will, more than anything else, in those who possess the wherewithal and power to make a difference.[15] Rees goes so far as to call for a world program of income/wealth redistribution as a way of "avoiding irreversible overshoot and 'irretrievably mutilating' our planetary home." For him, "income equalization is necessary because, apart from being morally reprehensible, gross income disparity will eventually lead to social unrest—possibly geopolitical chaos—thus making the achievement of ecosustainability impossible."[16]

How ought we to proceed? In a situation where *material* is placed over *relation*, there inevitably develops a social ontology that either ignores or obscures the importance of community in understanding justice. Needed, therefore, is a new understanding of economic justice in which, not just material distributive concerns, but also, and more important, the nonmaterial values that arise from the sociality of the human person are given the accent they deserve. Naturally, the justice demanded in the distribution of available resources to meet the needs of all people—a basic criterion both for personal and common good—has been a source of immense sociopolitical and economic interest down through the ages. Granted that global economic relations are not only between Christians, the reality is that even among those nations that gladly call themselves Christian, these relations have been practically removed from the realm of satisfying the needs of the human person redeemed by Christ, by reason of a notion of economic justice that undermines the human person. Rather than a disembodied distribution of "things," what is needed is a fundamental reconstruction of contextual social patterns, including our understanding of the human person in community.

The Human Person in Community

Traditional Catholic social thought has viewed the human person as a being created in its own right, with its own dignity, rather than as appendage to something else.[17] Human personhood, as embodied-yet-transcendent, along with our human dignity already mentioned, calls for participation in community, and in all the goods thereof. According to John Paul II's 1991 encyclical, *Centesimus Annus*, this dignity is "the main thread, and in a certain sense the guiding principle of . . . all the church's social doctrine."[18] The *Compendium of Catholic Social Doctrine* makes numerous references to "the inalienable dignity of the human person," "transcendent," and "trinitarian," which makes each person "superior to the material world."[19] In fact, the *Compendium* asserts that "a just society can become a reality only when it is based on the respect of the transcendent dignity of human persons,"[20] since in every person exists "the living image of God."[21]

In this anthropology, human dignity comes from God's generous free gift of creation and redemption, and it is this that has made all people fundamentally equal, irrespective of the personal achievements or the lack thereof.[22] There are several features of human uniqueness according to Catholic tradition. First, between human persons and God there is a permanent relationship, "which has implications for what it means to be human. . . . God sustains this relationship by divine faithfulness and love. As long as God offers divine love (i.e., grace) humans will ever remain God's image and enjoy a sacred dignity."[23] Second, St. Thomas explains that this link between God and humanity arises "in so far as the image implies an intelligent being endowed with free choice and self-movement,"[24] that is, from human intellect, free will, and power of self-determination. These faculties, says Lisa Sowle Cahill, "enable discernment of a common morality of which they themselves provide the basis."[25]

The implication of this equality is that all human persons are *equally* sacred and precious, and so must mutually recognize this sacredness in their relationships with one another. This invests them with a dignity that is not bound to the ephemeral criteria of this world, and is over and above rational calculations of merit or worth. Furthermore, this dignity demands equality of treatment not based on any such accidental criteria like race, nationality, gender, or any other human attribute, but on human *nature* itself.

God's Household as the Arena of Economic Justice

The problem as I see it lies in overemphasizing individual differences between persons and national economies at the expense of the common social nature of *all* human persons, for which community is an essential artifact. This, in fact, does *in*justice to the very essence of what it means to be human beings occupying a common household, our ecosphere.

The Greek verb *oikein*, from which we derive words such as "economics" and "ecology," espouses an incredibly capacious notion that not only denotes management of the *oikos* (household) but also connotes the activity of *habitation* of the world. The ancient roots of *oikein* constitute a spectrum sufficiently broad to include responsibility for the management of the *oikos* or household of the world in politics (secular and ecclesial), economics, and ecology. The relevance of this aspect of *oikein* to our discourse is clear, because it has to do, among other things, with the *rules* that govern the economic and distributional relationships within the human community, particularly at the crucial level of welfare or the satisfaction of needs.

The present set of household rules, and the way they are applied, has been primed to remain fundamentally unfair by excluding the vast majority of people who are deemed incapable of economic productivity as global market economics understands and practices it. There is sufficient reason to say that the enduring global asymmetry of power relations, economic and political, hardly reflects equity, fellowship, and participation of all in the burdens and benefits of the *oikos*. This is neither utopian nor beyond what has been identified as the basic human instinct for mutuality, understood in terms of "reciprocity, equality and justice."[26] Economics is a justice issue because it has to do, above all, with the crucial area of the welfare and well-being of human persons, through the production and distribution of scarce resources among all the inhabitants of this global household. It cannot, therefore, simply be a matter for private, exclusive, or elite scientific analysis.[27] It is rightfully a public responsibility toward justice, the baseline of which is to provide the opportunity for these basic human yearnings to be realized. There is a consensus, albeit with varied emphases, that unjust or unfair distribution of our present resources (or of production capacity for that matter) often means that some flourish and others deteriorate.[28]

Oikos presupposes both responsible habituation and responsibility for the habitat itself and its numerous and differentiated inhabitants. As can already be inferred from the semantic scope of the term, such stewardship responsibility was, at least, envisaged in the Jewish scripture to be *habitual*, that is, routine and a consistent part of human nature (Gen. 1:26, 28–29). In this sense the intended scope of what is included in *oikoumenè* is inexhaustible, and the centrality of human agency responsibly exercised is inestimable. Thus solicitude for the cosmos becomes the "public" responsibility of both present and future generations of humanity, traversing, as it were, the vast expanse of created reality, redeemed and sanctified by the same God, Creator.

Inclusive Ownership of Goods

One of the enduring support structures for the global asymmetry under focus is the way property rights are formulated in the individualist terms of positive law, which leaves room for the possibility that political might, economic capacity, or social advantage can determine economic right. This is an impoverished approach that needs to be rectified. Catholic theology can expand notions of property and community in important ways. Thomas Aquinas, for example, distinguishes between *usus* and *possessio*. This distinction is important for our understanding of what it means to own goods. It is clear from his *Summa Theologiae, II–II Partis*, at question 66, article 7, where he discusses theft and robbery under the virtue of justice, that human beings cannot own property absolutely, because absolute ownership belongs to God alone.

For Aquinas, property is justified only if it makes provision for the poor and those in need. Thomas immediately sets about addressing what must have been for him a most important value, namely, the responsibility that is inherent in private ownership: a person should hold his or her goods not as her or his own, but as common, so that she or he might readily give them to others whose need may be greater. In his own words, "A man's needs must therefore still be met out of the world's goods even though a certain division and apportionment of them is determined by law."[29] In saying this, Thomas makes "need" a criterion of title, and this becomes the main difference between Thomistic ownership and liberal, market-based criteria of private ownership.

There is, therefore, a twofold competence with which human beings could relate with material things: first, by way of stewardship and distribution, and second, by way of use and management of the world's resources. It would seem that Thomas did not see in property ownership the kind of exclusivity that would estrange those in need from what they need. Private property, for him, is first a determination of the unlimited rights that people have to the use of the goods of the earth (*usus*); second, private ownership (*possessio*) is natural, lawful, and necessary for effective human living under present conditions; and third, the only reason why it bears exclusivity is to facilitate procuring and dispensing, which includes the administration of goods (in charity) for the benefit of the poor. In William McDonald's interpretation, Thomas "attributes to it nothing of an absolute or unrestricted character but envisions it mainly as a system of private production and public consumption."[30]

Furthermore, Thomas makes the distinction between dominion and use, in order not to give the appearance that his teaching on dominion excludes others entirely from the fray of private ownership. His idea of common property or community goods refers to the *use* of material goods, which everyone needs to sustain life; but this, on its own, does not say anything about the extent of dominion that ownership should confer. However, certain of Thomas's emphases on the "communion" of goods portend a "communistic" availability of all things to all people, so much so that the owner enjoys no protective boundaries around his or her property.[31] In order to forestall this misinterpretation, Thomas provides a juridical definition of the scope of private ownership in this way:

> We say in the first place that he who is owner of a thing is also owner of the use of that thing. We say secondly that the real owner of a thing may transfer it to another gratis, or for a consideration or in exchange for another thing. Furthermore, we say thirdly that the owner can transfer the use and the fruit of his property. We say also, in the fourth place, that as the real owner of a thing, he can give or sell the property of the thing, or the fruit and use of the thing for all time, so he can also give or sell it for a fixed and particular time.[32]

It is clear from this that the one who owns something has, and can exercise, dominion over it in various ways including using, enjoying, and disposing of the thing owned, and not only in the management and administration of it. All these relate to the individual well-being of the owner, which it is lawful to satisfy before social concerns are addressed. However, private ownership within human competence and capacity obliges the owner not to forget the requirements of justice and charity, namely, that the rich help the poor, and that in time of need all property reverts to its natural state where it can be available for common use, in a "state of nature," as it were. In this regard, John Finnis is correct when he summarizes Thomas's view as follows:

> Everyone has a natural right to a fair share in the consumption of natural resources, and that no thing, no resource naturally belongs to some one person or group rather than another . . . any scheme for appropriating to

> particular persons or groups the management and distribution of things, though not contrary to nature, will equally be not natural, and so has moral or legal validity only by virtue of moral or legal principles and norms which, like all authentic moral and legal norms, are for *common good*.[33]

A Community-of-Interests in Justice

Justice is the crown of all virtue. Judeo-Christian scripture conceives of justice as a virtue far more extensively than is captured in our notion of the dispensation of justice. According to Ecumenical Patriarch Bartholomew, "The just person does more than comply with the law; the just person bears within oneself a higher conception of justice, namely of the perfect relationship of all things to one another."[34] Only with this understanding of justice is it possible, even probable, that a community-of-interests can be created based on a common pursuit of the good.

Christian ethics has long advocated a politics of the common good, and for Catholic social thought this requires a conversion of the whole person. Central to this is the cultivation of the stance of compassion "to create the emotional preconditions for the pursuit of solidarity," in Christopher Vogt's formulation.[35]

Christian ethics does not deny human individuality,[36] but balances this up with the equally valid human instinct for communion and community, and the solidarity that these require. Ethics is relational at core, and inevitably supplants any individualism that curtails possibilities beyond the self and the immediate. David Hollenbach has been a leading advocate for an "intellectual recognition that interdependence is a necessary quality of human existence and that this interdependence must be reciprocal if the equal human dignity of the participants is to be respected in action."[37] Such recognition should rescue discourse on economic justice from idealistic entanglement, while prodding action at the embodied level of the satisfaction of human need.

How might such an approach look in concrete situations? Nelson Mandela compares the irony of global inequality to the great social evils of slavery and apartheid, as "great scourges of our times"—times in which the world boasts of breathtaking advances in science, technology, industry, and wealth accumulation.[38] The suggestion is that this disjuncture is morally problematic. Others, such as Amartya Sen, have taken a different approach: namely, to recognize our plural affiliations, to accept that we inevitably occupy a common space, and depend on the same limited resources.[39] As such, shouldn't we be expanding ever wider the scope of our global solidarity and interdependence? Such a global ethic can be more readily attained when persons, communities, nations, and corporations are more compassionate in their economic relations with one another. Or, in light of the market's orientation toward perpetual growth, is this conviction as unrealistic as neoliberal market economists would have us believe?

Notes

1. See Donald Ludwig, Carl Walters, and Ray Hilbron, "Uncertainty, Resource Exploitation, and Conservation: Lessons from History," *Science* 260, no. 5104 (1993): 17–36.

2. Mancur Olson, *The Rise and Decline of Nations: Economic Growth, Stagflation, and Social Rigidities* (New Haven, CT: Yale University Press, 1982), 1, 2.

3. See Henry Bienen, *Political Conflict and Economic Change in Nigeria* (London: Frank Cass, 1985). According to Bienen the nationwide Udoji salary awards of 1974 were a typical case of a policy failure. With those awards the public sector wage bill increased by between 50 and 60 percent, at an estimated cost of over one billion US dollars at the time. The catastrophic inflation that ensued brought unprecedented economic difficulty, including a steep rise in unemployment and increased social and economic inequities to ordinary people and the poor. This undoubtedly signaled the gradual transformation and steady decline of the political economy of a once promising nation.

4. See Terry Lynn Karl, *The Paradox of Plenty: Oil Booms and Petro-States* (Berkeley: University of California Press, 1997). The absence of accountability is linked directly with the usual weakness of taxation in resource producers. This in turn weakens the citizens' resolve to demand accountability from an authoritarian regime.

5. See Alan Gelb et al., *Oil Windfalls: Blessing or Curse?* (New York: Oxford University Press for the World Bank, 1988).

6. Richard M. Auty, "The 'Resource Curse' in Developing Countries Can Be Avoided," Lancaster University.

7. Claudio Bravo-Ortega and José De Gregorio, "The Relative Richness of the Poor? Natural Resources, Human Capital and Economic Growth," *World Bank Policy Research Working Paper Series* WPS3484 (2005): 3.

8. Ehtisham Ahmad and Raju Singh, "Political Economy of Oil-Revenue Sharing in a Developing Country: Illustrations from Nigeria," *IMF Working Paper Series* WP/03/16 (January 2003): 3.

9. See Leif Wenar, "Property Rights and the Resource Curse," *Philosophy and Public Affairs* 36, no. 1 (2008): 2–32. For Wenar there are three overlapping "curses" that afflict these resource-rich nations: authoritarian governments, risk of civil conflict, and lower rates of growth.

10. Herman E. Daly, "Uneconomic Growth: In Theory, in Fact, in History, and in Relation to Globalisation," in *Clemens Lecture Series 11*, College of Saint Benedict and St. John's University (1999), http://www.csbsju.edu/.

11. Ibid., 6.

12. William Rees, "What's Blocking Sustainability? Human Nature, Cognition and Denial," *Sustainability: Science, Practice and Policy* 6, no. 2 (2010): 17.

13. Meidad Kissinger, William E. Rees, and Vanessa Timmer, "Interregional Sustainability: Governance and Policy in an Ecologically Interdependent World," *Environmental Science and Policy* 14 (2011): 965.

14. Ibid., 966.

15. Stephen A. Marglin, *The Dismal Science: How Thinking Like an Economist Undermines Community* (Cambridge, MA: Harvard University Press, 2008), esp. chap. 13.

16. Rees, "What's Blocking Sustainability?," 20.

17. *Catechism of the Catholic Church* (New York: Doubleday, 1995), nos. 27, 356,

and 358; Pontifical Council for Justice and Peace, *Compendium of the Social Doctrine of the Church* (Vatican City: Liberia Editrice Vaticana, 2004), no. 133.

18. John Paul II, "*Centesimus Annus*: On the Hundredth Anniversary of *Rerum Novarum*," in *Catholic Social Thought: The Documentary Heritage*, ed. David J. O'Brien and Thomas A. Shannon (Maryknoll, NY: Orbis Books, 1991), 446–47 (no. 11).

19. Pontifical Council for Justice and Peace, *Compendium*, nos. 37, 4, 34, and 128 respectively.

20. Ibid., no. 132.

21. Ibid., no. 105.

22. See Charles E. Curran, *Catholic Social Teaching 1891–Present: A Historical, Theological, and Ethical Analysis* (Washington, DC: Georgetown University Press, 2002), 132.

23. Richard M. Gula, *Reason Informed by Faith: Foundations of Catholic Morality* (Mahwah, NJ: Paulist Press, 1989), 64.

24. St. Thomas Aquinas, *Summa Theologiae: Latin Text and English Translation*, ed. Thomas Gilby, 60 vols. (Cambridge: Cambridge University Press, 2006), Prologue of Ia–IIae.

25. Lisa Sowle Cahill, "The Catholic Tradition: Religion, Morality and the Common Good," *Journal of Law and Religion* 5, no. 1 (1987): 75.

26. John Dominic Crossan, *Jesus: A Revolutionary Biography* (San Francisco: HarperSanFrancisco, 1994), 72.

27. Sallie McFague, "God's Household: Christianity, Economics, and Planetary Living," in *Subverting Greed: Religious Perspectives on the Global Economy*, ed. Paul F Knitter and Chandra Muzaffar (Maryknoll, NY: Orbis Books, 2002), 119–20.

28. See David Hollenbach, *The Global Face of Public Faith: Politics, Human Rights, and Christian Ethics* (Washington DC: Georgetown University, 2003); Martha Nussbaum, "Non-Relative Virtues: An Aristotelian Approach," in *The Quality of Life*, ed. Martha Nussbaum and Amartya Sen (Oxford: Oxford University Press, 1993), 242–70; Thomas M. Scanlon, *What We Owe Each Other* (Cambridge, MA: Harvard University Press, 1998).

29. St. Thomas Aquinas, *Summa Theologiae: Latin Text and English Translation*, ed. Thomas Gilby, vol. 37 (Cambridge: Cambridge University Press, 2006), IIa–IIae, q. 66, art. 7.

30. William J. McDonald, *The Social Value of Property according to St. Thomas Aquinas: A Study in Social Philosophy* (Washington, DC: Catholic University of America Press, 1939), 30.

31. Manfred Spieker, "The Universal Destination of Goods: The Ethics of Property in the Theory of Christian Society," *Journal of Markets & Morality* 8, no. 2 (Fall 2005): 335.

32. Cited in McDonald, *Social Value of Property*, 31.

33. John Finnis, *Aquinas: Moral, Political and Legal Theory* (Oxford: Oxford University Press, 1998), 190.

34. John Chryssavgis, ed., *On Earth as in Heaven: Ecological Vision and Initiatives of Ecumenical Patriarch Bartholomew* (New York: Fordham University Press, 2012), 163.

35. Christopher P. Vogt, "Fostering a Catholic Commitment to the Common Good: An Approach Rooted in Virtue Ethics," *Theological Studies* 68, no. 2 (2007): 405.

36. When scholars justifiably debate the possibility of a common good to which all must be drawn, it is probably because this is seen as undermining human individuality and subjectivity.

37. David Hollenbach, *The Common Good and Christian Ethics* (Cambridge: Cambridge University Press, 2002), 189.

38. Cited in United Nations Development Programme, *Human Development Report 2005: International Cooperation at a Crossroads: Aid, Trade and Security in an Unequal World* (New York: Oxford University Press for United Nations Development Programme, 2005), 5.

39. See Amartya Sen, "Global Justice: Beyond International Equity," in *Global Public Goods: International Cooperation in the 21st Century*, ed. Inge Kaul, Isabelle Grunberg, and Mark A. Stern (Oxford: Oxford University Press for United Nations Development Programme, 1999), 116–25.

By Night in a Pillar of Fire

A Theological Analysis of Renewable Energy

Erin Lothes Biviano

How do the histories of humanity and nature converge?

In an essay titled "The Climate of History: Four Theses," the historian Dipesh Chakrabarty documents an influential interpretation of the histories of humanity and nature in which these histories were largely viewed as distinct. This influential interpretation originates, perhaps, with a misreading by Benedetto Croce of the historian Giambattista Vico; but it is a famous and powerfully enduring misreading that marked twentieth-century historiography through its impact on R. G. Collingwood, who concluded that "all history properly so called is the history of human affairs."[1] Human persons remained the classic subject of historical narrative precisely as free agents.[2]

Against this current, Fernand Braudel, the influential leader of the Annales School, insisted on nature's role in the dynamic unfolding of history, protesting historiographies in which the environment was viewed as merely a stage, a "silent and passive backdrop."[3] In Braudel's more nuanced historiography, nature plays an active role in human history. In fact, nature's role was the more powerful. For most of history humanity has endured nature's power, passively experiencing storms, droughts, and floods, without affecting the earth in turn. Yet even acknowledging that "ships sail on a real sea that changes with the seasons," Braudel remained within a paradigm that viewed nature as essentially changeless—or changing at rates so slow to be virtually imperceptible.

Now the balance of power between nature and humanity is shifting at an accelerating rate. As Lynn White Jr. famously asserted in 1967, between the invention of agriculture and the "Baconian creed that scientific knowledge means technological power over nature," humans have exercised increasing power over nature.[4] And environmental historians such as Alfred Crosby Jr. further demonstrate how natural history and human history converge by exploring the concept of "biological agency." As biological agents, humanity may slaughter individual animals, alter the landscape via small-scale farming, and even trigger regional collapse.[5]

Lynn White Jr. wrote well before global, anthropogenic climate change was visible on the scientific horizon. And even Crosby's concept of biological agency, developed as recently as 1995, predates the awareness of humanity's present global impact. Chakrabarty describes this now ironically innocent awareness as "still a vision of man 'as a prisoner of climate,' as Crosby put it quoting Braudel, and not of man as the maker of it."[6] In the first decades of the twenty-first century, it is now quite clear that humanity as "the maker of climate" has taken over nature's ancient prerogative of setting the rhythms of seedtime and harvest, summer and winter. Humanity's power over the earth has expanded to the atmosphere itself.

Neither the paradigm of separate natural and human histories nor the paradigm of humanity passively enduring nature's power can be sustained. Historians join climate scientists and geologists to recognize that humanity has evolved from biological agent to geological force. The narrative of freedom in which humanity first played the prisoner is returning full circle. In the ecological suffering that is and will be caused by climate change, humanity is again the "prisoner of climate." Under the pressure of the radical new thesis of human geological agency, the narrative of freedom demands revision, and Chakrabarty concludes: the Anthropocene is a critique of freedom.[7]

The Anthropocene: The Colliding History of Nature and Humanity

Scientists and scholars in multiple disciplines agree that natural and human histories *have* converged; indeed, they have collided. Geologists assert that human action is the dominant shaper of the earth system by labeling the industrial era as a new geological era, the Anthropocene.[8] Climate scientists document the increasing scale and speed of humanity's impact on earth's multiple systems, causing increased greenhouse gas concentrations, melting surface ice, and increasing ocean acidification. Ecologists observe deforestation, desertification, and the loss of biodiversity. Political scientists identify the correlation between anthropogenic climate change and major social trends, such as climate refugees, internally displaced persons, mega-urbanization, and political unrest. Competition for contested resources then accelerates ecological exploitation and further alters the earth's geophysical contours in a vicious cycle.

Today, the risk of a global collapse of stable climate systems is a reality starkly assessed by the Intergovernmental Panel on Climate Change. The Fifth Assessment Report of September 2013 states that "increases in the intensity and/or duration of drought in the twenty-first century are likely, and increased incidence and/or magnitude of extreme high sea level is very likely." The report concludes that it is "extremely likely that human influence has been the dominant cause of the observed warming since the mid-20th century."[9]

To move forward into a renewed future, a new paradigm of freedom is needed, one that acknowledges the necessary limits of human impact on the earth and the restraint or elimination of technologies that disrupt nature's ancient patterns. Yet from a theological perspective, this paradigm of freedom with inherent limits is not new. The gift of human freedom is oriented to God's future, and its authentic exercise cannot contradict God's will that the gift of freedom be fulfilled in a history of salvation. What do we find at the convergence of these two paradigms—one pertaining to global climate, one theological? How do we theorize embodied human freedom within twenty-first-century limits?

The crisis of climate change is a critique of modern civilization and reveals the instability of a future civilization built on the apparent freedoms bought by fossil fuel. Yet a theological reading demands a second critique: a critique of the uncounted cost of those freedoms in the injustices absorbed by global civilization.

In what follows, I first retrieve a theological view of the moral dimensions of freedom that honors the limits of the earth, the limits of technology, and the claims of the vulnerable global neighbor. Next, since freedom is always exercised in concrete situations, I discuss the scale of renewable energy needed in a renewed future. The chapter concludes with a scriptural image of hope and transcendence, God in the pillar of fire leading former slaves into a new future.

Karl Rahner writes that God "has willed absolutely and attained the realization of the world's salvation, not only in the sense that he merely 'willed' to offer it to human freedom."[10] This powerful sign of hope amid the disruption of climate change also challenges humanity to transcend the current course of history with its specific energy technologies and act decisively. That such audacious hope can be realized is evident in the history of empires that have fallen, by the protest and resolve of those who reimagine freedom and creatively reshape history.

Freedom Betrayed: Climate Change and Suffering

The Enlightenment theme of freedom inspired the narratives of Kant and Hegel, of progress and class struggle, abolition, Nazi resistance, decolonization, and civil rights.[11] Industrialization itself belongs to this narrative of freedom as a quest for freedom from labor. Global warming is a bitterly unanticipated consequence of fossil-fuel technology, and so is an unwitting betrayal of the industrial age's desire for legitimate and often lifesaving improvements in lifestyle. Thus the first critique targets freedom as an "Enlightenment theme," a "blanket category for diverse imaginations of human autonomy and sovereignty" during the modern period. The industrial age has ironically betrayed its own hope for autonomy by creating the instability of climate, and the injustices of global capitalism have betrayed the hope of its underclass for sovereignty.

It must be acknowledged that the exercise of freedom depends on the stability of natural systems, just as culture flourishes during the stability of peacetime. In the Anthropocene, the *nature* of freedom itself (a phrase used advisedly) is called into question. Human civilization has occurred during the stability of nature's "long summer," the thousands of years of relatively mild weather that overlap with recorded history.[12] Modern civilization stands on artificial warmth, so to speak: "The mansion of modern freedoms stands on an ever-expanding base of fossil-fuel use. Most of our freedoms so far have been energy-intensive," avers Chakrabarty.[13] The United States Conference of Catholic Bishops concurred as early as 1981 that "cheap oil and natural gas not only powered the dramatic transformation of Western society in the 20th century, they underlie much of the material progress developing countries have made."[14]

Going forward, it is a bitter irony that now fossil fuels, far from establishing freedom, are unraveling the climate stability that has enabled human societies to flourish and within them, the pursuit of individual freedoms. Assertions that fossil-fuel use supports freedom and civilization must also now be revised, and carbon-free technologies sought. But the moral imperative goes beyond redeploying reason to invent new technologies in a similar global economy. Climate change, which most harshly affects the poor and vulnerable, is a forceful reminder that global capitalism has often betrayed those who labored, or were constrained to labor, without fully participating in capitalism's benefits. The benefits of capitalism, like the benefits of colonialism, are rarely equitably distributed. These economies were and are powered by slaves, sweatshop labor, and trafficked persons. Freedom in the industrial age meant freedom from toil, to be sure—for some, but not for all. The suffering "resulting from fossil fuel labor via the impacts of global warming mirrors the suffering inherent to human labor, and particularly to historical and contemporary slave labor."[15] Strikingly, the nexus of ecological exploitation and human trafficking is arguably stronger than ever today.[16]

Pope Francis uses the language of ethical limits to challenge unfettered economic freedom: "Just as the commandment 'Thou shalt not kill' sets a clear limit in order to safeguard the value of human life, today we also have to say 'thou shalt not' to an economy of exclusion and inequality. Such an economy kills."[17] Likewise, the carbon economy, like other environmental toxins, has a cost in human life borne disproportionately by persons who are economically poor and racially marked.[18] The most vulnerable are at risk, as witnessed in the suffering of those unable to flee from Hurricane Katrina. Their suffering is disregarded by what Patricia Williams has called the "actuarial devaluation of brown bodies."[19] The poor, the low-lying lands, and future generations are traded for fossil fuel—the contemporary equivalent of a biblical image: sold for a pair of sandals (Amos 8:6).

Climate change will intensify these inequalities as the costs of energy, food, and transport increase. Low-lying lands and nations without recourse to adaptation literally lose ground, and the future becomes saddled with the carbon debt of the present. The ethicist Michael Northcott compares these intensifying inequities to an assault, an invasion of developing nations by fossil-fuel use of the wealthy.[20] Yet all will, eventually, be affected. To continue a business-as-usual fossil-fuel-intensive civilization that disrupts the stability on which civilization depends is foolhardy at best; at worst, it is an insanely ecocidal desecration of creation.

Anthropogenic stress on the environment risks elevating the intersection of human and natural history from convergence to collision to collapse. Given that risk, the point, as Marx said, is not to interpret the world, but to change it. Collapse may be preventable—that is, if great change toward a path of renewable energy is accelerated through recourse to a truly transcendent and authentic freedom that seizes on new choices, partnering with God's grace in the task of co-creation.

Retrieving Theological Insights: The Moral Dimensions of Freedom

An Enlightenment view of freedom may have struck its limits. But a theological view has always understood freedom as a life-giving response to God's invitation to exercise transcendence in the concrete particularities of history. True freedom cannot be reduced to Enlightenment reason, still less to arbitrary choice, but is the creative response to God's invitation to become fully alive. By reconceiving limits as a foundation for freedom, inscribed in a narrative of sustainability, humanity may avoid being the prisoner of climate.

Although "the most common shape that freedom takes in human societies" may be politics, as Chakrabarty states, freedom is also expressed in economic decisions, cultural traditions, and moral choices. Likewise, freedom's limits are evident in each sphere of human activity, including the use of reason for environmental decisions. Environmental decision theory punctures the myth of the rational actor, showing the psychological determinants of economic choices. Social psychology and decision theory identify the influences that drive environmental decisions. Ecological economists question the imperative of growth, blind to physical resource flows and argue for prosperity within limits. Theological and ethical discourse analyzes the limits of cognition and behavior in ways that are not only fallible, but destructive—even sinful.

The moral dimensions of freedom include the material limits proper to creatures, and freedom's orientation to God as proper to a divine gift. Thus a theological analysis of freedom always affirms the material and moral limits of freedom's exercise. Such a reading of freedom has much to offer an analysis of the ecological crisis as the use of energy also has material and moral limits.

Material Limits as Earthly Creatures

Freedom is exercised in concrete, material situations as a moral response to God's invitation to salvation. Karl Rahner asserts, "History is ultimately the history of transcendentality itself." This is no idealistic assertion of unfettered reason because transcendence occurs in the world, in particular and historical contexts. God's self-communication is offered as an invitation to human freedom, and that invitation is accepted or rejected "in the concrete, historical corporeality of man and of mankind."[21] And humanity works out its freedom in relation to the material creation. As the theologian John Zizioulas writes, "The difference between divine and human freedom is that humans are dependent on the material and embodied order of creation for the constitution as agents." We depend on a right relationship with creation for our redemption and salvation.[22]

The contemporary context for exercising human freedom with its transcendence and limitations is climate change. Situating the human exercise of freedom in the context of this reality makes possible a renewed exercise of human freedom, guided by love of the vulnerable neighbor in history. Such love is capable of creative sacrifice for the beloved, discovering a kenotic freedom to change. This necessity, the necessity of exercising freedom in the context of a profound and heartbreaking, even terrifying and paralyzing, reality, is not an inhuman limit on freedom. The demands of the moral limits to freedom are the inescapable conditions of *human* freedom precisely because the human creature is not God.

Moral Limits as Freedom's Divine Orientation

The freedom of finite creatures is offered by the Creator God and must be shaped creatively in a life-giving way. The "spiritual movement of man in his transcendental knowledge and freedom is oriented towards the absolute immediacy of God, towards his absolute closeness."[23] Grace is a divine invitation that communicates God's own desire for a renewed earth. The history of freedom offered by God is oriented toward God and is an invitation not only to a sustainable future, but to an abundant future. In Jesus Christ, that invitation is made concretely again and again as an invitation for all to join an abundant banquet.

God makes space for human freedom by the very gift of creating free persons. Their freedom is enacted through the physical creation, the space of co-creation, a world whose future is not determined. Rahner writes, "Christianity conceives humankind's relationship to God as a reciprocal relationship of freedom, God's freedom and the freedom of humankind."[24] This history is "still running its course," and so the freedom of co-creation is an enormous responsibility and a difficult burden.

Thus the Anthropocene does not present a new, shocking ecological limit to freedom. In the light of faith, freedom has always been read as having moral limits that more profoundly express freedom as the invitation given to humanity to love God and the neighbor. It is in fact not freedom that faces limits, but freedom's unruly offspring, technology.

Technology and Its Discontents

Pope Benedict XVI has written that technology "is a profoundly human reality, linked to the autonomy and freedom of man." Thus technology is an invention of reason; it expresses human genius and freedom. Technology is a tool that "reveals man and his aspirations; it expresses an inner tension that impels him gradually to overcome material limitations." Technology is a "manifestation of absolute freedom, the freedom that seeks to prescind from the limits inherent in things." Yet although Benedict observes that technology enables humanity to transcend material limits, he also insists that, "human freedom is authentic only when it responds to the fascination of technology with decisions that are the fruit of moral responsibility." Technology must "serve to reinforce the covenant between human beings and the environment, a covenant that should mirror God's creative love."[25] In the final analysis, freedom cannot in fact prescind from the limits inherent in things precisely because of freedom's material expression—the moral use of materially expressed freedom must respect material limits.

The tension between technology and moral freedom thus immediately presents itself. Technology offers a way past material limits, while moral freedom must be a way of shaping its proper boundaries. In fact, as the philosopher Hans Jonas writes, responsibility increases in proportion to the impact of modern technological power. Modernity has made the gift of rationality more costly for the environment by orders of magnitude. There is a radical difference between the impact of a plow and the disruption caused by horizontal hydraulic fracturing, shearing underground layers of rock, saturating water tables with chemicals, and releasing toxic methane and benzene. Thus the question of moral responsibility, of heeding the moral limits of technology, becomes always more urgent, if not always answered. As John Paul II wrote in *Redemptor Hominis*, the "ascendancy of technology . . . demands a proportional development of morals and ethics . . . [which] seems unfortunately to be always left behind."[26]

The ascendant power of technology to take nature's common resources must accord with humanity's moral responsibility to serve the needs of the global community, prudently protect the common good, and respect the limits of the earth. The theological paradigm of freedom explored here requires humanity to accept limits to its technological choices without denying or willfully ignoring technology's real consequences, and to accelerate progress toward a new global energy system. The transcendence of freedom means precisely that free choices can be changed, when people are open to a conversion to reality and engage their consciences in the specific situation. Our immediate situation is the climate change crisis, and our moral choices must engage energy systems that minimize climate change and reduce greenhouse gas emissions.

Society must now choose realistically to assess and restrict the specific form of technology—fossil-fuel use—that has made so many institutions of advanced civilization seemingly effortless, but endlessly costly to the earth and its vulnerable living communities.

What are the specific, concrete choices for charting a new course in energy?

Correcting the Consequences: Choices in the Energy Mix of the Future

Models of global energy technologies for the twenty-first century predict different energy mixes, using diverse energy sources, deployment scales, speed, and costs. Scientists agree that a temperature increase above two degrees Celsius will create climate instability, ecosystem degradation, human suffering, and geopolitical strife: conditions that threaten the dignity and well-being of all life. In order to chart a path for achieving deep carbon-dioxide emissions reductions, and to remain below a two-degree Celsius temperature increase, all models agree that in 2100, at least half of all primary energy sources will need to be renewable.

How is this prediction attained? A recent study has examined six models that analyze a mix of global energy technologies that might emerge in the twenty-first century.[27] Each model predicts how coal, gas, oil, biomass, solar, wind, and nuclear energy will be used by 2100. These patterns of use are called patterns of technology diffusion, and they represent a potential global energy mix. Each model makes different assumptions about the rate of research, development, and implementation, as well as about land use, resource cost, and scarcity, in addition to assumptions about the modeling simulations themselves. As a result, each model predicts a global energy mix that includes different types of energy, with diverse deployment scales, speed, and costs. But by comparing multiple models, and finding trends within them, the study's authors reach well-grounded conclusions about the profile of energy use needed in 2100 to maintain a two-degree Celsius temperature increase.

Consider the chart on the next page. On the left, the six models are shown with their predicted energy mixes for 2050 and 2100. On the right, the same six models are shown for 2050 and 2100. The difference between the models on the left and the right is the stringency of environmental regulation assumed. The models on the left (labeled StrPol)[28] are "far from ambitious enough to reach a [two degree Celsius] maximum" increase. The models on the right (labeled RefPol)[29] simulate reductions in greenhouse gases deep enough to have a 70 percent probability of an increase of at most two degrees Celsius. Thus the models on the right are the only models that represent a viable future with a somewhat stable climate. All these models are based on 50–75 percent renewable energy sources.

The take-away from this complex graph is that if we are to have a 70 percent chance of remaining below a two-degree Celsius temperature increase by 2100, then by that time the global energy supply must use 50–75 percent renewable energy. All models expect fossil fuels plus nuclear energy to account for 25–50 percent of energy supply. Many of the models also depend on carbon capture and sequestration. This cross-analysis of technology models raises three important questions:

1. How will global society concretely achieve 50 percent renewable energy by 2100?
2. Will international governance mechanisms act strongly and in time to require and invest in renewable energy?
3. Will carbon capture and sequestration work?

Let us take them in reverse order.

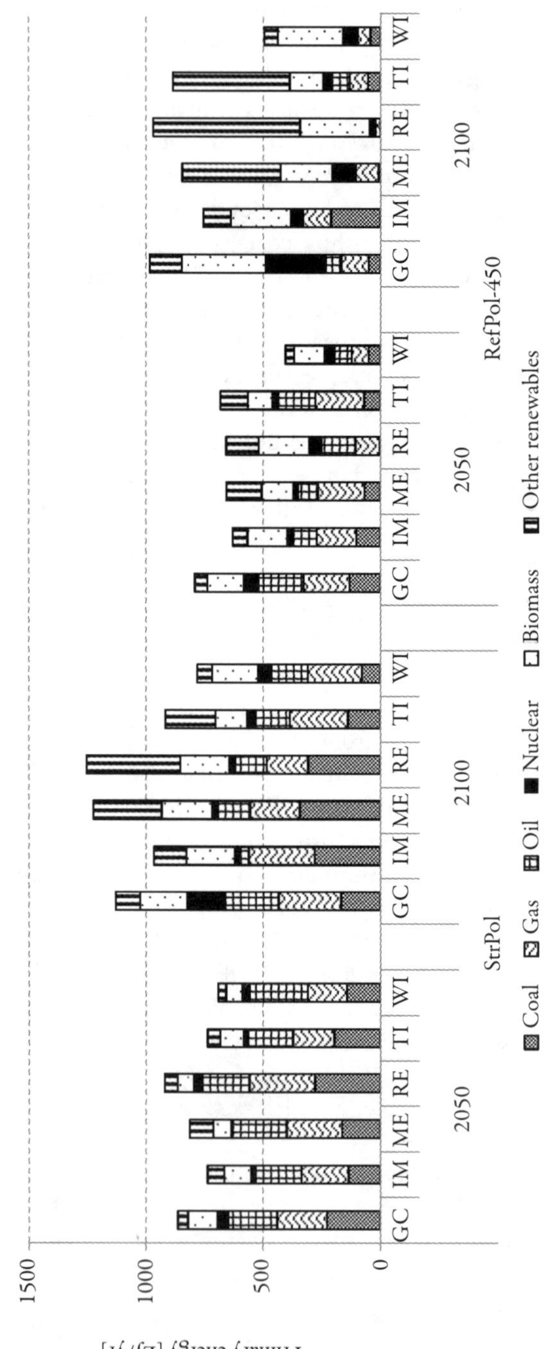

Global primary energy use in 2050 and 2100 in scenarios StrPol and RefPol-450. Bob van der Zwaan et al., “A Cross-Model Comparison of Global Long-Term Technology Diffusion under a 2° C Climate Change Control Target,” *Climate Change Economics* (2014).

Regarding the third question, assumptions about carbon capture and sequestration are deeply embedded in the models' calculations. If these assumptions fail, even more renewable energy will be needed. Additionally, critics of nuclear energy must acknowledge that without the contribution of nuclear energy, even more renewable energy will be needed.

Regarding the second question, if all nations do not cooperate in their commitments, those who seek to be the light forward into a new future—in our case, especially faith communities—must sponsor even more renewable energy. Can faith communities trust in the self-interest of competitive nations? Ban Ki-moon, the chief representative of the collective body of nations, the United Nations, does not express hope for this outcome.

Regarding the first question, a now-classic article published in 2004 by Stephen Pacala and Robert Socolow demonstrates that we have the needed technologies now.[30] It is time to use the currently available technology to leave the wasteland of an energy regime that undermines society's well-being.

Human actions have consequences. This is both a climatic reality and a theological datum. Indeed, Rahner acknowledges that "God . . . burdens man with the grace and the responsibility for his own accountable acts."[31] That burden lies heavy on the decision makers of this generation. Change will be difficult. Making the transition to renewable energy may even seem like a Galilean journey.[32] Rapidly transitioning to renewable energy means accepting the Galilean journey of suffering, struggling to change accepted and comfortable habits, making a sacrificial redirecting of resources, and confronting entrenched power—literally, the energy and power systems. The Galilean journey means change, uncertainty, lost income, investment portfolios in upheaval, conflicts with supervisors about commuting, changes in diets and traditional meals, shifting to efficiency and conservation from the habits of unthinking consumption. Yet the cross of this journey cannot be denied. It can only be deferred. The Galilean journey will be taken up by this generation or laid on the next, the Simon of Cyrenes of climate change.

As the climate ethicist Michael Northcott writes, the true power of the powerless is truth itself, and not simply effectiveness. Authenticity lies in part in "living true to the character of creation by bringing human making back into service of God's creation, and of local ecological and human communities." To cry out for authentic witness to the truth is not to abandon a claim for concrete agency that insists on change in the systems of political and economic power. Indeed, it is a necessary condition for it. For these reasons, Northcott calls for "proper accounting and confession" of the connection between global warming, modern imperialism, and neoliberal global capitalism.[33] This confession can be made by every modern first-world consumer. The powerless may be the first to protest, since they exist outside of the system of benefits linked to entrenched power and privilege. Good news can be seen: Their voices are already heard more loudly in corporate boardrooms, advocating for a sustainable future, from global activism efforts such as 350.org and fossil-fuel divestment campaigns in corporate governance and university contexts.[34]

Still, what can Christians hope for in an era of anthropogenic climate change? Theologically, as Pope Francis has said, hope is of God, and "God does not mislead hope."[35] St. Paul called for faith and hope to be fulfilled in love (1 Corinthians). Hope enables the struggle to continue in face of the overwhelming obstacles involved in transforming the global power system. Faith recalls the unimaginable liberating power of God recorded in the Exodus story, and sees that alongside the possibility of climate-induced disaster, there is also the possibility of an alternate future yet unseen. Faith is the evidence of things hoped for, writes the author of the Letter to the Hebrews. And love of God's earth and love for the global neighbor fuels the will, renewing the energy to struggle through the transitional desert toward a renewed energy economy.

Other theologians urge hope as well. Jürgen Moltmann points to God's ongoing creativity as a grace that approaches us as the incoming future. Karl Rahner identifies grace as the troubling awareness of a larger horizon beyond our comfortable, small island of knowledge, as the gift of questioning.[36] In this perspective, it may even be considered a grace to be troubled by the specter of climate instability, a grace to question the myths of affluenza. It is a grace to accept the responsibility invited by the question, to act decisively. This invitation is issued today by the negative contrast of global ecological suffering. Grace experiences the love of God poured out in our hearts, the presence of the Holy Spirit sharing her renewing love of all creation, inviting us to allow the earth to find favor with us.

Choosing a New Future: The Charge to Faith Communities

Faith communities are then obliged in conscience to seek ways forward out of concern for creation and the most vulnerable. What must be done?

Catholic magisterial teaching insists on humanity's responsibility to protect life and to care for creation.[37] The 1981 Statement by the Committee on Social Justice and World Peace of the United States Catholic Bishops, "Reflections on the Energy Crisis," offers principles for assessing energy choices. This document emphasizes finding energy solutions that are affordable for the poor, provide energy security, protect life, do not exploit the earth, finding the blessing of life beyond possessions, just economic distribution of benefits of energy, awareness of racial and global inequalities, and participation in decision making. Most significantly, the bishops call for the freedom to change our lifestyles. Energy savings, efficiency, and lifestyle changes are critical pathways to sustainability.[38]

Christian communities at many levels should respond diligently to the challenge of transitioning to a just, sustainable energy system, and advocating for the greater well-being offered by nonpolluting and sustainable systems. Catholics can act through their parishes through conservation and advocacy, in schools teaching about science and morality, in universities advancing the ethical and practical debates, in seminaries preparing social justice leaders, and in all Catholic organizations and interfaith coalitions.[39]

Recognizing the needed scale of change discussed above, faith communities should therefore choose institutional practices and prophetic education that leads society toward at least 50 percent renewable energy usage. Advocacy and systemic change are necessary parts of this work.

For example, the United States Catholic Bishops instruct Christians to work for the just distribution of energy and fair prices, and the transparent communication of energy sources and risks. Christians will "not only offer a neighborly hand to distressed individuals . . . they will back public energy assistance for all low-income people offered in a spirit of respect for the recipients' dignity."[40] Recognizing that the concentration of economic power in massive corporations risks granting such corporations undue political power and abuse, the bishops emphasize prudent prevention of the abuse of power through regulation and citizen participation. Such citizen intervention might take the form of "orderly protests to testimony at public hearing to consumer representation of corporate boards," as well as political advocacy for legislation.[41]

Fossil-fuel divestments—as well as leveraging positive investment—are critical options for Christians who find themselves shareholders and investors in large corporations. Indeed, investment in renewable energy is absolutely essential to reach the goals described above. Benedict XVI has already urged this transition to renewable energy.[42] The critical need to intensify investments that will deploy renewable energy at a massive scale cannot be emphasized enough. It is very likely that even more renewable energy is needed sooner than that.[43]

The Kenosis of Freedom

Faith communities must be a light dispelling the myth of carbon-based progress and integrate into their moral teaching the difference between livelihood necessity and luxury emissions. This is neither a call to asceticism nor to "shiver in the dark," but a faith invitation to reimagine the implications of authentic Christian freedom for energy decisions.[44]

Because fossil fuels ground many of society's current desires and visions of the good life, confronting the climate crisis and exercising freedom in light of its reality will mean individual, cultural, and global kenosis, a reimagining of freedom and the good life. The confrontation with freedom's ecological limits imposed by the climate crisis demands a reconfiguration of human consumption, a reconfiguration of global energy, but it is not a new vision of freedom as the always expressive, always kenotic, and creative enacting of one's life decisions within the limitations of one's concrete situation. Climate change invites the kenosis of freedom, a creative self-limiting of freedom that leads to renewal, even to Resurrection.

Following a Pillar of Fire

Making changes in institutional investments and communicating the urgency of change in wider society against the current energy regime are great challenges requiring enormous will. But history shows that regimes have fallen: Empires have fallen due to the unimaginable power of the powerless. In modern times, liberation has occurred in South Africa, in India, at the Berlin Wall, and during the abolition and Civil Rights movements. Although the full promise of liberation is still striving for fulfillment, history can point to times when a way has been made where there is no way.[45] Civil society can respond to changing paradigms of the person, the human species, biotic communities, human rights, market justice, and ecological limits, and it can confront existing patterns of governance and capital.

The stories and metaphors from Scripture can serve as succor for upsurges of collective cries for freedom. The Exodus is the paradigmatic story of the powerless whom God liberated from their crushing labor. In the present day, too, faith communities must move out of this desert waste, not looking back to the ways of the past, "the fleshpots of Egypt." Old ways, the old gods of outdated views of progress, must be renounced. Like the biblical Exodus, this is an uncharted and frightening journey into a new land, demanding openness to forms of life. The current fossil-fuel regime does not offer a viable future. It is an oppressive regime, and like the Israelites escaping their oppression, we must find a path forward through an uncertain landscape. The image of the pillar of light leading the people out of the wasteland testifies to God's will for a renewed future. As Rahner suggests: "God has offered this history as not merely a *possibility* of salvation but rather that God has through himself transformed this possibility of salvation into reality—and this in an irrevocable way."[46] Christians may look with the audacity of hope on a renewed future as an invitation from God, who leads as if by a pillar of fire.

God's creative will invites freedom to new choices. Sir John Houghton, the former chair of the Intergovernmental Panel on Climate Change, casts this choice as a way to "to chart a path for the future that quietly, radically and effectively will not only save us from the worst ravages of anthropogenic climate change but also bring about change toward a more sustainable, fairer, safer and happier world."[47] In theological perspective, God, as the "inmost dynamism and definitive goal offered and communicated . . . to the world," invites humanity to continue the forward journey of history, transcending the strictures of the past.[48] Faith communities and all people of goodwill can answer the scriptural invitation spoken by Moses to "choose life" and to chart a course toward a renewable, sustainable future.

Notes

1. Dipesh Chakrabarty, "The Climate of History: Four Theses," *Critical Inquiry* 35, no. 2 (2009): 203. Contemporary corrections to that misreading include Thomas Berry's interpretation of Vico, which interprets the successive ages of human history as defined by

distinctive types of consciousness, including the overly rational consciousness of the Enlightenment and contemporary ecological consciousness. Mary Evelyn Tucker, "Thomas Berry: A Brief Biography," *Religion and Intellectual Life* 5, no. 4 (1988): 109–10.

2. For the distinguished pedigree of natural history as distinct from human affairs, from Aristotle through the English parson-naturalists, see Donald Worster, *Nature's Economy: The Roots of Ecology* (San Francisco: Sierra Club Books, 1977).

3. Chakrabarty, "Climate of History," 204.

4. Lynn White Jr., "The Historical Roots of Our Ecologic Crisis," *Science* 155 (1967): 1203.

5. The devastation of societies as they overexploited their natural resources is documented in Jared Diamond, *Collapse: How Societies Choose to Fail or Succeed* (New York: Penguin, 2005). New interdisciplinary research further demonstrates the intersection of natural and human histories in events such as the Irish potato famine, the American Dust Bowl, the Darfur crises, and the Arab spring. Social upheaval can be plotted against changes in precipitation, agricultural yields, and other (formerly) natural conditions. Natural crises also lead to political, social, and theological crises, as the Lisbon Earthquake and the Black Death were watersheds in the history of European doubt. See Martin Stuber, "Divine Punishment or Object of Research? The Resonance of Earthquakes, Floods, Epidemics and Famine in the Correspondence Network of Albrecht Von Haller," *Environment and History* 9, no. 2 (2003): 171–93.

6. Chakrabarty, "Climate of History," 206.

7. Ibid. Chakrabarty also analyzes the limits of freedom through critiques of capitalist globalization. Although beyond the scope of this essay, for an excellent discussion of the limits of capitalism and earth's resources, see Tim Jackson, *Prosperity without Growth?* (London: Sustainable Development Commission, 2009).

8. Paul J. Crutzen, "Geology of Mankind," *Nature* 415 (2002): 23.

9. Working Group I Contribution to the Fifth Assessment Report, *Climate Change 2013: The Physical Science Basis* (Intergovernmental Panel on Climate Change, 2013), http://www.ipcc.ch.

10. Karl Rahner, "The Specific Character of the Christian Concept of God," in *Theological Investigations: Science and Christian Faith* (New York: Crossroad, 1988), 193.

11. Chakrabarty, "Climate of History," 208.

12. Tim Flannery, *The Weather Makers: How Man Is Changing the Climate and What It Means for Life on Earth* (New York: Grove Press, 2006), 63.

13. Chakrabarty, "Climate of History," 208.

14. United States Conference of Catholic Bishops, Committee on Social Development and World Peace, *Reflections on the Energy Crisis: A Statement by the Committee on Social Development and World Peace* (Washington, DC: United States Catholic Conference, 1981), "Introduction."

15. Joshua P. Howe, "History and Climate: A Road Map to Humanistic Scholarship on Climate Change," *Climatic Change* 105 (2011): 360.

16. See Kevin Bales, "The Deadly Link between Slavery and Environmental Destruction," in *Center for the Study of Science and Religion Seminar* (New York: Columbia University, 2012).

17. Francis, "Apostolic Exhortation *Evangelii Gaudium*" (2013), http://www.vatican.va.

18. Robert D. Bullard, Paul Mohai, Robin Saha, and Beverly Wright, *Toxic Wastes and Race at Twenty, 1987–2007: Grassroots Struggles to Dismantle Environmental Racism*

in the United States: A Report Prepared for the United Church of Christ Justice and Witness Ministries (Cleveland, OH: United Church of Christ, 2007).

19. Patricia Williams, "Looking for Lyricism: Black Maternity in an Unforgiving Land," in *Columbia University Seminar on Memory and Slavery* (New York: Columbia University, 2013). See also M. Shawn Copeland, *Enfleshing Freedom: Body, Race, and Being* (Minneapolis: Fortress Press, 2010).

20. Michael S. Northcott, *A Moral Climate: The Ethics of Global Warming* (Maryknoll, NY: Orbis Books, 2007), 59.

21. Karl Rahner, *Foundations of Christian Faith: An Introduction to the Idea of Christianity*, trans. William V. Dych (New York: Crossroad, 1976), 143.

22. John Zizioulas, "Proprietors or Priests of Creation?," in *Fifth Symposium of Religion, Science, and the Environment* (Vancouver: Regent College, 2003).

23. Rahner, *Foundations of Christian Faith*, 148.

24. Rahner, "Specific Character of the Christian Concept of God," 191.

25. Benedict XVI, *Caritas in Veritate* (2009), http://www.vatican.va, no. 69.

26. John Paul II, *Redemptor Hominis* (1979), http://www.vatican.va, no. 15.

27. Bob van der Zwaan, Hilke Rösler, Tom Kober, Tino Aboumahboub, Katherine Calvin, David Gernaat, Giacomo Marangoni, and David McCollum, "A Cross-Model Comparison of Global Long-Term Technology Diffusion under a 2° C Climate Change Control Target," *Climate Change Economics* (2014).

28. StrPol is the abbreviation for Stringent regional climate policies with enhanced Copenhagen Accord ("plus") pledges during the twenty-first century.

29. RefPol-450 is the abbreviation for Reference regional climate policies (Copenhagen pledges) until 2020 and global coordinated action to 2.8 W/m2 from 2020.

30. Robert H. Socolow and Stephen Pacala, "Stabilization Wedges: Solving the Climate Problem for the Next 50 Years with Current Technologies," *Science* 305, no. 5686 (2004): 968–72.

31. Rahner, *Foundations of Christian Faith*, 142.

32. Virgilio Elizondo, *Galilean Journey: The Mexican-American Promise* (Maryknoll, NY: Orbis Books, 1983).

33. Northcott, *A Moral Climate.*

34. Randall Smith, "A New Divestment Focus: Fossil Fuels," *New York Times*, September 5, 2013.

35. Antonio Spadaro, SJ, "A Big Heart Open to God," *America Magazine* 209, no. 8 (2013).

36. Jürgen Moltmann, *God in Creation: A New Theology of Creation and the Spirit of God*, trans. Margaret Kohl (Minneapolis: Fortress Press, 1985); Karl Rahner, "The Concept of Mystery in Catholic Theology," in *Theological Investigations*, vol. 4, trans. Kevin Smith (Baltimore: Helicon Press, 1966), 36–73.

37. Marjorie Keenan, *From Stockholm to Johannesburg: An Historical Overview of the Concern of the Holy See for the Environment, 1972–2002* (Vatican City: Pontifical Council for Justice and Peace, 2002).

38. Hannah Choi Granade, Jon Creyts, Anton Derkach, Philip Farese, Scott Nyquist, and Ken Ostrowski, *Unlocking Energy Efficiency in the U.S. Economy* (Milton, VT: McKinsey, 2009).

39. United States Conference of Catholic Bishops, *Reflections on the Energy Crisis*, V, "Conclusion."

40. Ibid., IV, "The Distribution of Energy."

41. Ibid., IV, "The Control of Energy."

42. Benedict XVI, "Address to the Diplomatic Corps" (2010), http://www.vatican.va.

43. The physicist Michael Oppenheimer notes that the effectiveness of carbon capture and sequestration is not currently known; furthermore, society needs intensified levels of renewable energy long before 2100. Personal communication.

44. Northcott, *Moral Climate,* 78. See also David Cloutier, "American Lifestyles and Structures of Sin: The Practical Implications of Pope Benedict XVI's Ecological Vision for the American Church," in *Environmental Justice and Climate Change*, ed. Jame Schaefer and Tobias Winright (New York: Lexington Books, 2013).

45. Delores S. Williams, *Sisters in the Wilderness: The Challenge of Womanist God-Talk* (Maryknoll, NY: Orbis Books, 1993).

46. Rahner, "Specific Character of the Christian Concept of God," 193.

47. John Houghton, Foreword to Michael S. Northcott, *A Moral Climate: The Ethics of Global Warming* (Maryknoll, NY: Orbis Books, 2007), ix.

48. Rahner, "Specific Character of the Christian Concept of God," 195.

Fostering Just Sustainability through Ignatian Spirituality

Daniel R. DiLeo

Throughout the history of Christianity, people of faith have been called to "cultivate and care for" God's good gift of creation (Gen. 2:15). In recent decades, however, unprecedented ecological challenges such as anthropogenic climate change have prompted the Catholic Church to reiterate and develop the belief that just sustainability is essential to both the active and spiritual aspects of Christian life.[1] Yet although it might be apparent to many Catholics why just sustainability requires tangible actions, how these activities involve the spiritual dimension of Christian life is perhaps less clear. Put another way, some persons of faith might be asking, "What does spirituality have to do with just sustainability?"

In order to begin answering that question, this essay first considers the concept of "just sustainability." Next, I describe what is meant by spirituality in the Catholic tradition, and why it is important to a faith-based pursuit of just sustainability. Finally, the spiritual tradition of St. Ignatius of Loyola will be described as one example of how a particular Catholic spirituality might help foster just sustainability in the world.

Just Sustainability

In the Catholic tradition, justice is recognized as "the firm and constant will to give God and neighbor their due."[2] At the same time, environmental sustainability is understood from a Catholic perspective as the process by which the concurrent pursuit of "economic development, social development, and environmental protection"[3] is inspired and animated by the Catholic tradition.[4] Given this framework, just sustainability in a Catholic context can be conceived of as the pursuit and fulfillment of actions that involve the environment and enable God and neighbor to receive their due.[5]

Catholic Spirituality

Spirituality is central to Christian life, and at its core it involves the Holy Spirit, the "wind/breath" of God, who enables people to discern God's call, "empower[s] persons to do God's work," and instills the hope that inspires people to persevere with God in their good actions (Rom. 15:13).[6] In addition to this, the presence of God's Spirit enables persons to both avoid and repent of "failure[s] in genuine love for God and neighbor" that fracture relationships and which the Church calls sin.[7] Given this understanding, Catholic spirituality has been described as "a way of living in relationship with God"[8] and creation such that "God's Spirit fill[s] us, work[s] in us, guide[s] us"[9] in all that we do.

Although all people are called to the same spirituality[10] of right "relationship with God" and God's creation,[11] the desire to live the Christian life in particular times and places[12] has led to the development of distinct Christian spiritual traditions. Examples include "Benedictine, Franciscan, Dominican, Ursuline, [and] Ignatian styles (or 'schools') of spirituality,"[13] and each tradition "emphasizes different aspects of the [one Christian] tradition."[14] Here, it is important to emphasize that different Catholic spiritual traditions should not be seen as competing with one another; rather, the various traditions should be understood as people's response to the common desire "to live the gospel life, to follow Christ fully and seriously to the best of [their abilities] and in response to the needs of their times."[15]

Just Sustainability and Catholic Spirituality

In view of the understanding that just sustainability entails ecologically conscious actions, as well as Catholics' belief that God's Spirit inspires, animates, and sustains all good actions and right relationships, it is thus clear that spirituality is at the core of pursuing just sustainability from a Catholic perspective. This is an important insight that warrants pause and appreciation on multiple accounts: first because, as John Coleman, SJ, observes, "usual accounts of Catholic social teaching"—within which creation care is a core commitment—"almost exclusively present it as a moral or ethical vision, un-rooted in the spiritual practices necessary to anchor [that teaching]."[16]

In addition to this, it is also important to recognize the centrality of spirituality to the pursuit of just sustainability from a Catholic perspective because personal sin and social sin—in the forms of "arrogance and acquisitiveness,"[17] environmentally deleterious "systems" of resource exploitation,[18] and a disordered "desire to exercise absolute domination over" creation[19]—are ultimately at the heart of all human-caused environmental degradation. Given this awareness, the promotion of just sustainability from a Catholic perspective must thus include the spirituality through which persons might be transformed by the Spirit to better care for God's creation and those unjustly harmed by environmental degradation.

Although spirituality is thus a requisite aspect of any Catholic effort to promote just sustainability, it is not enough to simply conclude with this theological observation. Rather, in order to sufficiently reflect on how spirituality might foster just sustainability from a Catholic perspective, it is necessary to offer a concrete, pastoral example of how a particular Catholic spirituality might be appropriated in light of contemporary environmental concerns.

The Franciscan spiritual tradition developed by St. Francis of Assisi has long been recognized as one of the church's deepest spiritual resources by which to care for God's creation, and it is an ongoing site for retrieval and renewal in contemporary Catholic scholarship and worship.[20] In addition, in recent years, the Ignatian spiritual tradition pioneered by St. Ignatius of Loyola has increasingly been plumbed for its ability to foster just sustainability. This is an innovative spiritual development, and the importance placed on creation care by Pope Francis—himself a Jesuit formed in the Ignatian spiritual tradition—provides a unique opportunity to further consider how Ignatian spirituality might uniquely foster just sustainability. Ignatian spirituality is especially characterized by the *Spiritual Exercises*, and three key aspects of the *Exercises* will now be considered in light of how they might help Catholics nurture just sustainability.

The Spiritual Exercises of St. Ignatius of Loyola

Iñigo López de Loyola was born in the Basque region of Spain in 1491. He became a soldier in 1517 and was critically wounded in the leg by a cannonball in 1521. During the subsequent recovery period, Iñigo had a deep spiritual conversation that inspired him to abandon his self-described former life "given over to the vanities of the world"[21] and ardently strive to emulate the life of Christ and those of the saints.[22] Toward this end, Iñigo—who later changed his name to Ignatius—traveled to Manresa when his leg was healed, and there spent a year praying, fasting, and guiding others in the process of developing a deeper Christian spirituality.[23]

While at Manresa, Ignatius began taking notes about his own spiritual conversion and the journeys of those to whom he gave direction.[24] He then spent the subsequent two decades revising and editing these materials,[25] and finally published them as the *Spiritual Exercises* in 1548. Since that time, the *Exercises* have come to be recognized as both "the primary gift of Ignatius to the world"[26] and "one of the main repositories for understanding the way of Ignatius."[27]

The *Spiritual Exercises* are essentially "a set of materials, directives, and suggestions for the person helping another through that course" of Christian spiritual development.[28] They are divided into four sections composed of meditations and contemplations. Each section—or "week"—invites a person to enter into deep personal, prayerful reflection about the life of Christ, to consider both meditations and contemplations in light of the particularities of one's own life, and to ultimately come into deeper relationship with God[29] and God's creation. In such a way, the *Spiritual Exercises* of St. Ignatius are designed to serve as a means through which the Spirit can transform, inspire, and animate the whole of a person's life—a process that, as noted, is at the core of all Christian spiritualities. Hence, further reflection on the *Exercises* can serve as a fruitful means by which to consider how particular elements of Ignatian spirituality can help foster just sustainability in the world.

The First Principle and Foundation

The First Week of the *Spiritual Exercises* begins with the First Principle and Foundation (no. 23), which seeks to situate teleologically the human person within the larger context of creation. Thus the First Principle and Foundation posits:

> Man is created to praise, reverence, and serve God our Lord, and by this means to save his soul. And the other things on the face of the earth are created for man and that they may help him in prosecuting the end for which he is created. From this it follows that man is to use them as much as they help him on to his end, and ought to rid himself of them so far as they hinder him as to it. For this it is necessary to make ourselves indifferent to all created things in all that is allowed to the choice of our free will and is not prohibited to it; so that, on our part, we want not health rather than sickness, riches rather than poverty, honor rather than dishonor, long rather than short life, and so in all the rest; desiring and choosing only what is most conducive for us to the end for which we are created.[30]

In his book *The Jesuit Guide to (Almost) Everything*, James Martin, SJ, observes that the First Principle and Foundation is premised on Ignatius's recognition that "disordered affections" and attachments to material possessions can "block the path to detachment, to growing more in freedom, growing as a person, and growing close to God."[31] The Church similarly recognizes that "perverse attachment to certain goods" is at the heart of personal and social sin.[32] Given this insight Martin notes that the First Principle and Foundation calls a person to a kind of "simple living"[33] that fundamentally challenges the consumerist ideology that claims that a person's innate desire to be in relationship with God and others can be placated through the never-ending consumption of material goods.[34]

Although the attempt to moderate the consumption of material goods according to reason—which, in a theological sense, is for the ends for which humans were created, that is, right relationship with God—is thus important to Ignatian spirituality, such simplicity and material temperance is also tremendously important to the fostering of just sustainability. This is first because much of the world's contemporary environmental degradation is the direct result of choices and systems that foster the unjust, sinful overconsumption of material goods.[35] In addition to this, environmental degradation wrought by overconsumption also pertains to justice because the adverse consequences of ecological destruction are often unjustly borne by those who contribute least to the problem.[36] Given that the First Principle and Foundation can help people of faith reduce their overconsumption of material goods, this pillar of the Jesuit tradition thus serves as an example of how Ignatian spirituality might help foster just sustainability in view of modern ecological challenges.

The Examination of Conscience

In addition to the First Principle and Foundation, the Examination of Conscience (sometimes called the Examen; nos. 24–43) is another core aspect of Ignatian spirituality that can help cultivate just sustainability. The Examen is designed to help a person recognize both the way in which God is relationally present and active in one's life and how a person has failed to lovingly respond to God's presence. It was intended by Ignatius to be practiced at least once per day,[37] and is made up of five core elements, including "(1) be grateful for God's blessings; (2) ask the help of the Spirit; (3) review the day, looking for times when God has been present and times when you have left God out; (4) express sorrow for sin and ask for God's forgiving love; (5) pray for the grace to be more totally available to God, who loves you so totally."[38]

Although the Examen has formally existed since Ignatius first published the Exercises in 1548,[39] David L. Fleming, SJ, notes that a vast number of Jesuits and followers of Ignatian spirituality have published different versions of the Examen in subsequent centuries in an effort to "emphasize certain things and to adapt to diverse audiences."[40] One example of how the Examen has been adapted is the "Ecological Examen"[41] written by Joseph Carver, SJ, which is intended to help people reflect more deeply about their relationship with God, self, neighbor, and creation.

This resource follows the traditional five-part structure of the Examen. Using this framework, the Ecological Examen thus proceeds as follows:

> We begin with thanksgiving and gratitude for the covenant God offers in the gift of God's self in all creation. Second, we specifically request to have our eyes opened by the Spirit as to how we might care for creation. Third, we review the challenges and joy experienced in this care. Asking God: "How was I drawn into God today through creation?" How were we being invited to respond to God's action in creation? Is there some part of our relationship with creation that is in need of change? Fourth, asking for a true and clear awareness of our sinfulness, whether it be a sense of superiority or a failure to respond to the needs of creation. Finally, hope. We ask for hope in the future, asking for greater sensitivity to trust in God's living presence in all creation.[42]

Based on this process, Carver observes that people of faith can thus be led to deeper "awareness, appreciation and commitment" regarding the natural world, and better recognize the ways in which particular lifestyles and choices promote or inhibit just relationships with God and creation.[43] In sum, then, the Examen provides another powerful way in which Ignatian spirituality can nurture just sustainability in the face of contemporary environmental challenges.

Contemplatio ad Amorem

Whether a person uses the original or an updated Examen, the third step in the process—reflecting on and noticing God's activity in the world—encapsulates one of the central themes of Ignatian spirituality: finding God in all things.[44] This is one of the most innovative insights of Ignatian spirituality,[45] and further pursuit of this ideal might foster just sustainability by helping people recognize and relate to God's sacramental presence in all creation.[46] Given that the "Contemplatio ad Amorem" ("Contemplation to Attain the Love of God," also known as the "Contemplatio," nos. 235–37) is an aspect of Ignatian spirituality that can especially foster such an understanding of creation, the Contemplatio might be seen as a third way in which the spiritual tradition of St. Ignatius of Loyola can help foster just sustainability in the world.[47]

The Contemplatio, which occurs in the Fourth Week of the *Exercises*, has been referred to as one of the "bookends of the Exercises."[48] It contains "four different focal points" that a person is invited to reflect on: "God's gifts to me . . . God's gift of [Godself] to me . . . God's labors for me . . . and God as Giver and Gift."[49] These movements invite a person to recognize the reality that God is always involved in creating and sustaining every aspect of the creation to which we relate,[50] an awareness known as "the Christian vision of a sacramental universe."[51] This vision can thus help humans recognize and "encounter" God in the natural world,[52] and as such has powerful implications with respect to the promotion of sustainability grounded in justice.

Initially, a sacramental understanding of God's ongoing creative and sustaining presence in all creation might inspire a newfound sense of awe deep within a person; she or he might appreciate more deeply, for example, St. Paul's awesome observation that God "is before all things, and in him all things hold together" (Col. 1:17). At the same time, however, a sacramental understanding of creation might also help a person appreciate that because God is truly present in all creation, she or he cannot offer the worship that is justly due to God (Exod. 20:1–3) without lovingly and prudently relating to and caring for creation in the way that God calls each of us (Gen. 2:15). In other words, a sacramental vision of creation can open one's eyes to see that irresponsible environmental degradation and sinful relationships with God's creation unjustly deprive God of the worship that is due to God.

In view of this insight, a greater recognition of God's presence in creation might subsequently inspire a person to more ardently pursue and support environmentally conscious lifestyles and choices out of a commitment to relate justly to God (i.e., giving to God the worship that is due to God)—a stance that can, in turn, lead to a deeper recognition of and devotion to the just sustainability that is part of what is due to others and to the whole of creation.[53] Given that the Contemplatio can be an avenue by which to awaken a deeper sacramental awareness and understanding of creation, this tenet of Ignatian spirituality thus offers a third means by which the spiritual tradition of St. Ignatius of Loyola might increasingly foster in the world sustainability that is rooted in justice.

In the face of unparalleled global ecological challenges—of which human-caused climate change is arguably the most pressing—the Church has explicitly and repeatedly called for efforts to promote and secure more just sustainability around the world. Aware that authentic justice must be rooted in personal and communal spiritual life, however, and conscious of the reality that unjust environmental degradation is symptomatic of deeper questions of sin against right relationships, the church also recognizes that "the root of the ecological crisis is a spiritual problem"[54] that requires spiritualities to foster just sustainability.

Given the rich mosaic of spiritual traditions through which Catholic spirituality has been expressed over time, Ignatian spirituality is but one way that Catholics might explore and encourage just sustainability in the modern world. The present focus on the spiritual tradition of St. Ignatius of Loyola is not meant to eclipse the unique ways in which other spiritual traditions might similarly cultivate just sustainability; rather, this chapter is intended to show how one tradition might be appropriated in light of modern ecological challenges. It is therefore my hope that this chapter will encourage others to reflect creatively on how the unique aspects of different spiritual traditions might similarly help Catholics better cooperate with the Spirit in order to promote just sustainability in the world for which God calls all people to "cultivate and care" (Gen. 2:15).

Notes

1. For examples, see Catholic Coalition on Climate Change, "Catholic Teachings." http://catholicclimatecovenant.org.

2. *Catechism of the Catholic Church* (Vatican City: Libreria Editrice Vaticana, 1993), no. 1807.

3. United Nations, *2005 World Summit Outcome* (Geneva: United Nations, 2005), 12.

4. Association of Catholic Colleges and Universities and Catholic Coalition on Climate Change, "Sustainability and Catholic Higher Education: A Toolkit for Mission Integration," (2011). http://catholicclimatecovenant.org/.

5. See Susan Hines-Brigger, "Environmental Justice: A Call to Stewardship" (2001), http://www.americancatholic.org.

6. Michael D. Guinan, "Christian Spirituality: Many Styles—One Spirit" (1998), http://www.americancatholic.org.

7. *Catechism of the Catholic Church*, no. 1807.

8. James Martin, *The Jesuit Guide to (Almost) Everything: A Spirituality for Real Life* (New York: HarperCollins, 2010), 2.

9. Guinan, "Christian Spirituality."

10. *Lumen Gentium*, 39–42, http:/www.vatican.va.

11. Martin, *Jesuit Guide*, 2.

12. Guinan, "Christian Spirituality."

13. Ibid.

14. Martin, *Jesuit Guide*, 2.

15. Guinan, "Christian Spirituality."

16. John A. Coleman, "Putting Spirituality and Catholic Social Teaching Together," *America Magazine*, June 14, 2012, http://americamagazine.org/.

17. United States Conference of Catholic Bishops, *Renewing the Earth: An Invitation to Reflection and Action on the Environment in Light of Catholic Social Teaching* (Washington, DC: United States Conference of Catholic Bishops, 1991), no. II, A.

18. United States Conference of Catholic Bishops, *Global Climate Change: A Plea for Dialogue, Prudence, and the Common Good* (Washington, DC: United States Conference of Catholic Bishops, 2001).

19. Benedict XVI, *2010 World Day of Peace Message: If You Want to Cultivate Peace, Protect Creation*, http:/www.vatican.va, no. 14.

20. E.g., Ilia Delio, Keith Douglass Warner, and Pamela Wood, *Care for Creation: A Franciscan Spirituality of the Earth* (Cincinnati, OH: St. Anthony Messenger Press, 2008); Ilia Delio, *A Franciscan View of Creation: Learning to Live in a Sacramental World* (St. Bonaventure, NY: Franciscan Institute, 2003).

21. Ignatius of Loyola, *The Autobiography of St. Ignatius* (New York: Fordham University Press, 1993), 1.

22. John W. O'Malley, *The First Jesuits* (Cambridge, MA: Harvard University Press, 1993), 24.

23. Ibid., 25.

24. Ibid.

25. Ibid.

26. Martin, *Jesuit Guide*, 19.

27. Ibid., 21.

28. O'Malley, *First Jesuits*, 37.

29. Harvey D. Egan, "Ignatian Spirituality," *The New Dictionary of Catholic Spirituality*, ed. Michael Glazier (Collegeville, MN: Order of St. Benedict, 1993), 522.

30. Ignatius of Loyola, *The Spiritual Exercises of St. Ignatius of Loyola*, trans. Elder Mullan (Berkeley Heights, NJ: P. J. Kenedy & Sons, 1914).

31. Martin, *Jesuit Guide*, 9–10.

32. *Catechism of the Catholic Church*, no. 1849.

33. Martin, *Jesuit Guide*, 186.

34. Ibid., 183.

35. See http:/www.vatican.va: John Paul II, *1990 World Day of Peace Message: Peace with God the Creator, Peace with All Creation*, no. 8; Benedict XVI, *Caritas in Veritate* (2009), no. 49.

36. Catholic Coalition on Climate Change, "Catholic Teachings".

37. David L. Fleming, *What Is Ignatian Spirituality?* (Chicago: Loyola Press, 2008), 20.

38. Ibid., 21.

39. Martin, *Jesuit Guide*, 87.

40. Fleming, *What Is Ignatian Spirituality?*, 21.

41. Joseph Carver, "Ecological Examen," (2010), http://catholicclimatecovenant.org/.

42. Joseph Carver, "Ignatian Spirituality and Ecology: Entering into Conversation," Social Justice and Ecology Secretariat of the Society of Jesus (2013), http://www.sjweb.info.

43. Ibid.

44. Martin, *Jesuit Guide*, 99–100.

45. Ibid., 5.

46. United States Conference of Catholic Bishops, *Renewing the Earth*, no. III, A.

47. Social Apostolate Secretariat of the Society of Jesus, "We Live in a Broken World: Reflections on Ecology," *Promotio Justitiae* 70 (1999), http://www.sjweb.info.

48. James Profit, "The Spiritual Exercises and Ecology," Social Justice Secretariat of the Society of Jesus (2011), http://www.sjweb.info.

49. David L. Fleming, *The Spiritual Exercises of St. Ignatius: A Literal Translation and a Contemporary Reading* (St. Louis, MO: Institute of Jesuit Sources, 1978), 139–43.

50. Martin, *Jesuit Guide*, 5.

51. United States Conference of Catholic Bishops, *Renewing the Earth*, no. III, A.

52. Ibid.

53. *Catechism of the Catholic Church*, no. 1807.

54. Profit, "Spiritual Exercises and Ecology."

Education for Just Sustainability in Malawi

Peter J. Henriot, SJ

The "warm heart of Africa"—that is the name, at least the "touristy" name, of Malawi, the beautiful country where I live in south-central Africa. Indeed, it is a country of warm people, wonderful natural resources, and enviable peace, with democratic processes in place. It has been easy for me to sit on the shores of the huge inland body of water that occupies almost 30 percent of our land mass, Lake Malawi, and imagine it as a warm heart of a heavenly spot. And yet I am very aware that Malawi is one of the poorest countries in the world, ranking 170th out of 187 on the Human Development Index of the United Nations. This means low life expectancy (approximately fifty years), low literacy rates (80 percent for men, 65 percent for women), and low income levels (53 percent living below the poverty line).[1] More than 80 percent of the fifteen million Malawians still live in rural areas, and the population is estimated to double in the next twenty-five years. Surely, this startling contrast between natural beauty and human suffering is something that strikes everyone who takes a good look at Malawi and its future development. How can the natural resources and human capabilities of this country be focused to improve the lives of all? And is it possible in fact, not just in theory, to improve the lives of people in a truly *sustainable* fashion?

To speak of "sustainable" is to raise a whole set of issues that are not always adequately attended to when "development" is the focus of public-policy planning. To be sustainable is to emphasize meeting the essential needs of the people of today without compromising meeting the essential needs of the people of tomorrow.[2] For me, this topic of sustainability is not simply an academic issue. It is something that personally challenges me for three reasons. First, as a resident of Malawi, I am disturbed to see what nonsustainable approaches in the economy mean for our environment now and in the future. Second, as a Jesuit, I am encouraged by religious calls to live a more sustainable lifestyle as a matter of social justice. Third, as a participant in a new school project in this country, I am challenged to implement a sustainable educational program right from the start. In this essay, I probe the possibilities of sustainability in several dimensions, in an attempt to articulate what "just sustainability" could look like in the "warm heart of Africa"—as a resident of Malawi, as a Jesuit, and as an official charged with establishing a school for the betterment of the children of the region.

Environmental Crises: The Challenge of Deforestation

I was born and raised in the Pacific Northwest of the United States, where rich evergreen forests occupy space not only in the national parks but also in the rural and urban lands all about. It is this association since my early childhood with green forests that initially made Malawi so attractive to me. From my first visit to that country in the early 1990s, I have been drawn to the northern forest reserves of Karonga and Mzuzu and the southern wooded plateaus of Zomba and the hills of Mulanje. Majestic indigenous trees like baobab and acacia have been located in mighty forests that have provided both game reserves and climate protection over many centuries. But I have been saddened to note over recent years the increasing barrenness of those forest reserves and wooded plateaus and hills, as tree after tree has been cut down to meet the economic demands of industry and the necessities of domestic life. And new trees have not been systematically planted. Deforestation has become all too common, both in speech and in action. This has had harsh environmental effects of less rain, hotter climates, and soil erosion. It is important to note that demands to cut these beautiful forests come from four major sources, all tied into a fifth overriding demand.

Cooking of family food has from time immemorial been done by collecting bits of wood or using charcoal, with a traditional three-stone arrangement to hold pots over fires. But many trees must be cut and burned to produce a much smaller quantity of charcoal. Although officially the government of Malawi discourages the preparation and sale of charcoal, it still occurs with considerable frequency. It is in fact a major source of livelihood for industrious individuals and small-scale firms. Moreover, since access to other energy sources (i.e., electricity and kerosene) is difficult or too expensive for many families, charcoal and wood remain in high demand. Indeed, it is estimated that 95 percent of households in Malawi use wood or charcoal for food-cooking purposes.[3]

Another demand for wood is for preparing the major component of both large-scale and small-scale construction, the *kiln-burnt brick*. These small blocks (usually eight inches by four inches) are first fashioned from local clay soil and then literally "cooked" in large kilns until hard enough to be used in construction. These kilns are used both by large commercial producers of bricks and by village entrepreneurs. Walls of office buildings, warehouses, shops large and small, commercial workplaces, and domestic dwellings alike are largely fashioned from these kiln-burnt bricks. And many a tree is cut down to fire up these kilns.

Tobacco is the number one agricultural product of Malawi, more than 80 percent of export earnings. Curing of the freshly cut tobacco (readying it for sale and transport) is done in both large and small huts warmed by wood and charcoal fires. These curing huts use wood in their basic construction. And they are structures that need to be replaced every one to two years. Thus the tobacco-curing process is a very large consumer of trees.

A fourth factor contributing to deforestation is the need to *clear land* for regular agricultural planting, with a "slash-and-burn" method used. As population increases in Malawi, forested land is extensively taken for ordinary planting of maize and other food crops, as well as for cash crops such as tobacco.

These four contributors to deforestation are of course all linked to the overriding concern of *income generation* for the large portion of Malawian society that is classified as seriously poor. Cutting trees and selling charcoal, manufacturing kiln-burnt bricks, curing tobacco for sale, and land clearing are all parts of everyday life in Malawi. They will continue to be so until alternatives are found. And the impact on the environment increases every year, as forests recede, microclimates shift as a result of lost forest cover, and runoffs from deforested lands pollute rivers and lakes.

The central problem, of course, is that a program of deforestation without parallel programs of reforestation is simply not sustainable. And that is not only a serious socioeconomic problem but also a profound ethical challenge because of its impact on a sustainable future.

Religious Calls for a More Sustainable Lifestyle

The election and inauguration of Cardinal Jorge Bergoglio as Pope Francis has stirred many hearts and challenged many minds. Of several topics he focused on when he initially began speaking of "a Church which is poor and for the poor" was a *respect for creation.* In remarks at his Installation Mass, the Holy Father said, "Please, I would like to ask all those who have positions of responsibility in economic, political and social life, and all men and women of goodwill: let us be 'protectors' of creation, protectors of God's plan inscribed in nature, protectors of one another and of the environment."[4]

This environmental concern of Pope Francis had already been demonstrated by his two immediate predecessors, Benedict XVI and John Paul II. In both their writings and statements (e.g., encyclicals and addresses) and in their actions (e.g., tree-planting on the Vatican grounds and solar panels in the papal audience hall), these two popes included care for the environment as central to the Church's social teaching. The 1990 World Day of Peace statement of John Paul II was titled "Peace with God the Creator, Peace with All of Creation." The pope made clear that "a new ecological awareness is beginning to emerge which, rather than being downplayed, ought to be encouraged to develop into concrete programs and initiatives."[5] And Benedict emphasized in his June 2009 encyclical, *Caritas in Veritate,*

> Today the subject of development is also closely related to the duties arising from our relationship to the natural environment. The environment is God's gift to everyone, and in our use of it we have a responsibility towards the poor, towards future generations and towards humanity as a whole.[6]

In addition, a clear call for ecological sustainability in Africa was made by Pope Benedict is his follow-up to the Second African Synod (October 2009). This is found in the Apostolic Exhortation, *Africae Munus*, issued in November 2011. His message was very strong:

> Some business men and women, governments and financial groups are involved in programmes of exploitation which pollute the environment and cause unprecedented desertification. Serious damage is done to nature, to the forests, to flora and fauna, and countless species risk extinction. All of this threatens the entire ecosystem and consequently the survival of humanity. I call upon the Church in Africa to encourage political leaders to protect such fundamental goods as land and water for the human life of present and future generations and for peace between peoples.[7]

Consistent with this papal stress on environmental care has been the recent emphasis coming from the offices of the Curia of the Society of Jesus in Rome. Fr. Adolfo Nicolás, SJ, Superior General of the Society of Jesus, urged in a 2011 letter to all Jesuits that more serious concern and action should be focused on respect for creation. He encouraged prayerful consideration of and practical responses to "Healing a Broken World," a document on ecology written by a task force composed of Jesuits and lay collaborators from around the world.[8] This document offers both theological and scientific analysis of today's ecological challenges. It also urges examination of the personal, communal, and institutional lifestyles of Jesuits in response to ecological challenges. Because of its very practical response to the issues of ecological sustainability, I believe it is worthwhile to quote in full what "Healing a Broken World" offers to those of us really committed to doing something about the problems of environmental degradation and human development. Its application obviously extends much beyond the Jesuit community and, in my opinion, raises special challenges involving African lifestyles.[9]

Concrete Suggestions for Jesuit Lifestyle and Ecology[10]

General

1. Examine our pattern and levels of consumption and firmly commit ourselves to a reduction in consumption.
2. Make the establishing of right (just) relationships with creation a theme of prayer in Jesuit communities. There is need to develop and share relevant texts and materials for common prayer or for community retreats.
3. Provide orientation to Jesuit and lay staff of our institutions on ecological perspectives, resources, and shared practices.

4. Provide tools and concepts that may help the community or the institution to plan for more sustainable ways of living: measurement of ecological footprint, buying from local markets, etc.
5. Develop eco-heritage sites at provincial level.

Mobility and communication

1. Examine modes of travel and actively search for alternatives. For example, limiting the use of cars and favouring public transportation and the use of cycles.
2. Offset the carbon-debt from air travel by investing in Jesuit ecology projects.
3. Provide facilities for video or Skype conferences instead of air travel.

Living spaces and buildings

1. Carry out energy audits and Environmental Impact Statements (EIS) and Environmental Resource Assessments (ERA) to assess the ecological footprint of our community, work, and province.
2. Act on them by establishing environment management plans that look closely at the running of our works, and obtain available certification of our (new) buildings.
3. This may lead us to invest in energy efficient heating/cooling systems, in appropriate electrical appliances, solar energy, and other forms of renewable energy, etc.
4. In all our communities and works, and especially in houses of formation, there should be a simple and constant practice of recycling perishable and imperishable materials.
5. Wherever applicable, we should recommend architects and engineers who are conscious of environmental issues and can help provinces in drafting building plans.
6. Any new construction of Jesuit institutions should examine ecotoilets, interlocking blocks, solar energy for heating water and allowing natural light into the building, water catchment and storage, biogas, and grey water.

Food

1. Offer training courses to learn about ways to render more sustainable our practices of buying food: promote organically grown, local, and seasonal fairly traded food.

2. Reduce food wastage as much as possible and compost organic kitchen waste.
3. Encourage vegetarian (meat-free) days or weeks in all communities, especially (but not exclusively) during Lent.
4. If possible, do not use bottled water.
5. Communities with outdoor space may want to grow vegetables.

Electronic devices, household appliances and other non-perishable goods

1. Follow the three Rs: reduce, recycle, and re-use in all our works and communities.
2. Examine our tendency to accumulate gadgets; ask always the question: do I really need this item?
3. Recycle appropriately all broken or unused consumer electronics.
4. When buying new devices/appliances, pay special attention to energy efficiency and longevity.
5. Use re-chargeable batteries.
6. Unplug your electronic devices. Do not leave them in standby mode.
7. When buying clothes, make sure they are made of natural, organically grown fibres and/or fairly traded.

Cleaning products

1. Use biodegradable cleaning products, especially if there are problems with waste water treatment.
2. Use paper-based hygiene products made from recycled materials.
3. Use cloth that can be washed rather than thrown away.

Financial management

1. FACSI could allocate some funds for environmental projects in the Society worldwide.[11]
2. Provinces should invest with socially and ecologically responsible criteria.

Educational Efforts toward Sustainability

Sustainability—in both its material and ethical dimensions—is especially concerned with the future. As demonstrated in what I have already presented, material sustainability in Malawi faces the challenges of deforestation. And the ethics of sustainability poses serious challenges to our lifestyle, not only of Jesuits but of the wider public all over the world.

Certainly a concern with the future is primary to the youth of today. That is why good education, in whatever form it takes today, must have a special focus on issues of sustainability for tomorrow. This is a guiding principle that lies behind the Zambia-Malawi Jesuit Province's commitment to make its new school in Malawi a "green institution" in many different ways. Loyola Jesuit Secondary School (LJSS), which opened for enrollment in September 2014, was designed with our hope that it will be noted for a serious commitment to ecological sustainability in construction, maintenance, and curriculum.[12]

When plans were being made to build a new secondary school in Malawi, there was wide-ranging consideration given to its location, enrollment, and orientation. To be honest, many presumed that our new Jesuit school would be somewhat traditional, that is, an all-boys private school located in the capital of the country, Lilongwe. But after much discussion, debate, and discernment, the planners came up with something quite different.

Indeed, LJSS is marked out from the start to be an "option for the poor." It is an effort by the Jesuits to give hope to at least some young women and men caught now in a very poor educational system in one of the poorest countries in the world. Loyola Jesuit is located in Kasungu, a poor rural municipality located seventy-five miles from the capital. In the capital there are already many secondary schools catering to various levels of society. Our school is coeducational from the start, aiming for a gender equity that promises more chances for women to enter creatively into future national development efforts. It will eventually be a boarding school for 500, Form One through Form Four (grades nine to twelve). And it will be a "grant-aided" school wherein the government of Malawi pays the salaries of the teachers, meaning that fees will be much lower and more available for families of lesser means.

We will of course make the effort to put into practice all the lofty ideals of "Ignatian Pedagogy," to produce "women and men for others," to educate youth not just to make a *living* but to make a *difference*. But central to our educational thrust will also be a concern for ecological sustainability. And this needs to be demonstrated in a variety of ways, with many practical applications.

1. *Planning*—Following government of Malawi regulations, an official "Environmental Impact Assessment" study was done to guide both the construction process and the ongoing activities of the school. Eighty pages of description and prescription laid out guidelines for responsible stewardship of land, air, and local environment.
2. *Location*—The fifty-acre site for LJSS is on a slightly sloping hillside, with good natural drainage toward a small stream that serves as one of the borders of school property. It was an empty plot used by only a few local people for minor cultivation. There was no necessity of moving local residents from their homes, something that would not only have angered them but would also have caused increased crowding in an already overpopulated area in our immediate neighborhood. The buildings are situated in such a way that sun and wind are taken into account to provide an optimal learning setting.

3. *Basic construction*—Admittedly we made an initial mistake in that the original perimeter wall surrounding our property was constructed of kiln-burnt bricks. But when plans for all the buildings of the school were drawn up and tenders for construction offered, we insisted with the architect, quantity surveyor, and contractor that so-called "stabilized soil blocks" (SSBs) would be used. These blocks are made on site, utilizing the good soil available, which is mixed with cement (ten to one ratio), molded in standard forms, and then sun-dried. No trees are destroyed to fire kilns to make bricks!
4. *Natural vegetation*—We did have to uproot some of the trees that dotted our site, but only as necessary. More trees, especially of local variety, will be planted around the campus, to be cared for by students. And local flowers will also beautify the campus.
5. *Water*—The school is connected to the municipality system for ordinary supply, but also will have available two boreholes and elevated water tanks. Something we need to explore is rainwater storage and water-recycling methods. Disposal of wastewater through methods like "eco-ponds" is already in the construction plans.
6. *Solar*—Wide-scale use of solar electricity is minimal in Malawi but is something that is growing. Large solar installations are still very expensive and a challenge to maintain. But we will initially utilize smaller solar installations such as solar water heating for showers, solar-powered night security lights, and solar generators for emergency electrical supplies.
7. *Wind power*—Our Kasungu site is on a hill, which can at times be quite windy. Some future exploration of windmills to generate and store electricity will be pursued. This will be particularly appropriate because we are in the district that a young Malawian, William Kamkwambe, made well known through windmill construction in his local village, portrayed in a *New York Times* best-selling book, *The Boy Who Harnessed the Wind*.[13]
8. *Carbon footprints*—There are available simple templates that students can use to monitor the amount of carbon dioxide and other greenhouse gases that their activities produce. Even in a poor country like Malawi, some habits of lifestyle can have negative ecological effect. Attention should be paid, for example, to use of electricity, taking care of food, and acquiring the latest IT technologies.
9. *Recycling*—From the start it was important to introduce all occupants of our LJSS site to good recycling habits. Disposal cans will be made available throughout the campus and in the residences for various types of garbage, including burnables, buriables, and more.
10. *Curriculum*—As part of the standard introduction to the education offered at LJSS, both new students and staff will be provided written and oral presentations wherein ecological concerns will be emphasized. Then there will be regular courses and special programs on environmental

topics, local, national, and global. As a Jesuit school, we will especially stress ethical issues and some of the practical lifestyle concerns mentioned earlier in this essay.[14]

11. *Service programs*—LJSS will require participation by all students and staff in service programs involving local residents, especially in our neighborhood, and children enrolled in nearby primary schools. Some of these programs will relate to environmental concerns such as use of ecological stoves, water concerns, and waste disposal.
12. *Spirituality*—LJSS is not an all-Catholic school staff and students. But it is a Catholic and Jesuit school in pedagogy and ethos. This will mean that ecological concerns should be integrated into religious education programs, liturgical and prayer experiences, and religious displays. An Ignatian emphasis on "finding God in all things" should open us up to a spirituality that is truly ecologically sensitive.[15]

This list of issues to focus on may look lengthy and complex. But we are learning in our sustainability efforts and are determined to make "sustainability and education" come alive in very practical ways at our new Loyola Jesuit Secondary School in Kasungu, Malawi.

Notes

1. Latest overall figures for Malawi can be found in United Nations Development Programme, *The Rise of the South: Human Development Report 2013: Human Progress in a Diverse World* (New York: United Nations Development Programme, 2013).

2. The commonly used definition is: "Sustainable development is development that meets the needs of the present without compromising the ability of future generations to meet their own needs." It was expressed in the Brundtland Commission Report presented to the United Nations March 20, 1987. See United Nations General Assembly, *Our Common Future: World Commission on Environment and Development* (New York: Oxford University Press, 1987).

3. See http://www.cleancookstoves.org.

4. http://www.vatican.va.

5. John Paul II, *Peace with God the Creator, Peace with All of Creation* (1990), http://www.vatican.va, no. 1.

6. Benedict XVI, *Caritas in Veritate* (2009), http://www.vatican.va, no. 48.

7. Benedict XVI, *Africae Munus* (2011), http://www.vatican.va, no. 80.

8. Task Force on Ecology, "Healing a Broken World: Special Report on Ecology," *Promotio Justitiae* 106 (2011).

9. A very important topic for research, education and practical application is the link between African cultural systems and environmental issues. See, for example, the work of the Institute for Culture and Ecology in Kenya: http://www.icekenya.org.

10. "Healing a Broken World: Special Report on Ecology," 51–53.

11. FACSI is the "Fundus Apostolicus et Caritativus Societatis Iesu," the charitable fund supporting apostolic activities of the Jesuits worldwide.

12. A full exposition of the vision and mission of Loyola Jesuit Secondary School (LJSS) in Kasungu, Malawi, can be found on our website: http://www.loyola-malawi.org.

13. See William Kamkwamba, *The Boy Who Harnessed the Wind: Creating Currents of Electricity and Hope* (New York: William Morrow, 2009).

14. Two books, written by authors with both academic and practical experiences that will be helpful in integrating environmental sustainability into our evolving LJSS curriculum are Donal Dorr, *Option for the Poor and the Earth: Catholic Social Teaching* (Maryknoll, NY: Orbis Books, 2012), and Sean McDonagh, *Climate Change: The Challenge to All of Us* (Dublin: Columba Press, 2006).

15. We will be assisted in this through the Jesuit offices in Rome and the Social Justice and Ecology Secretariat. See http://www.sjweb.info/sjs. Also see from this office *Promotio Justitiae* 111, no. 2 (2013), titled "A Spirituality That Reconciles Us with Creation." Moreover, an important academic effort to promote sustainability education and action with a strong ethical base is being developed at the Institute of Environmental Sustainability at Loyola University of Chicago. With a wide international outreach, the institute is organizing very helpful education materials. See http://www.luc.edu.

Contributors

Jacquineau Azétsop, SJ, earned a PhD in theological ethics with a focus on social ethics and bioethics (Boston College) and a Master's of Public Health at the Bloomberg School of Public Health (Johns Hopkins University). He lectures in bioethics, medical deontology, and public health at the University of N'Djaména (Chad). He also teaches public health and public health ethics at the Catholic University of Mozambique in Beira. Among his publications: *Structural Violence, Population Health and Health Equity: Preferential Option for the Poor and the Bioethics Health Equity in Sub-Saharan Africa* (2010).

Celia Deane-Drummond is currently professor in theology at the University of Notre Dame (Indiana). Her research interests are in the engagement of theology and natural science, including specifically ecology, evolution, animal behavior, and anthropology. Her most recent books include *Future Perfect* (2006); *Ecotheology* (2008); *Christ and Evolution* (2009); *Creaturely Theology* (2009); *Religion and Ecology in the Public Sphere* (2011); *Animals as Religious Subjects* (2013); and *The Wisdom of the Liminal* (2014).

Daniel R. DiLeo is a Margaret O'Brien Flatley Fellow and PhD student in theological ethics at Boston College, and works as Project Manager of the Catholic Coalition on Climate Change. He earned his MTS from the Boston College School of Theology and Ministry, and graduated magna cum laude from Cornell University. He served as a Mission Intern at the Catholic Health Association, and his research focuses on climate change, Catholic social thought, and public/political theology.

Denis Edwards is a professorial fellow of the Australian Catholic University. He is a priest of the Catholic Archdiocese of Adelaide. His research has been in the areas of Christology, trinitarian theology, the dialogue between science and theology, and ecological theology. Recent books include *How God Acts: Creation, Redemption and Special Divine Action* (2010); *Ecology at the Heart of Faith* (2006); and *Breath of Life: A Theology of the Creator Spirit* (2004).

Muhigirwa Rusembuka Ferdinand, SJ, has a doctorate in philosophy from the Gregorian University (Rome). He has taught social philosophy since 1997. Former coordinator of the Jesuit Social Apostolate in Africa, he directed the African Research Center on Social Action (CEPAS) until 2012, and he is the current director of the Arrupe Center for Research and Training in Lubumbashi (Democratic Republic of Congo).

Dennis T. Gonzalez teaches systematic theology at St. Vincent School of Theology (Quezon City, Philippines). He also teaches business ethics, public sector ethics, and leadership ethics and spirituality in the MBA, MPM, and PhD in Leadership Studies programs of the Ateneo de Manila University. He completed his Doctorate in Sacred Theology (STD) at the Catholic University of Leuven (Belgium). He is a member of the international Scientific Council of *Ordo Socialis*, which promotes Christian social teaching.

Mark Graham, PhD (Boston College), is an associate professor of theological ethics and the Director of the Undergraduate Program in the Theology and Religious Studies Department at Villanova University (Pennsylvania). He has authored two books: *Josef Fuchs on Natural Law* (2002) and *Sustainable Agriculture: A Christian Ethic of Gratitude* (2005). He is currently focusing his research on Christian environmental ethics and hopes to bring credibility to Thomas Berry's new creation story and the ethical code it entails. In addition to raising two precocious children, he tends an unruly garden, cares for his animal friends, and tries to find new ways to live lightly on planet Earth.

Peter J. Henriot, SJ, is a Jesuit priest trained as a political scientist. He served on the staff of the Center of Concern (Washington, DC) from 1971 to 1988, and on the staff of the Jesuit Center for Theological Reflection (Lusaka, Zambia) from 1990 to 2010. He currently is Director of Development for Loyola Jesuit Secondary School (Lilongwe, Malawi).

Francis X. Hezel, SJ, born in the United States, has spent nearly fifty years in Micronesia. He was director of Xavier High School in Chuuk and Jesuit mission superior in the islands for six years. In two terms, until 2010, he has served as director of a research-pastoral institute (Micronesian Seminar). During his years with the Micronesian Seminar, he has organized and lectured at dozens of conferences on public issues. He has also published eleven books and many articles on Micronesia. His last book, *Making Sense of Micronesia: The Logic of Pacific Island Culture*, was published in 2013.

Teresia Hinga received a BEd in English Literature and Religious Studies, an MA in Religious Studies (Nairobi University), and a PhD in Religious Studies (Lancaster University, UK). A founding member of the Circle of Concerned African Women Theologians, she is a member of the American Academy of Religion and the African Association for the Study of Religion. She has taught widely in Africa and the United States at such locations as Kenyatta University, Harvard Divinity School, and DePaul University. Since 2005, she has taught at Santa Clara University (California) on African religion, feminist theologies, and globalization. Her research interests include gendered perspectives on African Christianity, sustainability, and religion and the public square.

Christine Firer Hinze is professor of Christian ethics and Director of the Curran Center for American Catholic Studies at Fordham University (New York). Her teaching and research focus on foundational and applied ethical issues, with special emphasis on the dynamics of social transformation, Catholic social thought, and economic and work justice for vulnerable families and groups. Her recent publications include essays in *Theological Studies, Journal of the Society of Christian Ethics, Proceedings of the Catholic Theological Association of America, The Journal of Catholic Social Thought,* and *Studies in Christian Ethics.*

Dzintra Ilisko is associate professor at Daugavpils University (Latvia) and the Director of the University's Institute of Sustainable Education. Her fields of interest include sustainability, gender issues, and inclusive education. She is involved in numerous international research projects and is an active member of several international networks, including the Baltic and Black Sea Circle Consortium in Educational Research and the International Society of Religious Education and Values.

John Karuvelil, SJ, teaches moral theology at Jnana-Deepa Vidyapeeth in Pune (India), where he is also the head of the Department of Pastoral and Moral Theology and a specialist in biomedical ethics. He has a Doctorate in Theology from the Boston College School of Theology and Ministry. His recent publications include "Indian Health Care System under the Scanner" (2011); "Dignity of Women and Elective Abortions in India" (2012); and, in *Asian Horizons*, "Institutionalizing Ill-Health: Corruption and Health Care in India" (2011), "Gene Therapy: The Case for India" (2013), and "Stem Cell Therapies in India" (2013).

Before entering the Society of Jesus, South African **Peter Knox** worked as an industrial chemist. As a Jesuit, he has taught math and physical sciences in South Africa's townships, and was student chaplain and resident theologian at the Jesuit Institute in Johannesburg. He holds a doctorate in systematic theology from St. Paul University in Ottawa (Canada). He is currently Dean of Hekima College in Nairobi.

João Batista Libanio, SJ, earned a Doctorate in Theology (Frankfurt and Rome) and was professor emeritus of theology at the Jesuit Faculty of Philosophy and Theology in Belo Horizonte (Brazil). As Parochial Vicar in the city of Vespasiano, as well as a writer and lecturer, he authored *Introdução à Vida Intelectual* (4th ed., 2012); *A arte de formar-se* (6th ed., 2001); *Em busca de Lucidez* (2008); and *Os Caminhos de Existência* (2009). Fr. Libanio was born in 1932 in Belo Horizonte, Brazil, and died on January 30, 2014, in Curitiba.

Erin Lothes Biviano researches energy ethics and faith-based environmentalism, and is assistant professor of theology at the College of Saint Elizabeth (New Jersey). Dr. Lothes holds a PhD in Systematic Theology (Fordham University), a

Master's in Theology (Boston College), and an AB in English (Princeton University). She is author of *The Paradox of Christian Sacrifice: The Loss of Self, the Gift of Self* (2007) as well as articles in *New Theology Review*, *CrossCurrents*, and *Sustainability: Science, Practice & Policy*. From 2007 to 2010 she was an Earth Institute Fellow (Columbia University) and generated research on faith-based environmentalism, the subject of her in-process book manuscript. She is also convener of a task force developing an interdisciplinary energy ethics within the Catholic Theological Society of America.

Ann Marie Mealey is a senior lecturer in Theology and Religious Studies at Leeds Trinity University (UK) and author of *The Identity of Christian Morality* (2009). She has also published essays on moral conscience, stem cell research, and environmental issues in various theological journals and books. She is a member of the Catholic Agency for Overseas Development theological reference group in the UK.

Viviane Minikongo Mundele earned her doctorate in Theology and Human Sciences (Catholic University of Congo) with her thesis "*La mondialisation et l'altermondialisation remises en question: Approche théologique d'une éthique planétaire.*" She is part-time professor at the Higher Institute of Religious Pedagogy, the University of Saint Augustin, and the Reverend Kim University in Kinshasa (Democratic Republic of Congo). She teaches courses in Christian ethics, ethics and professional conduct, and bioethics. She is member of the Association of Women Theologians and Canonists of Kinshasa.

Constansia Mumma-Martinon received her PhD from Leipzig University (Germany). She is a lecturer in the Department of Political Science (University of Nairobi), the Institute of Peace Studies and International Relations (Nairobi), and the Austrian European Peace University. She is also Resident Reconciliation Consultant of the Kenyan Truth, Justice and Reconciliation Commission and works with the United Nations Development Programme–International Peace Support Training Center.

Benedict Chidi Nwachukwu-Udaku, a priest from Ahiara Diocese (Nigeria), received his PhD in Moral Theology and MA in Bioethics (Universidad Pontificia Comillas, Madrid). He also received a postdoctoral Master's Degree in Philosophy (Claremont Graduate University, California). Presently, he teaches at the Ministry Formation Institute, San Bernardino Diocese. He also chairs the Year of Faith program in the Diocese of San Bernardino.

Edward Osang Obi is a priest of the Missionary Society of St. Paul in Nigeria and an alumnus of the Catholic University of Leuven (Belgium). He teaches moral theology at the Catholic Institute of West Africa (Port Harcourt), where he also steers the church's engagement with extractive companies in pursuit of better and more just arrangements for local communities at the front lines of the oil and gas industry in the Niger Delta region.

Randy J. C. Odchigue is a priest of the diocese of Butuan (Philippines). He is the Vice President for Academic Affairs at Fr. Saturnino Urios University in Butuan City. He completed his doctorate in Sacred Theology at the Catholic University of Leuven (Belgium) with a dissertation titled "The Local Church in the Diverse Islands of Cultures: Towards a Filipino Ecclesiological Perspective" (2009). He is an active member of the Catholic Theological Society of the Philippines.

Christiana Z. Peppard is an assistant professor of Theology, Science, and Ethics at Fordham University (New York), with joint appointments in the programs in American Studies and Environmental Studies. She is the author of *Just Water: Theology, Ethics, and the Global Water Crisis* (2014) and coeditor with the late Arthur W. Galston of *Expanding Horizons in Bioethics* (2005). A graduate of Yale University (PhD, 2011), Yale Divinity School (MAR, Ethics, 2005), and Stanford University (BA, Human Biology, 2001), she writes and teaches about emerging ethical issues at the intersections of environment, water, science, and religion.

Nancy M. Rourke has a PhD in theology from the Pontifical Institute of St. Patrick's College of Maynooth (Ireland). She is associate professor of Religious Studies and Theology and Director of the Catholic Studies Program at Canisius College (Buffalo, New York). She teaches courses in Catholic ethics and religious studies and writes in areas of environmental ethics, health care ethics at the end of life, and meta-ethics.

Miguel Ángel Sánchez Carlos has a doctorate in Theology (Faculty of Theology of Granada, Spain), a Master's in Theology (Catholic University of Lyon, France), and a Bachelor's of Theology (Universidad Iberoamericana, Mexico City). A native of Mexico, he is professor of theological ethics and bioethics at the Universidad Iberoamericana in Mexico City and coordinator of the *Revista Iberoamericana de Teología*. He is a member of Catholic Theological Ethics in the World Church and of the Society of Christian Ethics (US).

John Sniegocki is an associate professor of Christian ethics and director of the Peace Studies minor at Xavier University in Cincinnati (Ohio). He is the author of *Catholic Social Teaching and Economic Globalization: The Quest for Alternatives* (1999), as well as numerous articles on Catholic social teaching, economic democracy, the ethics of war and nonviolence, food ethics, ecology, the Catholic Worker movement, and Buddhist-Christian dialogue.

Osamu Takeuchi, SJ, a native of Japan, is professor of moral theology at Sophia University (Tokyo). He received his STD from the Jesuit School of Theology at Berkeley (California). His areas of interest are fundamental moral theology, bioethics, and sexual ethics. He is the author of *Conscience and Culture: A Dialogue between the West and the East Concerning Conscience* (2010).

Andrea Vicini, SJ, MD, PhD (Boston College), and STD (Faculty of Theology of Southern Italy) is associate professor of moral theology at the Boston College School of Theology and Ministry. He is a member of the Planning Committee of Catholic Theological Ethics in the World Church, coeditor of the *Moral Traditions* series (Georgetown), and editorial consultant for *Theological Studies*. Among his publications are *Genetica umana e bene comune* (2008; Portuguese translation, 2011); "Bioethics: Basic Questions and Extraordinary Developments," *Theological Studies* (2012); "New Insights in Environmental and Sustainable Ethics," *Asian Horizons* (2012); and "Le neuroscienze e la bioetica," *La Civiltà Cattolica* (2014).

Markus Vogt studied philosophy and theology in Munich, Jerusalem, and Lucerne (Switzerland). Between 1992 and 1995, he worked at the council board for environmental issues of the German government. From 1998 to 2007, he was head of the Institute for Church and Environment of the German Bishops' Conference. Since 2007 he has been chair of Christian Social Ethics at the Ludwig-Maximilians-University in Munich, and since 2009 he has directed the Community of Christian Social Ethics in the German-speaking countries.

Kenneth M. Weare is adjunct professor of social ethics at the University of San Francisco. He is a member of the San Francisco Archdiocesan Board of Education and the Catholic Charities Catholic Youth Organization Board of Directors, and he is pastor of St. Rita Church in Fairfax (California). He earned a PhD in Religious Studies with a specialization in moral theology at the Catholic University of Louvain (Belgium). He has taught moral theology, environmental ethics, engineering ethics, agricultural ethics, and human rights at universities and colleges in Los Angeles, New York, and the US Midwest.

Index